THE GLOBAL BOURGEOISIE

The Global Bourgeoisie

THE RISE OF THE MIDDLE CLASSES
IN THE AGE OF EMPIRE

EDITED BY CHRISTOF DEJUNG,
DAVID MOTADEL &
JÜRGEN OSTERHAMMEL

PRINCETON UNIVERSITY PRESS

PRINCETON & OXFORD

Copyright © 2019 by Princeton University Press

Published by Princeton University Press
41 William Street, Princeton, New Jersey 08540
6 Oxford Street, Woodstock, Oxfordshire OX20 1TR

press.princeton.edu

LCCN 2019936039
ISBN 9780691195834
ISBN 9780691177342 (pbk.)

British Library Cataloging-in-Publication Data is available

Editorial: Eric Crahan, Thalia Leaf, and Pamela Weidman
Production Editorial: Debbie Tegarden
Cover design: Chris Ferrante
Cover credit: Pier of the Hotel de los Pocitos, Montevideo, Uruguay
Production: Erin Suydam
Publicity: Alyssa Sanford
Copyeditor: Gail K. Schmitt

This book has been composed in Arno Pro

Printed on acid-free paper. ∞

Printed in the United States of America

10 9 8 7 6 5 4 3 2 1

CONTENTS

ILLUSTRATIONS

ACKNOWLEDGMENTS

THIS BOOK IS the result of research carried out over the course of several years. It originated in a workshop at Gonville and Caius College, University of Cambridge, in the summer of 2015. We would like to thank Annina Clava-detscher, who assisted us in preparing the final manuscript for submission. Jeremy Lowe proofread parts of the text and saved us from many mistakes. We are also grateful to Sir Richard J. Evans, Janet Hartley, and Charles Jones, for their critical feedback and inspiring discussions. Moreover, we owe a debt of thanks to the anonymous readers for their helpful reports. Our editors at Princeton University Press, Brigitta van Rheinberg and Eric Crahan, believed in the book from the outset, and it was a great pleasure to work with them. Princeton University Press's Thalia Leaf, Amanda Peery, Stephanie Rojas, Gail Schmitt, and Pamela Weidman ensured its smooth production. Finally, we would like to acknowledge the support we received from the Fritz Thyssen Foundation, the Economic History Society, the German History Society, the Gottfried Wilhelm Leibniz Prize Program of the German Research Foundation, and the Smuts Memorial Fund of the University of Cambridge, which made this book possible.

The Editors, 2019

NOTES ON THE CONTRIBUTORS

ALISON BASHFORD is Research Professor in History at the University of New South Wales, Sydney. Previously she was the Vere Harmsworth Professor of Imperial History, University of Cambridge. Most recently, she is the author of *The New Worlds of Thomas Robert Malthus* (Princeton University Press, 2016, with Joyce E. Chaplin) and a coeditor of *Oceanic Histories* (Cambridge University Press, 2017).

HOUCHANG ESFANDIAR CHEHABI is Professor of International Relations and History at the Frederick S. Pardee School of Global Studies, Boston University. He is the author of *Iranian Politics and Religious Modernism* (Cornell University Press, 1990) and editor or coeditor of a dozen books, most recently *Erin and Iran: Cultural Encounters between the Irish and the Iranians* (Ilex Foundation, 2015).

SABINE DABRINGHAUS is Professor of Chinese History at Albert-Ludwigs-University of Freiburg. She is the author of *Territorialer Nationalismus in China: Historisch-geographisches Denken 1900–1949* (Böhlau Verlag, 2006), *Geschichte Chinas im 20. Jahrhundert* (C. H. Beck Verlag, 2009) and *Geschichte Chinas 1279–1949* (De Gruyter Oldenbourg, 2015).

CHRISTOF DEJUNG is Professor of Modern History at the University of Bern. He is the author of *Commodity Trading, Globalization and the Colonial World: Spinning the Web of the Global Market* (Routledge, 2018) and a coeditor of *Foundations of World-Wide Economic Integration: Power, Institutions and Global Markets, 1850–1930* (Cambridge University Press, 2013).

RICHARD DRAYTON is the Rhodes Professor of Imperial History at King's College London. He is the author of *Nature's Government: Science, Imperial Britain and the "Improvement" of the World* (Yale University Press, 2000) and

Whose Constitution? Law, Justice and History in the Caribbean (Judiciary of Trinidad and Tobago, 2016).

MARCUS GRÄSER is Professor of Modern and Contemporary History at Johannes Kepler University Linz. He is the author of "World History in a Nation-State: The Transnational Disposition in Historical Writing in the United States," *Journal of American History* (2009) and a coeditor of *The Transnational Significance of the American Civil War* (Palgrave Macmillan, 2016).

EMMA HUNTER is Senior Lecturer in African History at the University of Edinburgh. She is the author of *Political Thought and the Public Sphere in Tanzania: Freedom, Democracy and Citizenship in the Era of Decolonisation* (Cambridge University Press, 2015) and a coeditor of *African Print Cultures: Newspapers and their Publics in the Twentieth Century* (Michigan University Press, 2016).

JANET HUNTER is Professor Emerita of Economic History at the London School of Economics and a coeditor of the *Journal of Japanese Studies*. She is the author of *"Deficient in Commercial Morality"? Japan in Global Debates on Business Ethics in the Late Nineteenth—Early Twentieth Century* (Palgrave, 2016) and (with K. Ogasawara) "Price Shocks in Regional Markets: Japan's Great Kantō Earthquake of 1923," *Economic History Review* (2018).

KRIS MANJAPRA is Associate Professor of History at Tufts University, Medford, Massachusetts. He is the author of *Age of Entanglement: German and Indian Intellectuals across Empire* (Harvard University Press, 2014) and a coeditor of *Cosmopolitan Thought Zones: South Asia and the Global Circulation of Ideas* (Palgrave Macmillan Press, 2010).

ADAM MESTYAN is Assistant Professor of History at Duke University, Durham, North Carolina. He is the author of *Arab Patriotism: The Ideology and Culture of Power in Late Ottoman Egypt* (Princeton University Press, 2017). His most recent publication is a manuscript edition of *Primordial History, Print Capitalism, and Egyptology in Nineteenth-Century Cairo: Mustafa Salama al-Naggari's The Garden of Ismail's Praise* (Cairo: Ifao, 2019).

DAVID MOTADEL is Associate Professor of International History at the London School of Economics and Political Science. He is the author of *Islam and Nazi Germany's War* (Harvard University Press, 2014), which was awarded the Fraenkel Prize, and the editor of *Islam and the European Empires*

(Oxford University Press, 2014). In 2018, he received the Philip Leverhulme Prize for History.

JÜRGEN OSTERHAMMEL, until his retirement in 2018 Professor of Modern and Contemporary History at the University of Konstanz, is a Distinguished Fellow at the Freiburg Institute of Advanced Study (FRIAS). His publications in English include *The Transformation of the World: A Global History of the Nineteenth Century* (Princeton University Press, 2014), *Decolonization: A Short History* (coauthored with Jan C. Jansen, Princeton University Press, 2017), and *Unfabling the East: The Enlightenment's Encounter with Asia* (Princeton University Press, 2018).

DAVID S. PARKER is Associate Professor of History at Queen's University in Kingston, Ontario. He is author of *The Idea of the Middle Class: White-Collar Workers and Peruvian Society, 1900–1950* (Penn State University Press, 1998), a coeditor of *Latin America's Middle Class: Unsettled Debates and New Histories* (Lexington Books, 2013), and a contributor to López and Weinstein, eds., *The Making of the Middle Class, Toward a Transnational History* (Duke University Press, 2012).

UTSA RAY is Assistant Professor in History at Jadavpur University, Kolkata. She is the author of *Culinary Culture in Colonial India: A Cosmopolitan Platter and the Middle-Class* (Cambridge University Press, 2015) and has published in *Modern Asian Studies, South Asian History & Culture, Indian Economic and Social History Review*, and *History Compass*. She is also part of the editorial collective of the international journal on food studies, *Gastronomica*.

PADRAIC X. SCANLAN is Assistant Professor in the Centre for Industrial Relations and Human Resources and the Centre for Diaspora & Transnational Studies at the University of Toronto. He is the author of *Freedom's Debtors: British Antislavery in Sierra Leone in the Age of Revolution* (Yale University Press, 2017), which received the 2018 James A. Rawley Prize from the American Historical Association and the 2018 Wallace K. Ferguson Prize from the Canadian Historical Association.

ALISON K. SMITH is Professor of History at the University of Toronto. She is the author of *For the Common Good and Their Own Well-Being: Social Estates in Imperial Russia* (Oxford University Press, 2014) and articles including "A Microhistory of the Global Empire of Cotton: Ivanovo, the Russian Manchester," *Past & Present* (2019).

THE GLOBAL BOURGEOISIE

1

Worlds of the Bourgeoisie

Christof Dejung, David Motadel &
Jürgen Osterhammel

IN 1896, the Togolese businessman John Calvert Nayo Bruce traveled to Berlin for the Great Industrial Exposition. He was the manager of a company of nearly thirty men and women from Togo who were to stage an ethnographic exhibit, offering the German audience a supposedly authentic insight into the daily life of their home village. Bruce had specifically designed this *Togodorf* for the exposition. The son of a local chief, Bruce had been educated at a missionary school and worked many years as an interpreter for the German protectorate administration of Togoland. After the success of the show in Berlin, he toured with different companies through Europe and organized human zoos not only in Germany but also in France, Russia, Switzerland, and Italy, until his death, in 1916. He was, however, not merely an impresario interested in economic profit alone; he also expressed great interest in Western education. In an interview with the *Kölnische Zeitung* during the Berlin Exposition, he spoke about his daughter, who was attending a German school in order to "learn everything white girls learn and to become as civilized as them." Even though he praised German rule in Togoland, which is not surprising given that the *Togodorf* had been established with the explicit goal of propagating German colonialism, he criticized the atrocities committed against Africans by white hunters and travelers. And he took a swipe at the educational policy of the Germans in West Africa: "You see, our people would like to learn more, but the Germans don't want that. They think reading and writing is enough for the Negroes but it is not enough." Emphasizing the significance of higher education in Togoland, he added: "Many really want to study: law or medicine. We want to have black lawyers and medical doctors."[1]

By European standards Bruce would, no doubt, be ranked among the middle classes. His emphasis on learning, his striving for economic success as a businessman, and his urge to provide his people with education certainly qualified him as a bourgeois and, thus, a member of the social group that ranked between the established aristocratic elite on the one hand and the peasants and plebeian majority on the other, a group that had emerged as a result of increasing social and economic change after the end of the eighteenth century.

The long nineteenth century has often been described as the golden age of the bourgeoisie in Europe, but the emergence of middle classes and of bourgeois cultural milieus was by no means exclusive to European societies. One of the most striking features of the nineteenth century was the rise of similar social groups around the world. Merchants in Shanghai, lawyers in Delhi, bankers in New York, doctors in Cairo, professors in Vienna, and schoolteachers on the Gold Coast had much in common. A group between the old entrenched aristocratic classes and the peasants and workers, their social milieus were marked by its own lifestyles, tastes, and values. The members of this bourgeois middle class emphasized education and individual achievement. They were the product of the dramatic transformation of social structures, the progressive division of labor, and the increasing differentiation of societies. And they were often connected across countries and continents, standing at the very center of globalization. In fact, members of the middle classes acted as its most effective proponents, and an understanding of their history is vital for coming to grips with the transformation of the world in the modern age.

To be sure, this development was uneven. In the early nineteenth century, bourgeois social formations were most visible in Western Europe and its (current and former) settler colonies, but by the early twentieth century, bourgeois middle classes had emerged in various regions across the world. The global bourgeoisie was far from being a homogeneous social group. Its members competed with each other, both within one society and between countries. Non-European middle classes in the colonies, for example, were always demarcated (and to some extent excluded) from the white middle classes by the asymmetries of colonial rule and the mechanisms of "racial" exclusion. The global history of the rise of the bourgeois middle classes is a story not only of global

1. Rea Brändle, *Nayo Bruce: Geschichte einer afrikanischen Familie in Europa* (Zürich: Limmat, 2007), 15–16.

convergence and growing uniformity but also of divergences and mounting unevenness. Yet despite all differences and the frequent political and economic disparities among them, these middle classes were similar enough to allow us to study them across geographical boundaries.[2]

The history of the middle class and bourgeois culture has captured the interest of social historians for decades. Scholars working on European and American history, however, have long considered the middle class largely as a Western phenomenon.[3] Similar social groups in other parts of the world have been considered as merely a pseudo-bourgeoisie, if they have been considered at all. Historians have often referred to them using specific terms; one prominent example is the longtime interest of Africanists in the history of the African "elites"—among them Nayo Bruce—without explicitly comparing these "elites" to the middle classes of the Western world.[4] Such a restricted approach seems no longer expedient. The last decade has seen the publication of a great number of well-researched studies on the emergence of social groups in non-Western societies that can be described as bourgeois middle classes.[5] Still, most of these studies focus on particular countries and do not look at their rise as a global phenomenon by comparing middle classes across world or by tracing their global entanglements.

Drawing on recent research and combining the expertise of historians of the Western and non-Western worlds, this book provides the first truly global survey of the history of the bourgeoisie. It examines both the similarities and

2. Anil Bhatti and Dorothee Kimmich, eds., *Similarity: A Paradigm for Cultural Theory* (New Delhi: Tulika, 2018).

3. Hannes Siegrist, "Bourgeoisie/Middle Classes, History," in *International Encyclopedia of the Social and Behavioral Sciences*, ed. Neil J. Smelser and Paul B. Baltes (Amsterdam: Elsevier, 2001), 1307–1314, in particular 1312.

4. Carola Lentz, "African Middle Classes: Lessons from Transnational Studies and a Research Agenda," in *The Rise of Africa's Middle Class*, ed. Henning Melber (London: Zed, 2016), 17–53.

5. A. Ricardo López and Barbara Weinstein, eds., *The Making of the Middle Class: Toward a Transnational History* (Durham, NC: Duke University Press, 2012) provides first evidence for a transnational history of the middle classes, yet it has done so without closely investigating the role of the global entanglements and the imperial context that shaped their emergence. Christof Dejung, "Auf dem Weg zu einer globalen Sozialgeschichte? Neuere Studien zur Globalgeschichte des Bürgertums," *Neue Politische Literatur* 59, no. 2 (2014): 229–253, offers a survey of recent studies on the global history of the middle classes. Epistemological considerations can be found in Jürgen Osterhammel, "Gesellschaftsgeschichtliche Parameter chinesischer Modernität," *Geschichte und Gesellschaft* 28 (2002): 71–108.

differences between these groups in their various environments across the globe. Moreover, it demonstrates that the making of the middle classes across the world can be explained only by considering the increasing worldwide circulation of people, ideas, and goods. It was from its start closely connected to global interactions and interconnections in the age of empire. In fact, the middle classes, whether in European metropoles or in colonial peripheries, were deeply affected by global entanglements. Many social structures that emerged in the long nineteenth century can be traced back to activities of such cosmopolitan bourgeoisies and in turn can be considered a reason for the emergence of these groups.[6] Still, these structures were shaped by, and often the result of, highly uneven power relations, such as imperialism and the emergence of a global economy that was increasingly dominated by Western Europe during the long nineteenth century. The rise of middle classes in Asian and African colonies was undoubtedly fueled by European imperialism, yet their emergence was shaped not only by Western influences but also by local conditions. In some cases, colonial middle classes emerged *despite* the existence of global Western hegemony.

Global Social History

Since the beginnings of mankind, societies have been marked by inequality and hierarchy. In almost every human community, some groups have possessed more resources and enjoyed more privileges than others. To be sure, social stratification could vary significantly between different countries. In some societies it was more static and less permeable; in others it was more fluid and permitted more social mobility. But despite all the differences, the modern period saw transformations of class hierarchies across the globe that were remarkably similar.

Social historians tend to study societies within national boundaries, assuming the existence of distinct national societies. This framework may be justified in many cases, given that nation-states did indeed frequently emerge from distinct social communities. Moreover, following the foundation of nation-states, societies were shaped by each state's legal and political institutions and its efforts at nation building, which involved the invention of traditions and various attempts to introduce a feeling of national consciousness and solidarity among

---

6. Anthony Giddens, *The Constitution of Society: Outline of the Theory of Structuration* (Cambridge: Polity, 1984) discusses the mutual conditionality of structure and agency.

citizens.[7] But the nation-state is not always the best instrument to analyze societies historically. Often, it is rather pointless to make general statements about, say, Chinese, German, or American society. Even if the boundaries of national societies can be identified with some accuracy, taking into account border zones and areas of overlap and plural identities, the internal cohesion of society considered more or less congruent with a territory of national jurisdiction should not be overstated. Around 1800, it was hardly possible to speak of a "German" society, given the heterogeneity of all its individual regions. Similarly, the Qing Empire comprised more than half a dozen different regional societies. The United States had (and still has) various different societies across its regions, say between New England and the Southern slave states.

Consequently, scholars have moved beyond the nation as the main unit of analysis and have begun to examine historical processes both above and below the national level. On the one hand, they have focused on local historical processes, with local history becoming one of the most widely practiced forms of social history. On the other hand, they have examined transnational or even global historical processes, an endeavor that brings difficulties of its own, given all the local, national, regional, and continental particularities. While urban, local, national, and at times even regional and continental histories can examine single societies, global social history is confronted with the challenge that there is no observable world society; it thus lacks a clearly defined referent and space for the examination of the interplay of social processes. In practice, however, most global historians focus on a clearly defined locality—a city, a region, a nation-state—and examine its relation to other parts of the world and the consequences such entanglements had for its historical development. In fact, most historical accounts on the rise of the middle classes across the world focus on particular cities and towns such as Aleppo, Delhi, Lucknow, or Shanghai or countries such as Egypt, Japan, or Iran and explore how the middle classes emerged there in the context of transnational and imperial connections.

7. Benedict Anderson, *Imagined Communities: Reflections on the Origin and Spread of Nationalism* (London: Verso, 1983); Ernest Gellner, *Nations and Nationalism* (Ithaca, NY: Cornell University Press, 1983); and Eric Hobsbawm, *Nations and Nationalism since 1780: Programme, Myth, Reality* (Cambridge: Cambridge University Press, 1990) are the three classical accounts on the subject. Anthony D. Smith, *Nationalism: Theory, Ideology, History* (Cambridge: Polity, 2001); and the chapters in John Breuilly, ed., *The Oxford Handbook of the History of Nationalism* (Oxford: Oxford University Press, 2013) provide overviews.

A global social history also has to take into account the vast variety of social hierarchies across the world. But despite these enormous variations of social differentiation in diverse areas, the nineteenth and early twentieth centuries saw remarkably analogous developments in the transformation of societies around the world. Moreover, these developments were increasingly connected. Global labor history, for instance, has examined the interconnection of labor regimes in different parts of the world, demonstrating that forced and voluntary migration, such as the transatlantic slave trade, the Asian coolie trade, and after the turn of the nineteenth century, the emigration of millions of Europeans to the Americas and to Australia, often influenced each other and led to the emergence of new worker communities.[8] The global emergence of middle classes is a similar example of such transformative connectivity in the long nineteenth century. It was linked to global integration and has to be interpreted in the context of worldwide processes such as imperialism, the establishment of ever denser systems of transport and communication, and the breakthrough of global capitalism. In fact, many of the mercantile, scientific and political networks that came into being during the long nineteenth century were established by members of the middle classes such as businessmen, scholars, and intellectuals. It was the middle classes that staffed imperial bureaucracies and the offices of multinational companies, and it was they that ensured the effective operation of such global institutions.

Focusing on the middle classes, this book aims to set out a new trajectory for global historical research by helping define the field of global social history. It aims to reemphasize the importance of class and social stratification in global history and thus close a gap in current scholarship that has often been lamented.[9]

8. Richard Drayton, "The Collaboration of Labour: Slaves, Empires, and Globalizations in the Atlantic World, c. 1600–1850," in *Globalization in World History*, ed. A. G. Hopkins (London: Pimlico, 2002), 98–114, is a seminal article; Marcel van der Linden, *Workers of the World: Essays Toward a Global Labor History* (Leiden: Brill, 2008); and, for a concise reflection, see Andreas Eckert, "What Is Global Labour History Good For?," in *Work in a Modern Society: The German Historical Experience in Comparative Perspective*, ed. Jürgen Kocka (Oxford: Berghahn, 2010), 169–181; and the contributions to Karl-Heinz Roth, ed., *On the Road to Global Labour History: A Festschrift for Marcel van der Linden* (Leiden: Brill, 2017).

9. A more explicit focus on social history in global historical research has been suggested by Jürgen Osterhammel, "Transnationale Gesellschaftsgeschichte: Erweiterung oder Alternative?," *Geschichte und Gesellschaft* 27, no. 3 (2001): 464–479; Patrick Manning, *Navigating World History: Historians Create a Global Past* (New York: Palgrave Macmillan, 2003), 201–213; Peter Stearns, "Social History and World History: Toward Greater Interaction," *World History Connected* 2, no. 2 (2005); Jürgen Kocka, "Sozialgeschichte und Globalgeschichte," in *Dimensionen*

It thereby ties in with recent studies that explore other social groups, including the global history of interactions between European and non-European aristocrats and the global history of labor and workers.[10]

The emergence of the middle classes has to be considered in the context of the fundamental socioeconomic changes of the long nineteenth century, which led to social transformations throughout the world. In fact, both the establishment of transnational regimes of labor and the worldwide emergence of middle classes happened concomitantly; both can be considered a consequence of an emerging global economy and more generally of global entanglements.[11] There is a strong case to be made for examining social stratification as a result of global interaction and opens up a research trajectory that could eventually lead to the conceptualizing of a global social history as a new field of historical research.[12]

---

der Kultur- und Gesellschaftsgeschichte: Festschrift für Hannes Siegrist zum 60. Geburtstag, ed. Matthias Middell (Leipzig: Leipziger Universitätsverlag, 2007), 90–101; and Kenneth Pomeranz, "Social History and World History: From Daily Life to Patterns of Change," *Journal of World History* 18, no. 1 (2007): 69–98. Impulses also come from debates on global historical sociology: Jürgen Osterhammel, "Global History and Historical Sociology," in *The Prospect of Global History*, ed. James Belich, John Darwin, Margaret Frenz, and Chris Wickham (Oxford: Oxford University Press, 2016), 23–43; and the contributions to Julian Go and George Lawson, eds., *Global Historical Sociology* (Cambridge: Cambridge University Press, 2017). Among the few practical attempts to examine global history from an explicitly social historical perspective are Jürgen Osterhammel, *The Transformation of the World: A Global History of the Nineteenth Century* (Princeton, NJ: Princeton University Press, 2014), 744–778; and Jürgen Osterhammel, "Hierarchies and Connections: Aspects of a Global Social History," in *An Emerging Modern World, 1750–1870*, ed. Sebastian Conrad and Jürgen Osterhammel (Cambridge, MA: Harvard University Press, 2018), 661–888.

10. David Motadel, "Qajar Shahs in Imperial Germany," *Past and Present* 213, no. 1 (2011): 191–235; within an empire, David Cannadine, *Ornamentalism: How the British Saw Their Empire* (London: Penguin, 2001); and within Europe, Dominic Lieven, *The Aristocracy in Europe, 1815–1914* (New York: Macmillan, 1992), on the aristocracy and their regional and global encounters. Frederick Cooper, Thomas C. Holt, and Rebecca J. Scott, *Beyond Slavery: Explorations of Race, Labor, and Citizenship in Postemancipation Societies* (Chapel Hill: University of North Carolina Press, 2000); Van der Linden, *Workers of the World*; and, concisely, Eckert, "What Is Global Labour History Good For?"; and the contributions to Roth, *On the Road to Global Labour History*, discuss the global history of labor and the working class.

11. Sven Beckert, *Empire of Cotton: A Global History* (New York: Knopf, 2014), examines this interrelation.

12. Christof Dejung, "Transregional Study of Class, Social Groups, and Milieus," in *Handbook of Transregional Studies*, ed. Matthias Middell (London: Routledge, 2019), 74–81.

The Making of the Global Bourgeois Middle Classes

Scholars of the history of the bourgeoisie face the problem that it is difficult to define this social group according to objective criteria.[13] The middle class can be understood both in sociological and in cultural terms.[14] As a social formation, in the sense of Karl Marx or Max Weber, it can be seen as a group that distinguished itself from the aristocracy above it, which defined itself by genealogy and landownership, and peasants and the working classes below, which were defined by manual labor. Depending on the society, the middle class distinguished itself from the clergy as well. The difficulty of characterizing the bourgeois middle class stems not least from the fact that this social group could be very heterogeneous, comprising actors with varying social and economic statuses and different degrees of access to political power. It ranged from some of the richest people in the world, such as railroad magnates and owners of multinational banking corporations, to people with modest economic backgrounds, such as shopkeepers, schoolteachers, and train drivers. The bourgeois middle class may be divided into several subcategories by wealth and profession.[15] At its top was the upper bourgeoisie, a social elite that was composed of the old patricians, large landowners, and industrialists. At its core was the economic or entrepreneurial bourgeoisie, made up of merchants, businessmen, and bankers, as well as the educated or professional bourgeoisie, comprising lawyers, judges, teachers, medical doctors, scholars, architects, apothecaries, engineers, master artisans, and others. At its bottom was the petite bourgeoisie, or lower middle class, which included small shopkeepers and salespeople,

13. Some scholars have therefore even argued it was merely a myth that was established in the social imaginary to sustain particular notions of political power. For such an account, see Dror Wahrman, *Imagining the Middle Class: The Political Representation of Class in Britain, c. 1780–1840* (Cambridge: Cambridge University Press, 1995); and Sarah Maza, *The Myth of the French Bourgeoisie: An Essay on the Social Imaginary, 1750–1850* (Cambridge, MA: Harvard University Press, 2003).

14. Jürgen Kocka, "The Middle Classes in Europe," in *The European Way: European Societies in the 19th and 20th Centuries*, ed. Hartmut Kaelble (Oxford: Berghahn, 2004), 15–43. An early masterpiece on the history of the bourgeoisie is Edmond Goblot, *La barrière et le niveau: Etude sociologique sur la bourgeoisie française moderne* (Paris: Presses universitaires de France, 2010), first published in 1925.

15. Hartmut Kaelble, "Social Particularities of Nineteenth- and Twentieth-Century Europe," in *The European Way*, ed. Hartmut Kaelble, 276–317, at 282–284, proposes distinguishing between a bourgeois milieu in the narrow sense—the "upper middle class"—and a petit bourgeois milieu.

white-collar employees and lower-rank civil servants, artisans, policemen, and so on.[16] To be sure, the boundaries between these different strata within the bourgeois middle class were often fluid. While the upper bourgeoisie was at times eager to acquire an aristocratic lifestyle, the lower bourgeoisie, fearful of proletarization, was often anxious to distance itself from workers and peasants. There could also be frictions within the class. Middle-class men were confronted with the aspirations of middle-class women for political and economic equality; non-European middle classes living under colonial rule had to struggle for political and cultural equality and against racial prejudices and the imperial oppression they endured from their European middle-class rulers. And the significance of global connections could vary dramatically between the different segments of this class, ranging from the globally connected and mobile upper bourgeoisie to the more locally rooted petite bourgeoisie.

In cultural terms, the bourgeois middle class may be characterized by specific manners and social practices, as well as norms, values, ideals, and tastes, all forms of distinction by which its members marked out their social community and distinguished themselves from other social groups.[17] By focusing on cultural features, historians of the middle classes have pursued a similar approach to that proposed by E. P. Thompson and others for the history of the working class.[18] The distinct social practices of the bourgeois middle class were characterized by particular forms of sociability and associational life, taking place in coffeehouses, social clubs, and cultural organizations. Their forms of

16. Geoffrey Crossick and Heinz-Gerhard Haupt, *The Petite Bourgeoisie in Europe 1780–1914: Enterprise, Family and Independence* (New York: Routledge, 1995); and James R. Farr, *Artisans in Europe, 1300–1914* (Cambridge: Cambridge University Press, 2000), for Europe.

17. A cultural understanding of class was most prominently advocated by the Bielefeld research project "Sozialgeschichte des neuzeitlichen Bürgertums": Hans-Jürgen Puhle, ed., *Bürger in der Gesellschaft der Neuzeit: Wirtschaft—Politik—Kultur* (Göttingen: Vandenhoeck und Ruprecht, 1991); and Jonathan Sperber, "Bürger, Bürgertum, Bürgerlichkeit, Bürgerliche Gesellschaft: Studies of the German (Upper) Middle Class and Its Sociocultural World," *Journal of Modern History* 69 (1997): 271–297. On bourgeois culture, see Manfred Hettling and Stefan-Ludwig Hoffmann, eds., *Der bürgerliche Wertehimmel: Innenansichten des 19. Jahrhunderts* (Göttingen: Vandenhoeck und Ruprecht, 2000); Linda Young, *Middle-Class Culture in the Nineteenth Century* (New York: Palgrave, 2003); and Jerrold Seigel, *Modernity and Bourgeois Life: Society, Politics, and Culture in England, France, and Germany since 1750* (Cambridge: Cambridge University Press, 2012). On social distinction more generally, see Pierre Bourdieu, *Distinction: A Social Critique of the Judgement of Taste* (Cambridge, MA: Harvard University Press, 1987).

18. E. P. Thompson, *The Making of the English Working Class* (London: Victor Gollancz, 1963) is the most influential work to study the history of class as sociocultural history.

sociability included balls, reading circles, chamber concerts, and soirées. Their new institutions were theaters and operas, universities and polytechnics, public parks, and grand hotels. The bourgeois lifestyle involved new bodily practices, characterized by self-control, as well as new sartorial standards, often derived from Europe and marked by the suit and by specific headgear, such as the brimmed hat worn in imperial Europe or the fez in the Ottoman Empire.[19] They developed their own public sphere, forged in places like cafés and salons and in the press.[20] Generally, these institutions emerged in cities that grew dramatically in both centers and peripheries during the long nineteenth century. Urban spaces offered the bourgeoisie rooms to exercise and refine their repertoire of cultural practices.[21] The bourgeoisie can thus be considered mostly an urban phenomenon, even though rural elites were increasingly embracing middle-class lifestyles and cultures as well.[22]

Among their shared ideals were the control of emotions, the veneration of education and individual achievement, the development of an individual personality and pursuit of self-perfection, a particular work ethic, a belief in progress, and a distinct understanding of science, politics, and religion. They aspired to rise socially and were anxious about any potential loss of social status or downward social mobility. They sought individual prosperity but also valued the ideal of responsibility toward society as public-spirited citizens. To gain respectability, moreover, was a main goal of the bourgeois middle class; instead

19. Robert Ross, *Clothing: A Global History: Or, the Imperialists' New Clothes* (Cambridge: Polity, 2008).

20. Jürgen Habermas, *The Structural Transformation of the Public Sphere: An Inquiry into a Category of Bourgeois Society* (Cambridge, MA: MIT Press, 1989) is a translation of the German classic from 1962.

21. Edhem Eldem, "(A Quest for) the Bourgeoisie of Istanbul: Identities, Roles and Conflicts," in *Urban Governance Under the Ottomans: Between Cosmopolitanism and Conflict*, ed. Ulrike Freitag and Nora Lafi (London: Routledge, 2014), 159–186; Su Lin Lewis, *Cities in Motion: Urban Life and Cosmopolitanism in Southeast Asia, 1920–1940* (Cambridge: Cambridge University Press, 2016); and the contributions to the special issue "New Urban Middle Classes in Colonial Java," *Journal of the Humanities and Social Sciences of Southeast Asia* 173, no. 4 (2017) provide examples.

22. Michel R. Doortmont, *The Pen-Pictures of Modern Africans and African Celebrities by Charles Francis Hutchison: A Collective Biography of Elite Society in the Gold Coast Colony* (Leiden: Brill, 2005); and Lucie Ryzova, *The Age of the Efendiyya: Passages to Modernity in National-Colonial Egypt* (Oxford: Oxford University Press, 2014) on the links and shifting boundaries between urban middle classes and their relatives in the countryside in West Africa and Egypt.

of honor, the concern of the aristocrat, the bourgeois valued their own reputations and sought to appear respectable in society—creditworthy, law-abiding, and possessing moral integrity. Moreover, in many parts of the world, the bourgeois universe of values was characterized by the ideal of education—literary-philosophical in particular—or more generally, *Bildung* and an admiration of intellectual achievement and learning.[23] The bourgeois world honored the arts and sciences as performed in universities, museums, and galleries.

In their private lives, the middle classes developed distinct forms of domesticity, family relations, and gender roles.[24] In the bourgeois gender order, the public sphere of business and politics was for most of the nineteenth century a realm reserved for men. In contrast, women were supposed to organize the private sphere of home and family by making arrangements for the education of children and organizing dinner parties and establishing social ties.[25] This may be seen as evidence that in spite of its universalist pretentions, bourgeois society was often characterized by highly unequal gender relations. Social reality was often more complex, however, and women were by no means restricted to the household. They played an important role in social welfare organizations

23. For European examples, see Peter Lundgreen, "Bildung und Bürgertum," in *Sozial- und Kulturgeschichte des Bürgertums: Eine Bilanz des Bielefelder Sonderforschungsbereichs (1986–1997)*, ed. Peter Lundgreen (Göttingen: Vandenhoeck und Ruprecht, 2000), 173–194; and the contributions to Werner Conze and Jürgen Kocka, eds., *Bildungsbürgertum im neunzehnten Jahrhundert*, 4 vols. (Stuttgart: Klett-Cotta, 1985–92); for a non-European example: Cyrus Schayegh, *Who is Knowledgeable is Strong: Science, Class, and the Formation of Modern Iranian Society, 1900–1950* (Berkeley: University of California Press, 2009).

24. Kristin Mann, *Marrying Well: Marriage, Status and Social Change among the Educated Elite in Colonial Lagos* (Cambridge: Cambridge University Press, 1985); Ute Frevert, *Women in German History: From Bourgeois Emancipation to Sexual Liberation* (Oxford: Berg, 1989); Sanjay Joshi, *Fractured Modernity: Making of a Middle Class in Colonial North India* (Oxford: Oxford University Press, 2001); and Wilson Chacko Jacob, *Working Out Egypt: Effendi Masculinity and Subject Formation in Colonial Modernity, 1870–1940* (Durham, NC: Duke University Press, 2010), are examples providing insights into bourgeois gender relations.

25. Mary P. Ryan, *Cradle of the Middle Class: The Family in Oneida County, New York, 1790–1865* (New York: Cambridge University Press, 1981); Leonore Davidoff and Catherine Hall, *Family Fortunes: Men and Women of the English Middle Class* (Chicago: University of Chicago Press, 1987); Margaret MacMillan, *Women of the Raj* (London: Thames and Hudson, 1988); Marion A. Kaplan, *The Making of the Jewish Middle Class: Women, Family and Identity in Imperial Germany* (Oxford: Oxford University Press, 1991); and Elizabeth Buettner, *Empire Families: Britons and Late Imperial India* (Oxford: Oxford University Press, 2004).

and philanthropic movements. By raising funds, working as teachers, and making house calls in proletarian households, women contributed to shaping middle-class identity and culture.[26] Such ambivalence in middle-class gender relations also comes to the fore in terms of the women's movement. In both Western and non-Western countries, middle-class women could tie in with the bourgeois quest for equality.[27] As a consequence, throughout the world, middle-class women became exponents of the suffragette movements that emerged after the mid-nineteenth century in metropoles and at the colonial peripheries. In Egypt, for instance, suffragettes such as Nabawiyya Musa and Hifni Malak Nassef, both of whom came from middle-class families and were among the first women to attend the teachers colleges that had been established after the 1830s, advocated women's rights in newly founded feminist journals. Both were supported by male professionals such as Qasim Amin, a judge who called for the abolition of veiling and gender segregation.[28] In tsarist Russia, as well, feminists came mostly from the urban intelligentsia and were supported by their male companions.[29]

Comparing and Connecting Global Middle Classes

This book aims to provide a comparative view of middle classes and bourgeois cultures that emerged across the globe and to examine their interconnections. As a comparative history, it examines not only their similarities but also important differences, taking into account the diverse local and regional contexts.[30] A particular problem of a comparative history of the middle classes is that the designations of this group in different languages—such as *middle classes* in English, *Bürgertum* in German, *classe moyenne* in French, *efendiyya* in Arabic, and

---

26. Alison Twells, *The Civilising Mission and the English Middle Class, 1792–1850: The "Heathen" at Home and Overseas* (New York: Palgrave Macmillan, 2009).

27. Joshi, *Fractured Modernity*.

28. Margot Badran, "Competing Agenda: Feminists, Islam, and the State in Nineteenth- and Twentieth-Century Egypt," in *Global Feminisms since 1945*, ed. Bonnie G. Smith (London: Routledge, 2000), 13–44.

29. Bianka Pietrow-Ennker, *Russlands "neue Menschen": Die Entwicklung der Frauenbewegung von den Anfängen bis zur Oktoberrevolution* (Frankfurt: Campus, 1999).

30. R. Radhakrishnan, "Why Compare?," *New Literary History* 40, no. 3 (2009): 453–471; and some chapters in Bhatti and Kimmich, eds., *Similarity*, provide critical reflections on comparison.

bhadralok in Bengali—often have different meanings and connotations.[31] Historians have already discussed this problem of semantic heterogeneity in the European context, and it becomes even more crucial in a global comparison, where historians are confronted with more than just "three bourgeois worlds."[32] For practical reasons, and if not stated otherwise, this volume will use the terms "bourgeoisie" and "middle class" interchangeably, acknowledging the different meanings and connotations both terms carry in different English-speaking societies and, more crucially, the problems of using a European term as a category to analyze non-European societies.

Still, it is worth looking into the terminology used by historians. European social historians, most prominently in Germany and France, tend to use "bourgeoisie" and "middle class" as synonyms and range them in between the aristocracy above and the urban and rural underclasses below.[33] A similar tendency can be observed in Asian, Middle Eastern, and African studies. Whereas older publications described the new groups that emerged in these areas after the mid-nineteenth century as "bourgeoisies," studies published in the last fifteen years have tended to use the term "middle class" as a label for the very same groups; there is no discernible difference, however, with regards to content and theoretical approach between older and more recent studies on the histories of non-Western bourgeoisies and middle classes.[34] Exceptions are studies

31. *Efendi* originally describes a professional government employee in Arabic and Ottoman Turkish; *efendiyya* was used to describe an urban group of individuals with a middling cultural code, especially in Egypt after the turn of the twentieth century. This ambiguity is a striking example for the difficulties a comparative social history is confronted with in terms of terminology. Similar complex semantical evolutions can also be observed in other cases, from the German word *Bürgertum* to the English term "middle class."

32. Reinhart Koselleck, Ulrike Spree, and Willibald Steinmetz, "Drei bürgerliche Welten: Zur vergleichenden Semantik der bürgerlichen Gesellschaft in Deutschland, England und Frankreich," in *Bürger in der Gesellschaft der Neuzeit*, ed. Puhle, 14–58.

33. Kocka, "Middle Classes in Europe."

34. Examples of older publications on non-Western bourgeoisies are Leo Kuper, *An African Bourgeoisie: Race, Class, and Politics in South Africa* (New Haven, CT: Yale University Press, 1965); Alan Gregor Cobley, *Class and Consciousness: The Black Petty Bourgeoisie in South Africa, 1924 to 1950* (New York: Greenwood Press, 1990); Patrick Manning, "L' Affaire Adjovi: La bourgeoisie foncière naissante au Dahomey, face à l'administration," in *Entreprises et Entrepreneurs en Afrique*, ed. Alain Forest and Cathérine Cocquery-Vidrovitch, vol. 2 (Paris: Harmattan, 1983), 241–267; Marie-Claire Bergère, *The Golden Age of the Chinese Bourgeoisie, 1911–1937* (Cambridge: Cambridge University Press, 1989); Fatma Müge Göçek, *Rise of the Bourgeoisie, Demise of Empire: Ottoman Westernization and Social Change* (Oxford: Oxford University Press, 1996); and

on America. Scholars of American history generally use the term "bourgeoisie" as a Marxist category applied to the owners of means of production, while
they use the term "middle classes" to designate less wealthy yet well-educated
groups. This terminological differentiation corresponds to sociopolitical differences between the Old and the New World. In contrast to Europe, the
emerging bourgeoisies in the Americas did not have to sustain their position
against the claims of entrenched aristocratic elites. As Sven Beckert and others
have pointed out, it was exactly for this reason that the US-American bourgeoisie became one of the most eminent economic elites in the world in the
nineteenth century.[35] Yet its dominance was always contested by middle-class
radicalism, which argued for more political influence for the petite bourgeoisie
and a constraint on the hegemony of big business.[36]

When we turn to the non-Western world, the problem of terminology gets
even more complex. It should be obvious that sociological-historical concepts
of European origin, such as the bourgeoisie or the middle class, cannot be
smoothly applied to non-European history. First, the epistemological problem
of comparisons is that we selectively look for analogies, overlooking important
differences between Western and non-Western societies. Second, there is the
real danger that the application of models that are at the heart of Western his-
toricism to non-Western societies results in seeing the history of most of the
world in terms of a "lack"—such as the lack of the right social classes to initiate
the appropriate historical transitions to meet the Western standard. To completely renounce global comparisons for this reason, however, would reinforce
the othering of non-Western societies and abet their exoticism (which has been
rightly criticized by postcolonial theory as well). Without the adoption of common terms, cross-regional comparisons would be rendered impossible, which

Kumari Jayawardena, *Nobodies to Somebodies: The Rise of the Colonial Bourgeoisie in Sri Lanka*
(London: Zed, 2000).

35. Sven Beckert, *The Monied Metropolis: New York City and the Consolidation of the American
Bourgeoisie, 1850–1896* (Cambridge: Cambridge University Press, 2001); and Sven Beckert and
Julia B. Rosenbaum, eds., *The American Bourgeoisie: Distinction and Identity in the Nineteenth
Century* (New York: Palgrave Macmillan, 2010).

36. Stuart M. Blumin, *The Emergence of the Middle Class: Social Experience in the American
City, 1760–1900* (Cambridge: Cambridge University Press, 1989); Burton J. Bledstein and Rob-
ert D. Johnston, eds., *The Middling Sorts: Explorations in the History of the American Middle Class*
(New York: Routledge, 2001); and Robert D. Johnston, *The Radical Middle Class: Populist De-
mocracy and the Question of Capitalism in Progressive Era Portland, Oregon* (Princeton, NJ:
Princeton University Press, 2003).

is why they can be considered as "both inadequate and indispensable," as Dipesh Chakrabarty famously put it.[37]

Overall, differences in conceptualizing the relation between the bourgeoisies and middle classes in different world regions are no reason against their examination from a global historical perspective. On the contrary, the differences between the various historiographies reflect the diversity of relations between social groups in different parts of the world and may thus be a first step toward cross-societal comparisons.

A global history of the middle classes, however, needs to not only provide comparisons but also address the various connections between middle classes and bourgeois cultures across the globe. The chapters in this book thus also explore the ways in which the emergence of middle classes in different parts of the world (including Europe) was tied to global links of commerce, colonialism, and communication. Moreover, they examine the encounters between members of middle classes from different parts of the world, both in imperial and nonimperial contexts. In fact, the emergence of middle classes was closely tied to transnational and transimperial structures and can be examined as processes of socialization on a global level. Socialization, following the definition of Georg Simmel, means perceiving social order not as a static structure but as a process-related issue and as the result of social interaction.[38] Adopting such a course of action obviously ties in with, on the one hand, established approaches of social history that understand the formation of social classes as being a consequence of social practices. On the other hand, it can also be linked with the examination of networks and flows, which is so prominent in current global historical scholarship.

To some extent, the formation of the middle classes around the world was the result of the global spread of European bourgeois cultural standards and lifestyles among economically and socially independent groups. This can be observed in the cases of cultural ideals (such as gender roles) and aesthetics (such as fashion), in social practices (such as table manners), and in institutional standards (such as academic titles). Generally, these transfer processes were

37. Dipesh Chakrabarty, *Provincializing Europe: Postcolonial Thought and Historical Difference* (Princeton, NJ: Princeton University Press, 2000), 16.

38. Georg Simmel, *Soziologie: Untersuchungen über die Formen der Vergesellschaftung* (Leipzig: Duncker und Humblot, 1908); and, for a new edition, *Georg Simmel Gesamtausgabe*, vol. 11 (Frankfurt: Suhrkamp, 1992); and, for the English translation, Georg Simmel, *Sociology: Inquiries into the Construction of Social Forms*, 2 vols. (Leiden: Brill, 2009).

fueled by European imperialism and increasing integration. European bourgeois culture often served as a model for middle classes in other continents, as a reference point and even as a template for direct imitation. Studying this process for British India, Partha Chatterjee has argued that the Indian middle classes were nothing but an imitation of the Western model and therefore should be considered the product of a "derivative discourse."[39] Other scholars have maintained that non-Western middle classes were merely "comprador bourgeoisies," which assisted European imperialists in the exploitation of colonial possessions.[40]

And yet the global rise of the bourgeoisie was much more than a mere diffusion of European models. Rather than just passively adopting European ideas and practices, non-European middle classes modified them and merged them with their local cultures, which resulted in variations and hybridizations.[41] In general, bourgeois lifestyles and values were often understood in the non-European world, from Asia to Latin America, as "universal," "modern," and "civilized," and not as "European" or "Western" per se. Nor can non-Western middle classes be considered mere footmen of Europeans; throughout the world, they pursued political and economic agendas of their own and often were among the most explicit critiques of imperial rule.[42] It is obvious that a global historical study of the middle classes has to take such non-European agency seriously.[43] It was precisely their cosmopolitan attitude and the quest for social

39. Partha Chatterjee, *Nationalist Thought and the Colonial World: A Derivative Discourse?* (London: Zed, 1986); and Partha Chatterjee, *The Nation and Its Fragments: Colonial and Postcolonial Histories* (Princeton, NJ: Princeton University Press, 1993).

40. Frantz Fanon, *The Wretched of the Earth* (New York: Grove Press, 1963) is the most prominent example.

41. Homi K. Bhabha, *The Location of Culture* (London: Routledge, 1994); Jan Nederveen Pieterse, *Globalization and Culture: Global Mélange* (Lanham, MD: Rowman and Littlefield, 2004); and Marwan M. Kraidy, *Hybridity: On the Cultural Logic of Globalization* (Philadelphia, PA: Temple University Press, 2005).

42. Michael O. West, *The Rise of the African Middle Class: Colonial Zimbabwe, 1898–1965* (Bloomington: Indiana University Press, 2002) is a case study on this phenomenon.

43. C. A. Bayly, *Empire and Information: Intelligence Gathering and Social Communication in India, 1780–1870* (Cambridge: Cambridge University Press, 1996), 180–211; Joshi, *Fractured Modernity*; Margrit Pernau, *Ashraf into Middle Classes: Muslims in Nineteenth-Century Delhi* (Oxford: Oxford University Press, 2013); and Indra Sengupta, "Kolonialstadt und bürgerliche Kultur: Die 'Bhadralok' von Kolkata," in *Mumbai–Delhi–Kolkata: Annäherungen an die Megastädte Indiens*, ed. Ravi Ahuja and Christiane Brosius (Heidelberg: Draupadi, 2006), 269–282, have put forth this argument for colonial India.

and individual development that was at the core of the bourgeois worldview, and it was their ability to rearticulate and reinvent identities under conditions of global inequalities of power that turned the middle classes into a ubiquitous presence in the colonial world as well.

On the other side, the European bourgeoisie was not just the generator but also the product of global change. Emerging during the eighteenth- and nineteenth-century period of globalization, European middle classes were from the outset shaped by the international exchange of goods and ideas. The wealth of many members of the metropolitan bourgeoisie has actually been traced back to the trans-Atlantic slave trade and the Caribbean plantation system.[44] And recent research has revealed that the dual revolution of the late eighteenth century—the Industrial and the French Revolutions—that was crucial for the emergence of bourgeois societies can be interpreted as the result of processes of global entanglement. The French Revolution was, among other things, the consequence of the financial problems of the French state that had been caused by the costly wars fought in faraway places such as North America and India during the Seven Years War.[45] And the Industrial Revolution was not least the result of the endeavors of British entrepreneurs to produce luxury goods to compete with the high-quality imports from China and India.[46] The European bourgeoisie that came about in the wake of these revolutions had a global horizon. Seeing themselves as pioneers of modernity, they adjusted to the rapid social and economic transformations in the nineteenth century by redefining their relationship with societies on the colonial periphery and by assigning human civilizations in different parts of the world to different stages of development. Metropolitan sciences, which were established particularly by

44. Eric Williams, *Capitalism and Slavery* (Chapel Hill: University of North Carolina Press, 1944) is the classic study on this relation; and, for more recent accounts, see Thomas David, Bouda Etemad, and Janick Marina Schaufelbuehl, *La Suisse et l'esclavage des Noirs* (Lausanne: Editions Antipodes, 2005); and the contributions in Sven Beckert and Seth Rockman, eds., *Slavery's Capitalism: A New History of American Economic Development* (Philadelphia: University of Pennsylvania Press, 2016).

45. C. A. Bayly, *The Birth of the Modern World, 1780–1914: Global Connections and Comparisons* (Oxford: Blackwell, 2004), 86; and Lynn Hunt, "The Global Financial Origins of 1789," in *The French Revolution in Global Perspective*, ed. Suzanne Desan, Lynn Hunt, and William Max Nelson (Ithaca, NY: Cornell University Press, 2013), 32–43.

46. Maxine Berg, "In Pursuit of Luxury: Global History and British Consumer Goods in the Eighteenth Century," *Past and Present* 182, no. 1 (2004): 85–142; and also Giorgio Riello, *Cotton: The Fabric That Made the Modern World* (Cambridge: Cambridge University Press, 2013), 211–237.

members of the educated middle classes, sustained their claim to universalism by comparing plants and animals from all over the world. Indeed, even Enlightenment scholarship and the development of modern sciences were to some extent the result of a global transfer of ideas.[47] Moreover, bourgeois culture relied on the consumption of colonial commodities such as tea, coffee, cocoa, sugar, silk, and cotton, as well as on the display of non-European people and exotic plants and animals in anthropological museums and botanic and zoological gardens that were established in virtually every Western city during the nineteenth century. Thus, the rise of European middle classes cannot but be examined in the context of imperialism and globalization.[48]

Finally, the chapters of this book explore the encounters and interactions between middle classes from different parts of the world. Many members of the non-European intelligentsia were in close contact with their Western counterparts—whether they were educated in missionary schools or at Europe's great universities or communicated with scholars in Berlin, London, or Boston. The realms of scientific knowledge saw the emergence of global networks that were established by members of the educated middle classes from different parts of the world after the late nineteenth century. Membership in scientific societies and the exchange of ideas in scholarly publications and at international conferences led to the emergence of a global republic of letters in which, at least in theory, geographical origin was supposed not to be of importance.[49] Similar cooperation can be observed in terms of the global economy. Even though European, American, and, after the First World War,

47. Sebastian Conrad, "Enlightenment in Global History: A Historiographical Critique," *American Historical Review* 117, no. 4 (2012): 999–1027.

48. John MacKenzie, *Imperialism and Popular Culture* (Manchester: Manchester University Press, 1986); and the chapters in Frederick Cooper and Ann Laura Stoler, eds., *Tensions of Empire: Colonial Cultures in a Bourgeois World* (Berkeley: University of California Press); and in Catherine Hall and Sonya O. Rose, eds., *At Home with the Empire: Metropolitan Culture and the Imperial World* (Cambridge: Cambridge University Press, 2006) trace these colonial aspects of European bourgeois culture. Maya Jasanoff, *Edge of Empire: Lives, Culture, and Conquest in the East, 1750–1850* (New York: Knopf, 2005) examines them in the world of art; and Maya Jasanoff, *The Dawn Watch: Joseph Conrad in a Global World* (London: Penguin, 2017), in the world of literature.

49. Stefanie Gänger, *Relics of the Past: The Collecting and Study of Pre-Columbian Antiquities in Peru and Chile, 1837–1911* (Oxford: Oxford University Press, 2014); Stefanie Gänger and Su Lin Lewis, "Forum: A World of Ideas: New Pathways in Global Intellectual History, c. 1880–1930," *Modern Intellectual History* 10, no. 2 (2013): 347–351, on scholarly bourgeois cosmopolitanism; and Kris Manjapra, *Age of Entanglement: German and Indian Intellectuals across Empire*

Japanese capital and political power fundamentally transformed African, Asian, and Latin American economies, the integration of these areas into world capitalism would not have been possible without the assistance of local businessmen.[50] The cooperation between Western and non-Western businessmen was facilitated by similar business practices and a similar mercantile culture, which is why they can be described as joint members of a globally connected bourgeoisie.[51] Migration, too, could result in new connections, such as in the diaspora, where middle-class exiles routinely assimilated into the bourgeois milieu of the majority society.[52]

A global history of the middle classes also reveals that the world in the age of empire was characterized not only by racial discrimination and imperial arrogance but also by ideals of equality and development across geographical boundaries. As a consequence, global interactions between members of the respective middle classes were at times surprisingly egalitarian and free from cultural prejudices and conflict, whereas in other cases, they were tainted by racist and colonial attitudes and confrontation.[53]

The temporal focus of this book ranges roughly from the 1850s to the 1950s. To be sure, social history knows no schematically defined periods with sharp cutoff dates. Origins and ends are often less interesting than trajectories and phases of intensification and accelerated change. In the most general terms,

---

(Cambridge, MA: Harvard University Press, 2014) on more general intellectual cosmopolitanism are important case studies.

50. C. A. Bayly, *Rulers, Townsmen and Bazaars: North Indian Society in the Age of British Expansion, 1770–1870* (Cambridge: Cambridge University Press, 1983); Yen-p'ing Hao, *The Commercial Revolution in Nineteenth-Century China: The Rise of Sino-Western Mercantile Capitalism* (Berkeley: University of California Press, 1986); and Rajat Kanta Ray, "Asian Capital in the Age of European Domination. The Rise of the Bazaar, 1800–1914," *Modern Asian Studies* 29 (1995): 449–554, on the significance of local businessmen for European trade in Asia.

51. Eric L. Jones, *The European Miracle: Environments, Economies and Geopolitics in the History of Europe and Asia* (Cambridge: Cambridge University Press, 1981); Charles A. Jones, *International Business in the Nineteenth Century: The Rise and Fall of a Cosmopolitan Bourgeoisie* (Brighton: Wheatsheaf, 1987); Ulrike Freitag, *Indian Ocean Migrants and State Formation in Hadhramaut: Reforming the Homeland* (Leiden: Brill, 2003); and Christof Dejung, *Commodity Trading, Globalization and the Colonial World: Spinning the Web of the Global Market* (New York: Routledge, 2018).

52. David Motadel, "Islamische Bürgerlichkeit: Das soziokulturelle Milieu der muslimischen Minderheit in Berlin 1918–1939," *Tel Aviver Jahrbuch für deutsche Geschichte* 37 (2009): 103–121.

53. Cannadine, *Ornamentalism*, refers to the importance of class and social status with regard to the interaction between members of European and non-European elites within the British Empire.

modern bourgeois middle classes emerged outside Western Europe and the East Coast of the United States during or after the middle decades of the nineteenth century. At the same time, they achieved unprecedented cultural, economic, and even political power in the West. By around 1880, clusters of bourgeois classes could be found in the densely populated parts of every continent, and by the 1920s, they had matured almost everywhere. The various stories told in this book thus begin at the outset of what James Gelvin and Nile Green have termed "the age of steam and print" and end with the decline of European imperial domination after 1945.[54] Some of the authors have chosen to highlight a particular section of time and to stop a long way before empires did in fact exit from the stage of history. In other cases, they look at long-term societal changes crossing the caesuras of political history and extending their narratives to the postimperial world. We would like to see this as a virtue of the volume and would be unhappy with the rigid enforcement of clear temporal boundaries.

This book addresses the global history of the emergence of middle classes and bourgeois cultures in five thematic parts, looking at the relations between the middle classes and the state (Part I), the importance of colonialism in the emergence of global middle classes (Part II), the role of culture and religion in the global history of the bourgeoisie (Part III), the frictions and limits of the emergence of global middle classes (Part IV), and the intersection of global capitalism and the emergence of bourgeoisies around the world (Part V). To be sure, the lines between these thematic segments are not clear-cut and there is significant overlap between them. Yet, overall, the chapters provide a colorful panorama of the global rise of the bourgeoisie in the age of empire.

State and Class

Over the course of the nineteenth and twentieth centuries, the bourgeoisie became an increasingly influential political force, trying to take control and set the rules of society and state. They challenged aristocratic powers and entrenched elites, such as in the great bourgeois revolutions in 1848–49 (mainly in Europe) and 1905–11 (mainly in Asia). Yet even though the long nineteenth century has often been described as the golden age of the bourgeoisie, societies with a "bourgeois" political system were rare. Only in a small number of states, such as Switzerland, the Netherlands, France after 1870, and on the east coast

---

54. James L. Gelvin and Nile Green, eds., *Global Muslims in the Age of Steam and Print* (Berkeley: University of California Press, 2014).

of the United States, could the bourgeoisie realize their ambition of determining the course of society. In the rest of the world—particularly on Europe's fringes and outside Europe but also in European countries such as Germany, Great Britain, or Austria-Hungary—the middle classes often existed in a symbiotic relationship with the aristocracy, or, in colonial possessions, with the colonial state, without taking over state power themselves.[55]

Around the world, however, the state became an important frame for the formation of the middle classes. The modern state became more and more reliant on a bureaucratic bourgeoisie of civil servants, military officers, teachers, and university professors. Often they were classes in the service of the state and created by the state as part of modernization and nation-building programs. In his chapter "The Rise of the Middle Class in Iran before the Second World War," Houchang Chehabi traces the formation of a modern middle class that emerged as a result of Reza Shah's rigorous modernization policies in the 1920s and 1930s. The state expanded the educational system and bureaucracy, reaching down from the court to the village level. At the same time, it fostered lifestyles and consumption patterns modeled on those of Europe, which this new and increasingly secular middle class embraced, setting it apart from the rest of society. Given its reliance on state employment, this was not a bourgeoisie *stricto sensu*. This new middle class existed next to the traditional mercantile elite, which was centered on the bazaar and closely allied to the clergy. In the 1920s, however, many Iranian businessmen adopted a middle-class lifestyle, and, as a consequence, a modern business bourgeoisie gradually emerged that was to some extent a link between the traditional mercantile elite centered on the bazaar and the modern middle class.

In America, as Marcus Gräser shows in his chapter "'The Great Middle Class' in the Nineteenth-Century United States," the middle class has historically been more than just a diverse group of middling sorts. In self-awareness as well as in the descriptions made by foreign observers, the middle classes after the eighteenth century appeared as embodiments of the new society that had developed in the colonies of settlers on North American soil. This resulted not least from the fact that typical elements of European societies—above all the aristocracy but also the clergy as a separate estate—were absent. Since the state was relatively weak, the core tasks of civil society, such as poor relief or the

55. Iván T. Berend, *History Derailed: Central and Eastern Europe in the Long Nineteenth Century* (Berkeley: University of California Press, 2003), 196, for Eastern Europe; Pernau, *Ashraf into Middle Classes*, for India; and Ryzova, *Age of the Efendiyya*, for Egypt.

establishing of institutions—museums, libraries, symphony orchestras—
relied on the private initiatives of the American bourgeoisie and middle class,
respectively. In reality, however, the "great American middle class" was much
more fragmented than the emphasis placed on it in political discourse might
suggest. One important reason for this was racial exclusion. Although the
emergence of an Afro-American middle class succeeded in the last third of the
nineteenth century, its rise was restricted by a variety of racially motivated
discriminations.[56] Overcoming such racial segregation was hardly possible
until the second half of the twentieth century.

The establishment of a viable middle class relied not least on the relative stability of the political order. In China, for instance, the bourgeois middle class,
which had emerged in coastal cities after the mid-nineteenth century, could not
take hold because it was not backed by state power and had no influence on the
social and economic conditions in the rural interior of the country. As a consequence, the bourgeoisie came under pressure during the civil wars of the 1920s
and 1930s and was finally crushed after the establishment of the Communist
People's Republic in 1949.[57] In Japan, in contrast, the Meiji oligarchy took on
social modernization as a state task after the 1860s. What is more, after the seventeenth century, a rural proto-middle class had established economic structures in the countryside that paved the path for the implementation of the transformations after the late nineteenth century.[58] In this context, a relatively
strong middle class could emerge even though it had only limited political influence before the end of the Second World War.

In the twentieth century, states even aimed to implement new ideas of population planning in order to foster the emergence of stable middle classes. The
control of fertility became an integral part of the global history of the middle
classes, as Alison Bashford shows in her chapter "Population Planning for a
Global Middle Class." Because the nuclear family was at the core of middle-class
lifestyle and a prerequisite for its reproduction and economic capacity, states

---

56. On the history of the Afro-American middle class, see William A. Muraskin, *Middle-Class
Blacks in a White Society: Prince Hall Freemasonry in America* (Berkeley: University of California
Press, 1975); Lawrence Otis Graham, *Our Kind of People: Inside America's Black Upper Class*
(New York: Harper Collins, 1999); and Joseph O. Jewell, *Race, Social Reform, and the Making of
a Middle Class: The American Missionary Association and Black Atlanta, 1870–1900* (Lanham, MD:
Rowman and Littlefield, 2007).

57. Bergère, *Golden Age of the Chinese Bourgeoisie*.

58. Edward Pratt, *Japan's Protoindustrial Elite: The Economic Foundations of the Gōnō* (Cambridge, MA: Harvard University Press, 1999).

across the globe resorted to population planning after the early twentieth century. For economic and political planners immersed in adapted Malthusian arguments, limiting fertility was a means by which widespread poverty could be mitigated and standards of living raised at a population level to allow everyone to afford middle-class lifestyles. Population control was thus part of the dream of, and for, a global middle class.

The bourgeois worldview was certainly characterized by the striving for individual freedom and political participation. However, the middle classes were not always the backbone of a moderate, democratic political center, as modernization theory would have it. This can be exemplified by the case of Latin America. In contrast to historians of modern Europe, where shared bourgeois values and practices were considered unifying bonds between the bourgeoisie consisting of financiers and wholesalers on the one hand and the lower middle classes on the other, scholars of Latin American social history emphasize the antagonism between these two social strata.[59] They argue that as a consequence of the marginal influence of the middle classes, neither democratic institutions nor a viable civil society could take hold.[60] Social instability, in turn, made the middle classes prone to political repression. Various attempts to establish a social order shaped by the economic and political ideals of the middle classes were accompanied by military coups and the assassination of trade unionists or massacres among Indians and revolting peasants.[61] At the same time, European fascist regimes were supported by both higher and lower middle classes, which were anxious about the aspirations of radicalized working classes to seize political power. This may be a reminder that the middle classes can become the promoters of authoritarian regimes and counterrevolutions if they fear the loss

59. David S. Parker, *The Idea of the Middle Class: White-Collar Workers and Peruvian Society, 1900–1950* (University Park: Pennsylvania State University Press, 1998); Brian P. Owensby, *Intimate Ironies: Making Middle-Class Lives in Modern Brazil* (Stanford, CA: Stanford University Press, 1999); Rodolfo Barros, *Fuimos: Aventuras y Desventuras de La Clase Media* (Buenos Aires: Aguilar, 2005); and, for an overview, David S. Parker and Louise E. Walker, eds., *Latin America's Middle Class: Unsettled Debates and New Histories* (Lanham, MD: Lexington, 2013).

60. Louise E. Walker, *Waking from the Dream: Mexico's Middle Classes after 1968* (Stanford, CA: Stanford University Press, 2013), on the shattered hopes of the Mexican middle class and their increasing estrangement from the ruling Partido Revolucionario Institucional after the mid-1960s.

61. Greg Grandin, *The Last Colonial Massacre: Latin America in the Cold War* (Chicago: University of Chicago Press, 2004).

of the influence and wealth they have accumulated.[62] Such acts of discrimination and repression can be considered the dark side of the ideology of modernity and of the bourgeois quest for universal equality and progress.[63] In particular, colonialism discloses the inherent contradictions of the bourgeois project, as Frederick Cooper and Ann Laura Stoler pointed out, because colonial racism stood in obvious contrast to the claim of universal equality of all humans.[64]

Globally oriented middle classes also interacted to pursue joint political agendas. An exemplary case concerns the British, Indian, and American social reformers who aimed at solving the "woman question" through transoceanic cooperation.[65] Also, middle-class actors not only benefited from and sustained imperial structures, they also were among the most fervent critics of imperialism. The resistance against colonial rule caused the emergence of "cosmopolitan thought zones," which allowed intellectuals from different parts of the world to create an anti-imperial repertoire of ideas. These political activists often established ties across ethnic and geographical borders after the turn of the twentieth century. Scholars have, for instance, emphasized the cooperation of proponents of national independence movements in Ireland, India, Egypt, and South Africa. These movements opposed British hegemony by closely observing anti-imperial strategies in other parts of the world and were supported by British activists in this endeavor. Such cooperation relied not least on the fact that many of these activists—from Gandhi to Bourguiba—had a middle-class background and had received their education at European or American schools and universities.[66]

62. Marc Mulholland, *Bourgeois Liberty and the Politics of Fear: From Absolutism to Neo-Conservatism* (Oxford: Oxford University Press, 2012).

63. Jeffrey C. Alexander, *The Dark Side of Modernity* (Cambridge: Polity, 2013); and, of course, the classic study by the two main exponents of the Frankfurt School, Max Horkheimer and Theodor W. Adorno, *Dialectic of Enlightenment* (New York: Verso, 1986), originally published in 1947.

64. Ann Laura Stoler and Frederick Cooper, "Between Metropole and Colony: Rethinking a Research Agenda," in *Tensions of Empire*, ed. Cooper and Stoler, 1–56.

65. Clare Midgley, "Liberal Religion and the 'Woman Question' between East and West: Perspectives from a Nineteenth-Century Bengali Women's Journal," *Gender & History* 25 (2013): 445–460; and Clare Midgley, "Mary Carpenter and the Brahmo Samaj of India: A Transnational Perspective on Social Reform in the Age of Empire," *Women's History Review* 22 (2013): 363–385.

66. Elleke Boehmer, *Empire, the National, and the Postcolonial, 1890–1920: Resistance in Interaction* (Oxford: Oxford University Press, 2002); Sugata Bose and Kris Manjapra, eds.,

Colonialism and Class

The impact of European imperialism on the emergence and evolution of middle classes around the world can hardly be overestimated. Middle classes could be found on both sides of the colonial divide. The colonial state gave rise to the emergence of colonial middle classes, from West Africa to South Asia. Early non-Western colonial middle classes emerged in the late nineteenth century, most notably in India, but most developed in the first half of the twentieth century. Their ascent was often (but not always) linked to the colonial state, with its educational system, bureaucracy, and army, all of which created a caste of educated professionals—from bureaucrats to merchants—who merged European middle-class culture with their own into distinct forms of colonial middle-class culture. Still, it was often difficult for this group to acculturate with Europeans living in the colonies and to be accepted as equals (even though in some cases, cooperation between European and non-European middle classes was indeed possible and characterized by a remarkable lack of racist discrimination). Faced with mounting discrimination, resentment among members of the African, Asian, and Oceanic bourgeoisie grew, eventually turning this class into one of the most passionate opponents of empire. In particular, in 1919, middle classes across the colonial world embraced nationalist politics to challenge the European empires.[67]

Looking at colonial East Africa, Emma Hunter's chapter, "Modernity, Print Media and the Middle Class in Colonial East Africa," captures this ambiguity. On the one hand, her chapter shows that the colonial economy and racial hierarchies of East Africa offered little potential for the growth of an African bourgeoisie. On the other hand, she demonstrates that in the cultural rather than the economic sphere, a slightly different picture emerges. Looking at the Swahili-language government and the mission newspapers of colonial Zanzibar and Tanganyika between the 1880s and the 1930s, she reveals the ways in which a small but growing literate elite in late nineteenth and early twentieth-century East Africa used the medium of print in order to allow them to do what Hunter terms "jumping scale," that is, "[produce] a new geographical scale above

Cosmopolitan Thought Zones: South Asia and the Global Circulation of Ideas (New York: Palgrave Macmillan, 2010); Nico Slate, *Colored Cosmopolitanism: The Shared Struggle for Freedom in the United States and India* (Cambridge, MA: Harvard University Press: 2012); and Manjapra, *Age of Entanglement*.

67. Erez Manela, *The Wilsonian Moment: Self-Determination and the International Origins of Anticolonial Nationalism* (New York: Oxford University Press, 2007).

that of the colonial territory, a space in which new collectivities could be imagined and identities constructed." The particular space offered by newspapers and periodicals thus provided a possibility for African middle classes to create a distinct public sphere and to assert their distinctiveness by rhetorically identifying with, and making a claim of belonging to, an imagined global bourgeoisie.

Similarly, Utsa Ray, in "Domesticity, Cooking and the Middle Class in Colonial India," demonstrates that, while scholars have long focused on the economic origins of this class, it is crucial to understand the ways in which it fashioned itself. Although the universe of the Indian middle class revolved around contesting colonial categories, the chapter shows that the project of self-fashioning of the Indian middle class was not an instance of alternative modernity, nor did the locality of the middle class in colonial India result in producing some sort of indigenism. This middle class borrowed, adapted, and appropriated the pleasures of modernity and tweaked and subverted it to suit their project of self-fashioning. An area in which such cosmopolitan domesticity can be observed was the culinary culture of colonial Bengal, which utilized both vernacular ingredients and British modes of cooking in order to establish a Bengali bourgeois cuisine.[68] This process of indigenization was an aesthetic choice that was imbricated in the upper caste and in the patriarchal agenda of middle-class social reform, and it developed certain social practices, including imagining the act of cooking as a classic feminine practice and the domestic kitchen as a sacred space. It was often this hybrid culture that marked the colonial middle classes.

The colonial world also saw the emergence of middle classes among European emigrants. In settler colonies, such as Canada, New Zealand, Australia, and South Africa, as well as in the United States and Latin America, European middle-class structures were often reproduced in complex ways, creating distinct social groups with particular cultures and lifestyles.[69] In contrast to Europe, these bourgeoisies did not have to deal with an aristocracy, and they often formed the new ruling elites. They ranked in social status above the majority

68. Kristin L. Hoganson, *Consumers' Imperium: The Global Production of American Domesticity, 1865–1920* (Chapel Hill: University of North Carolina Press, 2007); and Toufoul Abou-Hodeib, *A Taste for Home: The Modern Middle Class in Ottoman Beirut* (Stanford, CA: Stanford University Press, 2017) provide other examples of such cosmopolitan domesticity.

69. James Belich, *Replenishing the Earth: The Settler Revolution and the Rise of the Angloworld* (Oxford: Oxford University Press, 2011).

of lower-class whites and the local populations. Moreover, settler colonies gave rise to new middle classes—from *colons* in Algeria, who formed a petty bourgeoisie, to mining barons in South Africa, who formed a wealthy upper bourgeoisie—that had little to do with the bourgeoisies in their home countries. In most non-settler colonies, however, the group of middle-class Europeans—merchants, officers, government officials—was too small, and their presence often too temporary, for them to form deeper local social structures. What is more, members of these European colonial middle classes did not usually mix with the emerging non-European middle classes, with color bars remaining crucial.

Europe's colonial expansion not only influenced the emergence of middle classes in the colonial world but also in Europe itself. The colonial world shaped the lifestyles and homes of bourgeois middle-class families in the metropolis. As Padraic X. Scanlan shows in his chapter, "Emancipation and the Global British Middle Class," Europe's colonial expansion and imperial economic exploitation contributed to the rise of European middle classes and at the same time shaped European bourgeois culture and values. He points out that Britain's nineteenth-century middle class—famous for its culture of high-minded rectitude, self-discipline, and austere morality and infamous for its hypocrisy, rigidity, and pious sadism—was as much a product of imperial expansion and the integration of global markets as it was one of religious introspection or the politics of bourgeois respectability. Scanlan's chapter reveals that the Victorian middle class made, and was made by, the domestic and imperial reform movements of the nineteenth century. Campaigns for reform in imperial governance, for the end of slavery in British colonies, and for the expansion of the British missionary movement shared practices, ideas, and key personnel with many vigorous domestic reform programs, including campaigns for labor regulation and discipline, temperance, the education and supervision of the urban poor, and the "correction" of convicts. The chapter locates the connections between the imperial and domestic faces of Victorian values in the history of Britain's place in an emerging global capitalism and points to the spread of "Victorianism" far beyond the British archipelago.

Capitalism and Class

Capitalism was not only a defining force in the forging of the middle classes, it also determined the increasing global interaction of their members. The economic bourgeoisie, characterized by their ownership of the modes of production, their control of trade networks, and their command of the financial system, was a global phenomenon from the beginning. Often they grew out of early modern merchant classes, although the path was anything but straightforward. The grand bourgeoisie of Northern Germany, so wonderfully portrayed in Thomas Mann's novel *Buddenbrooks* (1901), grew out of old Hanseatic patrician merchant families. In India, the Bania had acquired enough wealth to make even the British partly dependent on them. In China, the Hong merchants, who had controlled the country's trade with the Europeans before the Opium War, emerged as a distinct mercantile community. After the turn of the nineteenth century, these merchant classes tended to adopt the cultural canon of the educated bourgeoisie, which led to a rapprochement between them. Such a reorientation can be observed in different parts of the world. In nineteenth-century Western Europe, merchants and businessmen generally had a classical education and embraced the values and lifestyle of the educated middle classes.[70] Merchants in the colonial world often came to the conclusion that a Western education would be crucial for their offspring. The mercantile elite of Calcutta, for instance, was the driving force behind the foundation of Hindu College in 1817, which became the role model for the foundation of similar institutions on the subcontinent, institutions that would become the cradles of the Indian middle class until the late nineteenth century.[71]

The involvement of the families of the economic bourgeoisie in trade, finance, and industry gave them the wealth they needed to cement their status in society, and, at the same time, the connections to the outside world. "The need of a constantly expanding market for its products chases the bourgeoisie over the entire surface of the globe. It must nestle everywhere, settle everywhere, establish connexions everywhere," remarked Karl Marx and Friedrich Engels in *The Communist Manifesto* in 1848.[72] Operating on an increasingly

70. Hartmut Berghoff and Roland Möller, "Unternehmer in Deutschland und England 1870–1914: Aspekte eines kollektiv-biographischen Vergleichs," *Historische Zeitschrift* 256 (1993): 353–386.

71. Kapil Raj, *Relocating Modern Science: Circulation and the Construction of Knowledge in South Asia and Europe, 1650–1900* (New York: Palgrave Macmillan, 2007). Other authors, however, have emphasized the differences between the economic and educated middle classes in colonial India in terms of their different affiliation to the state, see, most importantly, Claude Markovits, *Merchants, Traders, Entrepreneurs: Indian Business in the Colonial Era* (New York: Palgrave Macmillan, 2008), 167–183.

72. Karl Marx and Friedrich Engels, *Manifesto of the Communist Party* (London: George Allen, 1954), 124, first published in 1848.

global scale, bourgeois merchant and industrial classes forged networks across continents and oceans. In the age of empire, the European and North American bourgeoisie had a significant advantage in global operations. Non-European mercantile elites often suffered under Europe's imperial expansion, which could rob them of markets and monopolies.[73] Outside Europe, major industrial projects, from railways to telegraph wires, as well as lucrative plantations, were in the hands of entrepreneurs from Europe and the United States. But in non-Western countries as well, members of the economic bourgeoisie could benefit by taking part in a global market that offered a space for economic actors from different parts of the world to interact.

Global trade and business contacts were frequently facilitated through brokers, who could link local trade networks to the global economy. The economic penetration of Asia, for example, would have been impossible for Europeans without the assistance of local intermediaries. Often they acted as middlemen who could link local trade networks to the global economy.[74] Such intermediary positions were filled by minorities—Jews, Greeks, and Armenians in the Mediterranean, Parsis in India, Germans and Jews in Hungary. Émigré communities across the world were involved in long-distance trade as well, such as the Chinese across Southeast Asia or Indian traders in East Africa.[75] Global trade offered minorities a possibility to rise socially, although, as nonhegemonic groups, they often had no protection in times of crisis. However, non-Western economic elites, such as Indian and Chinese merchants, were not restricted to the status of intermediaries; they increasingly engaged

73. Jacques Pouchepadass, "The Agrarian Economy and Rural Society (1790–1860)," in Claude Markovits, ed., *A History of Modern India, 1480–1950* (London: Anthem Press, 2002), 294–315, 310; Claude Markovits, "Merchants and Cities (1760–1860)," in Markovits, ed., *History of Modern India*, 316–329, 325–326; and Weng Eang Cheong, *The Hong Merchants of Canton: Chinese Merchants in Sino-Western Trade, 1684–1798* (London: Routledge, 1997), 303–304.

74. Bayly, *Rulers, Townsmen and Bazaars*; Hao, *Commercial Revolution*; Ray, "Asian Capital"; Dejung, *Commodity Trading*; and Corey Ross, *Ecology and Power in the Age of Empire: Europe and the Transformation of the Tropical World* (Oxford: Oxford University Press, 2017), on the European expansion into Asia.

75. Christine Dobbin, *Asian Entrepreneurial Minorities: Conjoint Communities in the Making of the World Economy, 1570–1940* (Richmond, UK: Curzon, 1996), 47, 69, 171, on Chinese traders across Southeast Asia; and Pedro Machado, *Ocean of Trade: South Asian Merchants, Africa and the Indian Ocean, c. 1750–1850* (Cambridge: Cambridge University Press, 2014), on Indian traders in East Africa; and, more generally, Claude Markovits, "Trading Networks in Global History," in *Explorations in History and Globalization*, ed. Cátia Antunes and Karwan Fatah-Black (New York: Routledge, 2016), 63–75.

in world markets and sometimes even became global players. By doing so, they benefited not least from an infrastructure that had been established by imperial governments.[76]

The rise of capitalism, consumerism, and welfare states was intimately linked to the emergence of the middle classes. This could be observed most prominently in modern Japan.[77] As Janet Hunter shows in her contribution, "Modern Business and the Rise of the Japanese Middle Classes," economic processes played a crucial part in the emergence of this new social group in the country between the Meiji Restoration of 1868 and the First World War.[78] Having a certain level of income was integral to any lifestyle that might be viewed as "middle class," and the pattern of income distribution and economic activity helped determine the changing shape of class and social relations and the discourse surrounding them. The chapter shows that patterns of consumption drew on both "traditional" Japanese and "Western" patterns in a very specific way. It also demonstrates that the emergence of a Japanese middle class relied not least on transformations of the Japanese economy that date back as far as the seventeenth century.

The global rise of capitalism also produced new global professional groups, which formed mobile bourgeois communities. As Kris Manjapra points out in his chapter "Middle-Class Service Professionals of Imperial Capitalism," economic globalization, free trade, and liberal imperialism gave rise to an expanding elite of experts—managerial, scientific, and scribal professionals—during the nineteenth century. This new class of worldwide circulating service professionals was involved in establishing new industries, setting international standards and measures, managing new markets, and surveilling and controlling land and labor across the Global South. With backgrounds ranging from the petty bourgeoisies to financially independent bourgeois elites, this caste was characterized by mobility and middle-class lifestyles.

76. Claude Markovits, *The Global World of Indian Merchants, 1750–1947: Traders of Sind from Bukhara to Panama* (Cambridge: Cambridge University Press, 2000) provides an example.

77. Sheldon Garon, *Molding Japanese Minds: The State in Everyday Life* (Princeton, NJ: Princeton University Press, 1997); and, more generally, the chapters in Sheldon Garon and Patricia L. Maclachlan, eds., *The Ambivalent Consumer: Questioning Consumption in East Asia and the West* (Ithaca, NY: Cornell University Press, 2006) provide insights into the history of the Japanese middle class.

78. David Ambaras, "Social Knowledge, Cultural Capital, and the New Middle Class in Japan, 1895–1912," *Journal of Japanese Studies* 24 (1998): 1–33.

Religion and the Betterment of the World

As middle classes were influenced by ideas of the Enlightenment, with science and notions of rationality being an integral part of bourgeois culture, religion allegedly played a lesser role for them than it did for members of premodern societies. Recent research has demonstrated, however, that religion remained an important part of the middle-class worldview, not least in the field of charity. Even though the state was an important frame for establishing middle classes, the emerging bourgeoisie pursued philanthropic activities and created spaces of civil society that allowed them to become involved in public affairs outside the state domain. Their clubs, salons, and associations engaged in a wide range of charitable activities, ranging from poor and disaster relief to the founding of hospitals, orphanages, and libraries. In many cases, organized philanthropy was the innocuous starting point for a wider preoccupation with public affairs. Adam Mestyan's chapter, "The Muslim Bourgeoisie and Philanthropy in the Late Ottoman Empire," demonstrates the ways in which philanthropic organizations in Ottoman provincial capitals emerged from the mid-1870s with the mission to foster public education and health care through charity. In places like Izmir, Cairo, Beirut, and Damascus, emerging bourgeoisies organized theater performances, concerts, and balls to raise money for charity, which they perceived as being patriotic activities. Such charity events were occasions when the middle class could not only exercise its habitus but also show patriotism. Public religiosity and religious sociability were central to this Ottoman civil society, shaping the emergence of a public middle-class culture in the cities. This middle-class culture was thus the result of private initiative and took place beyond state institutions.

Religion was crucial not only in the formation of middle classes in their respective homelands but also in the diaspora. In his chapter, "Worlds of a Muslim Bourgeoisie," David Motadel explores the bourgeois world of one such exile group. Looking at the sociocultural milieu of the Muslim minority in interwar Berlin, he shows that they combined Islamic and bourgeois lifestyles and values into a hybrid form of Islamic bourgeois culture. The majority of the Muslim community in Berlin was financially independent and highly educated. Most of them came from the upper middle classes of their home countries. In the diaspora situation, they could base their community on two bonds—class and religion. The sociocultural background of the Muslims in Berlin, their lifestyles, and the nature of their associations meant that they came into contact with educated middle-class Germans, particularly academics, students, diplomats, and businessmen, and to some extent were able to connect with bourgeois segments of the majority society.

Religion also played a role in addressing a primary cleavage of the long nineteenth century, namely the conflict between the middle classes and the urban underclasses. The middle classes attempted to examine ways to enhance the social conditions of the underclasses, for example, by fostering education and cleanliness and fighting drunkenness. In his chapter, "From Global Civilizing Missions to Racial Warfare," Christof Dejung describes such civilizing missions, which were organized by philanthropic societies that were established by bourgeois circles in both the European and non-European worlds. The emerging middle classes in the Middle East or in India, for instance, became engaged in civilizing missions in quite a similar manner to the European home missionary movement.[79] In addition, journalists, scholars, and members of philanthropic societies time and again compared the European underclasses to colonial subjects and used their alleged "primitiveness" in order to claim the modernity of the European bourgeoisie. This may be evidence of the fact that the European middle classes did not consider social developments in European and non-European regions as distinct phenomena but rather as shared aspects of worldwide modernization—without, however, taking into account the emergence of colonial middle classes in that very period. The chapter further demonstrates that the belief that social problems could be solved by social modernization under bourgeois hegemony was ever more challenged after the mid-nineteenth century. Politically conservative circles expressed anxiety about the supposed degeneration of bourgeois culture on the one hand and about the insurgency of colonial savages and metropolitan underclasses on the other. The fact that both the quest for modernity and fears about the loss of bourgeois hegemony were expressed by making worldwide comparisons can be considered evidence of the truly global reach of the cultural canopy of the metropolitan middle classes.

---

79. Keith David Watenpaugh, *Being Modern in the Middle East: Revolution, Nationalism, Colonialism, and the Arab Middle Class* (Princeton, NJ: Princeton University Press, 2006); Prashant Kidambi, *The Making of an Indian Metropolis: Colonial Governance and Public Culture in Bombay, 1890–1920* (Aldershot: Ashgate, 2007); and, on a broad range of civilizing missions, the contributions to Boris Barth and Jürgen Osterhammel, eds., *Zivilisierungsmissionen: Imperiale Weltverbesserung seit dem 18. Jahrhundert* (Konstanz: Universitätsverlag Konstanz, 2005).

Failures and Fringes

Global middle-class formation faced numerous obstacles. In parts of the world—notably Imperial Russia, Latin America, and China—middle classes were allegedly "missing." Here, the claim of European and North-American middle classes to be the epitome of modernity led to a sense of deficiency among the emerging middle classes. In late nineteenth- and early twentieth-century South America, as David S. Parker shows in his chapter, "Asymmetric Globality and South American Narratives of Bourgeois Failure," intellectuals witnessed European and US industrial progress, imperial power, and apparent cultural modernity, against which they compared their own nations, usually unfavorably. One major strain of national self-criticism focused on the supposed absence of a genuine bourgeois middle class or, if existent, its inability to carry out the "historical mission" attributed to its European counterpart. The diagnoses ranged from a focus, in midcentury, on the legacies of Spanish oppression, to racial and climatic theories from the late nineteenth century to the First World War, to more radical, materialist, nationalist, vanguardist, and anti-imperialist perspectives in the 1920s. Yet ideologically divergent explanations of middle-class failure often had common themes, many of which persisted into the 1970s and inspired both cultural and *dependencia* theories of Latin American underdevelopment that still echo today. Finding similar debates in Argentina, Chile, and Peru—countries whose economic and demographic fortunes varied considerably—Parker shows that narratives of a missing or flawed bourgeoisie may have accurately reflected the knock-on effects of Latin America's successful insertion into the global economy as a primary product exporter and an importer of manufactured goods, but they also invoked a heavily mythologized *bourgeoisie conquérant* wresting power from the feudal aristocracy and implanting liberal capitalism, an idea in which few modern historians of Europe believe anymore.

The situation in Russia was not dissimilar. Alison K. Smith's chapter, "The 'Missing' or 'Forgotten' Middle of Tsarist Russia," shows that the idea that Imperial Russia lacked a middle class was well established by the middle of the nineteenth century. Starting from that point, contemporary commentators and later historians debated the existence of that middle class, variously denying it existed, seeking to identify why Russia lacked it, or attempting to find elements of that elusive "missing" bourgeoisie, from merchants and entrepreneurs, to professionals, to public associations, and to cities meant to support it.[80] These discussions have taken place in dialogue with a vision of the "West" that served as Russia's opposite, something given all the more weight in discussions of nineteenth-century Russia, when Russian (or, perhaps more generally, Slavic) tradition was increasingly seen as opposed to a modernity seen as Western, or even global. The result has often been a kind of self-othering, in which the lack of an obvious middle class is read as indicative of a pervasive particularity in Russian social structures. This tendency to see Russia in contrast to this outside other, viewed as more properly normal, has served to obscure the existence of the middle of Russian society, in particular by erasing some groups that fit neither the model of absence nor the ideal of a prosperous, politically active middle class (the *meshchane*, or petty bourgeois, the artisans, and the honored citizens) from the record. Furthermore, it ignores Imperial Russia's role in a world economy—granted, one of trade and not of capitalism—through its long-standing Eurasian networks. Examining these groups and networks, and the way they were interpreted by contemporary observers, Smith shows that only in the context of a global middle class envisioned in Western European terms did Russia suffer from a "missing" bourgeoisie.

In China, the political turbulences of the twentieth century prevented the emergence of a viable middle class, as Sabine Dabringhaus and Jürgen Oster-hammel point out in their chapter, "Chinese Middle Classes between Empire and Revolution." Until the late nineteenth century, China seemed to remain static, not susceptible to social change and institutional reform, while Western Europe developed a new kind of dynamic bourgeois society underpinned by industrialization and fueling imperial expansion. This situation changed after the opening of the treaty ports, which became important places for the entry of Western modernity into China. This was particularly true for Shanghai, which was globally connected to a much greater extent than any other Chinese city, with the exception of colonial Hong Kong. In these coastal cities, it is possible to speak of the emergence of a social group that resembled the

---

80. Louise McReynolds, *Russia at Play: Leisure Activities at the End of the Tsarist Era* (Ithaca, NY: Cornell University Press, 2003) demonstrates the existence of a middle class in the tsarist era by pointing out the cultural similarity of Russian middle-class culture to that of Western Europe. Elise Kimerling Wirtschafter, "The Groups Between: Raznochintsy, Intelligentsia, Professionals," in *The Cambridge History of Russia: Imperial Russia, 1689–1917*, ed. Dominic Lieven (Cambridge: Cambridge University Press, 2006), 245–263, provides an overview. Janet M. Hartley, *A Social History of the Russian Empire 1650–1825* (London: Longman, 1998) offers a brilliant, more general overview of the origins of social hierarchies in early Imperial Russia.

Western middle class, at least from the second decade of the twentieth century. On the one hand, it involved an entrepreneurial elite; on the other, a new generation of Western-educated Chinese, who either joined the private economic sector, found employment as teachers in the rapidly expanding schools and universities, or tried to make a living as freelance intellectuals. This short period, however, described as the "golden age of the Chinese bourgeoisie" by Marie-Claire Bergère, came to an end after the Japanese invasion in 1937, and completely disappeared after 1949, when any remnants of middle-class society were ruthlessly eradicated by the Communist Party.[81] This is why there are extremely few links between the new Chinese middle class that came into being as a consequence of economic reforms after the 1980s and its forerunner in the early twentieth century. This distinguishes China not only from Western Europe and the post-aristocratic immigrant societies of North America but also from Asian countries such as Japan or India, where twenty-first-century middle classes can very well be traced back to the nineteenth century. And it is striking evidence for the claim that the existence of a middle class relied not least on a stable political framework that safeguarded individual and property rights.

Paths from Past to Future

In the final chapter of this book, "Race, Culture and Class: European Hegemony and Global Class Formation, c. 1800–1950," Richard Drayton takes a broader perspective, demonstrating that the middle class in every society has been both "middle" in terms of status, and "middle" in terms of its capacity for engagement with social groups above or below. The history of the global middle class is in essence the history of global processes of mediation, linked to the intensification of the integration of economy, politics, and culture across the world. The post-1500 early modern forms of globalization, which reached maturity in the early nineteenth century, had three key effects. First, the moment of European hegemony in the period from circa 1750 to 1950 was correlated with the internal integration of Western Christendom and its diasporas on the basis of ideas of "civilization" and "whiteness" and with an ever-expanding external regime of links between Western European and non-European social formations. Second, connected to these processes of integration (often in the midst of competitive warfare) and external linkages (again

81. Bergère, *Golden Age of the Chinese Bourgeoisie.*

often associated with violence and constrained consent) was the production, and growth in importance, of mediating groups—negotiators, brokers, merchants, translators, middlemen, subaltern "fixers," overseers, work captains, gang masters, accountants, managers, skilled artisans—in every corner of the globe, of which the European bourgeois was a local and privileged expression. Third, linked to this violent integration of international society, and the associated primacy of mediation and mediators, was a process of standardization of social imaginaries, manners, and customs, a pressure toward the reduction of specific complexity into general categories, toward uniformity. An integrated world could only be made sense of, indeed could only be created, through forms of simplification and the disregard of complexity. Race, through which social precedence was premised on ideas of somatic and cultural types, was within this system a critical currency through which Weber's triad of class, status group, and party were negotiated in international social history. At the center of the history of the global middle class thus lies the mass production and mass marketing of regimes of status.

Taken together, the chapters of this book demonstrate that the emergence of middle classes around the world was closely linked to imperialism and the rise of global capitalism. They show that this emergence has a rich history. It is not a history of European exceptionalism; rather, the volume decenters the social transformation of the long nineteenth century. Looking at social stratification as a result of global interaction, the book opens up a research trajectory that could eventually lead to global social history as a new field of historical research. Such a history needs to come to terms with various research questions, which are also raised in this book. Historians will have to examine the relations between local structures and global influences. How did these two interact and to what extent did these interactions differ around the world? Historians will have to look at the relations between the middle class and other parts of society, such as the aristocracy, the working classes, and the peasantry, in different parts of the world; particularly in the colonies, the rapprochement of middle classes and peasantry was crucial for the success of national liberation movements. Historians also need to address the relations between different segments of the bourgeoisie, such as the educated and the economic middle classes: under what conditions did these two groups merge into a discernible social entity, and what conditions might have hindered such convergence in other areas? Also, we might ask in which countries the middle classes were able to achieve discernible political influence and in which places this was not the case.

Future research will also need to close the gap in our knowledge of the history of the middle class between the 1940s and the 1990s.[82] As is the case with the vast majority of studies on the subject, the chapters in this book focus mostly on a period that begins in the nineteenth century and ends with the Second World War. Fewer studies, however, have been published on the period between the 1950s and the turn of the twenty-first century, perhaps with the exception of African studies, in which the African "elites" were considered the key players for social development in the newly independent nation-states and hence have been examined by scholars and institutions of development aid. In the industrialized world, the distinctions between working classes and middle classes at times became blurred as a result of the expansion of the welfare state and the spread of mass consumption; some social historians have thus even asked whether a history of the bourgeoisie post-1945 makes any sense at all.[83] In communist countries, the middle classes came under pressure from regimes determined to establish a classless society (as was the case in Eastern Europe), or they were completely eradicated by state power (as was the case in China and North Korea). In the Global South, ultimately, the history of the middle classes seems not to provide the key to understanding the impoverishment and economic stagnation in what was to become the "Third World." Around the world, to be sure, the middle classes remained part of the social tableau, but scholarly attention has focused more on political processes such as the history of decolonization and the Cold War, rather than on the history of social conflict and the bourgeoisie.

This gap becomes particularly noticeable when we compare the lack of research for the period between the end of the Second World War and that of the Cold War with the renewed interest in the global middle classes after the 1990s.[84] Scholars of sociology, anthropology, economics, and political science have written extensively on the rise of "new middle classes" in the Global South in recent years.[85] Indeed, in debates about the future of the liberal world order, one social

82. William I. Robinson and Jerry Harris, "Towards a Global Ruling Class? Globalization and the Transnational Capitalist Class," *Science and Society* 64, no. 1 (2000): 11–54, provides some valuable observations on the post-1970s.

83. Gunilla Budde, Eckart Conze, and Cornelia Rauh, eds., *Bürgertum nach dem Bürgerlichen Zeitalter: Leitbilder und Praxis seit 1945* (Göttingen: Vandenhoeck und Ruprecht, 2010) offers chapters questioning this distinction in the case of Western Europe.

84. Rachel Heiman, Carla Freeman, and Mark Liechty, eds., *The Global Middle Classes: Theorizing through Ethnography* (Santa Fe, NM: School for Advanced Research Press, 2012).

85. Among the most important studies are Jie Chen, *A Middle Class without Democracy: Economic Growth and the Prospects for Democratization in China* (Oxford: Oxford University

group is mentioned again and again: the middle classes.[86] Be it China, Egypt, Russia, or Iran, the question of whether these countries might develop into stable democracies seems to depend most on the possible triumph of bourgeois values and the establishment of a vibrant middle-class society. The middle classes, more than any other social group, are seen as the promoters of education, science, and the rule of law, as well as the pillars of capitalist market economies and an open public sphere. They seem to be the prerequisite for the emergence of civil society and the project of modernity as a whole. Indeed, the subject has fired the imagination of global corporations and institutions such as the World Bank, McKinsey, or Credit Suisse, as they consider these groups the promoters of free markets, liberalism, and democratic institutions. It has regularly been argued that the future of a liberal world depends not least on the influence of the Russian, Chinese, Indian, African, and Arab middle classes in their societies.

Nevertheless, hopes for the triumph of liberalism advanced by a new middle classes have often remained unfulfilled. European and American middle classes voice increased criticism of the consequences of globalization, which they

---

Press, 2014); Leela Fernandes, *India's New Middle Class: Democratic Politics in an Era of Economic Reform* (Minneapolis: University of Minnesota Press, 2006); Minna Saavala, *Middle-Class Moralities: Everyday Struggle over Belonging and Prestige in India* (New Delhi: Orient Black Swan, 2010); Christiane Brosius, *India's Middle Class: New Forms of Urban Leisure, Consumption and Prosperity* (London: Routledge, 2010); Henrike Donner, ed., *Being Middle-Class in India: A Way of Life* (London: Routledge, 2011); Jim Rohwer, *Asia Rising: How History's Biggest Middle Class Will Change the World* (London: Brealey, 1995); Diane E. Davis, *Discipline and Development: Middle Classes and Prosperity in East Asia and Latin America* (Cambridge: Cambridge University Press, 2004); Vali Nasr, *Forces of Fortune: The Rise of the New Muslim Middle Class and What it Will Mean for Our World* (New York: Free Press, 2009); Walter Russell Mead and Rachid Sherle Ouissa, "Blocked Middle Classes as an Engine of Change in the Arab World?," in *Euro-Mediterranean Relations after the Arab Spring: Persistence in Times of Change*, ed. Jakob Horst, Annette Jünemann, and Delf Rothe (New York: Palgrave Macmillan, 2013), 123–142; Henning Melber, ed., *The Rise of Africa's Middle Class* (London: Zed, 2016); and Lena Kroeker, David O'Kane, and Tabea Scharrer, eds., *Middle Classes in Africa: Changing Lives and Conceptual Challenges* (New York: Palgrave Macmillan, 2018). Abhijit V. Banerjee and Esther Duflo, "What Is Middle Class about the Middle Classes around the World?," *Journal of Economic Perspectives* 22 (2008): 3–28, points out common features of the middle classes in the Global South.

86. The argument that a strong bourgeoisie is crucial for the establishing of democratic societies has been put forth by Barrington Moore, *Social Origins of Dictatorship and Democracy: Lord and Peasant in the Making of the Modern World* (Boston: Beacon Press, 1966); Francis Fukuyama, "The Future of History: Can Liberal Democracy Survive the Decline of the Middle Class?," *Foreign Affairs* 91 (2012): 53–61.

(and many members of Western underclasses as well) perceive as a threat to their prosperity and social position.[87] The rise of populist leaders throughout the Western world is considered not least the result of growing material inequality and the relative economic stagnation of the middle classes.[88] Some even see a decline and disintegration of the old Western middle classes.[89] At the same time, Asian, African, and Middle Eastern societies are redefining their attitude toward both the West and the Western project of modernity; this process is often accompanied by conflicts between the respective non-Western middle classes on the one hand, which are partial to a Western way of living, and governments, conservative political groups, and religious fundamentalists on the other, which vehemently repudiate Western influences.

The study of the history of the global middle classes therefore bears high political relevance besides its historiographical potential. A global history of the middle classes, in particular if it aims at creating research trajectories leading toward the establishment of global social history as a field of historical study, may be an antidote to any liberal daydreaming, as it emphasizes the contradictions and social conflicts that are intrinsically linked to the rise of the middle classes both past and present. At the same time, a global history of the bourgeois middle classes may also point out global similarities of and cooperation between social groups, challenging notions of civilizational and cultural boundaries.[90]

87. Olivier Zunz, Leonard Schoppa, and Nobuhiro Hiwatari, eds., *Social Contracts under Stress: The Middle Classes of America, Europe, and Japan at the Turn of the Century* (New York: Russell Sage, 2002) provides insightful essays on this development.

88. Branko Milanović, *Global Inequality: A New Approach for the Age of Globalization* (Cambridge, MA: Harvard University Press, 2016); and, for the case of the United States, Ganesh Sitarman, *The Crisis of the Middle-Class Constitution* (New York: Knopf, 2017).

89. Christophe Guilluy, *No Society: La fin de la classe moyenne occidentale* (Paris: Flammarion, 2018).

90. The argument of an incommensurateness of cultures is put forth by authors as different as Edward W. Said, *Orientalism* (New York: Pantheon, 1978); and Samuel P. Huntington, *The Clash of Civilizations and the Remaking of World Order* (New York: Simon and Schuster, 1996).

PART I

State and Class

2

The Rise of the Middle Class in Iran before the Second World War

H. E. Chehabi

THE RISE OF THE IRANIAN MIDDLE CLASS is usually said to have begun with the Constitutional Revolution of 1905–11, which put an end to monarchical absolutism in Iran.[1] It continued with the reforms of Reza Shah Pahlavi (r. 1925–41), under whom the modern Iranian state was created, a state whose administrations and agencies provided employment for a new and growing educated middle class. The rise continued during the rule of the last shah, Mohammad Reza Pahlavi (r. 1941–79), under the impact of the country's rising prosperity due to oil. The middle classes continued their ascension after the Islamic Revolution of 1979, which ousted the old elite and brought to power people from a traditional lower-middle-class background whose aspirations for middle-class status were finally met under the new dispensation. This narrative brings to mind David Hackett Fischer's quip that "if the middle class had in fact been rising as powerfully as this, it should presently be somewhere in the disciplinary jurisdiction of astronomers, who alone could measure its continuous ascension with their powerful instruments."[2]

---

1. The author thanks the editors as well as Ali Gheissari, Rudi Matthee, and Cyrus Schayegh for their valuable help and comments on earlier drafts.

2. David Hackett Fischer, *Historians' Fallacies: Toward a Logic of Historical Thought* (New York: Harper Torchbooks, 1970), 150.

To avoid what Fischer calls the "interminable fallacy,"[3] I shall disaggregate the subject of the "rise of the middle class" by looking at three distinct processes. The first is the attainment of what Tocqueville called "equality of condition," by which he meant the disappearance of ascriptive status distinctions.[4] The second is the bifurcation of Iranian society into one group consisting of people whose lifestyles and values came to be directly inspired by bourgeois European models, and another group, the majority, who were more resistant to cultural change based on foreign models. The first group included the court and many elite members of society, which is why it is important to distinguish this process from the third process, namely the appearance of a modern middle class after the Constitutional Revolution. This group came to dominate society, only to lose its hegemony after the Islamic Revolution of 1979. Before the Islamic Revolution, it was the object of a number of studies emphasizing its contribution to modernization.[5] Marxist-oriented scholars analyzed its heterogeneity.[6] Since the revolution, a number of studies have focused on its failure to retain power.[7] Only recently has an engagement with the cultural identity of this stratum begun, as a number of historians of the Reza Shah era have striven to analyze the ways members of this stratum shaped state policy.[8]

3. Fischer, *Historians' Fallacies*, 149.

4. Alexis de Tocqueville, *Democracy in America*, vol. 1 (New York: Vintage Books, 1945), chapters 2 and 3.

5. Ehsan Naraghi, "Elite ancienne et élite nouvelle dans l'Iran actuel," *Revue des Etudes Islamiques* 25 (1951): 69–80; Ehsan Naraghi, "Les classes moyennes en Iran," *Cahiers internationaux de sociologie*, n.s. 4 (1957): 156–173; Enrico Cerulli, "Origines et développement de la classe moyenne en Iran," in *Development of a Middle Class in Tropical and Sub-tropical Countries*, International Institute of Differing Civilizations, Record of the 29th session held in London 13–16 September 1955 (Brussels: n.p., 1956), 262–270; James A. Bill, *The Politics of Iran: Groups, Classes, and Modernization* (Columbus, OH: Charles Merrill, 1972).

6. Hoseyn Adibi, *Tabaqeh-ye motevasset-e jadid dar Iran* [The new middle class in Iran] (Tehran: Jame'eh, 1979).

7. Azadeh Kian-Thiebaut, *Secularization of Iran: A Doomed Failure? The New Middle Class and the Making of Modern Iran* (Paris: Peeters, 1998); Farhad Khosrokhavar, *The Iranian Middle Classes between Political Failure and Cultural Supremacy* (Amsterdam: Sadighi Research Fund, 2015).

8. Cyrus Schayegh, *Who Is Knowledgeable Is Strong: Science, Class, and the Formation of Modern Iranian Society, 1900–1950* (Berkeley: University of California Press, 2009) and the various articles in *Culture and Cultural Politics under Reza Shah: The Pahlavi State, New Bourgeoisie and the Creation of a Modern Society in Iran*, ed. Bianca Devos and Christoph Werner (Abingdon: Routledge, 2014).

Iran's Traditional Classes and Status Distinctions

To approach the topic of the evolution of the middle strata in Iranian society, it is best to take a look at how Iranians themselves conceived of stratification in their society. Medieval Islamic philosophers, influenced by Greek and Persian thought, defined the ideal society as consisting of a hierarchy of classes such as priests, warriors, bureaucrats, peasants, and artisans.[9] In practice, however, society was more often conceptualized in terms of elites, *khawass al-nas* (literally, "special people"), and the rest, *'awamm al-nas* (literally, "common people"). The former included the ruling dynasty, high state officials, tribal chieftains, rich merchants, and the upper strata of the ulema. Sometimes, however, we find references to a middle stratum, *awaset al-nas* (middle people), which consisted of merchants, mid-level state officials, and mid-level ulema.[10] For instance, when the Qajar prince Nader Mirza finished his education, his impoverished father told him that he had to get a job in the state bureaucracy because he could not provide him with more than clothes befitting the *awaset al-nas*.[11] This seems to indicate that what characterized membership in the middle stratum was education plus the need to seek gainful employment.

Between the various strata there was permeability and mobility, largely because of the arbitrary nature of the governance and the concomitant weakness of property rights. Although wealth and social influence were often hereditary in prominent families, political upheavals could spell the end of their privileged position, while the shah's command could easily propel a talented man from a position of obscurity to one of great influence. An often cited example is that of the reformist vizier Amir Kabir (1807–52), whose father was a cook and who ended up marrying the shah's sister—before the same shah had him strangled (though not because of the marriage). The absence of rigid status distinctions as observed in Europe or India made an impression on European observers of nineteenth-century Iran, such as Lady Sheil, the wife of the British minster in Tehran, who wrote in 1845: "In Persia and other

---

9. A.K.S. Lambton, "Islamic Society in Persia," in *Peoples and Cultures of the Middle East: An Anthropological Reader*, vol. 1, ed. Louise E. Sweet (New York: National History Press, 1970), 74–101, 74–75.

10. Ahmad Ashraf and Ali Banuazizi, "Class System V: Classes in the Qajar Period," in *Encyclopaedia Iranica*, vol. 5, ed. Ehsan Yarshater (Costa Mesa, CA: Mazda Publishers, 1992), 667.

11. Nader Mirza, *Tarikh va joghrafi-ye Dar al-Saltaneh-ye Tabriz* [History and geography of the abode of kingship Tabriz], ed. Gholam-Reza Tabataba'i Majd (Tehran: Entesharat-e Sotudeh, 1994), 384.

Mahommedan countries there is a large fund of personal equality, and obscurity of descent is not an obstacle to advancement."[12]

If we look for an Iranian equivalent of a bourgeoisie in the economic sense of the word, we find merchants and artisans, two groups that are often lumped together because of their physical proximity in the bazaars. In the course of the nineteenth century, however, their fortunes diverged. Given Iran's semicolonial status as a formally sovereign state subject to *pénétration pacifique*, foreign goods started flooding Iranian markets, leading to a decline of traditional manufacturing and thereby of the artisans who produced goods and to a lesser extent of the merchants who traded in them.[13] Western penetration also affected the financial system, and the opening of European-owned banks, such as the British Bank-e Shahanshahi (Imperial Bank) drove many traditional money lenders, *sarrafs*, into bankruptcy.[14] Merchants were better able to cope with Western economic penetration, because they developed their own transnational networks. Most famously, the merchant Hajj Mohammad Hoseyn Amin al-Zarb had trading offices in Marseille, London, Paris, and China, in addition to real estate in Moscow and Nizhny Novgorod.[15] In spite of its relative isolation, Iran in the late Qajar period was connected to its neighboring regions through a number of long-established commercial routes, which were important in the economic and social, and, as we shall see, intellectual history of the country. Iran was linked to the Ottoman Empire mainly via the road from Tabriz to Istanbul (through Trabzon: opened in the 1830s); to the Caucuses and Russia via Rasht and Anzali to Baku and beyond; and to India via Bushehr to Bombay. In addition to these there were the pilgrimage routes to the shrine cities of Iraq and to Mecca, which also had certain commercial significance.[16] Exports included

12. Lady Mary Leonora Sheil, *Glimpses of Life and Manners in Persia* (London: John Murray, 1856), 201.

13. Ahmad Ashraf, "Historical Obstacles to the Development of a Bourgeoisie in Iran," in *Studies in the Economic History of the Middle East: From the Rise of Islam to the Present Day*, ed. M. A. Cook (London: Oxford University Press, 1970), 308–332.

14. Hoseyn Mahbubi Ardakani, *Tarikh-e mo'assasat-e tamaddoni-ye jadid dar Iran* [The history of the institutions of modern civilization in Iran], vol. 2 (Tehran: Entesharat-e Daneshgah-e Tehran, 1997), 88.

15. Z. Z. Abdullaev, quoted in *The Economic History of Iran 1800–1914*, ed. Charles Issawi (Chicago: University of Chicago Press, 1971), 43.

16. Ali Gheissari, "Merchants without Borders: Trade, Travel and a Revolution in Late Qajar Iran (The Memoirs of Hajj Mohammad-Taqi Jourabchi, 1907–1911)," in *War and Peace in Qajar*

carpets, animal skins, and agricultural products, while imports consisted of watches, knives, textiles, sugar, matches, tea, porcelain, and glass dishes. While these imports contributed to the decline of the artisanal class, they also led to a certain standardization of consumption patterns that helped the appearance of a national market.[17]

At the end of the nineteenth century, the extravagant expenditures of the court and the foreign loans taken out to finance Mozaffar al-Din Shah's (r. 1896–1907) lengthy trips to Europe led to considerable social ferment in Iran. Critical newspapers were published by Iranian exiles and smuggled into Iran. There were more and more modern schools, which increased the numbers of educated Iranians who adopted critical attitudes. As the economic situation deteriorated, the "impecunious Qajar state became more predatory and the confiscation of land and merchant capital more frequent."[18]

Dissatisfaction with the political status quo was rife, and it is interesting for our purposes that what triggered the events that would later be called the Constitutional Revolution was the ill-treatment of two merchants by state officials.[19] In December 1905 two traders in Tehran were accused of overcharging and humiliatingly bastinadoed in public. This outrage caused merchants to close the bazaar of Tehran. The Shiite ulema and the nascent intelligentsia rallied to their cause. At first Mozaffar al-Din Shah seemed to accept the need for change, but then he prevaricated, as a result of which in July 1906, twelve thousand men, representing around seventy guilds, began a long sit-in in the grounds of the British legation to demand an end to absolutist rule. The shah granted the principle of a parliament in August, and elections were held in the autumn. The electoral law provided for representation by estates: guilds, princes of the imperial family, ulema, notables, merchants, and finally landlords and peasants.

Persia: Implications Past and Present, ed. Roxane Farmanfarmaian (London: Routledge, 2008), 183–212, 189.

17. Ehsan Tabari, *Forupashi-ye nezam-e sonnati va zayesh-e sarmayehdari dar Iran* [The decline of the traditional order and the birth of capitalism in Iran] (Stockholm: Tudeh Publishing Centre, 1354/1975), 56.

18. Hadi Enayat, *Law, State, and Society in Modern Iran: Constitutionalism, Autocracy, and Legal Reform, 1906–1941* (New York: Palgrave Macmillan, 2013), 47.

19. Mangol Bayat, *Iran's First Revolution: Shi'ism and the Constitutional Revolution of 1905–1909* (New York: Oxford University Press, 1991).

This parliament, which convened in October, embodied the apogee of "bourgeois" power in Iran: 26 percent of the deputies were guild elders, and 15 percent were merchants.[20] The chamber lost no time declaring itself a constituent assembly and hurriedly drafted a constitution that was signed by the ailing shah on his deathbed in late December 1906. Marxist theorists have a point when they classify the Constitutional Revolution of 1906 as a "bourgeois democratic" revolution that put an end to "feudalism" and "absolute monarchy"—except that the revolution did not inaugurate democracy or rule by the bourgeoisie. The new ruler, Mohammad 'Ali Shah, disbanded parliament in 1908 and a civil war ensued. The shah's supporters lost, and in 1909 the capital was taken by a coalition of activists from Tabriz and Gilan and tribal forces from Isfahan. The constitution was reinstated and new elections were held, this time with a unified electorate. The number of "bourgeois" representatives (guilds and merchants) declined precipitously, allowing big landowners and ancien régime statesmen to remain in power.[21]

The years between 1909 and 1921 were difficult ones, and the country seemed to fall apart. Russian forces occupied the northern parts of the country in 1909, leading to the northwest becoming the arena of fighting between Ottoman and Russian forces in the First World War. In the south, the discovery of oil in 1908 led to a British presence that in the course of the war came to constitute a military occupation as well. The authority of the central state weakened in the outlying provinces, begetting the usual consequences of insecurity and banditry. As the state disintegrated, however, the Second and Third Parliaments (1909–11 and 1914–15) proceeded to lay the foundations of a centralized state by creating new institutions and reforming the legal system with the elaboration of new commercial, criminal, and civil codes, even though it would take many years for these reforms to be implemented in practice. The Second Parliament instituted universal male suffrage and passed a law instituting the registration of property in 1911.[22] Traditionally, land had been assigned to notables by the state, which then confirmed the arrangement with their heirs. With the new legislation,

20. Ervand Abrahamian, *Iran between Two Revolutions* (Princeton, NJ: Princeton University Press, 1982), 87–88.

21. Mansureh Ettehadieh (Nezam-Mafi), *Majles va entekhabat az mashruteh ta payan-e Qajarieh* [Parliament and elections from the constitution to the end of the Qajars] (Tehran: Nashr-e tarikh-e Iran, 1375/1996), 18.

22. Enayat, *Law, State, and Society*, 152. More property registration acts were passed in 1923 and 1928.

landed property came to be guaranteed by law and could now change hands as a result of commercial transactions. This new situation was exploited by the middle and upper classes at the expense of the peasants.[23] While it also impoverished a few members of the elite, because properties were divided, it led to the strengthening of those with money, who could now buy land.[24] The Constitutional Revolution thus ended up strengthening the power and influence of the old ruling class; earlier, their power and position had been dependent on the goodwill of the shah, whereas now they could attain all sorts of government positions through political activity.[25]

At the societal level, however, the middle strata gathered momentum. The old merchant bourgeoisie was still socially prominent, but it left the political scene after the Second Parliament, concentrating on making demands of an economic nature rather than seeking direct political influence.[26] More important for the future was a new class of state employees: provincial elites, journalists, and educated nonaristocratic young people.

It is a reflection of the rise of this class that while until roughly the First World War challenges to the central authority of the state had come from rival claimants to the throne, after 1914 such challenges came from decidedly non-elite regional quarters. One of the rebellions that did succeed was that of Reza Khan Pahlavi, a man of humble background who had risen to become the commander of the country's main organized military force, the Cossack Division. In February 1921 he staged a coup together with the journalist Seyyed Ziya al-Din Tabataba'i, who became prime minister of a government that called itself "revolutionary." Seyyed Ziya's inaugural declaration was rife with anti-elite rhetoric, and he lost no time having some leading members of the old ruling class arrested. His tenure in office, however, was brief. The military leader of the coup, Reza Pahlavi, assumed ever more power over the next few years, allying himself with more progressive elements of the old elite and the intelligentsia, including socialists. Given the political chaos engendered by the Constitutional Revolution, many politically articulate Iranians came to conclude that

---

23. Enayat, *Law, State, and Society*, 189.

24. Abbas Zaryab Kho'i, "Zendegi-ye man" [My life], *Bokhara* 104 (1393/2015): 185–217, 197.

25. Ettehadieh, *Majles*, 15.

26. Soheila Torabi Farsani, "Merchants, Their Class Identification Process, and Constitutionalism," in *Iran's Constitutional Revolution: Politics, Cultural Transformations and Transnational Connections*, ed. H. E. Chehabi and Vanessa Martin (London: I. B. Tauris, 2010), 117–130 and 433–435.

the general population was too unsophisticated to justify universal suffrage, leading them to clamor for a strong leader. In 1925 Reza Khan toppled the Qajar dynasty and inaugurated the new Pahlavi dynasty. The middle strata, which had welcomed the Constitutional Revolution in 1906, effected a "Brumarian abdication" in 1924–25.[27]

However, while the Constitutional Revolution's promises of *political* democracy remained unfulfilled, democratization in the Tocquevillean sense was indeed advanced in the first quarter of the twentieth century. The constitution and the legal reforms that followed it created a concept of Iranian citizenship that proclaimed, and to a large measure instituted, the equality of all citizens.[28] Subsequent legislation, decrees, and policies contributed to the equalization of status. The new civil code made ownership unequivocally individualistic, its presupposition being that equal property-owning individuals entering voluntarily into agreements that would then come with obligations and rights.[29] In 1925 the onomastic regime of the Iranians was reformed, obliging Iranians to choose and register family names for themselves. At the same time, the (non-hereditary) titles proudly worn by members of the old elite were abolished. A few days later, universal male conscription was introduced, affecting rich and poor, urban and rural, literate and illiterate. In 1928 the capitulations were ended, which meant that Iranian subjects could no longer evade their country's jurisdiction by placing themselves under the protection of a foreign power. In 1929, slavery was abolished. Between 1928 and 1936 the state issued a number of decrees regulating how people had to dress, with men forced to wear European suits and hats and women forced to unveil. What few status distinctions had existed until the end of the nineteenth century were eroded as Iran became a modern nation-state.

Although the first decades of the twentieth century saw the birth of a new citizenry that attempted to do away with former distinctions based on ethnicity, the tribal-rural-urban divide, and even religion, the Europeanization propagated by the state after 1925 also begat a new cleavage in society, as some strata actively embraced the state's policies, while others rejected it. To this cleavage we must now turn.

27. The term is Alfred Stepan's; see his *Arguing Comparative Politics* (Oxford: Oxford University Press, 2011), 76.

28. Except that Muslim men remained somewhat "more equal" than Muslim women and non-Muslims, which in the context of the early twentieth century was not exceptional.

29. Enayat, *Law, State, and Society*, 137.

Emergence of a Dual Society

In Iran the adoption of European bourgeois cultural patterns began not among the middle strata of society but at the elite level. In 1811, the first group of young Iranian men was sent to Western Europe to get acquainted with modern sciences and arts, and throughout the "bourgeois century" more followed, although their overall numbers remained small. As more Iranians traveled abroad, many of them came to ascribe Europeans' perceived superiority to the latter's culture, especially the political culture and more egalitarian gender relations. Upon returning home, the Iranians' lifestyles came to show the effect of their European experience. The Caucasus, in particular, played a major role, since many Iranians traveled to such relatively developed cities as Tiflis and Baku, where they became acquainted with Russian culture.[30] Iranian merchants dealing with Europe and India also gradually adopted European cultural practices, and in this Istanbul and to a lesser extent Cairo played a major role, because these cities were host to large expatriate communities.[31] The British presence in the south influenced everyday culture in southern Iran.[32]

At the same time a growing number of Iranians became acquainted with European ideas and cultural patterns through interaction with European residents of Iran, be they missionaries, diplomats, merchants, military instructors, or teachers. These Europeans had their greatest impact in the northwestern province of Azerbaijan, which was connected by long-established trade routes to the Caucasus and the Ottoman Empire and which contained a large and compact number of Christians and more European and Russian merchants than other parts of the country.[33] Its capital, Tabriz, had a modern theater many years before Tehran; it had been created at the initiative of local Armenians who had staged *Othello*

30. Afshin Matin-asgari, "The Impact of Imperial Russia and the Soviet Union on Qajar and Pahlavi Iran: Notes toward a Revisionist Historiography," in *Empires and Revolutions: Iranian-Russian Encounters since 1800*, ed. Stephanie Cronin (London: Routledge, 2012), 11–46.

31. Thierry Zarcone and Fariba Zarinebaf-Shahr, eds., *Les Iraniens d'Istanbul* (Tehran: Institut Français de Recherches en Iran and Istanbul: Institut Français d'Etudes Anatoliennes, 1993).

32. Morteza Nouraei, "Ordinary People and the Reception of British Culture in Iran, 1906–41," in *Anglo-Iranian Relations since 1800*, ed. Vanessa Martin (London: Routledge, 2005), 67–79.

33. Fariba Zarinebaf-Shahr, "The Iranian (Azeri) Merchant Community in the Ottoman Empire and the Constitutional Revolution," in *Les Iraniens d'Istanbul*, ed. Zarcone and Zarinebaf-Shahr, 203–212, 209.

in translation as early as the 1880s.[34] Missionary-educated Assyrian Christians in the area west of Lake Urmia arguably constituted the first elements of what would become Iran's modern middle class, but during the First World War the area was occupied by Ottoman troops, and Assyrians were decimated in the course of the genocide of 1915, so they left little impact on the country at large.

Among Muslims, the adoption of European cultural patterns began at Court.[35] It was the Qajar shahs and princes who first adopted European clothes, filled their palaces with European furniture and accessories, placed their well-being in the hands of European doctors, and learned foreign languages, usually French. This trend was given a fillip by Naser al-Din Shah's European tour of 1873, the first visit to Europe by any Iranian ruler. Wishing to be taken seriously by his European hosts, European diplomats were asked to teach the shah and other court officials the use of cutlery for eating. Such anecdotes suffice to show that court life gradually took on a European veneer, and it was a bourgeois veneer.

The court and the Qajar princes were soon emulated by the upper-class notables. What these self-conscious innovations entailed in practice is spelled out in chapter 8 of a book written by E'temad al-Saltaneh, Naser al-Din Shah's minister of publications, in 1888 to celebrate forty years of that shah's rule. It begins by stating that during that ruler's reign, the Iranian state had propagated modern industry and science, as well as transformations of habits and customs, all characteristics of the modern age. It concludes that "this great nation, which fate had destined (like the other states of Asia) to fall behind the great states of the world, had now rejoined the ranks of civilized nations." Innovations listed include the popularization of tea, which had hitherto only been enjoyed by the elite; chocolate; European bread (baked by Muslims!); potatoes, now eaten by rich and poor; and umbrellas. Iranians, both elite and middle strata, had developed a taste for such luxuries as crystal chandeliers and chairs, while men dressed and adorned themselves differently from previous generations. At the same time, and this is very important, the text emphasizes that the shah had also acted within the bounds of Islam and actually strengthened Islam by instituting new customs.[36]

---

34. Christoph Werner, "Drama and Operetta at the Red Lion and Sun: Theatre in Tabriz 1927–41," in *Culture and Cultural Politics*, ed. Devos and Werner, 201–232, 205 and 210.

35. Norbert Elias, *The Civilizing Process* (Oxford: Blackwell, 1994).

36. Mohammad Hasan Khan E'temad al-Saltaneh, *Ketab al-ma'aser va al-asar* [The book of effects and testimonies] (Tehran: Dar al-Taba'eh-ye Dowlati, 1306/1927), 101–129.

While elite Iranians adopted European practices, they also adapted them to their specific needs. True, the use of cutlery gradually displaced eating with one's right hand, but rice came to be eaten with a spoon, a practice not unknown elsewhere in Asia. Chairs and armchairs were acquired, but they were placed next to the walls on the perimeter of rooms rather than arranged in seating groups.[37] Elite men started wearing European clothes but kept their heads covered indoors, as mandated by Muslim etiquette (cf. the Ottoman fez).

In parallel with the changes in domestic life, the city of Tehran began to be transformed as well. In the 1860s it was expanded northward, with three straight tree-lined paved avenues connecting the old center to the northern suburbs, enabling both foreign residents and members of the Iranian elite to use carriages.[38] In 1873 a grand theater, the Takiyeh-ye Dowlat, was opened as a venue for the traditional Shiite passion plays that had become ever more popular since the eighteenth century.[39] Clearly, the capital was beginning to acquire the public spaces characteristic of a bourgeois urban milieu.

The downward diffusion of European cultural practices is usually credited to Iran's small intelligentsia, whose growth resulted from the development of a modern educational system. In 1851 the country's first modern school was set up, the Dar al-fonun (named after the Ottoman Darülfünûn, or House of Multiple Sciences, founded in 1846), where children of the elite were taught by European teachers.[40] The founding of this school was of tremendous importance, because from then on "modern education" meant an education disembedded from its religious context. As more modern schools followed, the old *maktab*s and madrasas did not disappear, however, leading to a dual educational system that was one of the contributors to the emergence of Iran's dual society.[41]

37. Samuel R. Peterson, "Chairs and Change in Qajar Times," in *Modern Iran: The Dialectics of Continuity and Change*, ed. Michael E. Bonine and Nikki R. Keddie (Albany: State University of New York Press, 1981), 383–390.

38. John D. Gurney, "The Transformation of Tehran in the Later Nineteenth Century," in *Téhéran: Capitale bicentenaire*, ed. Chahryar Adle and Bernard Hourcade (Paris: Institut Français de Recherche en Iran, 1992), 51–71.

39. Farrokh Gaffary, "Lieux de spectacle à Téhéran," in *Téhéran*, ed. Adle and Hourcade, 141–152, 144–148.

40. Maryam Ekhtiar, "Nasir al-Din Shah and the Dar al-Funun: The Evolution of an Institution," *Iranian Studies* 34, nos. 1–4 (2001): 153–162.

41. Roy Mottahedeh, *The Mantle of the Prophet* (New York: Simon and Schuster, 1984).

By the end of the nineteenth century, the number of modern schools had increased. The Alliance Israélite Universelle in Paris founded schools for Iran's downtrodden Jews, and Indian Parsis helped establish schools for the even more downtrodden Zoroastrians. These schools, and the earlier Christian missionary schools, also attracted Muslim pupils whose parents just wanted their children to get a good education. Later, Iran's Baha'is set up the Tarbiat schools, which also attracted a few Muslims. Modernist Muslims, some of whom had spent time in the Ottoman Empire (Istanbul and Beirut), also founded schools, including schools for girls, and these schools were routinely attacked and ransacked by mobs instigated by conservative clerics who feared the intrusion of Western culture on society.[42] They were waging a losing battle, however, since the Constitutional Revolution ended in the victory of the modernists, after which the modern educational system expanded under state protection and the conservative clerics were cowed—at least until 1979.

Contact with the West, the development of modern schools, and a burgeoning diasporic press, which was printed in India and the Ottoman Empire (including Egypt) but disseminated in Iran, all contributed to the diffusion of ideas usually associated with a bourgeoisie. The first such idea, was the importance of the rule of law: arbitrary government was rendered responsible for Iran's backwardness. In 1870 a book appeared whose titled said it all: *Yek kalameh*, "one word," that word being "law," signifying that no one, not even the shah, should be above the law. The Constitutional Revolution of 1906 seemed to be the fulfilment of the clamor for a *Rechtsstaat*, but as we have seen, its triumph was short-lived. Increasing Europeanization of a segment of Iran's urban population gradually led to tensions within society. Iranian men dressed in European costume came to be derided as *fokkoli*, people who wear a *faux-col*, a detachable collar (cf. the Turkish *şapkalı*, "hat-wearer"). But *fokkoli*-hood was about more than a devotion to European fashion: it connoted an alienation from customary practices more generally, as seen in language use, gender relations, literary tastes, and of course consumption patterns. Originally a tiny minority in Iran's overall population, the size of the modern segment grew sharply after the Constitutional Revolution. By the 1920s the chasm between traditional and modernist Iranians was so obvious that it became a popular theme in Persian literature. The title of the founding short story of modern Persian literature, Mohammad 'Ali Jamalzadeh's "Persian Is Sugar," refers to two Iranians' inability to understand

---

42. David Menashri, *Education and the Making of Modern Iran* (Ithaca, NY: Cornell University Press, 1992), 91–154.

each other while speaking the same language, as one keeps showing off with incomprehensible Gallicisms while the other encumbers his speech with Arabic words derived from religious discourse. In the widely popular play *Ja'far Khan has Returned from Europe*, the protagonist scandalizes his parents by returning to Iran with a little lap dog, dogs being considered defiling by Muslim Iranians.

The establishment of Pahlavi rule between 1921 and 1925 seemed to herald the triumph of modernists. The tensions this created were visible even in smaller towns. In an autobiographical piece, one of Iran's top literary scholars wrote about the northwestern Iranian town of Khoy:

> The transition from Qajar to Pahlavi rule divided the people of Khoy into two groups that viewed each other with hate. The modernists and Europeanized saw in Pahlavi [rule] and the new institutions harbingers of a better future, believing that these institutions, the new dress codes, and superficial freedom for women would make Iran an equal of Western countries. Traditionalists ... believed that the new institutions, clothes, and schools would result in people losing their faith and that unveiling would be conducive to general moral corruption. Both sides persisted in their simplistic views, and after 1941 an unbridgeable gap appeared in society whose consequences became visible later.[43]

The "modernists and Europeanized" in this passage refer not to an elite, either social or intellectual, but to ordinary Iranians who thought of themselves as partaking of the dominant zeitgeist, thus pointing to a widening of the circles who had, or at least affected to have, a more cosmopolitan and less traditional outlook on life. These are the people often referred to as the modern middle class, a subset of Iran's cosmopolitan-minded population, to which we can now turn.

State-Building and the Modern Middle Class

Although the modern middle class, defined here as people with a bourgeois lifestyle whose livelihood was dependent neither on landownership nor on economic activities concentrated on the bazaar, came into its own starting in the 1920s, its origins lie a few years earlier. In late Qajar times the state made cautious attempts to centralize power, leading to the creation of jobs in the provinces, but fiscal penury meant that these measures did not go very far, although

---

43. Zaryab Kho'i, "Zendegi-ye man," 190–191.

a few employment opportunities were created for non-elite people. In the aftermath of the Constitutional Revolution, municipal governments were established in major cities, and in the capital various administrations were created to govern the entire country.[44] The state took an active role in promoting the employment of the graduates of the new schools: in the legal field, for instance, laws and decrees were passed that specified that judges and lawyers had to be graduates of the new schools, including a law school, which was a direct challenge to the madrasa-trained ulema, who had hitherto dominated the legal field.[45] When property registration offices were set up, these too were placed in the hands of civilian officials, again depriving clerics of a lucrative occupation,[46] not to mention the new schools themselves, which were luring pupils away from the traditional *maktab*s and madrasas. While it is true that the institution-building policies of the centralizing state marginalized and antagonized the ulema, who had constituted the traditional intellectual elite, it should also be emphasized that many clerics adapted to the new situation by abandoning their turbans, shaving their beards, putting on a tie, and taking a few courses at state schools to learn the new procedures.[47]

After the coup d'état of 1921, the pace of institution-building accelerated and its scope widened, made possible by rising incomes due to increased oil revenues. Given the centrifugal tendencies mentioned above, the establishment of the state's monopoly of legitimate force was of the essence, and to that end various military forces were amalgamated to create a modern army under the supervision of Reza Khan (later, Reza Shah). The army's importance grew throughout the interwar years, and many officers were appointed as heads of other state agencies. The officer corps was coddled by the state and came to be one of the pillars of the new middle class.[48]

The Pahlavi state also expanded the educational system, with elementary education becoming compulsory in 1927. The numbers of state elementary and high schools increased, and in 1934 various institutions of higher learning were

44. Reza Mokhtari Esfahani, "Municipalities and Constitutionalism in Iran," in *Iran's Constitutional Revolution*, ed. Chehabi and Martin, 99–113 and 431–432.

45. Enayat, *Law, State, and Society*, 110.

46. Ahmad Mahdavi Damghani, "Tarikhcheh-ye mahzar va daftar-e asnad-e rasmi" [A history of registries], *Bokhara* 89–90 (1391/2002): 122–137.

47. Mohammad Faghfoory, "The Impact of Modernization on the Ulama of Iran, 1925–1941," *Iranian Studies* 26 (1993): 277–312.

48. Stephanie Cronin, "Režā Šāh and the Paradoxes of Military Modernization in Iran," *Quaderni di Oriente Moderno*, n.s. 23, no. 5 (2004): 175–203.

merged to become the University of Tehran. In the 1920s the state instituted a program to send Iranian high school graduates abroad for tertiary education, and as they returned to Iran they staffed not only the university but also the higher echelons of other state administrations. They brought with them Western lifestyles and often also European wives.

A territorial administration was set up, and the country was divided into a number of provinces having equal status vis-à-vis the center, each province in turn being divided into districts, these into subdistricts, and so on. At each level, state officials appointed by the ministry of the interior administered the affairs of the local populations. The power of the state now reached down to the grassroots of society all over the country. In addition, as the various ministries, such as transportation, education, public health, agriculture, and interior, were expanded, they set up offices in the various provincial capitals. The new National Bank opened branches in the provinces. The provincial administrations, the local offices of the ministries, the teachers, the bank managers, the judges, and the local army officers constituted the modern middle class in the provinces, although the term "middle" has to be taken with a grain of salt in the case of the poorer provinces, where the state officials were incomparably better off than the vast majority of the locals. In fact, it was often the local notables such as landlords who managed to secure jobs in these agencies for their offspring.

Under Reza Shah much money was poured into infrastructural projects. The capital Tehran was transformed. "The classical bourgeois is a 'man about town,'" writes Jürgen Osterhammel,[49] but it was difficult to be a dapper flaneur in the winding, narrow, and often mud-covered alleys of Iranian cities, where one had nothing to look at to boot, since the alleys were boarded by the blind walls of inward-looking houses centered on a courtyard. In the nineteenth century, straight streets had been laid outside the old town, but under Reza Shah, wide tree-lined avenues were driven through the old neighborhoods with little regard for the inhabitants. An entire neighborhood, Sangelaj, was razed to create a park. The American embassy estimated the number of destroyed houses at between fifteen and thirty thousand and noted that Tehran looked as though it had been destroyed by an earthquake.[50]

49. Jürgen Osterhammel, *The Transformation of the World: A Global History of the Nineteenth Century* (Princeton, NJ: Princeton University Press, 2014), 777.

50. Talinn Grigor, "The King's White Walls: Modernism and Bourgeois Architecture," in *Culture and Cultural Politics*, ed. Devos and Werner, 95–118, 99.

As we saw earlier, the outward appearance of Iranians was regulated to conform to European tastes, but public venues were also created where these modern citizens could exhibit their modernity. In 1933, for instance, the municipal government of Teheran opened a café that featured a band whose players wore oversized bow ties and played a mix of Western and Iranian tunes.[51] In 1938 the construction of an opera house was begun, but it was never finished. In 1939 new zoning regulations mandated that new buildings face the street and have at least one story above the ground floor.[52]

Outside Tehran, new roads were built and existing roads paved, and in 1927 the construction of the Trans-Iranian Railway was begun.[53] Although much of the work was done by European engineering firms, many of the Iranian students sent abroad returned as engineers, providing a technical component for the new middle class. Engineers were also needed in the new industries set up by the state, whose economic policies were statist, especially after the world economic crisis of 1929. To counter the effects of that crisis, in 1930 the Iranian state nationalized foreign trade. The Soviet Union and Kemalist Turkey had done so earlier, the combined result of these measures being that merchants in northern Iran could no longer engage in transborder trade. Many of them sought employment with state agencies, contributing to the growth of the modern middle class.[54]

The state also regulated the liberal professions, for instance, the medical field. The graduates of European medical schools lobbied for the marginalization of traditional medicine, and the possession of a diploma from a modern medical school became a condition sine qua non for the practice of medicine.[55] By the same token, the state also began supervising and regulating midwifery.[56] Self-employed professionals, many of them educated in Europe, thus became another component of the new middle class.

51. Ruhollah Khaleqi, *Sargozasht-e musiqi-ye Iran* [History of Iranian music], vol. 2 (Tehran: Ebn-e Sina, 1956), 335–336.

52. Mohsen Habibi, "Réza Chah et le développement de Téhéran (1925–1941)," in *Téhéran*, ed. Adle and Hourcade, 199–206, 203.

53. Patrick Clawson, "Knitting Iran Together: The Land Transport Revolution, 1920–1941," *Iranian Studies* 26 (1993): 235–250.

54. Zaryab Kho'i, "Zendegi-ye man," 197.

55. Schayegh, *Who Is Knowledgeable*, 56–57.

56. Elham Malekzadeh, "Giving birth to a new generation: Midwifery in the public health system of the Reza Shah era," in *Culture and Cultural Politics*, ed. Devos and Werner, 249–265.

The importance of education in the shaping of the modern middle class had an unanticipated consequence. The necessity of certification by the state led to a quest for diplomas, a phenomenon that has been called "credentialism," a classical middle-class phenomenon based on the idealization of knowledge and meritocracy. The old highfalutin titles had been abolished in 1925, but the new middle class adopted *doktor* and *mohandes* (engineer), placed before the family name, as new markers of distinction. In fact, the everyday use of family names itself was a sign of being modern, since the lower classes continued to rely on first names and informal epithets for all unofficial purposes, while among the old elites the abolished titles lingered on for a while.

The aim of education was to enable people to develop the country so that Iranians could catch up with Europe, and this meant that technical fields acquired more prestige than the humanities, mastery of which had characterized the traditional elites. The educational system was modeled on the French one and aimed at forming an educated citizenry by teaching the history and geography of faraway lands in addition to those of Iran, but the steel mills of the United States and the lists of English kings were too removed from the everyday concerns of Iranians to constitute the basis of the encyclopedic *culture générale* or *Allgemeinbildung* prized by continental Europe's *Bildungsbürgertum* (educational bourgeoisie). Moreover, artistic and aesthetic concerns were given spectacularly short shrift by the educational system: Iranians were taught at school to admire Cyrus the Great, but few school classes were taken to Tehran's Archaeological Museum, designed by the French architect André Godard and opened in 1937. The best secondary schools were those that offered high-quality instruction in the sciences and mathematics, subjects that allowed graduates to go on and study engineering or medicine. In these secondary schools, the humanities track came to be seen as appropriate for girls and not-very-bright boys. In a way the civil servants and the members of the liberal professions I have been describing constituted what Rainer Lepsius called a *Dienstleistungsbürgertum* (services bourgeoisie) a sector of the *Bildungsbürgertum*,[57] although I am tempted to coin the neologism *Ausbildungsbürgertum* (professionally trained bourgeoisie), since *Bildung*, in the sense of seeking personal fulfilment through constant cultural self-improvement, was not a priority, and the acquisition of diplomas was to some extent an end in itself, allowing the

57. M. Rainer Lepsius, "Das Bildungsbürgertum als ständische Vergesellschaftung," in *Demokratie in Deutschland: Soziologisch-historische Konstellationsanalysen: Ausgewählte Aufsätze* (Göttingen: Vandenhoek und Ruprecht, 1993), 303–314, 307.

recipients to hold a government job that provided a steady income and thus stability and social prestige.

However, the new middle class also contained a commercial component. Some trade activity moved out of the traditional bazaars into the newer neighborhoods. Often the new stores were run by scions of the merchants active in the bazaar, and initially they maintained links with the old commercial centers. But gradually they became absorbed by the modern segment as their lifestyles changed. Thus a modern business bourgeoisie gradually emerged that was to some extent a link between the traditional middle class centered on the bazaar and the modern middle class.

What about the values held by the modern middle class? Most of all, its members were nationalists. Love of Iran and pride in its heritage and ancient history were inculcated by the state, intellectuals, the press, and the educational system. This glorious heritage was insufficiently appreciated by Westerners, who pushed Iranians around, and to gain the strength to withstand the West, Iranians had to emulate the West. The adoption of European cultural practices was part of this emulation, as was the acquisition of a European language, which replaced the emphasis on Arabic that had characterized traditional Iranian education. Being up-to-date with the latest trends in Europe became a matter of status and generated cultural capital. While proud of an idealized Iran as embodied in the pre-Islamic empires, many educated Iranians were weary of the actual conditions in Iran, being ashamed of their less sophisticated compatriots, their dwellings, their clothes, their manners. Gradually, a geographical segregation set in. Traditionally, rich and poor urban Iranians had cohabited in the same neighborhoods and participated in the same rituals. Most Iranians continued living in traditional neighborhoods, with their winding alleys, cul-de-sacs, and bazaars, but beginning in the late 1920s, cosmopolitan-minded Iranians could stroll on the sidewalks of paved streets lined by shops with carefully decorated window displays.[58] Here, restaurants serving European fare and cafés were opened, affording modernist Iranians spaces where they could put their new lifestyle on display and gain prestige by consuming European (more often than not Russian) dishes.[59] Alcoholic beverages, hitherto consumed in private, became available in these venues, allowing modern Iranians

58. Martin Seger, "Segregation of Retail Facilities and the Bipolar City Centre of Tehran," in *Téhéran*, ed. Adle and Hourcade, 281–297.

59. Farhad Khosrokhavar, "La pratique alimentaire," in *Entre l'Iran et l'Occident*, ed. Yann Richard (Paris: Editions de la Maison des Sciences de l'Homme, 1989), 143–154.

to flaunt their indifference to religious strictures publicly (and signaling to traditionalists that the state was not only tolerating but actually *promoting* vice). As non-Muslim Iranians became educated and left their traditional neighborhoods, they moved into these new parts of Tehran, which were located to the north of the old city. Indeed, one of the characteristics of the modern middle class was that it included Baha'is, Christians, Jews, and Zoroastrians, who commingled more easily with their Muslim compatriots than in the past. In Tehran, where the modern middle class was concentrated, the residential segregation between the two segments of society deepened after the Second World War, leading to the dual-city phenomenon that by the late 1970s had divided the capital into a prosperous and cosmopolitan North and a poorer, more traditional South.[60]

The press, by now tightly controlled by the state, propagated the adoption of new ways: the semiofficial daily newspaper *Ettela'at* advised readers on how to use calling cards or how to doff one's hat when meeting an acquaintance in the street. The same newspaper featured advertisements for private language and music lessons, books and bookshops, cinemas and theaters, Singer sewing machines, and foreign cars and watches.[61] In 1928 a municipal decree in Tehran codified table manners, prohibiting, for instance, eating with one's fingers in restaurants.[62] In that same year, regulations were published regulating the behavior of theater audiences: whistling, stamping with feet, and clapping hands out of place were not permitted.[63] Arguably the most decisive state policy was the prohibition of veiling in January 1936, a policy begun when the queen and several daughters of the shah appeared at an official graduation ceremony dressed in European garb with hats on their heads. Reza Shah, ultimately a traditional Iranian patriarch, admitted in private that he hated to see his womenfolk unveiled but that he insisted on the measure so that Europeans would not look down on Iranians.[64] Hailed by modern Iranians as the liberation of women, unveiling was seen as an intolerable intrusion into the innermost private sphere of the citizenry and was rescinded after Reza Shah's abdication in 1941, following Iran's occupation by Allied powers. Between 1941 and 1979, women's veils became the most visible markers of their families' appurtenance to the traditional

60. Mahvash Alemi, "The 1981 Map of Tehran: Two Cities, Two Cores, Two Cultures," *A.A.R.P. Environmental Design* (1985): 74–84.

61. Schayegh, *Who Is Knowledgeable*, 26.

62. *Ettela'at*, no. 609 (26 Mehr 1307/18 October 1928), 4.

63. Werner, "Drama and Operetta," 208.

64. As reported by the queen herself; see *Yaddashtha-ye 'Alam*, 1353 ['Alam's diaries, 1353 (1974–75)], ed. 'Ali Naqi 'Alikhani (Bethesda, MD: Ibex, n.d.), 298.

or modern segments of society, and women of the modern middle class increasingly internalized the idea that veiling was a sign of backwardness and subjugation.

Although the modern middle class grew in size, it did not achieve political power. Under Reza Shah, Iran was a royal dictatorship with a constitutional facade, and most of its most influential officials—such as prime ministers and cabinet members—hailed from the old elite, which, with few exceptions, had weathered the regime change of 1925 rather well. But members of the modern middle class gained prominence in intellectual life, the media, and the arts. Quite a few used their public positions to carve out private economic benefits for themselves.

Conclusion

The departure of Reza Shah in 1941 opened up Iranian politics, and for the next twelve years Iran had a semblance of constitutional government. As organized religion made a comeback, the modern middle class now had to face an increasingly self-confident traditional bazaar-based middle class. Many members of the intelligentsia sympathized with the Communist Tudeh party, among whose founders members of the modern middle class clearly dominated.[65] But others came together with the bazaar to support the National Movement, led by Mohammad Mosaddeq, whose ouster in the coup d'état of 1953 spelled the end for the bazaar as a force in prerevolutionary national politics.

Mohammad Reza Shah's White Revolution of 1963, whose cornerstone was land reform, destroyed Iran's landowning elite as a class. The cosmopolitan segment now came to be coterminous with a bourgeoisie of which the modern middle class was the most important component. While powerless politically under the dictatorship of the shah, this class was nonetheless culturally hegemonic. Its members staffed the expanding institutions of the state and constituted a modern business elite whose habitus allowed it to be far better connected to the state than the more traditional merchants of the bazaar, thus benefiting more from the oil boom of the 1970s.[66] The revolution of 1978–79 was again propelled by an alliance of the bazaar, clerics, and the modern intelligentsia, but the leaders of the traditional segment of Iran's population had learned their

65. Abrahamian, *Iran*, 158–161.

66. Djavad Salehi-Isfahani, "The Political Economy of Credit Subsidy in Iran 1973–1978," *International Journal of Middle East Studies* 21, no. 3 (1989): 359–379.

lesson and ruthlessly swept aside the modern middle class from positions of power. Although the modern middle class has reproduced itself in Iran since 1979 and even seems to be growing, the institutions of the Islamic Republic are set up in such a way as to keep it politically powerless.

One outcome of these frustrated ambitions has been massive emigration to the West. Beginning in the early twentieth century, many Iranians hoped that adopting a European habitus would be conducive to international respect. On an individual level, they succeeded spectacularly. Although as a country Iran is perceived by many people in the West as a pariah nation governed by mad mullahs, Iranian immigrants in Europe, North America, and Australia have been very successful, their integration hailed as a model for others.

In the United States, the emphasis on education that characterizes Iran's modern middle class combined with the meritocracy prevailing in America to produce a chief business officer of Google, the founder of e-Bay, a former chief executive officer of YouTube, a chief executive officer of Expedia, and a former chief technology officer of Yahoo, not to mention the first female space tourist and the first woman mathematician to win the Fields Medal. In the German Bundestag, thanks to proportional representation, members of Iranian or partially Iranian background are found in the parliamentary caucuses of the Left, the Greens, and the Christian Democrats, while the Social Democrats had a secretary general until 2015 who bears the surname of her Iranian immigrant father. More tellingly still, in 2010 an Iranian immigrant, Amir Shafaghi, was named Carnival Prince in the Federal City of Bonn and enthroned as Prince Amir I, surely the highest accolade an integrated immigrant can receive.[67]

67. "Karnevalsprinz kommt aus dem Iran," *Kölner Stadt-Anzeiger*, 7 February 2010.

3

"The Great Middle Class" in the Nineteenth-Century United States

Marcus Gräser

THE AMERICAN MIDDLE CLASS has been (and still is) more than just a diverse group of middling sorts. In self-awareness as well as in the description of foreign observers, the middle class since the eighteenth century appeared as the embodiment of the new society that had developed in the colonies of settlers on North American soil. The *Pennsylvania Journal* wrote in 1756:

> The people of this province are generally of the middling sort, and at present pretty much upon a level. They are chiefly industrious farmers, artificers or men in trade; they enjoy and are fond of freedom, and the meanest among them thinks he has a right to civility from the greatest.[1]

And Alexis de Tocqueville wrote in his travel notebook in May 1831: "What strikes me thus far is that the country exhibits the outward perfection of the middle classes, or, to put it another way, the entire society seems to have fused into one middle class."[2] What he saw on his trip through the United States was the middle class of the hometowns, who for a few decades reasonably felt they could control their provincial society—before the Civil War and the

---

I would like to thank Daniel Hanglberger, Hans-Jürgen Puhle, the three editors of this volume, and the anonymous reviewers for their critical comments and advice.

1. Quoted in Richard Hofstadter, *America at 1750: A Social Portrait* (New York: Vintage Books, 1973), 131.

2. Quoted in Oliver Zunz, *Alexis de Tocqueville and Gustave de Beaumont in America: Their Friendship and Their Travels* (Charlottesville: University of Virginia Press, 2010), 365.

dynamics of capitalism finally undermined the stability of the hometowns and their middle class.[3] In fact, use of the term "middle class" had been common in public discourse since the 1830s.[4] In 1850, the New York–based journalist George Foster euphorically wrote about the "great middle class," which he saw growing in the urban population, where one could develop a certain prosperity and "wisely fall short of that snobbish longing after social notoriety which so many of their class mistake for exclusiveness and aristocracy."[5] Thinking of oneself as being middle class, and assuming that being middle class is the "normal" position one should have in society, is a typical middle-class idea, which fell on especially fertile ground in the US. This idea of the middle class as a "general" class finally found its way into scientific theory: "consensus history," which was predominant among American historians in the 1950s and 1960s, operated on the belief that a conflict-free development of society based on middle-class values prevailed. The sociological theory of modernization, which originated in the same decades, condensed its normative model of modernization from a similar image of American social development, in which democracy and the middle class seemed to be inextricably linked.[6]

Although "consensus" and "modernization" are no longer key terms in social historical research, the middle class has not yet completely lost its function

3. For the middle class in the hometowns of the Middle West, see the trilogy by Timothy R. Mahoney: *River Towns in the Great West: The Structure of Provincial Urbanization in the American Midwest, 1820–1870* (Cambridge: Cambridge University Press, 1990); *Provincial Lives: Middle-Class Experience in the Antebellum Middle West* (Cambridge: Cambridge University Press, 1999); and *From Hometown to Battlefield in the Civil War Era: Middle Class Life in Midwest America* (Cambridge: Cambridge University Press, 2016).

4. Jonathan Daniel Wells, *The Origins of the Southern Middle Class, 1800–1861* (Chapel Hill: University of North Carolina Press, 2004), 12.

5. George G. Foster, *New York by Gas-Light: With Here and There a Streak of Sunshine* (New York: Duwitt and Davenport, 1850), quoted in Stuart M. Blumin, "The Hypothesis of Middle-Class Formation in Nineteenth-Century America: A Critique and Some Proposals," *American Historical Review* 90 (1985): 299–338, 311.

6. For a critical perspective on "consensus history" as well as on modernization theory, see Peter Novick, *That Noble Dream: The "Objectivity Question" and the American Historical Profession* (Cambridge: Cambridge University Press, 1988), 333ff.; Ellen Fitzpatrick, *History's Memory: Writing America's Past 1880–1980* (Cambridge, MA: Harvard University Press, 2002), 188–238; and Peter N. Stearns, "Toward a Wider Vision: Trends in Social History," in *The Past before Us: Contemporary Historical Writing in the United States*, ed. Michael Kammen (Ithaca, NY: Cornell University Press, 1980), 205–230.

as being a "general class." Almost no one who talks about the middle class in public debate fails to point out that it is "America's backbone." This, by the way, makes nervousness about its condition very widespread: "The phrase has become laden with a feeling of anxiety of not being able to get into that group, falling out of it or never climbing beyond it."[7] Surprisingly, historians have contributed less to this debate than one might expect; their interest is, in fact, inversely proportional to the dominance of the middle class in the public self-description of the US. Writing about the "well born, the rich, and the powerful" has always been popular, especially in the genre of biography.[8] And when attention shifted to social classes—in the ascendancy and implementation of social history as an academic field—interest in the working class was almost unrivaled. There are prestigious journals and book series on working-class history, but there is nothing like it for the vast middle class.[9] In fact, it seems to be much more possible to summarize an ideological history of thinking about the middle class than to write a summary of the research on the social history of it.[10] Why is there so little interest in the social history of the subject? There are three explanations at hand. First, the ideological overloading of the middle class as the incarnation of the American creed may have encouraged demystification at the level of intellectual history, but it has not led to a precise view of those social groups that might be usefully analyzed under the term "middle class." Second, a great many American historians still rank ethnic and religious configurations and cleavages higher than aspects of class.[11] Finally, the undisputed difficulties in defining the middle class—who

7. Derek Willis, "The Rise of 'Middle Class' As an Ordinary American Term," *New York Times*, 14 May 2015. For a general and quick overview on discussions about the American middle class, see Marina Moskowitz, "Aren't We All? Aspiration, Acquisition, and the American Middle Class," in *The Making of the Middle Class: Toward a Transnational History*, ed. A. Ricardo López and Barbara Weinstein (Durham, NC: Duke University Press, 2012), 75–86.

8. Frederic Cople Jaher, ed., *The Rich, The Well-Born, and the Powerful: Elites and Upper Classes in History* (Urbana: University of Illinois Press, 1973).

9. Just to name a few for the working class: *Labor History, Labor: Studies in Working Class History of the Americas*, and the book series The Working Class in American History, published by the University of Illinois Press.

10. See Burton J. Bledstein, "Introduction: Storytellers to the Middle Class," in *The Middling Sorts: Explorations in the History of the American Middle Class*, ed. Burton J. Bledstein and Robert D. Johnston (New York: Routledge, 2001), 1–25.

11. Lee Benson, "Group Cohesion and Social and Ideological Conflict: A Critique of Some Marxian and Tocquevillian Theories," *American Behavioral Scientist* 16 (1973), quoted in Blumin, "Hypothesis of Middle-Class Formation," 302.

belongs to it and why?—have contributed to a certain unpopularity of the topic in historical research. Not only the sheer size and regional variety of the American middle class(es) but the fuzzy edges and subsequently the lack of "sufficient analytical clarity" have led to less interest in this social group, which has been described as either an "elusive middle class" or the "Imperial Middle."[12]

Why is it so difficult to delimit the American middle class? From a European point of view, it was, among many reasons, the somewhat mysterious ubiquity of middle-class values in combination with a lack of tradition in America's social fabric that was particularly noticeable. "There are," the German sociologist Charlotte Lütkens wrote in 1929, "specifically bourgeois virtues that constitute the American type of society, . . . they are attainable for every human being, regardless of his or her origin . . . by the explicit exclusion of all special talents inherited from descent or acquired through other relations with tradition."[13]

Colonial Beginnings

If one wants to find out about the framework that gave the American middle class its special appearance, one has to go back to colonial times and to the settler society that happened to be a unique experiment in social history: The American colonies of settlers grew into a commercial, market-driven society, and the market was dominant not because it was huge, but because other factors

12. Sven Beckert, *The Monied Metropolis: New York City and the Consolidation of the American Bourgeoisie, 1850–1896* (Cambridge: Cambridge University Press, 2001), 6. See also Clifton Hood, *In Pursuit of Privilege: A History of New York City's Upper Class and the Making of a Metropolis* (New York: Columbia University Press, 2017); Stuart M. Blumin, *The Emergence of the Middle Class: Social Experience in the American City, 1760–1900* (Cambridge: Cambridge University Press, 1989), 1–16; Sylvie Murray, "Rethinking Middle-Class Populism and Politics in the Postwar Era: Community Activism in Queens," in *Middling Sorts*, ed. Bledstein and Johnston, 267–284, 283.

13. Charlotte Lütkens, *Staat und Gesellschaft in Amerika: Zur Soziologie des amerikanischen Kapitalismus* (Tübingen: Mohr, 1929), 187. The comparative gaze of contemporaries as well as of the historical research is indispensable if a global social history is to be considered. See Susanna Delfino, Marcus Gräser, Hans Krabbendam, and Vincent Michelot, "Europeans Writing American History: The Comparative Trope," *American Historical Review* 119, no. 3 (2014): 791–799; A. Ricardo López and Barbara Weinstein, "Introduction: We Shall Be All: Toward a Transnational History of the Middle Class," in *Making of the Middle Class*, ed. López and Weinstein, 1–25.

of status allocation were weak or absent.[14] Typical elements of European societies—above all the aristocracy, but also the clergy as a separate estate—were missing. The absence of an aristocracy saved the middle class from the social and political conflict typical of Europe's Age of Revolution. Also significant for the configuration of the middle class was the absence of the city as a corporation. Hence, the legal status of the city citizen (the burgher), who for a long time closely linked the city and citizenship in large parts of Europe, was unknown in the colonies and also later in the US. The settler colonies set up no legal boundaries defining the middle class, at least not any that would have imposed barriers on the growing self-awareness of the colonies as being middle-class societies. British colonial rule created not so much a caste of educated bureaucrats as ample room for the self-government of the colonists, which was widely used by the middle class.[15] The weakness of the state in its administrative capacities, legislative ambition, and educational and cultural institutions—in colonial society as well as in the American republic—also contributed to the fact that American society was able to emerge as a legally egalitarian, market-regulated society of owners (and those who aspired to become owners).

The fact that the middle class was given such a broad, open, legally unrestricted leeway raises doubts as to whether it is possible to speak of a social class in a strict sense, or whether it is, rather, a huge and also fragmented section of American society that at best allows us to speak of middle classes, in the plural. Most of the historians, however, who deal with the middling sorts in the US are of the opinion that the division of labor in the market society and through industrialization allows us to speak of a middle class as a recognizable and acting social group, a social formation with its own forms of self-expression that "set itself off in specific ways from the rest of American society."[16] Certainly, the middle class is much more than a "rhetorical device whose characteristics are created mainly to illuminate groups above and below."[17] Stuart Blumin, who

14. Hans-Jürgen Puhle, "Soziale Ungleichheit und Klassenstrukturen in den USA," in *Klassen in der europäischen Sozialgeschichte*, ed. Hans-Ulrich Wehler (Göttingen: Vandenhoeck und Ruprecht, 1979), 233–280, 234–235.

15. The question of a national bourgeoisie creating a state in the American Revolution, which should primarily serve its interest, is discussed in Edward Countryman, "The Uses of Capital in Revolutionary America: The Case of the New York Loyalist Merchants," *William and Mary Quarterly: A Magazine of Early American History and Culture* 99, no. 1 (1992): 3–28.

16. Blumin, "Hypothesis of Middle-Class Formation," 299.

17. Peter N. Stearns, "The Middle Class: Toward a Precise Definition," *Comparative Studies in Society and History* 21, no. 3 (1979): 377–396, 378.

published one of the pioneering studies on the history of the middle class in 1989, argues that "Americans (or at least urban Americans) of middling economic and social position were formed and formed themselves into a relatively coherent and ascending middle class during the middle decades of the nineteenth century"—which corresponds to the time period in which the term "middle class" came into use in the public debate.[18]

"The Great Middle Class"

Who belongs to the middle class? The sociologist Alfred Meusel, who wrote the article on the "middle class" for Edwin Seligman and Alvin Johnson's *Encyclopaedia of the Social Sciences*, described the middle class as "a mixture of heterogenous elements, some in undisguised conflict." While in his article "the simple producer of goods," "the artisans," "the small shopkeeper and tradesman," or, in short, "the old middle class," as well as the "new middle class" of "official(s) and salaried employee(s)" and the "free professions," were described as essential parts of the middle class, the dividing line between them and the upper strata was not drawn without difficulty. For the sake of determining the position of a "middle class" in the international context, Meusel excluded the "trust bourgeoisie" as a component and allowed only middling and small-sized entrepreneurs to stay in the middle class. The question about the role of the peasants in the middle class was also not easy for him to answer. He decided to look at the peasants as a genuine part of the middle class only where they had never been part of a feudal society—a decision that made the American farmer a part of the middle class. Despite these uncertain boundaries defining the middle class as a social phenomenon, Meusel emphasized "the tendencies towards unification . . . both on a national and international level."[19]

The greatest difficulty in the attempt to get the middle class historiographically under control is the demarcation upward. What can be meaningfully described as upper class if there is no aristocracy? Is the American bourgeoisie not part of the "great middle class"? Peter Stearns and Sven Beckert have presented good arguments for this view, as have Meusel and Blumin.[20] There are

18. Blumin, *Emergence of the Middle Class*, 12.

19. Alfred Meusel, "Middle Class," in *Encyclopaedia of the Social Sciences*, ed. Edwin R. A. Seligman and Alvin Johnson, vol. 10 (New York: MacMillan, 1933), 407–415.

20. Stearns, "Middle Class," 393; Sven Beckert, "Propertied of a Different Kind: Bourgeoisie and Lower Middle Class in the Nineteenth-Century United States," in *Middling Sorts*, ed.

indeed sharp boundaries between the bourgeoisie—who have substantial capital, do not have to work for wages, and do not work with their own hands in their own businesses—and the lower middle class of artisans and shopowners, boundaries that translated into political conflicts.[21] But are there also clear distinctions between a bourgeois and a professor of economics at a prestigious university? Certainly there may be significant differences in financial wealth and, based on that, in lifestyle. But it is questionable whether such differences are really categorical or just gradual. In cultural taste and worldview, few differences may be recognizable.

After all, the boundaries between a broad middle class and the upper class of the business elite were permeable, more permeable, at any rate, than the borders between the bourgeoisie and the aristocracy in Europe. Within a self-proclaimed democratic society, the upper strata—as well as the middle class—must have room for newcomers. In any case, the middle class will not be substantially smaller if the bourgeoisie is excluded, for this is, of course, a share of the population below 1 percent. How many people do we talk about when we talk about the middle class? The term does not appear in the census; the statisticians counted according to occupations. But the estimate of Clifton Yearley, that around 1890 roughly one-third of the population had middle-class status, has never been contradicted, and it also coincides with assessments available for European countries.[22] This is the "great middle class" of the nineteenth century, which extends to the lower middle class but excludes the bourgeoisie and the farmers, because the latter maintain a different way of life, regardless of their ownership status.[23]

Bledstein and Johnston, 285–295; Sven Beckert and Julia Rosenbaum, "Introduction," in *The American Bourgeoisie: Distinction and Identity in the Nineteenth Century*, ed. Sven Beckert and Julia Rosenbaum (New York: Palgrave Macmillan, 2010), 1–8, 2; Blumin, "Hypothesis of Middle-Class Formation," 304; Meusel, "Middle Class," 410.

21. Robert D. Johnston, *The Radical Middle Class: Populist Democracy and the Question of Capitalism in Progressive Era Portland, Oregon* (Princeton, NJ: Princeton University Press, 2003).

22. Clifton K. Yearley, "The 'Provincial Party' and the Megalopolises: London, Paris, and New York, 1850–1910," *Comparative Studies in Society and History* 15, no. 1 (1973), quoted in Burton J. Bledstein, *The Culture of Professionalism: The Middle Class and the Development of Higher Education in America* (New York: W. W. Norton, 1976), 35. For Germany, see Hans-Ulrich Wehler, *Deutsche Gesellschaftsgeschichte*, vol. 4: *Vom Beginn des Ersten Weltkriegs bis zur Teilung der beiden deutschen Staaten, 1914–1949* (Munich: C. H. Beck, 2003), 284–299.

23. For the problem of how to relate the lower middle class to the middle class, see Andrew Wender Cohen, "Obstacles to History? Modernization and the Lower Middle Class in Chicago,

Cohesive Forces and Distinctions

But what binds the "great middle class" together? What justifies the subsuming of quite disparate parts of a numerically large group under one term? First of all, what has to be taken into account is that *being* middle class is the result of self-assessment. The political scientist Arthur Holcombe, who wrote in the 1940s about the middle class as a political actor, briefly noted: "There is no middle class, politically speaking, but thinking makes it so."[24] A very important element in the self-interpretation of being middle class, besides owning property, was the trust in social mobility. For those who conceived themselves as middle class, the blurring of the boundaries of this social group has never been a problem; on the contrary, it has served as a self-evident expression of a society that not only allows social advancement, but makes it the norm.[25] By 1850, Ralph Waldo Emerson had already wanted to understand the society of his country as showing an escalator effect in the generational sequence. He only distinguished between "conservative and . . . democratic classes; between those who have made their fortunes, and the young and the poor who have fortunes to make."[26] The myth that came to the fore here did not, of course, completely contradict reality, and the popularity of the middle class as a self-denotation in American society can also be read as the perception of a scope of possibilities. Believing in being middle class and in having plenty of opportunities went hand in hand and also served as a way of conceiving the difference between America and Europe, insofar as most Americans believed that their society offered more opportunities than the rigid European societies. This belief rested upon the higher consumption standards and had linked, since the late nineteenth century, middle class and consumer status in a way that was unknown in Europe at that time.[27]

1900–1940," in *Middling Sorts*, ed. Bledstein and Johnston, 189–200; and Sven Beckert, "Propertied of a Different Kind," in *Middling Sorts*, ed. Bledstein and Johnston, 285–295.

24. Arthur N. Holcombe, *The Middle Classes in American Politics* (Cambridge, MA: Harvard University Press, 1940), 49; and, for a similar assessment, Alfred M. Bingham, *Insurgent America: The Revolt of the Middle Classes* (New York: Harper, 1935), 47.

25. Bledstein, *Culture of Professionalism*, 20.

26. Ralph Waldo Emerson, "Napoleon; or, the Man of the World," in *Essays and Lectures* (New York: Library of America, 1983), 727–745, 727.

27. Otherwise, Europe was much needed as a resource for distinction; see Maureen E. Montgomery, "'Natural Distinction': The American Bourgeois Search for Distinctive Signs in Europe," in *American Bourgeoisie*, ed. Beckert and Rosenbaum, 27–44.

But being middle class was not all about self-attribution; no one enrolled in the middle class voluntarily, under circumstances of his or her own choosing. A middle-class existence also became manifest within the social relations of production. The ideals of independence and self-reliance, with which one could differentiate oneself from the working class and its dependent employment relationships, needed a foundation in the social division of labor. In fact, one of the most difficult tasks in social history is to find out "how the position in the social structure interacted with particular collective identities."[28]

But the simple anchoring of a social group to the division of labor and the social relations of production is not sufficient if one wants to find the cement that binds disparate parts of the middling sorts together. The constitution of a social class—or, less strictly speaking, the coherence of a social class—does not depend on indistinguishability or uniformity. For Max Weber, a social class is an ensemble of neighboring class positions in which market-dependent, as well as market-independent, criteria can be decisive. In his research on the German middle classes, the sociologist Rainer Lepsius suggested that a certain unity of the *Bürgertum* should be seen as the result of a process of socialization (*Vergesellschaftung*) of otherwise disparate middle classes.[29] Property and position in the social relations of production certainly do play a role in this process of middle-class-building, but they are not the only ones. What is more important are ways of living, overarching cultural repertoires, and patterns of interpretations and justifications, which ensure that the middle class is recognizable both to the outside and to the inside. This way of living also may contain a normative idea of life that can be passed on to the next generation. Tocqueville had precisely such circumstances in mind when he formulated his remarkable observation that American society "seems to have fused into one middle class." His impression did not arise from observing the financial circumstances of Americans or their position in the social relations of production, and he did not reflect on the spatial displacement of the indigenous population as a prerequisite of settler conquest. Tocqueville instead gained his impression of a

28. Sven Beckert, "Comments on 'Studying the Middle Class in the Modern City,'" *Journal of Urban History* 31, no. 3 (2005): 393–399, 395.

29. M. Rainer Lepsius, "Zur Soziologie des Bürgertums und der Bürgerlichkeit," in *Bürger und Bürgerlichkeit im 19. Jahrhundert*, ed. Jürgen Kocka (Göttingen: Vandenhoeck und Ruprecht, 1987), 79–100. For a general overview of the German *Bürgertum* as a middle class, see Jürgen Kocka, "Middle Class and Authoritarian State: Toward a History of the German 'Bürgertum' in the Nineteenth Century," in *Industrial Culture and Bourgeois Society: Business, Labor, and Bureaucracy in Modern Germany* (New York: Berghahn Books, 1999), 192–207.

coherent middle class through the perception of everyday behavior (among people of European descent): "All the Americans we have met so far, right down to the simplest shop clerk, seem either to have been well brought up or to wish to appear so. Their manners are serious, poised, and reserved, and all dress the same way."[30]

An important question middle-class people had to ask themselves is, what separates us from those whom we wish to regard as standing below us? Property and nonmanual labor are undoubtedly important markings; a way of life, however, develops not as a deduction from a given set of material conditions, but rather comes as a result of "daily routines and social networks," of the interplay between the perception of other people and the wish to identify within one's own group.[31] Most important for defining the way of life of the middle class was a group that was quite visible and could be used as a perfect counterpart: the poor. The "untraditional existence" of the poor "was an effective folio for the social significance of the citizen."[32] Middle-class people and the poor together formed one of the main antagonistic social figures of modernity. Just as the poor man only comes to his social consciousness as being poor through an opponent who recognizes him in his poverty, so the middle-class person needs a social opposite who confirms his or her own social position. This interaction between the poor and the middle class was not a theoretical affair. In the US, more than in other countries, poor relief was the task not of the state or the city but of civil society, and the agents of civil society, those who became engaged in all kinds of social work, were usually middle-class people. Attitudes and values that usually are considered typically middle class—self-reliance, a solid work ethic, a certain purposefulness—were modeled in a contrast with the poor and their unreliable, unclean, unsteady way of life.[33] Every presentation of middle-class values in advice books from the nineteenth century always looked like a prescription for the poor. This demarcation between a middle class and those below, which was formed around a work ethic, was, moreover, one of the factors that the lower middle class always tied to the "great middle class."

30. Quoted in Zunz, *Tocqueville*, 365–366.

31. Blumin, *Emergence of the Middle Class*, 297.

32. Käthe Bauer-Mengelberg, "Der Bürger," *Kölner Vierteljahreshefte für Soziologie* 8 (1929): 190–200, 192.

33. Marcus Gräser, *Wohlfahrtsgesellschaft und Wohlfahrtsstaat: Bürgerliche Sozialreform und Welfare State Building in den US und in Deutschland 1880–1940* (Göttingen: Vandenhoeck und Ruprecht, 2009), 61–81.

The middle-class standard of respectability was helpful not only in separating the middle class from the folks of the lower class but also in providing a weapon against the elite or upper class at a moment when the wealth and power of the upper class seemed to be overwhelming the traditional social environment of the middle class. The rise of the bourgeoisie and its "merchant princes" earlier in the nineteenth century had challenged the local hegemony of the older middle class, which had been recognizable not only by its way of life but also by its seniority ("old stock"). "New actors," observed William Ellery Channing in Boston 1837, "hurry the old ones from the stage," adding: "The former stability of things is strikingly impaired. The authority which gathered around the aged has declined."[34] What happened here was a "struggle between their own homogenous patrician society and a rising materialistic middle class without education and tradition, who were winning cultural and economic power and changing the tone of American life."[35]

Education and Culture

Education, culture, politics, and the family were invariably important places in the process of middle-class-building. Here, in both public and private spaces, essential facets of the middle-class way of life can be clearly seen, and here they also span the differences that might be given by the various occupations and ownership structures among the middling sorts. In the course of the nineteenth century, the acquisition and use of education not only became an essential component of the way of life of the middle class, it also became more and more important for the professional success of middle-class men. Is it therefore possible to speak of an educated middle class that resembled the German *Bildungsbürgertum*? There have always been debates among social historians who engage in comparative history about whether the German *Bildungsbürgertum* is a special case. The state guarantee of educational patents and the great demand for a trained staff by a strong administrative state naturally resulted in a favorable situation for university-trained people, and it gave a certain esprit de

34. William Ellery Channing, "The Philanthropist: A Tribute to the Memory of the Rev. Noah Worcester D. D. Boston, November 12, 1837," in *The Works of William E. Channing, D. D.* (Boston: American Unitarian Association, 1903), 599–607, 602.

35. William Charvat, "American Romanticism and the Depression of 1837," *Science and Society* 2 (1937/38): 67–82, 80–81.

corps to the German *Bildungsbürgertum*. From that point of view, German observers have always been skeptical about an American *Bildungsbürgertum*. Charlotte Lütkens, whose analytic and insightful reflection *Staat und Gesellschaft in Amerika* (State and society in America) is one of the best books on America from the years of the Weimar Republic, was quite sure on that

> a society which believes in success that can be measured by the amount of the available money, as the American society does, has no room for a class that derives its peculiarity from the possession of education. . . . So in America there are people with knowledge, with training and spiritual interests— but no intellectual middle class.[36]

There was a certain amount of left-wing *Kulturkritik* in Lütkens's statement— she was disappointed that there was no visible movement that aimed to intellectually transcend the current state of affairs in the US. But Lütkens also figured that the lack of an intellectual middle class was inextricably bound up with the weakness of a "leisure class," which Lütkens understood to mean "a broader, stationary social group of inherited prosperity that has retreated from business, or especially a stratum of agrarian retirement, which as consumers or patrons would provide the economic basis for the existence of the intellectuals."[37] At first sight, Lütkens's analysis contradicted that in Thorstein Veblen's famous *Theory of the Leisure Class*. In it, Veblen had criticized the emergence of absentee ownership, which had produced a leisure class who tended toward a ceremonialization of education and the establishment of conservative curricula in the educational institutions.[38] But Veblen's leisure class was in favor of conspicuous consumption; hence, he was as equally pessimistic as Lütkens. His book *The Higher Learning in America*, published in 1918, presented a furious critique of what seemed to him a miserable subordination of the universities to the economic interest.

It seems indisputable that the social esteem of higher education in the US was significantly lower than it had been in nineteenth-century Germany. Most universities in the US were private, not connected in any way to the state, and the American state had long been without a large bureaucracy; there were few

36. Lütkens, *Staat und Gesellschaft in Amerika*, 132–133.

37. Lütkens, *Staat und Gesellschaft in Amerika*, 134, 136.

38. Thorstein Veblen, *Theorie der feinen Leute: Eine ökonomische Untersuchung der Institutionen* (1899; Frankfurt am Main: S. Fischer, 1986), 362.

opportunities for academics in the civil service in the nineteenth century. Nevertheless, there was a demand for professionally trained staff. The many private colleges and universities needed professors, and the growing demand of companies for skilled employees furthered education as a prerequisite of professional success. There was also social esteem in the achievement of knowledge, and it existed in what Burton Bledstein called a "culture of professionalism": "The middle-class person in America owns an acquired skill or cultivated talent by means of which to provide a service. And he does not view his 'ability' as a commodity, an external resource, like the means of production or manual labor."[39] Only against this background does the gradual depreciation of the term "amateurish" become meaningful. The "great middle class" had room for at least some American *Bildungsbürger*.

Culture, especially high culture, was another field that was shaped by, and shaped, the middle class. The creation of a "class-segregated public sphere" was accompanied by the development of a certain understanding of what culture means and what high culture consists of: a decidedly exclusive aesthetic that was not meant to be open to everyone.[40] High culture (which, in the nineteenth century, was mostly learned or imported from Europe) was something that brought together the bourgeoisie and the middle class in a taste community: "Merchants and industrialists, Jews and Gentiles, immigrants and natives, local manufacturers and the heads of large national corporations, all rubbed shoulders listening to the music of Mozart and Beethoven."[41] At the same time, however, it separated them. The bourgeoisie created many of the domestic institutions—museums, libraries, symphony orchestras—with their assets and controlled them on the boards of trustees, while the middle class formed the audience.[42] This private initiative was necessary because neither the state nor the cities were considered to be essential actors in cultural policy. Middle-class interest, and the approach to democratizing art and transforming it into a consumable good, also led to a "middlebrow culture," which found its expression in the first half of the twentieth

39. Bledstein, *Culture of Professionalism*, 4.

40. Beckert, *Monied Metropolis*, 268–269.

41. Beckert, *Monied Metropolis*, 269. See also Michael Broyles, "Bourgeois Appropriation of Music: Challenging Ethnicity; Class, and Gender," in *American Bourgeoisie*, ed. Beckert and Rosenbaum, 233–246.

42. Compare the example of Chicago: Helen Lefkowitz Horowitz, *Culture and the City: Cultural Philanthropy in Chicago from the 1880s to 1917* (Chicago: University of Chicago Press, 1989), 93–125.

century in the establishment of book clubs and the emergence of literary or scientific radio programs.[43]

Politics

In the field of politics, especially municipal politics, the American middle class was acting with major disadvantages. The legal construction of the city in most parts of Europe, which had produced a strong nexus between municipal rule and the corporate group of burghers, gave predominantly upper- and middle-class people privileged access to political rights. Universal manhood suffrage in the US (from about 1830 onward, but with a long tradition of black disfranchisement) and the rapid naturalization of (most) immigrants by political means, left no space for any kind of class-based suffrage or property requirements for voting rights.[44] The city councils in most American cities were anything but happy hunting grounds for the respectable middle class. The link between the self-administration of cities and the rise of the middle class never did exist in the US, to mutual disadvantage: low competence for self-administration and the political weakness of the middle class went hand in hand. Occasionally, in the upper class, and also in those parts of the middle class that were interested in municipal reform, the attempt was made to correct the democratization of suffrage through the introduction of voting rights restrictions. The motive was quite clear: New York's Citizens' Association, which agitated for corresponding changes in the state constitution, argued in the late 1860s that "it is not safe to place the execution of the laws in the hands of the classes against which they are principally to be enforced."[45] But these attempts failed in the election. Lower-class voters who were accustomed to the democratization of suffrage could of course not be persuaded to give up this right to vote.

Whereas the European middle class, which had been affected by the process of the gradual democratization of electoral law since the last third of the nineteenth century, was able to withdraw to the bureaucracy, thereby preserving a small share of power and rule, the educated middle class (and significant parts

43. Joan Shelley Rubin, *The Making of Middlebrow Culture* (Chapel Hill: University of North Carolina Press, 1992).

44. Luella Gettys, *The Law of Citizenship in the United States* (Chicago: University of Chicago Press, 1934), 31–61.

45. Quoted in Beckert, *Monied Metropolis*, 184.

of the middle class overall) in American cities had only the option to retreat to private endeavor. The politics of the educated middle class took place primarily within the orbit of associations and clubs, which created their own political terrain during the heyday of Progressivism with the intent to principally reform the political regime, especially at the local level, but they basically had no success. Middle-class politics ended up creating something like a parallel structure consisting of many organizations and institutions that focused on nearly every aspect of municipal politics but that was devoid of power and rarely reached into the heart of political decision-making in the cities.[46] The rather weak position of the middle class in the political power structure of the (big) cities had some severe consequences. Without political clout, the middle class—and in this case especially the upper middle class—was not in a position to protect itself against the excesses of urbanization and the rapid growth of the cities. Residential areas, which once had been desirable and were favored by the well-to-do, changed their social composition within a generation. Zoning laws, which in European cities protected upper- and middle-class residential areas from social decomposition, came much too late in American cities and were less successfully implemented and enforced by a bureaucratically weak administration.[47] Suburbia has been the refuge of the middle class since the last third of the nineteenth century, but here again it did not escape the desire to differentiate itself from "undesirable" people.[48]

Family and Privacy

Family life in private was another constituent factor of the middle class way of life.[49] Urbanization and industrialization allowed for a separation between home and work, enabling the private home to function as a retreat. Whether one looks at the completely overloaded interiors of the Victorian Age or at the

---

46. Jon C. Teaford, *The Unheralded Triumph: City Government in America, 1870–1900* (Baltimore: Johns Hopkins University Press, 1984), 25.

47. Marcus Gräser, "Urbanisierung ohne administrative Kompetenz: Chicago 1880–1940," in *Megastädte im 20. Jahrhundert*, ed. Wolfgang Schwentker (Göttingen: Vandenhoeck und Ruprecht, 2006), 27–55, 51.

48. Robert M. Fogelson, *Bourgeois Nightmares: Suburbia, 1870–1930* (New Haven, CT: Yale University Press, 2005).

49. On middle-class family life, see the groundbreaking study by Mary P. Ryan, *The Cradle of the Middle Class: The Family in Oneida County, New York, 1790–1865* (Cambridge: Cambridge University Press, 1981).

more unpretentiously designed rooms of the architects of the Prairie School as a comparison, the modern house of the middle-class family moved the effort of design inward to a great extent. The parlor became the central place in the house and a demonstration object of refinement, even though, as Katherine Grier mocks, the middle class had thereby created a room "that none of them needed."[50] The high level of attention paid to the house reflected the need to ensure the emotional quality of the family members' relationships and to guarantee emotional stability, which of course was not always possible; the civic home could be a place of neuroses.[51] The middle-class home was basically made for the nuclear family—the parents and the children. But the family structure of the American middle class in fact reflected the relative social openness of the "great middle class." In addition to the nuclear family, the type of the "extended family" and the hybrid form of "extended family cohesion" (a "middle region . . . between related nuclear families") existed. [52] The extended family (which, besides parents and children, included additional family members) was by no means a remnant of a distant rural past. Rather, the extended family was in some respects much better prepared for the needs of the modern urban industrial society: the assistance provided by a family network allowed for an intensive relationship between several family members. The nuclear family, on the other hand, was predestined for stagnation. In fact, the American middle class in its openness acted as an extended class that was quite able to maintain a "powerful ethos of inclusion in the face of great economic stratification."[53] This ethos of inclusion also allowed for political coalition-building with

50. Katherine C. Grier, *Culture and Comfort: Parlor Making and Middle Class Identity, 1850–1930* (Washington DC: Smithsonian Institution Press, 1988), vii; and also Katherine C. Grier, "The 'Blending and Confusion' of Expensiveness and Beauty: Bourgeois Interiors," in *American Bourgeoisie*, ed. Beckert and Rosenbaum, 87–100.

51. Especially men from the middle class had various chances to escape from a world that seemed to consist only of "manners." The California Gold Rush, for example, attracted a great number of middle-class men and offered one of the possibilities to escape the world of manners and to experience adventures. See Karen Halttunen, *Confidence Men and Painted Women: A Study of Middle-Class Culture in America, 1830–1870* (New Haven, CT: Yale University Press, 1982), 193–197; Brian Roberts, *American Alchemy: The California Gold Rush and Middle-Class Culture* (Chapel Hill: University of North Carolina Press, 2000).

52. Richard Sennett, *Families against the City: Middle Class Homes of Industrial Chicago* (1970; Cambridge, MA: Harvard University Press, 1984), 62–77, 230.

53. Debby Applegate, "Henry Ward Beecher and the 'Great Middle Class': Mass-Marketed Intimacy and Middle-Class Identity," in *Middling Sorts*, ed. Bledstein and Johnston, 107–124, 110–111.

segments of the working class, which was necessary in order to maintain a degree of political influence in a political atmosphere that was shaped by universal manhood suffrage.[54]

The middle-class woman had the task of shaping domesticity. Her job was to manage the household, but not alone, because the middle-class income was usually high enough to employ domestic staff. The ideal of domesticity was the perfect expression of the interpretive pattern of the separate spheres, which had been established since the early nineteenth century and which constructed gender relations diametrically. Whereas the public realm—earning a living and politics—was reserved for men, the house and the family were considered the given sphere of women. The idea of republican motherhood was not meant as a pathway to political participation, for the mothers did not have to embody the republic, but only educate their sons as good republican citizens. Yet the distribution of roles between men and women in the middle-class family—for example, in the education of the children—was in fact much less clear than the interpretive pattern of the separate spheres suggests. Fathers played a greater role in the education of the children than previously thought, "in such a way that emotion has to be considered as one of the defining characteristics of middle-class father-child relationships."[55]

Domesticity should not be underestimated; it did not prevent women from getting a growing sense of self-confidence that ultimately extended beyond the borders of the family and the household. In the last third of the nineteenth century, the woman's role in the family became a reason for the growing public commitment of many middle-class women who engaged in social reform (as well as in the women's suffrage movement). A new generation of middle-class women was concerned with societal motherhood and "municipal housekeeping," working toward a modern welfare policy focusing on poverty not as a moral but as a social problem and trying to build institutions that arranged for the integration of immigrants into American society. "Women's place is home," wrote the journalist Retha Childe Dorr, "but home is not contained within the four walls for an individual house. Home is the community. The city full of people is the family. . . . And badly do the Home and the family need their mother."[56]

54. Johnston, *The Radical Middle Class*, 270.

55. Shawn Johansen, *Family Men: Middle-Class Fatherhood in Early Industrializing America* (New York: Routledge, 2001), 138.

56. Quoted in Kirsten Delegard, "Women's Movements, 1880s–1920s," in *A Companion to American Women's History*, ed. Nancy E. Hewitt (Chichester: John Wiley, 2008), 328–347, 332.

"Great," but Fragmented

Was there a *national* middle class that could have set *national* standards—in cultural consumption, in attitudes to politics? In fact, several related processes stood in the way: the economic opportunities of middle-class status and the experiences of a middle-class way of life were not, nor simultaneously, available in all regions of the country. The variety of middle-class experiences gradually emerged from the opening up of the continent and the growing density of the settlements and left room for the diffusion of certain standards that were already established on the East Coast and could be learned at the frontier. This diffusion of opportunities and style also left room for distinct regional varieties— the middle class in the southern states participated in the system of slavery, as did the merchants in New York City who participated in the cotton trade.[57] None of them saw a contradiction between middle-class values and slavery or racism; nonetheless, abolitionism could also muster considerable middle-class support.

Racial exclusion was another factor that made the "great middle class" less inclusive. Although a successful black middle class emerged in the last third of the nineteenth century, its rise was restricted by a variety of racially motivated discrimination. Yet the genesis of the black middle class was structurally analogous to the genesis of every middle class: property, and position in the social relations of production, created the conditions for a black middle class (and a numerically small black bourgeoisie), which in its lifestyle sought to adapt to long-established patterns of typical middle-class behavior. Crucial to the emergence of the black middle class was the creation of educational institutions, colleges, and universities from which a black, educated middle class could not only graduate, but could also increasingly use job opportunities and care for the Talented Tenth.[58] The black middle class was more open to people who, generally considered, would not have qualified as being middle class: "In the

On female intellectual culture in the nineteenth century, see Jonathan Daniel Wells, *The Origins of the Southern Middle Class, 1800–1861* (Chapel Hill: University of North Carolina Press, 2004), 116–132.

57. Wells, *Southern Middle Class*, 89–90; James Oakes, "Epilogue: Middle Class Masters?," in *The Southern Middle Class in the Long Nineteenth Century*, ed. Jonathan Daniel Wells and Jennifer R. Green (Baton Rouge: Louisiana State University, 2011), 285–295; Beckert, *Monied Metropolis*, 87–88.

58. David Levering Lewis, *W.E.B. Du Bois: Biography of a Race, 1868–1919* (New York: Henry Holt, 1993), 546–549.

1880s, the old wealthy . . . were gradually accepting a newer middle class: postal workers, some municipal employees, and eventually Pullman porters." The key here was not the income but a respectable lifestyle: "economically secure, churchgoing," and participating in civic organizations.[59]

Overcoming racial segregation was, however, hardly possible until the second half of the twentieth century. The blacks desire for middle-class norms, as well as their rejection by the white middle class, was exemplified by the phenomenon of Freemasonry. In the antebellum period, black Masonic lodges had been established on the East Coast, and their significance for the development of African American political life should not be underestimated. However, the attempt to obtain recognition and acceptance by the white "brethren" failed—racial exclusion prevailed and violated basic Masonic principles and goals. In 1945, two sociologists, St. Clair Drake and Horace Cayton, wrote about an "almost complete isolation of the Negro middle class," and this observation had been all the more valid for the nineteenth century.[60]

Did globalization in the nineteenth century have an impact on the shape of the American middle class? That "the much vaunted American standard of living has depended on an imperial system of consumption" is certainly true, but that did not differentiate the American middle class from its European counterparts.[61] What really made the American middle class unique was its character as an extended class in a country full of immigrants, some of whom already had middle-class status or aspired to earn that status in the US. This does not mean that the middle class had been able to ignore ethnicity. Although integration into the bourgeoisie succeeded quickly—"what mattered most was ownership of capital"[62]—ethnicity and racial segregation resulted in a different pathway

59. Margaret Garb, *Freedom's Ballot: African American Political Struggle in Chicago from Abolition to the Great Migration* (Chicago: University of Chicago Press, 2014), 53.

60. St. Clair Drake and Horace R. Cayton, *Black Metropolis: A Study of Negro Life in a Northern City* (Chicago: University of Chicago Press, 1993), 283; For the emerging black middle class in the late nineteenth century, see also Stephen Kantrowitz, "'Intended for the Better Government of Man': The Political History of African American Freemasonry in the Era of Emancipation," *Journal of American History* 96 (2009/10): 1001–1026; Beckert, *Monied Metropolis*, 368; Lawrence Otis Graham, *Our Kind of People: Inside America's Black Upper Class* (New York: Harper Collins 1999), 9; and Stephen Tuck, *We Ain't What We Ought To Be: The Black Freedom Struggle from Emancipation to Obama* (Cambridge, MA: Belknap Press of Harvard University Press, 2010), 111.

61. Kristin Hoganson, *Consumer's Imperium: The Global Production of American Domesticity, 1865–1920* (Chapel Hill: University of North Carolina Press 2007), 11.

62. Beckert and Rosenbaum, "Introduction," 4.

to the middle class. A brewer with German descent would likely have felt he was much more a part of an American middle class than a businessman in Chinatown.[63] Anti-Semitism acted as a powerful mechanism of exclusion from institutions (like Ivy League universities) and professions, and anti-Catholicism hurt the middle-class aspirations of immigrants from Ireland, Italy, and Poland.[64] But the attractiveness of the "great middle class" in the "first international nation" naturally depended on its absorption power.[65]

Should we think about the American middle class as the first international middle class? Of course, not everything that contributed to the constitution and the size of the American middle class was due to global interaction and interconnections. The effects of the global exchanges of goods and ideas varied in the different segments of the middle class. And yet, the "great" American middle class is unique because over a period of about a hundred and fifty years—from 1750 to 1900—it embarked on a path for which there is no equivalent in any other world region. A middle class that was globally configured at its start because of its colonial dependency became a globally dominant social player during this period: first in the realm of American imperialism in the Caribbean, in Latin America, and the Pacific, then also in Europe.[66] The European middle class gradually lost its importance as a model for middle classes across the globe. The discussion of an Americanization of the world that began around 1900 was explicitly or implicitly based on the idea of a particular lifestyle

63. For the situation of Chinese businessmen in Chicago around 1900, see Adam McKeown, *Chinese Migrant Networks and Cultural Change: Peru, Chicago, Hawaii, 1900–1936* (Chicago: University of Chicago Press, 2001), 178–223.

64. John Higham, *Strangers in the Land: Patterns of American Nativism 1860–1925* (New York: Atheneum, 1965); Martin E. Marty, *Pilgrims in Their Own Land: 500 Years of Religion in America* (New York: Penguin, 1984), 273–276; Leonard Dinnerstein, *Antisemitism in America* (New York: Oxford University Press, 1994), 35–57.

65. Randolph S. Bourne, "Trans-National America" (1916), in *Randolph S. Bourne, War and the Intellectuals: Collected Essays 1915–1919*, ed. Carl Resek (Indianapolis: Hackett, 1999), 107–123, 117.

66. For the appeal of the American middle class in Puerto Rico and the Philippines, see Gervasio Luis Garcia, "I Am the Other: Puerto Rico in the Eyes of North Americans," *Journal of American History* 87, no. 1 (2000): 39–64, 63; Vince Boudreau, "Methods of Domination and Modes of Resistance: The U.S. Colonial State and Philippine Mobilization in Comparative Perspective," in *The American Colonial State in the Philippines: Global Perspectives*, ed. Julian Go and Anne L. Foster (Durham, NC: Duke University Press, 2003), 256–290; Julian Go, *American Empire and the Politics of Meaning: Elite Political Cultures in the Philippines and Puerto Rico during U.S. Colonialism* (Durham, NC: Duke University Press, 2008).

inseparably linked to the American middle class. The formation of middle classes in the twentieth century was most often inspired by American middle-class standards.

The search for context and conditions of middle-class-building in the US is a way to clarify not only the question of whether (and if so, how) we can speak of a middle class. Factors that worked against a coherent middle class—regional disparities, racial and ethnic divisions—must be weighed. Analyzing them contributes to a picture of the middle class, even where they contradict the idea of the coherence of *one* middle class. The idea of an American middle class is a working hypothesis that can clarify many aspects of American social history, even if uncertainty regarding the questions about the size and delineation of the middle class remains. The American middle class developed itself in a dialectics of general aspiration and regional variety; in other words, the "great middle class" in this huge country was achieved only with consideration of a great amount of internal differentiation. Paradoxically, it was the great economic potential for a middle class, in conjunction with the great public emphasis on the middle class, that made the real middle class in this diverse country look rather fragmented.

4

Population Planning for a Global Middle Class

Alison Bashford

REPRODUCTION AND ITS REGULATION have a spectacular modern world history. At the end of the eighteenth century, population growth was not a world problem, nor was it perceived to be. European and Asian commentators alike generally presumed a relatively stable population, even though changes in fertility and mortality in societies across the globe were already objects of economic and ethnographic interest. A century later, accelerating rates of global population growth were recognized to be unprecedented historically, and correctly so. By the end of the First World War, world population growth was targeted as a political and economic problem for intervention by a series of internationally oriented organizations and by demographers, geographers, and economists, again from Europe and Asia, the Old World and the New, the north and the south. And in the postwar period, it was an alarming, even catastrophic, planetary problem that national and international bodies were soon actively to address in policy terms.[1]

The modern history of accelerating global population growth was accompanied by a dramatic, if geographically uneven, fertility decline. Counterintuitive to the uninitiated, the coincidence of population growth and fertility

---

1. Alison Bashford and Joyce E. Chaplin, *The New Worlds of Thomas Robert Malthus: Rereading the Principle of Population* (Princeton, NJ: Princeton University Press, 2016); Alison Bashford, *Global Population: History, Geopolitics, and Life on Earth* (New York: Columbia University Press, 2014).

decline was largely due to changes in infant mortality. That the average number of births per woman across the world dropped from around 7 in 1880 to 2.5 in 2015,[2] is both a commonplace observation (the first and second fertility transition) and *so* commonplace that historians often fail to see this change for what it is: perhaps the single most consistently converging trend of modern world history. This was, quite literally, the embodiment of modernity.

What might this enduring global phenomenon (fertility decline and population growth) tell us about the rise of a global middle class over the same modern period? The question is hampered somewhat by the terms in which population has been understood in the past, and, in turn, by historians of that past. Determining and asserting fertility differentials by class was standard in all kinds of national analyses of fertility changes from the late nineteenth century—in northwestern Europe, in North America, in Australasia. This class analysis persisted as a conceptual and substantive constant in later historical demographies. In other words, when applied to *national* contexts, "class," sometimes reformulated as "occupation," has fundamentally driven historical research on population for decades.[3]

When scaled up to the world, however, historians rarely analyze fertility transitions in terms of class, still less in terms of a global middle class. The reason is partly because historians have focused so strongly on critiquing mid-twentieth-century population control, development, demographic transition, and modernization theory as empirically erroneous; as a form of neo-imperialism; and as a problematically forced if not formally compelled manifestation of improper state powers exercised over racialized, subaltern men

2. United Nations, *World Fertility Patterns, 2015: Data Booklet*; International Monetary Fund, *Global Demographic Transition, 1700–2050*. See also Jay Winter and Michael Teitelbaum, *The Global Spread of Fertility Decline: Population, Fear, and Uncertainty* (New Haven, CT: Yale University Press, 2013).

3. For example, Michael R. Haines, "Social Class Differentials during Fertility Decline: England and Wales Revisited," *Population Studies* 43 (1989): 305–323; Eilidh Garrett, Alice Reid, Kevin Schürer and Simon Szreter, *Changing Family Size in England and Wales: Place, Class and Demography, 1891–1911* (Cambridge: Cambridge University Press, 2001); Simon Szreter, *Fertility, Class and Gender in Britain, 1860–1940* (Cambridge: Cambridge University Press, 1996); James C. Witte and Gert G. Wagner, "Declining Fertility in East Germany after Unification: A Demographic Response to Socioeconomic Change," *Population and Development Review* 21 (1995): 387–397; Jane C. Schneider and Peter T. Schneider, *Festival of the Poor: Fertility Decline and the Ideology of Class in Sicily, 1860–1980* (Tucson: University of Arizona Press, 1996); Michael B. Katz and Mark J. Stern, "Fertility, Class, and Industrial Capitalism: Erie County, New York, 1855–1915," *American Quarterly* 33 (1981): 63–92.

and women.[4] In short, historical interpretation of the globalization of population control or fertility decline is generally framed *from* (national) class *to* (global) race.

This chapter suggests that population planning is part of the history of a global middle class for three key reasons. First, fertility control has long been conceptualized, promoted, and analyzed as a micro- and macroeconomic matter. Economists and demographers in many world regions sought to raise the standard of living of the poor. Further, from around 1900, experts assessing relationships between family size and standards of living (class on one measure) actively sought to "globalize" the trend they observed nationally: that smaller families and more wealth (or less poverty) correlated. This was a discussion of the relationship between smaller families and savings that might be spent on commodities or "luxuries" or reinvested in business or education.[5] This is not a claim about the accuracy of their observation, or even its political implications; a vast amount of scholarship investigates both. It is, rather, a reminder that for most of the modern period, fertility control was part of economic planning in the first instance. And what *is* economic planning, if not an intervention into wealth production, consumption, and distribution; if not, in some way, about class?

It is important to recognize "economy" as simultaneously a household, sexual, and public policy matter. That "class" is displayed and created in the domestic sphere is a staple observation.[6] It is embodied and performed in changing experiences of gender: in relation to fatherhood, motherhood, income,

4. See, for the empirical question, Simon Szreter, "The Idea of Demographic Transition and the Study of Fertility Change: A Critical Intellectual History," *Population and Development Review* 19 (1993): 659–701; and Mohan Rao, *From Population Control to Reproductive Health: Malthusian Arithmetic* (New Delhi: Sage, 2004). For the neo-imperial and subaltern argument, Jacqueline Kasun, *The War against Population: The Economics and Ideology of Population Control* (San Francisco: Ignatius Press, 1988); Matthew Connelly, *Fatal Misconception: The Struggle to Control World Population* (Cambridge, MA: Harvard University Press, 2008); Betsy Hartmann, *Reproductive Rights and Wrongs: The Global Politics of Population Control* (Boston: South End Press, 1995); Sarah Hodges, "Malthus Is Forever: The Global Market for Population Control," *Global Social Policy* 10 (2010): 120–126.

5. R. A. Easterlin, "The Economics and Sociology of Fertility: A Synthesis," in *Historical Studies of Changing Fertility*, ed. Eilidh Garrett (Princeton, NJ: Princeton University Press, 1978), 57–134.

6. For example, Marion A. Kaplan, *The Making of the Jewish Middle Class: Women, Family and Identity in Imperial Germany* (Oxford: Oxford University Press, 1991); Mary P. Ryan, *Cradle of the Middle Class: The Family in Oneida County, New York, 1790–1865* (New York: Cambridge

work, and culture.[7] Being middle class required a particular display of masculinity and femininity in relation to the family and to reproduction.[8] In other words, the great change to smaller families did not just accompany middle-class formation; over time it fundamentally defined a new middle class.

Second, the very attribute of "planning"—foresight, control, delayed rewards, investment in the future—were values and modes of conduct strongly associated with upward mobility and with middle-class consciousness and culture. Family planning on the one hand, and political and economic planning on the other, came to be aligned in polities across the world. Population or fertility control at a global level served to bring to light a new way of problematizing the world's poor, against whom a transnational middle-class increasingly defined itself. And that was not just an attribute of Euro-Americans. This chapter focuses on the Indian case, showing how class, population, and fertility control were discussed in the late colonial and early postcolonial period. In the developmental model, the project of raising standards of living across India was strongly linked to fertility control for birth control organizations, for the Indian National Congress, and in Nehru's successive five-year plans. Middle-class commodity consumption, effected through family planning, was an aspiration in the early to mid-twentieth century and a realization several generations on.

Third, a correlation between wealth and family size is firmly maintained by scholars interested in a global middle class in the twenty-first century. When two economists recently asked, "What is middle class about the middle classes around the world?," one clear answer was "smaller families." Middle-classness is signaled, and perhaps even achieved, by having fewer children compared with the poor: "The number of children per adult woman in the household falls sharply as incomes rise."[9] This is neither a new phenomenon nor one newly

University Press, 1981); Leonore Davidoff and Catherine Hall, *Family Fortunes: Men and Women of the English Middle Class* (Chicago: University of Chicago Press, 1987).

7. T.H.C. Stevenson, "The Fertility of Various Social Classes in England and Wales from the Middle of the Nineteenth Century to 1911," *Journal of the Royal Statistical Society* 83 (1920): 401–444; J. R. Gillis, "Gender and Fertility Decline among the British Middle Classes," in *The European Experience of Declining Fertility, 1850–1970: The Quiet Revolution*, ed. John R. Gillis, Louise A. Tilly, and David Levine (Cambridge, MA: Blackwell, 1992), 31–47.

8. Douglas E. Haynes, "Masculinity, Advertising and the Reproduction of the Middle Class Family in Western India, 1918–1940," in *Being Middle Class in India: A Way of Life*, ed. Henrike Donner (London: Routledge, 2011), 23–46.

9. Abhijit V. Banerjee and Esther Duflo, "What Is Middle Class about the Middle Classes around the World?," *Journal of Economic Perspectives* 22 (2008): 3–28, 22.

observed. One way or another, fertility changes and class have gone together for a very long time. And yet "class" needs to be reinserted into the global history of fertility control, just as fertility needs to be inserted into the project of historicizing a global middle class.

Fertility Decline and the Standard of Living

When fertility began to decline at the end of the nineteenth century in parts of France and in England, North America, and Australasia, it was immediately perceived to be both a geographically specific and class-specific phenomenon. Working-class fertility was generally concluded to be higher than that for the middle- or wealthier classes, which had begun moving toward a small family norm from the 1880s (in England, Simon Szreter and Eilidh Garrett argue, from 1816).[10] The relation between class and fertility was a standard element of social and biological investigation in which particular urban, rural, or national populations were analyzed in terms of differential fertilities. This was one field of late nineteenth- and early twentieth-century social science inquiry that had class as a central axis of empirical, as opposed to theoretical, observation. In short, class-based studies emerged and endured as an entirely familiar mode of demographic inquiry.

In populations where fertility decline was early apparent, it was seized upon as characteristic of an aspiring working class. Early twentieth-century British economists almost immediately imagined fertility control as usefully "spreading" as knowledge and practice to working class families over time. In a classic Malthusian model, many argued that working-class families would be better off at the household economy level if they had fewer children. Fertility control brought upward mobility in which surpluses of various kinds might be accumulated or reinvested. Crudely, "surplus" children—those who might well die in infancy—could be converted into surplus food or goods to exchange or into surplus monies to invest. While the economic analogy is open to obvious critique, it is more productive to observe how high infant mortality was conceptualized as wasteful in energy-systems terms. Ecology and economy were early related, conceptually.[11]

10. Simon Szreter and Eilidh Garrett, "Reproduction, Compositional Demography, and Economic Growth: Family Planning in England Long before the Fertility Decline," *Population and Development Review* 26 (2000): 45–80.

11. Bashford, *Global Population*, chapter 5.

Population and the idea of rising standards of living for households, and later for national polities, went together for most early twentieth-century economists. Indeed, the very idea of a measurable standard of living—within and across nations and across the world—was introduced by economists in this demographic context. Many considered that a nation's living standard was an indicator of over-, under-, or optimal population.[12] The reverse was also held to be true: overpopulation itself reduced the overall standard of living. Long-term changes in fertility and mortality came to be theorized as demographic transitions that were either necessary for, or an effect of, economic development.

Although historians often understand this analysis to be brought to the extra-European world via post-1945 demographic transition and modernization theories ("development"), the correlation between fertility, standards of living, and changing perception of class was already part of Asian economy and demography by the early twentieth century. Likewise, world-level comparisons and global ambitions for fertility control were common enough in an earlier period. None of this, in other words, was an exclusively British, North American, or European observation or aspiration.

Indian economists—themselves middle-class—made the connection routinely. In 1933, for example, the Bengali economist Radhakamal Mukerjee explained that "fecundity is lower in the higher economic and social strata compared with the lower layers of the population."[13] The claim was common, recognizable, and widely held. Vepa Ramesam, founder of the Madras Neo-Malthusian League in the 1920s, also asserted the correlation between family size and what he explicitly labelled "class." Most human societies, including his own, could be divided into four, he claimed in a version of demographic transition theory: "1) Rich men with small families, 2) Rich men with large families, 3) Poor men with small families, 4) Poor men with large families."[14] In countries with birth control, he espoused, the disparity between the first and the last group was reduced, and this was a promising trajectory. The relationship

12. T. N. Carver, "Some Needed Refinements of the Theory of Population," and Henry Pratt Fairchild, "Optimum Population," in *Proceedings of the World Population Conference, 1927*, ed. Margaret Sanger (London: Edward Arnold, 1927).

13. Radhakamal Mukerjee, "The Criterion of Optimum Population," *American Journal of Sociology* 38 (1933): 688–698, 695.

14. Sripati Chandrasekhar, "The Madras Neo-Malthusian League: A History," typescript, box 61, folder 10, p. 19, Sripati Chandrasekhar Papers, Ward M. Canaday Center for Special Collections, University of Toledo, Ohio; hereafter, Chandrasekhar Papers.

between fertility and class was rarely understood as static; it always "developed." Something could and (for neo-Malthusians like Ramesam) *should* be done about it.

The idea that fertility control connected household microeconomies to national macroeconomies—to standards of living across a polity—and that this connection should be actively managed, was, again, by no means limited to Euro-American commentators: "heightening the standard of living, class by class," as the sociologist Benoy Kuma Sarkar put it in 1936.[15] And to take another example, the International Labor Organization economist Rajani Kanta Das contributed "The Standard of Living in Asia" to the 1933 Birth Control in Asia conference in London. He presented a progressive agenda: "In order to bring about such changes, India needs compulsory education, universal suffrage, abolition of caste and other social evils, industrialisation of production, and the raising of the standard of life."[16] The feedbacks between fertility, prosperity, and a range of social and political privileges held by the wealthier, but entitled by the poorer, were clearly articulated by Europeans and Asians alike. It was already a world conversation that was shaped to a considerable extent by both colonialism and anti-colonialism.

Globalizing a Middle-Class Trend

That there was feedback between fertility control and economic growth was a modern idea that became globalized and had great influence in terms of intellectual, policy, and social history. Yet it is worth recalling that the long modern history of thinking about fertility transition (actual and aspirational) had a globalizing dynamic written into it from the start. Classic demographic transition theory, in which poor countries modernized from high fertility and high mortality to low fertility and low mortality, developing their economies in the process, was an extension of eighteenth- and nineteenth-century stadial theorizing: economic development from a hunter-gatherer "savage" stage to a commercial "civilized" stage, one version of universal or world history. This was so not least for Thomas Robert Malthus, whose foundational *Essay on the*

---

15. Benoy Kuma Sarkar, *The Sociology of Population with Special Reference to Optimum, Standard of Living and Progress* (Calcutta: N. M. Chowhury, 1936), 35.

16. R. K. Das, "The Standard of Living in Asia," in *Birth Control in Asia: A Report of a Conference Held at the London School of Hygiene & Tropical Medicine, November 24–25, 1933*, ed. Michael Fielding (London: Birth Control International Information Centre, 1935), 37.

Principle of Population must be read as late-Enlightenment stadial theory. It is an economic history of the world, in fact, in which poverty might be amelio-rated and world economies and societies develop, or so he hoped.[17] The Mal-thusian tradition of scholarship itself, in other words, was never *not* interested in the world, even if it originally saw that world very much from Europe. One hundred years after Malthus's own interventions, and in response to an unprecedented global population growth in that century, the so-called neo-Malthusians still pursued active fertility control on a global scale. This is where and when early versions of demographic transition were articulated. The idea of a "league of low-birth-rate nations" became common. But far from being exclusive, the whole point was that it would enlarge, embracing, for example, India, China, Russia, and Japan as well as Britain, France, Ger-many, Canada, Sweden, and Australia. Birth control was to disseminate not just from a middle class to a working class within any one polity but across the world.

Retrospectively, the globalization of the idea of demographic transition has been analyzed firmly within a tradition of anti-racist and feminist critiques of neo-imperialism. And rightly so. Some of those who propounded population control across the world did so in highly patrician ways, as squarely linked to raced and classed eugenics as it was possible to be. Demographic transition thinking always had class implications precisely because standards of living were affected and effected.

Yet the conventional critique of population planners sometimes overlooks the fact that the globalization of middle-class fertility control was often an ambition of leftist progressives, who earnestly sought a redistribution of wealth and power (and food) across the globe. Physicians, economists, geog-raphers, and lawyers were sometimes eager to reduce the economic gap be-tween nations, in part by planning for a growing global middle class. This was the case for John Boyd Orr, for example, an agriculturalist, physician, and first director of the Food and Agriculture Organisation. Early in his career he was deeply concerned with Scottish poverty and later sought greater global equal-ity, even if that meant (as he perceived it inevitably would) a reduction of what he called "white man's power." Stabilizing population growth and raising standards of living was the means by which global poverty might also be ameliorated. "I hope and believe that there will happen all over the world

17. Bashford and Chaplin, *New Worlds of Thomas Robert Malthus.*

what has happened in Western Europe: the birth rate will fall, and, though the death rate must fall too, we may hope to get a stable world population."[18] In his international work, he sought to close a gap between what he figured as the West and the East, soon to be called the developing world, the Third World, and later the Global South.

The critique of neo-imperial population control also ignores the fact that nationalists in China and India often took a demographic (transition) turn. In 1948, Lt. General Kin Cheung spoke to an international audience on population in China, then engaged in a bloody civil war. Was China over-populated? It all depends, he explained, on the standard of living which one expected:

> If we are aiming merely at sustaining a subsistence level of living, I think that China can provide enough food and shelter for 4000 million people in peace. If we wish to claim a standard which ensures sufficient cultural and material facilities, it is necessary either to increase our national wealth or else decrease our population.[19]

Twentieth-century visions for a higher standard of living across the world were thus not just Euro-American plans for a "league of low birth-rate na-tions" to grow internationally, they were simultaneously aspirations *of* those in the high birth-rate nations who recognized that the demographic division of the world was also the economic division of the world. In this context, it is important to recall that the very term "Third World" arose out of this de-mographic context. The population economist Alfred Sauvy first wrested "third estate" from its original bourgeois political moment—the French Revolution—and applied it to the great global changes of the mid-twentieth century: "ce Tiers Monde ignoré, exploité, méprisé comme le Tiers Etat, veut lui aussi, être quelque chose."[20] The world's third estate wanted some-thing economically and was itself thinking in demographic terms about how to get it.

18. John Boyd Orr, *Proceedings of the International Congress on Population and World Resources in Relation to the Family* (London: Family Planning Association, 1948), 10.

19. Lt. General Kin Cheung, "Population in China," *Proceedings of the International Congress on Population*, 106.

20. Alfred Sauvy, "Trois Mondes, Une Planète," *L'Observateur*, 14 August 1952. See also Alfred Sauvy, *Fertility and Survival: Population Problems from Malthus to Mao Tse-Tung* (London: Chatto and Windus, 1961).

Middle-Class Malthusians in India

Middle-class identity was in part self-fashioned through the act of speaking in the interests of those of lower status. Certainly one of the defining features of the middle class in India was its "role as the articulator and representative of the interests of the masses," as Lancy Lobo and Jayesh Shah argue in their study of the economy, etiquette, and ethics of the South Asian middle class.[21] Thus, when Indian men and women began to theorize and act on population as a social and economic problem from the 1920s onward, they did so as one expression and performance of their own middle-class status, as a self-defining act. As Anshu Malhotra has shown of the adjacent field of birth (not birth control), "The issue of gaining control over women's reproductive health was central to securing a middle class life."[22]

The mission of fertility control was itself a class-styled enterprise, the business of middle-class men and women in India in the 1920s and 1930s. Some middle-class Indian women politicized and publicized birth control. The All-India Women's Conference, founded in 1928, certainly middle class, was described as "patriotic, highly educated, and professional," and included women who were "wives of high-ranking men who held distinguished positions in Indian Public life."[23] It endorsed birth control explicitly at its 1935 meeting. During the same period, the Madras Neo-Malthusian League was a middle-class organization for men, its members largely lawyers but also teachers and minor governmental officials; Weber's intelligentsia perhaps.[24] Across the world such civil society organizations were themselves an important form of middle-class culture. The league published leaflets and pamphlets in English and in Tamil, including "Hindu Methods of Birth Control" and "Poverty of Mother India."[25]

---

21. Lancy Lobo and Jayesh Shah, "Introduction," in *The Trajectory of India's Middle Class: Economy, Ethics, and Etiquette*, ed. Lancy Lobo and Jayesh Shah (Newcastle: Cambridge Scholars Publishing, 2015), 1–12, 1.

22. Anshu Malhotra, "Of Dais and Midwives: 'Middle-Class' Interventions in the Management of Reproductive Health in Colonial Punjab," in *Reproductive Health in India: History, Politics, Controversies*, ed. Sarah Hodges (Delhi: Orient Longman, 2006), 199–226, 200.

23. Chandrasekhar, "Madras Neo-Malthusian League: A History," 7.

24. For intelligentsia and Indian middle classes, see Christophe Jaffrelot and Peter van der Veer, "Introduction," in *Patterns of Middle Class Consumption in India and China*, ed. Christophe Jaffrelot and Peter van der Veer (Delhi: Sage, 2008), 11–34, 13–17.

25. Sripati Chandrasekhar, "The Madras Neo-Malthusian League: An Appeal," typescript, box 61, folder 10, Chandrasekhar Papers.

The intention was to influence conduct across individual, household, national, and world levels, the multi-scalar rationale for fertility control that was entirely typical for the period.

The founder of the league was Vepa Ramesam, a lawyer born in 1875 into what the demographer Sriptai Chandrasekhar, writing in the 1950s, called "a middle class orthodox Andhra (Telugu speaking) Hindu family."[26] Ramesam's vision of fertility control was squarely social and economic, concerned with poverty and its possible alleviation through smaller families. His own intergenerational history is telling. Vepa Ramesam and his second wife had fourteen children, but he exhorted all of them to practice birth control themselves. One of his daughters had twelve children, but the remaining eleven had no more than three each.[27] The generational shift was not unique and was, indeed, to generalize across India in subsequent generations.

The Madras Neo-Malthusian League offered the familiar refrain that birth control was necessary to ameliorate poverty: "All suffering, famines, destitution and poverty can be prevented by the adoption of the methods of Birth Control."[28] The poor was the category that united and defined Malthusians across the world in a middle-class "global network of contraceptive evangelism," as Sarah Hodges has named it.[29] The president of the league, Sir Sivaswami Aiyer, wrote of the "misery, hardship, suffering and despair" in Marie Stopes's England, "the most civilized country in the world," thereby emphasizing how much worse the situation was in his own country: "If India is ever to arise out of the depth of her poverty and degradation, she can only do so by learning to control births and raising the mothers of India to a higher standard of life, health and happiness."[30] Their work and their ideas were directed at the rural peasantry as well as at the urban poor in classic Malthusian fashion. Sarah Hodges explains how these men found common cause with

26. Sripati Chandrasekhar, "Sir Vepa Ramesam: A Brief Biography," typescript, box 16, folder 50, p. 2, Chandrasekhar Papers. See also Eleanor Newbigin, *The Hindu Family and the Emergence of Modern India: Law, Citizenship and Community* (Cambridge: Cambridge University Press, 2013), 114–115.

27. Chandrasekhar, "Madras Neo-Malthusian League: A History."

28. Chandrasekhar, "Madras Neo-Malthusian League: An Appeal."

29. Sarah Hodges, *Contraception, Colonialism and Commerce: Birth Control in South India, 1920–1940* (Aldershot: Ashgate, 2008), 47.

30. Sir Sivaswami Iyer, review of *Mother England*, by Marie Stopes, quoted in Chandrasekhar, "Madras Neo-Malthusian League: A History."

their international equivalents, Malthusians and birth control advocates in England, especially.[31]

Yet it is apposite that aristocratic elites were sometimes the object of Malthusians' campaigns as well. The Madras Neo-Malthusian League directed one of its 1929 appeals to the wealthy local *zamindar*, suggesting to them the expedience of fertility control for intergenerational wealth retention. This would render unnecessary the "large sub-division of their princely fortune among numerous children." With just two or three children, "their families can remain millionaires for ever. Thus Birth Control is the key to the retention of prosperity."[32] Appealing to peasants and the urban poor on the one hand and to aristocratic *zamindar* on the other, the league situated itself squarely in the middle. They were, indeed, an urban, educated middle class, keen to instruct and recommend fertility control to those above and below.

This was a middle-class enterprise in process, as well as in ideology. The lawyers in the league pursued their Malthusian interests, undertaken on behalf of a mass poor, in an honorary fashion. Their "work" was demonstrably middle-class precisely because it was voluntary and philanthropic. It was a kind of improvement society that appealed to the evolution of a "higher humanity in the motherland and the uplift of mankind in general."[33] Neo-Malthusians themselves knew that the reach of their work was limited, and few historians actually credit them with effecting the great decline in fertility that was to unfold in later generations. Their more local influence, as Hodges argues, was to reaffirm traditional conjugal practices and laws in a changing modern Madras: contraception was useful in orthodox arguments to retain child marriage.[34] Their larger and longer influence was discursive, the fixing of a link between population and economic development that was to thrive and drive policy in early independent India.

The Madras Neo-Malthusian League was mainly made up of Brahmin men with an investment in, and a certain allegiance to, late colonial bureaucracy. For others during the 1930s, the link between birth control, economic development, and Indian independence was firm. It was drawn by any number of public figures and across a range of political positions within the Indian National

---

31. Hodges, *Contraception, Colonialism and Commerce*, 47.

32. Chandrasekhar, "Madras Neo-Malthusian League: An Appeal."

33. Chandrasekhar, "Madras Neo-Malthusian League: An Appeal."

34. Hodges, *Contraception, Colonialism, and Commerce*, 50, 73–75.

Congress. The Parsi politician Minoo Masani, for example, an anti-colonial activist and later the leader of the Swantantra Party, remembered the 1930s as a point at which he supported birth control and did so as a socialist though not a Marxist. "I would be the last to suggest that birth control was a remedy for all ills but urged that it was certainly one of the ways of combating poverty."[35] Jawaharlal Nehru recorded his economic interest in birth control in his *Autobiography*.[36] And Subhas Chandra Bose agreed that population growth was a major problem, indeed "the first problem," of India.[37] The extensive economic and political discussion of population and its regulation in the 1930s by an Indian middle class and its political elite prepared the ground for the conjoined family planning, political planning, and economic planning that was to ensue in the post-independence era.

Planning: Middle-Class Culture

By 1947, birth control was redirected into the project of Indian nation-building itself. It transformed into "population planning" and became part of the new nation's path to economic development and, as some would have it, to India's freedom. R. K. Nair of the Neo-Malthusian League in Gandhipuram, Coimbatore, wrote in 1950 that "implementation of the Art of BC and its technique should be Nationwide for the Emancipation of our country."[38] In truth it already was.

Well-established arguments about the feedback relationship between standards of living and fertility rates were written into India's Five Year Plans from the beginning. Population control was part of Nehru's First Plan, his policy following the then-dominant conviction that developing the economy would in itself slow birth rates. In 1954 the minister for health argued that "raising the standards of living of the people [will] bring down the birth rate." He noted that "fantastic sums" would be required to implement birth control as a truly national

35. Minoo Masani, *Bliss Was It in That Dawn: A Political Memoir up to Indian Independence* (Arnold-Heinemann: Bombay, 1977).

36. Jawaharlal Nehru, *Autobiography* (London: Bodley Head, 1936), 44.

37. Subhas Chandra Bose, "Presidential Address to the Fifty-First Session of the Indian National Congress," [1938], in *Crossroads: Being the Works of S. C. Bose, 1938–1940* (New York: Asia Publishing House, 1962).

38. R. K. Nair to Sripati Chandrasekhar, 3 June 1950, box 1, folder 8, Chandrasekhar Papers.

measure.[39] And yet this is precisely what unfolded over the Second and Third Five-Year Plans as demographic transition and modernization theory reversed the relationship: the active promotion of birth control was reconceptualized as a key driver of economic growth.

The Third Five-Year Plan (1961) established a national policy that the rate of population growth should be reduced to ensure economic and social stability. It sought to turn around "low levels of consumption, saving, productivity and employment." And "special efforts should be made to reduce the rate at which population is increasing."[40] Economic planning and family planning were twinned:

> The objective of stabilising the growth of population over a reasonable period must therefore be at the very centre of planned development. The programme of family planning, involving intense education, provision of facilities and advice on the largest scale possible and widespread popular effort in every rural and urban community has therefore the greatest significance.[41]

For Nehru, family planning *was* political and economic planning.

The phenomenon and habit of "planning"—rational decision-making with the future in mind coupled with an efficiency-oriented vision—came to be one sign of middle-class identity itself. In post-1947 India, it was certainly a governmental ambition that small families become a norm and that family planning be "accepted as a 'way of life.'" Part of the problem of implementation, however, was not just "low standards of living" but also "low aspirations."[42] Altering expectations, embedding the vision of a more prosperous future household by household, and instilling the need to project forward—these were all middle-class ways of thinking and being.

Demographic thought has a long history of advocating just this kind of individual and household endeavor for greater prosperity. Malthus, for example, had written of Ireland that education would help people plan ahead, marry later, have fewer children, and aspire to and expect more wealth.[43] In the 1920s, the

39. Derrick Kaur, minister for health, India to Shri D. V. Krishna Rao, 4 January 1954, box 1, folder 14, Chandrasekhar Papers.

40. Government of India, *Third Five Year Plan*, introduction and chapter 2.

41. Government of India, *Third Five Year Plan*, chapter 2, clause 13.

42. B. P. Patel, "India: Mass Communication in the Family Planning Programme," paper presented to UNESCO Conference on Family Planning Mass Communication, June 1969, box 49, folder 13, Chandrasekhar Papers.

43. See Bashford and Chaplin, *New Worlds of Thomas Robert Malthus*, 220–221.

sociologist Henry Pratt Fairchild explained that "one type of society is held by the checks of actual starvation. Another type is held by the desire for comforts and luxuries."[44] The best global future, he and others thought, would be when the former converted into the latter, progressively.[45] "Desire" is the key word here, one that signaled both consumption of goods, purposeful planning, and conscious choice. This is where demographic development met consumer capitalism. The objective for Malthusians might have been to create a working class that was above the poverty line, but over time, and with consumer capitalism in good working order, those whose domestic economy included a planned sexual economy might contribute to the ranks of a growing middle class. The long modern world story of fertility decline—the "small-family system"—is part of the history of global capitalism, ironically implemented most overtly in socialist and communist polities: India and later China.

In India, the closest of connections between class, family size, and consumerism was signaled in the vast industry of family-planning propaganda. Posters, stamps, and brochures displayed two parents with two children in domestic contexts endowed with all kinds of postwar household consumables, the unmistakable markers of high modernity and upward mobility. Small families were happy families, as the posters not just implied but actively stated. The promise was prosperity, brought about by the classic middle-class virtues of moderation, prudence, and planning. The reward was, apparently, content middle-class domesticity.

Conclusion

One trajectory of these economic and demographic plans at the governmental level was the much-criticized sterilization programs of Mrs. Gandhi's Emergency Period. Over time, however, another trajectory was a steady change toward a small-family norm and the expectation of upward mobility that accompanied it.[46] The Indian middle class was on its way.[47] Indeed, if scholars of

44. H. P. Fairchild, "Migration," Harris Foundation Round Table, 20 June 1929, typescript in Margaret Sanger Papers, Box 192, Library of Congress, Washington, DC, United States.

45. Fairchild, "Migration."

46. Corinna Unger, "The Making of the Small Family Norm in Post–1947 India," *Contemporanea* 18 (2015): 483–488.

47. Banerjee and Duflo, "What Is Middle Class?," 3–28; Daron Acemoglu and Fabrizio Zilibotti, "Was Prometheus Unbound by Choice?," *Journal of Political Economy* 105 (1997): 709–751.

twenty-first-century India recognize that "the middle class has historically been linked to the question of development, especially in the post-colonial context," then the history of population control and of fertility decline need to be assessed and addressed squarely as class-shaping or, at the very least, class-related phenomena.[48] However politically uncomfortable it may be, population control was a central plank of economic development and of the emergence of an Indian, and arguably a global, middle class.

Fertility rates have dropped across the world. Dramatically so. The most startling period of change was not in the age of empire but in its aftermath, in the mid-twentieth-century moment when decolonization, development, and demography folded into one another. Today, India's fertility has declined to 2.6 children per woman, less than half of the 1950s level.[49] It is so low in part because single-child families are becoming the norm in a quickly growing middle class, albeit a geographically differentiated trend. This familial structure is increasingly familiar in urban, upper-income, educated families. As Alaka Basu and Sonalde Desai put it, "The growing literature on the growth of a middle class in India would suggest that elite Indians live lives that are closer to a global middle class in the West and participate in the kind of ideational transformation reflected in this second demographic transition."[50] In other words, precisely what Indian economists and neo-Malthusians sought in the early and mid-twentieth century has materialized. And not just in India. In China the projection is that any loosening of the one-child policy will not significantly change fertility rates; many couples will continue to reproduce once only, a household economy decision linked to the capacity for commodity consumption, education, and other "middle-class" activities and aspirations.[51]

48. Lobo and Shah, "Introduction," 1.

49. K. Bruce Newbold, *Six Billion Plus: World Population in the Twenty-Frist Century* (Lanham, MD: Rowman and Littlefield, 2007), 8–10; Carl Haub and James Gribble, "India on the Path to Replacement?," *Population Bulletin* 66 (2011): 8–9, 8.

50. Alaka M. Basu and Sonalde Desai, "Hopes, Dreams and Anxieties: India's One-child Families," *Asian Population Studies* 12 (2016): 4–27; Fernandes Leela, "Restructuring the New Middle Classes in Liberalizing India," *Comparative Studies of South Asia, Africa and the Middle East* 20 (2000): 88–104.

51. Xiaoying Zheng, "The Challenges of Population and Development in China," paper delivered to the conference Malthus: Food, Land, People, University of Cambridge, 21 June 2016; Susan Greenhalgh, "Fertility as Mobility: Sinic Transitions," *Population and Development Review* 14 (1988): 629–674.

The global fertility transition represents significant changes in reproduction, in familial life, and in meanings of masculinity and femininity, all of which have accompanied, and in some ways actually formed, a global middle class. There are few sustained global trends so unambiguously embodied and so pivotal to economic and social change over the long modern period. Limiting fertility—the smaller family—was comprehended by individuals, households, and national planners alike to *be* modernity, to *be* "civilization." Fertility decline is a key element of the modern, global story, part of the pattern of upward mobility and of a form of global capitalism in which one of the most recognizably shared and converging middle-class values, and at the same time signifier of class, was the small family. Population control was part of the dream of and for a global middle class, one that continues to unfold as a very real phenomenon in the late modern world.

PART II

Colonialism and Class

5

Modernity, Print Media, and the Middle Class in Colonial East Africa

Emma Hunter

TO WHAT EXTENT, and by what means, were middle classes and bourgeois cultures created in Eastern Africa in the age of empire? This question might at first seem misplaced. The period was one of upheaval, as the region increasingly came under the control of European empires and was drawn into colonial economies. Older forms of connection across the Indian Ocean became harder to maintain, and new kinds of social hierarchies emerged, often defined in racial terms. The colonial economy and racial hierarchies of East Africa offered limited potential for the growth of an African bourgeoisie in any economic sense of the term.

And yet the history of bourgeois cultures in the age of empire is not only a history of social and economic change. It is also a history of intellectual and cultural change, of shifting norms for how society ought to be organized, a history closely linked to changing understandings of the naturalness and desirability of "progress." It is a history of performance, in which new identities were embraced and enacted.[1] And it is a history also of argument, as individuals battled over what constituted progress. Eastern Africa provides a vital perspective on this story.

1. Although he rarely uses the term "performance," the best introduction to a "performative" approach to class remains Pierre Bourdieu, *Distinction: A Social Critique of the Judgement of Taste* (London: Routledge, 2010).

This chapter focuses on the Swahili-language government and mission newspapers of colonial Tanganyika (formerly German East Africa) from the 1880s to 1939. It explores the ways in which a small but growing literate elite in late nineteenth- and early twentieth-century East Africa used the medium of print, and the particular type of space offered by newspapers and periodicals, to assert distinction through rhetorically identifying with, and making a claim of belonging to, an imagined global bourgeoisie. While the groups discussed here did not use the terms "middle class" or "bourgeois" to describe themselves, reading their words through this lens draws our attention to the ways in which the new social and cultural practices they claimed for themselves and praised in others served as a means of identifying with an imagined social identity that transcended the colonial territories in which they lived.

Histories of the Middle Classes in East Africa

The first decades of the twenty-first century have appeared to show the sudden and dramatic growth of Africa's middle classes. For economists, this growing middle class has been taken as both a sign of Africa's increasing prosperity and an engine of further growth.[2] For some political scientists, it seems to promise the arrival of new cultures of democratic government on the continent.[3] Others have been more critical, questioning whether Africa's middle classes are indeed growing as dramatically as has been claimed and challenging the normative assumptions made about the implications of a growing middle class.[4] Those critics have called for more specificity and for

2. Charles Leyeka Lufumpa, Maurice Mubila, and Mohamed Safouane Ben Aïssa, "The Dynamics of the Middle Class in Africa," in *The Emerging Middle Class in Africa*, ed. Mthuli Ncube and Charles Leyeka Lufumpa (London: Routledge, 2015), 9–33.

3. For a critical discussion of these themes, see Ncube and Lufumpa, eds., *Emerging Middle Class in Africa*; Dominique Darbon and Comi Toulabor, eds., *L'invention des classes moyennes: Enjeux politiques d'une catégorie incertaine* (Paris: Karthala, 2014); and Nicholas Cheeseman, "'No Bourgeoisie: No Democracy'? The Political Attitudes of the Kenyan Middle Class," *Journal of International Development* 27 (2015): 647–664.

4. Henning Melber, *The Rise of Africa's Middle Class: Myths, Realities and Critical Engagements* (London: Zed books, 2016); Roger Southall, *The New Black Middle Class in South Africa* (Woodbridge, UK: James Currey, 2016).

historically and contextually rooted studies of middle-class cultures in practice.[5]

Such studies are beginning to emerge, as geographers and anthropologists describe the ways in which new middle-class identities are performed through social and cultural practice, in studies ranging widely from anthropologies of middle-class sexualities and careers to discussions about the use of space and the architecture of the houses of the new middle class.[6] Yet many of the cultural forms identified in the present not only are products of historical processes but also have historical antecedents.[7]

For historians of Africa, however, studying middle-class cultures in the past poses a particular challenge. Even to ask where the middle classes might have been is to step into a historiographical and conceptual minefield. For the colonial officials and ethnographers of early colonial Africa, the hierarchies of African societies, where they were recognized at all, were not understood in terms of a straightforward class hierarchy. As they, and their social scientist successors, became more attuned to the social change happening around them in the mid-twentieth century, they paid growing attention to the specific question of whether a working class might be said to be emerging but concluded eventually that it was not.[8] The formation of a middle class attracted less attention,

5. In their recent, edited volume, Tabea Scharrer, David O'Kane, and Lena Kroeker summarize a range of approaches that have in common an insistence "that it is cultural factors through which people of the middle class distinguish themselves from others, and that the middle class's social distinctiveness is expressed in cultural preferences and behaviours. Investigations of middle classes in Africa would benefit, we argue, from a greater emphasis on these factors, defined qualitatively and emically." "Introduction: Africa's Middle Classes in Critical Perspective," in *Middle Classes in Africa: Changing Lives and Conceptual Challenges*, ed. Lena Kroeker, David O'Kane, and Tabea Scharrer (Cham: Palgrave Macmillan, 2018), 1–31, 8.

6. Rachel Spronk, "Exploring the Middle Classes in Nairobi: From Modes of Production to Modes of Sophistication," *African Studies Review* 57, no. 1 (2014): 93–114; Rachel Spronk, *Ambiguous Pleasures: Sexuality and Middle Class Self-Perceptions in Nairobi* (New York: Berghahn Books, 2012); Claire Mercer, "Middle Class Construction: Domestic Architecture, Aesthetics and Anxieties," *Journal of Modern African Studies* 52, no. 2 (2014): 227–250.

7. Dominique Connan, "La décolonisation des clubs Kényans: Sociabilité exclusive et constitution morale des élites africaines dans le Kenya contemporaine" (PhD diss., Paris 1, 2014).

8. This literature is helpfully reviewed in Carola Lentz, "African Middle Classes: Lessons from Transnational Studies and a Research Agenda," in *The Rise of Africa's Middle Class*, ed. Henning Melber (London: Zed Books, 2016), 17–53.

and where social scientists did explore the emergence of new middle classes, it tended to be in those regions and societies where the social hierarchy was forged through settler colonialism and in urban contexts—for instance, in South Africa and Zimbabwe, in which an African "middle class" could be said to have sat between a European elite above and a poorer section of society below.[9]

Yet, as the anthropologist Carola Lentz has recently reminded us, the same observers and commentators who were so cautious about the "middle classes" were nevertheless very aware of a group whom they termed "elites."[10] As independence approached for many parts of Africa, social scientists began looking for those groups who would take over when the colonial power had withdrawn. Their attention focused on those who had been to school or in some cases university, who were fluent in European languages, and who had joined white-collar professions as clerks or district officers in colonial service or as lawyers, teachers, or doctors. In West Africa, this was a large group that encompassed both the coastal elites whose wealth lay in the era of the Atlantic slave trade and the newer elites.[11] In Eastern Africa, attention focused on "new" elites, who were distinct from an older Islamic coastal elite. They were often Christian and were the product of government or mission schools, with their roots lying in rural areas.

For historians of eastern Africa, the interest of these groups lay particularly in the fact that they were the leaders of nationalist movements and staffed postcolonial bureaucracies.[12] These groups, of course, followed in the wake of earlier forerunners, in particular, the colonial clerks who were early converts

9. Leo Kuper, *African Bourgeoisie: Race, Class and Politics in South Africa* (New Haven, CT: Yale University Press, 1965); Alan Gregor Cobley, *Class and Consciousness: The Black Petty Bourgeoisie in South Africa, 1924–1950* (New York: Greenwood Press, 1990), 229–233.

10. Lentz, "African Middle Classes," 19–20.

11. Michel R. Doortmont, "Producing a Received View of Gold Coast Elite Society? C. F. Hutchison's *Pen Pictures of Modern Africans and African Celebrities,*" *History in Africa* 33 (2006): 473–493; Stephanie Newell, "Introduction," in *Marita: Or the Folly of Love* (Leiden: Brill, 2002), 1–37; Richard Rathbone, "West Africa: Modernity and Modernization," in *African Modernities: Entangled Meanings in Current Debate*, ed. Jan-Georg Deutsch, Peter Probst, and Heike Schmidt (Oxford: James Currey, 2002), 18–30.

12. Benjamin N. Lawrance, Emily Lynn Osborn, and Richard L. Roberts, "Introduction: African Intermediaries and the 'Bargain' of Collaboration," in *Intermediaries, Interpreters, and Clerks: African Employees in the Making of Colonial Africa*, ed. Benjamin N. Lawrance, Emily Lynn Osborn, and Richard L. Roberts (London: University of Wisconsin Press, 2006), 3–34, 24.

and attendees of mission schools in the late nineteenth and early twentieth centuries. Yet such people were of less interest to Africanist historians, for whom they fell on the wrong side of an imagined collaborator/nationalist divide. It is only relatively recently that those colonial-period groups have attracted the attention of a new generation of historians that is less confined by nationalist frameworks. A growing body of work has produced rich social histories revealing the difficult paths such groups navigated as they forged new identities in a colonial world.

The question of where these groups of colonial intermediaries or elites sit in a global history of the middle classes is therefore an interesting one. Economically, their position was fragile and their capacity for career advancement was fundamentally limited by the racial politics of settler societies, particularly in German East Africa (later, Tanganyika) and British East Africa (later, Kenya). Unlike the middle classes of colonial West Africa or India, they were often "new men," who had not enjoyed wealth or status in the precolonial era.[13] Under the watchful eye of repressive colonial states, there was very little scope for the collective organizing engaged in by middle-class communities in other parts of the colonial world. In particular, the potential for forming pan-ethnic or national associations was highly restricted, and so local forms of social distinction did not necessarily translate easily into identification with a *national* collective.

It is therefore not surprising that historians have rarely used the label "middle-class" to describe such groups. While Michael West's study of the middle class in Zimbabwe stands as a relatively rare exception, other scholars of Zimbabwe conspicuously avoid the term.[14] Timothy Burke's classic study of twentieth-century Zimbabwe chooses the term "elites" to describe the principal characters in his story.[15] Others come closer. In her study of schooling in colonial

---

13. Newell, "Introduction," 14; Sanjay Joshi, "Thinking about Modernity from the Margins: The Making of a Middle Class in Colonial India," in *The Making of the Middle Class: Toward a Transnational History*, ed. A. Ricardo López and Barbara Weinstein (Durham, NC: Duke University Press, 2012), 29–44.

14. Michael O. West, *The Rise of an African Middle Class: Colonial Zimbabwe, 1898–1965* (Bloomington: Indiana University Press, 2002); Sean Redding, "Peasants and the Creation of an African Middle Class in Umtata," *International Journal of African Historical Studies* 26, no. 3 (1993): 513–539.

15. Timothy Burke, *Lifebuoy Men, Lux Women: Commodification, Consumption, and Cleanliness in Modern Zimbabwe* (Durham, NC: Duke University Press, 1996), 43.

Zimbabwe between 1918 and 1940, Carol Summers at times refers to this group as "middle people."[16]

This social group, whose voices we can hear in newspapers designed by the colonial state to be spaces of didacticism and edification, worried out loud in the pages of these newspapers about many things that concerned middle classes elsewhere. During the 1930s, Burke argues, "Western ideals of cleanliness, appearance, and bodily behavior became increasingly powerful within African communities," and within public discourse, cultures of bodily hygiene came to stand as a totemic symbol within wider struggles "between 'traditional' and 'modern' life, 'African' and 'European' ways, 'heathenism' and 'Christianity.'"[17] The languages of "the modern" and of "civilization" were frequently invoked. As one correspondent to the *Bantu Mirror*, cited by Burke, wrote, "We let our children go almost naked. We call ourselves civilized, yet we do not show the fruits of that civilization."[18] Yet strikingly, what does not appear in these newspapers is a language of class or of the middle or the term "bourgeoisie."

If languages of class seem largely not to have been employed by our historical actors themselves, is there nevertheless a case for concepts of class in general and of the "middle class" in particular to be employed by historians as a category of analysis? A growing body of literature suggests that there may be.

In their recent transnational history of the middle classes, the historians A. Ricardo López and Barbara Weinstein argue that

> middle-class modernities were not originally European, uniquely North American, homogeneously Anglo, alternatively Indian, genuinely African, or differently Latin American, but rather transnational historical formations through which the meanings, subjectivities and practices of being middle class were mutually—and coevally—constituted across the globe.[19]

Taking a transnational perspective, they fold the colonial experience into a wider global story rather than seeing it as exceptional. Thus, they write, "Colonial practices, gender hierarchies, class segmentations, racial categorizations, and religious projects were indeed constitutive of—rather than opposed or marginal to—the historical experiences of modernity *throughout the world*."

16. Carol Summers, *Colonial Lessons: Africans' Education in Southern Rhodesia, 1918–1940* (Oxford: James Currey, 2002), xxviii.

17. Burke, *Lifebuoy Men, Lux Women*, 43.

18. Burke, *Lifebuoy Men, Lux Women*, 43.

19. *Making of the Middle Class*, ed. López and Weinstein.

The approach taken in that volume, both by the editors and their contributors, serves to break down dichotomies between the West and the world beyond Europe and America and to challenge the contrast between studies of the middle class focused on its discursive construction and those that privilege material practices, all of which is immensely productive. But at the same time, their focus on a process leading to a sense of "belonging to a collective middle class" forces us to think more seriously about the African case, where the language of bourgeoisie or middle-classness was relatively absent; in other words, to consider what the case of colonial Africa means for a global history of the middle classes, and vice versa.

In her review of the literature on Africa, Carola Lentz hesitates to go as far as López and Weinstein, but she does argue for

> striking continuities of current middle-class formation in the Global South with processes in the nineteenth and early twentieth centuries in Europe and America, namely the centrality of "boundary work"; the role of education, "intelligent" work and meritocratic values; new ideals of domesticity and gender relations; practices of consumption and middle-class sociability and political engagement.[20]

And indeed, she makes a compelling case for using the term "middle class" "both for historical and contemporary social formations" on the grounds of the "comparative perspective" that it allows.[21] For Lentz, culture is at the heart of definitions of the middle class. She cites approvingly the historian of Europe Jürgen Kocka, who writes that

> membership in voluntary associations—based on an emerging common culture and centred on family and work—ideas of progress and a strict moral code, education and sometimes religion held these middle-class groups together. This culture implied a post-aristocratic, modern vision of life frequently advocated with outright criticism of the old order and the aristocracy.[22]

While Kocka's gaze is firmly focused on Europe, this definition lends itself easily to comparative analysis and perhaps helps explain why, in colonial Africa,

---

20. Lentz, "African Middle Classes," 26.

21. Lentz, "African Middle Classes," 26.

22. Jürgen Kocka, "The Middle Classes in Europe," in *The European Way: European Societies during the Nineteenth and Twentieth Centuries*, ed. Hartmut Kaelble (London: Berghahn Books, 2004), 15–43, 29.

talk of "the modern" provided a space in which new cultural forms were articulated.

Yet Lentz also draws attention to areas in which the African experience may be historically distinctive, notably the importance of paying attention to scales, and to the ways in which "sub-national horizontal memberships and loyalties, organized around locality, region, ethnicity, or religion, defy, intersect with, or drive the emergence of national middle classes," an approach that echoes recent work on other parts of the Global South.[23] The global is also important to her analysis. "In what ways," she asks, "are the aspirations of African middle classes inspired by global discourses on middleclassness and imaginaries of middle-class lives?"[24]

With this in mind, let us turn now to the newspapers and print media of German East Africa and Tanganyika in which a sense of collective belonging to an imagined social formation that bore the cultural hallmarks of what in other places would be termed "middle class" was rhetorically constructed, and we will do so with attention to the question of scales highlighted by Lentz.

"There Are More African Newspapers in Africa Than Europeans Generally Think"[25]

In the late nineteenth and early twentieth centuries, East Africa was in flux. European power was growing, but the region remained part of an Indian Ocean world. It was in this context that people living in the region were compelled to confront the great questions of the age. What constituted "modernity"? What did "progress" mean? Was there one definition of "civilization" or many? On the Islamic Swahili-speaking coast, elite conceptions of what constituted "civilization" shifted over the course of the nineteenth century.[26] By the end of the century, both on the coast and inland, the growing power of the German and British Empires and the arrival of Christian missionaries were providing alternative conceptions of what it might mean to be "civilized." At the same time,

---

23. Lentz, "African Middle Classes," 45; Joshi, "Thinking about Modernity."

24. Lentz, "African Middle Classes," 45.

25. Hilda Lemke, "Die Suaheli-Zeitungen und Zeitschriften in Deutsch-Ostafrika" (PhD diss., University of Leipzig, 1929), 12.

26. Randall L. Pouwels, *Horn and Crescent: Cultural Change and Traditional Islam on the East African Coast, 800–1900* (Cambridge: Cambridge University Press, 1987), 72.

the rise of colonial power coupled with a new hardening of racial thought meant that posing, and answering, these questions acquired a new urgency.

In these discussions, newspapers and periodicals played an important role. In contrast to Anglophone West Africa, home from the early nineteenth century to an important press that understood its role as akin to a "fourth estate," in which power could be critiqued in the absence of other opportunities to pursue political rights, the first newspapers printed in nineteenth-century East Africa, as distinct from those published elsewhere but circulating in the region, were produced by missions and governments.[27]

While colonial states were often divided among themselves over what "progress" might look like, there was broad agreement that whatever it was, newspapers were both an index by which it could be measured and a weapon through it could be achieved—through spreading literacy in general and through the didactic content the newspapers contained. For missionaries, newspapers and periodicals held particular importance in strengthening Christian communities, but a language of "progress" was present there too.[28]

We can see this in the commitment from colonial states and missions to creating newspapers. The UMCA Mission on the island of Zanzibar, which had introduced a press soon after it arrived on the island in 1865, at first used it to publish various religious texts as well as other printed matter to assist in their conversion attempts. In 1888 a periodical called *Msimulizi* (The Reporter) was launched, produced by the African students studying at Kiungani College in Zanzibar. Alongside news of the college, the periodical published contributions

27. Newell, "Introduction," 21; Derek Peterson and Emma Hunter, "Print Culture in Colonial Africa," in *African Print Cultures: Newspapers and Their Publics in the Twentieth Century*, ed. Derek Peterson, Emma Hunter, and Stephanie Newell (Ann Arbor: University of Michigan Press, 2016), 1–45; Philip C. Sadgrove, "The Press, Engine of a Mini-Renaissance in Zanzibar (1860–1920)," in *History of Printing and Publishing in the Languages and Countries of the Middle East*, ed. Philip C. Sadgrove (Oxford: Oxford University Press, 2005), 151–178, 153.

28. On the history of literacy in colonial Africa, see Karin Barber, "Introduction: Hidden Innovators in Africa," in *Africa's Hidden Histories: Everyday Literacy and Making the Self*, ed. Karin Barber (Bloomington: Indiana University Press, 2006), 1–24. While colonial rulers were keen to promote literacy, they were also conscious of the risk that widespread literacy could pose to their rule, which at times led them to promote vernacular languages over the teaching of European languages such as English or German. Derek Peterson, "Language Work and Colonial Politics in Eastern Africa: The Making of Standard Swahili and 'School Kikuyu,'" in *The Study of Language and the Politics of Community in Global Context*, ed. David Hoyt and Karen Oslund (Oxford: Lexington Books, 2006), 185–214.

from local people, the first of which was an article by a teacher, Mildred Maua.[29] The paper lapsed in 1895 but reappeared in 1904 and continued publication until the First World War.

On the mainland in German East Africa, by 1914 there were four Swahili-language newspapers published by missions and government and intended for an African readership. *Habari za Mwezi, Pwani na Bara*, and *Rafiki Yangu* were all published by missions, while *Kiongozi* was published by the Government School in Tanga, eventually with financial support from the German colonial government. Although the newspapers were to some degree rivals, they spoke to each other as friends. Thus the UMCA newspaper *Habari za Mwezi* greeted the arrival of *Kiongozi* in 1905 with warm words. An editorial explained that they were two different people, but their cause was the same, for they shared the aim of encouraging people to read and write, to increase their knowledge, and to be aware of world news.[30] The circulation of these four newspapers was small, generally around two thousand copies per newspaper, but circulation grew steadily until interrupted by the First World War.[31] Although three of the four newspapers were published by missions, missionaries with journalistic aspirations discovered early on that for a newspaper to be successful it could not be too focused on religion.

The UMCA publishers of *Habari za Mwezi* learned this the hard way. The newspaper was launched in 1895 but briefly folded in 1907. In his January 1907 editorial, the last before it closed, the editor wrote that when he started the newspaper he hoped that "many people would be prepared to pay 2 Hellers each month because many had learned to read and there were not many books." And yet, he had come to understand that there were not many who were willing to pay for it, and so he had decided to abandon it. When it reappeared the following year, now edited by Samuel Sehoza, it was a very different undertaking, with less of the paternalist tone of its earlier incarnation and much more "secular" content—such as folk tales, translations of short stories and books by such authors as the Brothers Grimm and Leo Tolstoy, reprints of articles published in other newspapers such as the Lutheran *Pwani na Bara*, and reprints of encyclopedia entries.[32]

---

29. Sadgrove, "Engine of a Mini-Renaissance in Zanzibar," 157.

30. "Kiongozi," *Habari za Mwezi*, July 1905, printed in Lemke, "Die Suaheli-Zeitungen," 29.

31. In the case of *Kiongozi*, it was originally intended for former pupils of the Government School in Tanga, but by the end of its life it had expanded beyond that relatively narrow base.

32. Martin Sturmer, *The Media History of Tanzania* (Ndanda: Ndanda Mission Press, 1998); Lemke, "Die Suaheli-Zeitungen."

The missionary newspapers addressed a Christian audience and were in part a means of building up a new Christian community, but they did not exclude others. When *Pwani na Bara* was established by the Protestant evangelical missions in 1910, it was explicitly noted that the fight against Islam should not be a primary aim of the newspaper. *Kiongozi* adopted a secular standpoint. Even though all four papers folded during the First World War, after the British assumed the League of Nations Mandate of Tanganyika, officials moved quickly to establish a new government periodical, *Mambo Leo*, which began publication in 1923.

Newspapers in early colonial Tanganyika and Zanzibar, then, had in common a normative conception of the newspaper as both an agent and a symbol of progress. In 1895, the government newspaper in Zanzibar, the *Gazette*, greeted news of the establishment of a Swahili monthly newspaper by the UMCA Mission in mainland Tanganyika with the hope that this "new venture in journalism in East Africa . . . may be the beginning of a great change in the life and views of the educated native races around us." Newspapers brought progress, the *Gazette* declared: "The evolution of society is working out before our eyes, there can be no retrogression, we have moved on from the past and there can be no return thereto, and the Press is one of the greatest factors at work even in Africa."[33] In a 1929 editorial, the editor of *Mambo Leo* told his readers, "When you buy a newspaper, or when you bring us news and questions, you are following the example of other peoples of the world who rely on the newspaper as one way of modernizing [lit. civilizing themselves]."[34]

The content of mission and government newspapers demonstrates the nature of the kind of "progress" imagined and was similar to that found in newspapers in other parts of the colonial world, both at the time and earlier. In his recent study of the history of the black middle class in South Africa, Nkululeko Mabandla discusses the role of mid-nineteenth-century missionary periodicals in promoting new kinds of cultural practices, such as the building of square houses rather than the traditional *rondavel*.[35] As Jean and John Comaroff have shown, this was part of a wider missionary project of remaking cultures, itself,

33. Sadgrove, "Engine of a Mini-Renaissance," 159.

34. Editorial, "Faida ya gazeti kama hili letu," *Mambo Leo*, September 1929, 2.

35. N. Mabandla, *Lahla Ngubo: The Continuities and Discontinuities of a South African Black Middle Class* (Leiden: African Studies Centre, 2013), 19.

they argue, part of an endeavor by a British middle class in formation to "secure its cultural hegemony."[36]

These newspapers were tools of colonial states and missions, understood as instruments for the creation of new kinds of colonial subjecthood. In that sense, they take us to the heart both of the colonial and missionary projects of creating new cultural forms and of the anxieties and indecision of those institutions about what kinds of colonial subjects and Christian subjects they sought to create.

But newspapers and periodicals were never simply a colonial export imposed on colonial territories. In Tanzania, a small but growing group of African readers, writers, and editors embraced newspapers and periodicals, conscious of the potential they offered and agreeing that they were a universal index of progress.[37] They also shared the view that they could be used to encourage new cultural practices, the adoption of which would constitute "progress." The pages of newspapers like *Mambo Leo* served as a space in which the "bourgeois culture" described by Jürgen Kocka and Carola Lentz were inculcated, both by European editors and contributors and by African editors and writers. This was true of the government and mission press.[38] But it was also true of the independent press. As John Lonsdale has shown for 1920s Kenya, it was in the pages of the Kikuyu-language newspaper *Muigwithania* that Kenya's future president, Jomo Kenyatta, sought to develop a "vision of modernizing reform."[39]

Yet at the same time, the readers saw them as a space in which to debate what "progress" could and should mean. A close reading of these newspapers suggests the importance of global discourses in shaping new identities in late

36. Jean Comaroff and John Comaroff, "Home-Made Hegemony: Modernity, Domesticity, and Colonialism," in *African Encounters*, ed. Karen Tranberg Hansen (New Brunswick, NJ: Rutgers University Press, 1992), 37–74, 39; Lentz, "African Middle Classes," 32.

37. Letter from "Msomaji," "Kila kitu na dawa yake," *Mambo Leo*, April 1931, 72.

38. Katrin Bromber, "*Ustaarabu*: A Conceptual Change in Tanganyika Newspaper Discourse in the 1920s," in *The Global Worlds of the Swahili*, ed. Roman Loimeier and Rüdiger Seesemann (Berlin: Lit, 2006), 67–81; Emma Hunter, "'Our Common Humanity': Print, Power and the Colonial Press in Interwar Tanganyika and French Cameroun," *Journal of Global History* 7 (2012): 279–301.

39. Bruce Berman and John Lonsdale, "Custom, Modernity, and the Search for *Kihooto*: Kenyatta, Malinowski and the Making of *Facing Mount Kenya*," in *Ordering Africa: Anthropology, European Imperialism and the Politics of Knowledge*, ed. Helen Tilley and Robert Gordon (Manchester: Manchester University Press, 2007), 173–198, 175.

nineteenth- and early twentieth-century East Africa, and that imperialism and colonial rule played a key role in propagating such discourses. It was precisely in texts such as these with their firmly didactic overtones that readers were exposed to a discourse in which self-help, associational life, and respectability were elements of a potentially universal conception of "modern" life, as applicable in East Africa as it was in Lucknow or Aleppo.[40]

But the interactions that took place in these pages, both between readers and between readers and editors, reinforces the point made for other times and places that the question of what constituted "modernity" was something to be argued over. These arguments thus took shape in different forms in different places, always drawing on older social formations and social and cultural practices and characterized more by contradictions than by homogeneity.[41]

Running through the pages of Tanzania's late nineteenth- and early twentieth-century newspapers is a persistent questioning of what "progress" should mean in an East African context. The language used to do so in this period was one of "civilization," or ustaarabu.[42] While the term had been used in the second half of the nineteenth century to indicate a coastal Islamic culture, which distinguished the coast from inland areas, in the late nineteenth and early twentieth century, alternative associations were offered, ones associated with the modern West. At the same time, others wrote back against these definitions. In Kenya in the 1930s, the Islamic reformer Sheieikh al-Amin Mazrui used his Arabic-script Swahili newspaper to question "Western" civilization. He asked the question, "How are we imitating the Whites?" (Namna gani twaigiza Wazungu) and criticized Muslims on Kenya's coast who adopted bad customs from the British, such as drinking and dancing, rather than what he saw as more positive customs which he associated with Western civilization, such as hard work and commitment to education.[43]

40. Jürgen Osterhammel, The Transformation of the World: A Global History of the Nineteenth Century (Princeton, NJ: Princeton University Press, 2014), 771

41. Joshi, "Thinking about Modernity." I discuss these themes in more detail in Hunter, "'Our Common Humanity'" and Emma Hunter, Political Thought and the Public Sphere in Tanzania: Freedom, Democracy and Citizenship in the Era of Decolonization (Cambridge: Cambridge University Press, 2015), chapter 1.

42. Bromber, "Ustaarabu."

43. Kai Kresse, "On the Skills to Navigate the World, and Religion, in Coastal Kenya," in Articulating Islam: Anthropological Approaches to Muslim Worlds, ed. Magnus Marsden and Konstantinos Retsikas (New York: Springer, 2013), 77–99, 89; Kai Kresse, Guidance (Uwongozi) by Sheikh Al-Amin Mazrui: Selections from the First Swahili Islamic Newspaper (Leiden: Brill, 2016).

Newspapers, then, were understood to represent a universal form, the adoption of which was itself a measure of modernity. Yet they also provided a space in which to argue over the specifics of what progress should look like in particular contexts.

Global Imaginaries

Newspapers in East Africa quickly became a space in which new kinds of identities were performed. The act of writing to a newspaper or reading a newspaper or claiming an identity as a reader was a performance of a particular kind of subjectivity. In Carola Lentz's terms, this was part of "doing being middle class."[44] In the pages of the newspaper, readers could assert distinction over nonreaders by celebrating the cultural codes to which they adhered and critiquing those who failed to adopt the modes of behavior they had adopted for themselves. Like the contemporary Kenyan middle classes recently studied by Dominique Connan, they did so by inserting themselves into an imagined global bourgeois culture.[45] Thus those who were mocked for spending hard-earned money on a newspaper could write in to air their frustrations, knowing that fellow readers agreed that newspapers were an essential element of a "modern" life.

In their own towns and villages, these groups were often in a relatively insecure position. Their economic situation was not necessarily substantially superior to that of their neighbors. Their everyday working lives in a colonial society were characterized by negotiating the racial hierarchies of a colonial state. Their letters and autobiographies bring to life the challenges they faced in the workplace and their attempts to mobilize patrons to support their career trajectories.[46] Their writings also capture the parallel challenges they faced in their social lives, where the demands of respectability in a colonial setting often contradicted existing social constructions of successful manhood.[47] Focusing on Zimbabwe in the years between 1920 and 1945, Carol Summers describes the

44. Lentz, "African Middle Classes," 42.

45. Connan, "La décolonisation des clubs Kényans."

46. Andreas Eckert, "'I Do Not Wish to Be a Tale-Teller': Afrikanische Eliten in British-Tanganyika; Das Beispiel Thomas Marealle," in *Lesarten eines globalen Prozesses: Quellen und Interpretationen zur Geschichte der europäischen Expansion*, ed. Andreas Eckert and Gesine Krüger (Hamburg: Lit, 1998), 172–186.

47. Stephan Miescher, *Making Men in Ghana* (Bloomington: Indiana University Press, 2006), 11–13.

ways in which young African men working at Christian mission stations employed marriage strategies to resist the tag of "mission boy" and assert their claim to independent manhood as "relatively independent Christian men."[48] Very often, then, the everyday life of this group was characterized as much by struggles with and against marginalization and marginality as by the power that derives from "elite" status. The act of engaging with a newspaper, and the "boundary work" embodied in it, is perhaps helpfully understood in this context.

At the same time, such engagement provided a means of claiming authority over existing local elites. For Jomo Kenyatta, who came of age in colonial Kenya in the 1920s, the pages of *Muigwithania* offered a space in which he could speak with authority. In the oral context of the *baraza*, or public meeting, wealth and seniority gave men the authority to speak. How, it was asked, could a man with one goat dare to speak to a man with one hundred? The short answer was that while in the public meeting he could not, in print he, and indeed she, could. As Bruce Berman and John Lonsdale write, "No *Muigwithania* correspondent counted his goats before writing; women wrote too, overcoming a nervousness that must have been more crippling in speech. Print had a power of its own; it could convey *kihooto* irrespective of an author's status."[49] Print offered a space that was both egalitarian and inegalitarian, its boundaries sharply policed yet in theory open to all.

If the everyday life of East Africa's "middle people" at work and at home was characterized simultaneously by power and marginality, particularly in rural areas and small towns, print provided a domain in which they could claim their place as members of a collective that transcended locality and that was pan-territorial, pan-African, or indeed global.

Exploring the creation of bourgeois cultures in the pages of newspapers and periodicals, then, reminds us that while much of the literature on the making of the middle classes focuses on their formation in national contexts, in colonial settings a national framing takes us only so far. Colonial regimes in East Africa did their best to prevent organization on a national scale, and it was in any case not clear what would be gained from such organization. But in the pages

48. Summers, *Colonial Lessons*, 176.

49. Berman and Lonsdale, "Custom, Modernity," 176. Though women's voices remained rare, as suggested by a letter published in *Mambo Leo* in 1931 asking why the women who had intervened in debates over the education of girls in the pages of *Mambo Leo* in 1926 and 1927 had fallen silent. Joseph M. B. Tibeiya, letter to the editor, *Mambo Leo*, September 1931, 172.

of the newspaper, readers could insert themselves into a global story of progress, engage in comparison and address an imagined global audience. Even when they wrote in vernaculars understood within a relatively confined geographical space, correspondents to early colonial newspapers understood themselves to be addressing a readership that transcended space and linguistic barriers. This was as true of the Yoruba newspapermen in West Africa, studied by Karin Barber and Rebecca Jones, as it was of Jomo Kenyatta and the writers who constructed a Kikuyu modernity in the pages of *Muigwithania*.[50] This imagined global readership informed the way in which readers and correspondents disciplined each other, as when a regular correspondent to the Tanganyikan government periodical *Mambo Leo* criticized a fellow correspondent who had sent in a story of a wife who had turned into an elephant. He demanded his fellow correspondents send in only news whose veracity they could attest to, for *Mambo Leo* was read around the world and to publish untrue stories would be a source of shame. In a similar vein, when funds were being raised in Scotland to create a museum in memory of the missionary David Livingstone, a letter writer calling himself Rafiki (friend) called on Tanganyikans to contribute so that "our name of Tanganyika" would have its rightful place on the public list of those who had contributed.[51]

At first glance, this insistence that everything published in the newspaper could be read anywhere in the world might suggest either a certain naivety or a more concrete attempt to construct a diasporic nationalism. Yet we might also detect something else at work. Employing print might tentatively be understood as an attempt at "jumping scale," an act of producing a new geographical scale above that of the colonial territory in which new collectivities could be imagined and identities constructed. In this way, even as readers and correspondents appeared to endorse the hegemony of new cultural constructions of bourgeois life advocated by colonial officials and missionaries, the act of participating in a colonial public sphere simultaneously constituted a mode of resistance to the boundaries imposed by colonial rule in Africa.[52]

50. Rebecca Jones, "The Sociability of Print: 1920s and 30s Lagos Newspaper Travel Writing," in *African Print Cultures*, ed. Peterson, Hunter, and Newell, 102–124; Karin Barber, "Experiments with Genre in Yoruba Newspapers of the 1920s," in *African Print Cultures*, ed. Peterson, Hunter, and Newell, 151–178; John Lonsdale, "Kenyatta, God and the Modern World," in *African Modernities*, ed. Deutsch, Probst and Schmidt, 31–65.

51. Hunter, "'Our Common Humanity,'" 288, 293.

52. Neil Smith, "Contours of a Spatialized Politics: Homeless Vehicles and the Production of a Geographical Scale," *Social Text* 33 (1992): 54–81, 60.

There were nevertheless limits to this imaginative insertion into the global, and we can see this especially in writing about government and political power. The normative idea of the newspaper, then as now, was as a space where power is critiqued. Yet in the pages of the UMCA newspaper *Habari za Mwezi*, when the state appears it is a power to be obeyed and not to be challenged. These lines from an article in 1906 are telling in this regard. Following a news item, the editor wrote:

> This news has been published in order that we remember that we must obey the Government, and if we obey the Government and respect it, if we fear it and follow its orders, then it will respect us in turn. Because if a child doesn't obey his father, that father has no alternative but to reproach his son, and so it is with us, if we don't obey the orders of the Government, the Government has no alternative but to reproach us.[53]

As the editors of this volume make clear, attention to global comparison must not be at the expense of local political and social context.

Conclusion

To return, then, to the questions with which we started, what implications can we draw for a global history of the middle classes by looking again at a particular group of people engaging in a particular space, that of newspapers and periodicals published in East Africa in the early colonial period and intended specifically for an African readership? While the groups I have examined here did not use the term "middle class" to describe themselves, considering them through the lens of the emergence of a "global bourgeoisie" draws our attention to the extent to which the new cultural practices they embraced for themselves and labeled "modern" or "civilized" were similar to those embraced by similar groups across the world in the same period.

Yet it also reminds us of the *imagined* quality of this social collective. In the pages of these newspapers, we encounter individuals whose wealth was insignificant in global terms, who lacked the political rights increasingly enjoyed by the middle classes across Europe and America, and who could not physically travel to build the sorts of cosmopolitan connections created by an ever more mobile global bourgeoisie. Nevertheless, within the tight constraints of a colonial public sphere that limited the emergence of an independent press, print

53. "Zigua kwa Sonyo," *Habari za Mwezi*, April 1906.

allowed them imaginatively to insert themselves into a collective which transcended space and the repressive confines of colonial rule.[54]

This suggests two conclusions. First, we may suppose that in approaching the global history of the middle class, we need to be attentive to scale, not only as a means of incorporating older social formations and alternative allegiances into our reading of the global making of the middle classes, but also to appreciate the ways in which "jumping scale" was fundamental to the ways in which middle-classness was experienced and performed in this period. Second, and at the same time, this East African case study reinforces the point that the story of the global middle classes is a story of particularity and of "diverse local and regional contexts" as much as it is a story of similarities and convergences.

54. The term "colonial public sphere" has been used in different ways. For some, it is used to simply to describe a specific context; for others, as an analytical tool. For recent helpful discussions of the concept, see, for example, Stephanie Newell, *The Power to Name: Aa History of Anonymity in West Africa* (Athens: Ohio University Press, 2013); Tony Ballantyne, "What Difference Does Colonialism Make? Reassessing Print and Social Change in an Age of Global Imperialism," in *Agent of Change: Print Culture Studies after Elizabeth L. Eisenstein*, ed. Sabrina Alcorn Baron, Eric N. Lindquist, and Eleanor F. Shevlin (Amherst: University of Massachusetts Press, 2007), 342–352; Neeladri Bhattacharya, "Notes Towards a Concept of the Colonial Public," in *Civil Society, Public Sphere and Citizenship: Dialogues and Perceptions*, ed. Rajeev Bhargava and Helmut Reifeld (New Delhi: Sage Publications, 2005), 130–156.

6

Cosmopolitan Consumption

DOMESTICITY, COOKING, AND THE MIDDLE CLASS IN COLONIAL INDIA

Utsa Ray

SCHOLARS HAVE LONG DEBATED THE ORIGINS of the middle class in colonial India. While traditional scholarship has focused on its economic origins, in recent years scholars have become increasingly interested in the ways in which this class fashioned itself. This self-fashioning was of course relational, based on its interactions and negotiations with other classes. But scholars have debated the degree to which the middle class maintained distance from the other. Some have pointed to the fact that middle-class prioritization of education and the subsequent emphasis on respectability was intended to separate it from the peasants and the working class, as well as from the aristocrats it perceived as decadent, while at the same time maintaining caste status and privileges of rank.[1] Others have urged us to look at the complexities involved in the marking of such boundaries.[2] Scholars acknowledge that the politics of the Indian middle class revolved around contesting colonial categories; however, drawing on Pierre Bourdieu's concept of cultural capital, they try to delve into the

1. Tithi Bhattacharya, *The Sentinels of Culture: Class, Education, and the Colonial Intellectual in Bengal (1848–85)* (New Delhi: Oxford University Press, 2005); Bidyut Chakrabarty, "Social Classes and Social Consciousness," in *History of Bangladesh, 1704–1971*, vol. 3: *Social and Cultural History*, ed. Sirajul Islam (Dhaka: Asiatic Society of Bangladesh, 1992); S. N. Mukherjee, *Calcutta: Myths and History* (Calcutta: Subarnarekha, 1977).

2. Swarupa Gupta, *Notions of Nationhood in Bengal: Perspectives on Samaj, c.1867–1905* (Leiden: Brill, 2009).

contradictory forces that marked the self-fashioning of the middle class. In this essay, I argue that the Indian middle class borrowed, adapted, and appropriated the new pleasures that had followed the establishment of colonial rule and then tweaked and subverted them to suit its project of self-fashioning. This project was not an instance of alternative modernity, nor did the locality of the middle class in colonial India result in some sort of indigenism. The middle class all over the world has been a product of cross-cultural ideas. Notwithstanding the brutal impact of colonialism and imperialism the colonial middle-class demonstrated their own ways of negotiating with modernity. These negotiations were not without resistance or challenge as the global language of modernity translated into the local.[3]

The Making of the Colonial Middle Class in British India

The assumption of power by the British crown in 1857 carried along with it a systematic imperial intervention into the political and socioeconomic structure of the colony. On the one hand, the British state feigned distance from its subjects, yet on the other, there was a much more rigorous imperial intervention instituted through bureaucratic modes of power. It was in dialogue and resistance to this new imperial intervention that the colonial middle class formulated a new discourse of politics. The particular socioeconomic context of colonial Bengal and the peculiar position of the Bengali middle class within it produced this discourse. From the second half of the eighteenth century and into the early nineteenth century, Calcutta was being transformed from a small European settlement into a prosperous commercial city.[4] By 1850, its population had reached four hundred thousand. Long before the take over of India by the Crown, Calcutta began to attract European institutions, communities of merchant and indigenous professional classes.[5] One consequence of these transformations was the emergence of a Bengali middle class in colonial Calcutta.

In eastern India, racially discriminatory administrative policies encouraged an exclusively European-dominated economy of Calcutta and its hinterlands

---

3. Andrew Gordon, *Fabricating Consumers: The Sewing Machine in Modern Japan* (Berkeley: University of California Press, 2012).

4. Mukherjee, *Calcutta: Myths and History*, 16.

5. P. J. Marshall, "General Economic Conditions under the East India Company," in *History of Bangladesh, 1704–1971*, vol. 2: *Economic History*, ed. Islam, 79–80.

at least until the outbreak of the First World War. The result was a check to the growth of Indian enterprise. There was, however, no dearth of professional and service groups, whose numbers continued to rise thanks to the needs of British commerce and the British administration. Rajat Kanta Ray has described this process of the decline of Bengali entrepreneurship and the rise of the professional Bengali elites as a two-tiered formation of the middle class.[6] The first stage in the formation of social groups in Calcutta involved the making of compradors attached to the officers of the East India Company or private British traders. There were a few entrepreneurs who emerged from their ranks and made huge fortunes through speculative and commercial activities in the first half of the nineteenth century. However, as the industrial capitalism of Britain made further inroads into the economy of Bengal, the European business houses, which acquired local expertise themselves, no longer needed Bengali partnerships. Bengalis were thus not taken on as partners in the new export-oriented manufacturing ventures, which developed in the second half of the nineteenth century. This led to a collapse of Bengali industrial enterprise and the increasing dependence of middle-class families on income from land. This growing reliance on land and concomitant adoption of the lifestyle of the older landlords of Bengal turned the new rich families of Calcutta into landed notables within two or three generations.

The second stage in the formation of the middle class involved the making of an intermediate social layer that populated the new apparatuses of the colonial government after the rebellion of 1857. They were the products of Western education, which in turn had transformed the traditional groups of rent-receiving literati into an English-educated professional class. Soon, however, this group of people discovered that, despite their qualifications, they would always lag behind in the administrative structure of the colonial state.

The grievances of both these groups constituted middle-class politics in colonial Bengal. According to Ray, British economic interests did not allow for overall development of the economy by Bengali entrepreneurs. Instead, British capital twisted the economy into a colonial mold that impaired the organic connections between the literate and rustic levels of Bengali society.[7] The urban professional Bengalis had no independent position in the economy, nor did they

6. Rajat Kanta Ray, *Social Conflict and Political Unrest in Bengal, 1875–1927* (Delhi: Oxford University Press, 1984).

7. Ray, *Social Conflict*, 11.

control the new productive forces that could be invested in their struggle for political power. This lack of a productive role, Ray argues, disconnected the middle-class society of Calcutta from the working population of Bengal.[8] Higher education in the English language, the sole means of entry into a profession, remained confined to Bengali middle-class men. Their concentration in the urban professions created the enormous distance of this group from the sphere of social production.[9] The distortion of the economy of Bengal shaped the cultural refashioning of the middle class. Thus, its critique of colonial rule took a strange form, allowing it to appropriate the colonial state's critique of it and use that critique as a vantage point.

Focusing on a book called *Bengal Sweets*, I look at the making of the Indian middle class in relation to the situation of the European middle class in colonial India. Written around 1921 by a woman named J. Haldar, *Bengal Sweets* is a significant example of the situatedness of the colonial middle class.[10] The book is about 135 pages long and carries recipes for no less than at least 160 recipes for sweets as well as *jolkhabar* (a snack that people consumed for breakfast or early in the evening). Haldar wrote in detail about the ingredients used in her cooking as well as the utensils needed for making sweets. These tedious explanations were not least necessary, because the book was written for European ladies. But at the same time the author also addressed women of the newly emerged middle class, women who had been schooled by the colonial education system.[11] The fact that the book was written in English warrants that the book was not accessible for the lower classes; neither was it destined for upper-class women who had enough hands in their kitchens to help them out. Although the book was written by a Bengali middle-class woman, the author claimed that she was encouraged by several European women to publish her recipes on Bengali sweets and that her recipes were tried out in England. It is difficult to assess the authenticity of Haldar's claims. However, this text and several other cookbooks and memoirs written by Europeans residing in colonial India allude to a middle-class lifestyle. Focusing on these texts, my essay asks whether we can describe this lifestyle as a product of colonial experience. I also

8. Ray, *Social Conflict*, 29–35.

9. Partha Chatterjee, *Bengal 1920–1947: The Land Question*, vol. 1 (Calcutta: K. P. Bagchi, 1984).

10. Mrs. J. Haldar, *Bengal Sweets* (Calcutta: Chuckervertty, Chatterjee, 1926).

11. Meredith Borthwick, *The Changing Role of Women in Bengal 1849–1905* (Princeton, NJ: Princeton University Press, 1984).

delve into the question of whether the colonial middle class can be described as a cosmopolitan social group.

This essay is divided into three sections. In the first section, I contextualize my essay within the larger historiography of the middle class. More specifically, I use J. Haldar's book to see how taste and consumption aided in the self-fashioning of the middle class. Here, I chiefly draw on the works of scholars who refuse to identify economic indicators as the only decisive factors behind the rise of a middle class. In many senses, the cosmopolitan nature of Bengali taste emerged from gendered negotiations. Surprisingly, women wrote cookbooks from within a public/professional domain instead of a private/domestic one. The innumerable recipes that women produced cannot be explained away as being engendered by the hand of patriarchy. Writing as a mode of self-expression could take several forms. It is in this context that we need to reconceptualize the "public" and the "private." Through the production of recipes, cooking as a domestic act crossed the boundaries of house and home; through their writing, women created new identities for themselves, which were not much different from those of the men who also wrote recipes.

The second section more broadly tries to contextualize the history of the middle class within the environs of Bengal. Here, I examine what it meant to be Bengali. How far did regional nationalism define the contours of the colonial middle class in Bengal? In responding to these issues, I argue that the regionalism of the colonial middle class in Bengal was also intertwined with a strange sense of cosmopolitanism. This characteristic of the Bengali middle class holds true not only for other regions in India but also for other settings where such self-fashioning of the middle class was visible.

In the third section of this essay, I then explore how this process of assimilation was not just experienced by the colonial middle class, but how even the Europeans residing in India incorporated several elements from Bengali gastronomic culture, even though they never became oblivious to the racial hierarchy that prevailed in colonial society.

The Colonial Middle Class:
A Product of Self-Fashioning?

In the past, the Indian middle class was defined as a product of colonial education and the administrative structure introduced by the British colonial state in India. In his classic study on the Indian middle class, B. B. Mishra argues that it "remained divided into water-tight status groups according to the caste to which they belonged."[12] Thus it was British rule that produced the Indian middle class and elevated the "Indian bourgeoisie as controllers of money power, whose influence became more widespread with the growth of modern towns and cities."[13] This attempt to label the middle class as a "status group"[14] has more recently been challenged by those who have seen the middle class as a de facto social group.[15] Yet these approaches have been critiqued sharply for their tendency to treat the middle class as a fully formed sociological category determined chiefly by economic factors. While acknowledging the role of colonial education in the creation of the middle class, scholars such as Partha Chatterjee and Dipesh Chakrabarty have focused instead on the creativity of indigenous responses to British rule. While they agree that several ideas related to bourgeois domesticity, privacy, and individuality, all of which created modern, educated Indians, came from European modernity, they also argue that the colonial Indian middle class had its own version of modernity that made it different from the European middle class and gave it its unique identity.[16]

If one needs to take into account how the middle class constructed its own identity, economic factors are not enough to guide us. Of course, a myriad of different social groups, including doctors, lawyers, traders, merchants, and even clerks, might fall under this rubric; the "middle class," whether in India or in Europe, has never been a fixed category. Certain characteristics, such as education, deportment, and refined manners, did define people's sense of being

12. B. B. Misra, "The Middle Class of Colonial India: A Product of British Benevolence," in *The Middle Class in Colonial India*, ed. S. Joshi (New Delhi: Oxford University Press, 2010), 33–46, 40–41.

13. Misra, "Middle Class," 44.

14. J. H. Broomfield, *Elite Conflict in a Plural Society: Twentieth-Century Bengal* (Berkeley: University of California Press, 1968).

15. Pradip Sinha, *Nineteenth Century Bengal: Aspects of Social History* (Calcutta: Firma K. L. Mukhopadhyay, 1965), 91–92; John McGuire, *The Making of a Colonial Mind: A Quantitative Study of the Bhadralok in Calcutta, 1857–1885* (Canberra: South Asian History Section, Australian National University, 1983), 10; S. N. Mukherjee, *Calcutta: Essays in Urban History* (Calcutta: Subarnarekha, 1993).

16. Partha Chatterjee, *Nationalist Thought and the Colonial World: A Derivative Discourse?* (Delhi: Oxford University Press, 1986); Partha Chatterjee, *The Nation and Its Fragments: Colonial and Postcolonial Histories* (Princeton, NJ: Princeton University Press, 1993); Dipesh Chakrabarty, "Postcoloniality and the Artifice of History: Who Speaks for 'Indian' Pasts?," in "Imperial Fantasies and Postcolonial Histories," special issue, *Representations* 37 (1992): 1–26; Dipesh Chakrabarty, *Provincializing Europe: Postcolonial Thought and Historical Difference* (Princeton, NJ: Princeton University Press, 2000).

middle class,[17] but encouraged by a growing trend in the history of consumption and the middle class, a number of scholars have more recently come together to delve deeper into what they consider to be one defining characteristic of middle-class consumption in present-day India.[18] These scholars believe that, even though there was no such thing as a mass consumer society in India, consumption practices have played a strong role in the constitution of South Asian society, culture, and economy since the eighteenth century.

The other category that these scholars purport to problematize is the category of the middle class itself. They argue that there was not one single Indian middle class but, instead, "a varied set of actors characterized by anxieties that reflected often-straitened material circumstances, ambivalences steeped in their own contradictory strivings for new identities, and ethical conceptions that frowned upon the embrace of material goods."[19] These scholars have argued that economic position can never be used as the exclusive analytical tool for defining the middle class. Some people who described themselves as middle class were quite wealthy, whereas others had limited access to resources, making them resemble the upper ranks of the working class. Thus, traditional sociological indicators of income and occupation are not sufficient to understand the nature of the Indian middle class.[20] Being middle class implied embracing patterns of consumption that would distinguish a person from Indian princes and rural magnates on the one hand and from workers, artisans, and villagers on the other.[21] As Sumit Sarkar rightly observes, this middle class distanced itself from what its members considered the luxury and corruption of the aristocracy, as well as from the ways of those who soiled their hands through manual labor.[22]

Increasingly, then, consumption patterns are becoming much more significant indicators of the formation of the middle class than economic position. The middle class very carefully and selectively chose what it consumed. One

17. Margrit Pernau, *Ashraf into Middle Classes: Muslims in Nineteenth-Century Delhi* (New Delhi: Oxford University Press, 2013).

18. D. E. Haynes, A. McGowan, T. Roy, and H. Yanagisawa, eds., *Towards a History of Consumption in South Asia* (New Delhi: Oxford University Press, 2010).

19. Haynes et al., *Towards a History of Consumption*, 4–5.

20. Sanjay Joshi, *Fractured Modernity: Making of a Middle Class in Colonial North India* (New Delhi: Oxford University Press, 2001).

21. Joshi, *Fractured Modernity*.

22. Sumit Sarkar, "The City Imagined: Calcutta of the Nineteenth and Early Twentieth Centuries," in *Writing Social History* (Delhi: Oxford University Press, 1997), 159–185, 169.

can indeed find a rapid increase after the turn of the twentieth century in patterns of consumption that led to the formation of new categories of the middle class all over the world. However, consumption aided in the self-fashioning of the middle class much earlier than this. Drawing on Pierre Bourdieu's concept of "cultural capital," scholars pointed out the contradictory forces that marked the self-fashioning of the middle class. In his book on the colonial middle class in North India, Joshi argues that being middle class was a project of self-fashioning that was accomplished through public-sphere politics and cultural entrepreneurship in colonial north India.[23] In some ways, this form of self-fashioning of the middle class was not necessarily peculiar to colonial conditions. Recent research has examined the emergence of middle classes around the world in a comparative and connective framework.[24] On the one hand, these approaches challenge the assumption that the middle class was a phenomenon particular to Western societies; on the other hand, they point out that these Western middle classes by no means originated in a purely local context completely severed from any transnational influence.[25]

Although a certain set of values encompasses middle-class culture all over the world—and there are certain traits that are common to the formation of a global middle class—we also need to take into account local and national contexts. Undoubtedly, the idea of refined taste is also integral: a marker of standards of good and bad, acceptance of some things, rejection of some others and, in Pierre Bourdieu's apt phrase, "disgust for other tastes."[26] However, in situations such as colonial or postcolonial India, the modern middle class had a double task First, it had to define itself as modern while maintaining distance from the so-called Western modern. Second, the acts of consumption that defined this middle class had to draw boundaries separating it from other classes. Recent works on the Indian middle class—such as Emma Tarlo's book on dress and identity politics in India, A. R. Venkatachalapathy's essay on consumption

23. Joshi, *Fractured Modernity*, 2.

24. A. Ricardo López and Barbara Weinstein, eds., *The Making of the Middle Class: Toward a Transnational History*, (Durham, NC: Duke University Press, 2012).

25. John Smail, *The Origins of Middle-Class Culture: Halifax, Yorkshire 1660–1780* (Ithaca, NY: Cornell University Press, 1994). For a critique of such self-contained emergence of the middle in the West, see Simon Gunn, "Between Modernity and Backwardness: The Case of the English Middle Class," in *Making of the Middle Class*, ed. López and Weinstein, 58–74.

26. While refined taste is also a marker of aristocracy, aristocrats do not need to fashion themselves into aristocrats. The middle class, in contrast, needs to claim its status by cultural means.

of coffee among the middle class in colonial Tamilnadu, Abigail McGowan's essay on consumption and the construction of an elite identity in the Bombay presidency, and Markus Daechsel's book on the Urdu middle class milieu in mid-twentieth century India and Pakistan—focus on taste and consumption in order to figure out how exactly the Indian middle class tried to achieve this balance.[27] Similar processes can be observed in other parts of the non-Western world as well.[28]

In this essay, I argue that while writing *Bengal Sweets*, J. Haldar did not hide the fact that she was writing about the confectionary of Bengal. In fact, she mentioned that the sweets of Bengal are prepared with such skill that they have almost attained the highest stage of perfection. This perfection makes it almost redundant for the Bengalis to try out any other form of confectionary: "Most of the Bengal sweets are prepared at home by prudent housewives and freshly served in tiffin, lunch or breakfast and constitute substantial repast. They take the place of biscuits, cakes, chocolates, etc., in the Bengali household."[29] Haldar's writing style, however, took her beyond any parochialism. She definitely wrote about a regional cuisine, but her readers were not confined to Bengal. Haldar had first published the recipes for Bengali sweets in the columns of the Sunday editions of the *Statesman*.[30] She later compiled these recipes in book form. From the preface to both the first and the second editions of her book, it is clear that Haldar was definitely addressing a European public. In fact, she wrote that she was encouraged by Anglo-Indian ladies—British women residing in India—to publish her book. Like their contemporary male recipe writers, women like J. Haldar took a professional interest in writing recipes. One cannot just explain away these cookbooks and columns as a mode of education

27. Emma Tarlo, *Clothing Matters: Dress and Identity in India* (Chicago: University of Chicago Press, 1996); Abigail McGowan, "An All-Consuming Subject? Women and Consumption in Late-Nineteenth and Early-Twentieth Century Western India," *Journal of Women's History* 18, no. 4 (2006): 31–54; A. R. Venkatachalapathy, *In Those Days There Was No Coffee: Writings in Cultural History* (New Delhi: Yoda Press, 2006); Markus Daechsel, *The Politics of Self-Expression: The Urdu Middle Class Milieu in Mid-twentieth Century Indian and Pakistan* (London: Routledge, 2006).

28. Toufoul Abou-Hodeib, "Taste and Class in Late Ottoman Beirut," *International Journal of Middle East Studies* 43 (2011): 475–492; Johan Fischer, *Proper Islamic Consumption: Shopping among the Malays in Modern Malaysia* (Copenhagen: Nias Press, 2008).

29. Haldar, *Bengal Sweets*, 8.

30. The *Statesman* was an English language newspaper founded c. 1875 and published in Calcutta.

for "new" women. Culinary education was definitely deemed necessary for the modern woman considered not to be adept at cooking; however, this body of writing also took on an almost academic dimension.

Bengal Sweets was so popular that Haldar brought out a second edition of the book. She of course took pride in the fact that Bengal was the cradle of the finest confectionary in the world, but she did not want this object of art to be preserved within the four walls of Bengali domesticity. One of the primary aims of her writing was to ensure that no one would miss the cosmopolitan character of Bengali sweetmeats. This cosmopolitanism did not merely entail incorporating foreign ingredients into Bengali food; rather, the cosmopolitanism of Bengali sweets lay in its quality to be appreciated by people across the world.[31] Notions of genteel taste connected bourgeois women like Mrs. Haldar to her counterparts in other parts of the world. Genteel taste was not a style of individual choice; it was rather "an expression of adherence to middle-class values" characterized by restraint and self-control.[32]

> The spontaneous manifestation of the popularity of the book is demonstrated by the insistent demand for it among all sorts of people. The book has made its way not only to different parts of India but also to the United Kingdom. Indeed I feel legitimate pride to learn that the *Rasagolla* has been successfully prepared in far-off England with the help of this book and that Europeans stationed in this country have greatly enjoyed *Sandesh* themselves making the same.
>
> The book has therefore been so modified as to assist even the foreigners in easily comprehending the processes and in preparing the sweets according to the recipes without encountering the least difficulties.[33]

What becomes quite apparent from the above passage is, then, the fact that being middle class was, after all, a process. In order to become middle class, one needed to be open to new changes while being cautious at the same time. These

---

31. In her book, Christina Hodge has argued how gentility as a cultural value was adopted by the "middling sorts." This value was used by the Americans in the former British colonies, as well as by many other national and racial collectives across the country, which also included the industrial middling and working classes. See Christina J. Hodge, *Consumerism and the Emergence of the Middle Class in Colonial America* (New York: Cambridge University Press, 2014).

32. W. Walton, *France at the Crystal Palace: Bourgeois Taste and Artisan Manufacture in the Nineteenth Century* (Berkeley: University of California Press, 1992).

33. *Rasagolla* is a sweet made from cottage cheese, or *chhana*. It looks like a ball and is cooked in sugar syrup. Haldar, *Bengal Sweets*, i.

are the traits that connect the history of the middle class. However, there are also certain particularities of the colonial middle class that one should not ignore. In order to understand how gastronomy became central to the self-fashioning of the Bengali middle class, the history of the colonial middle class in Bengal needs to be mapped out.

Situating Bengaliness: Material Culture, Food, and the Middle Class

For the emerging Bengali middle class, colonial rule, which was established after 1857, entailed certain inevitable changes in the material environment of Bengal. Refinement in food, education, music, literature, and deportment also embodied the essence of "Bengaliness" for this middle class.

Print media enabled people of the new middle class to voice their opinions through various forms of literature, such as journals, memoirs, and autobiographies. While this literature provides evidence of a sense of loss that the middle class experienced under the oppressive new working conditions in Calcutta, a loss expressed in images of a supposed idyllic life in the villages, what needs to be remembered is that this blissful "traditional" village life was more of an imagined ideal than a reality. Along with these publications, print also made available a number of other sources—the cookbooks, the recipe columns published in periodicals, and domestic manuals. These recipes evinced that the new life in colonial Calcutta was bringing with it certain forms of pleasure. While stew, for example, became part of the diet, it was now made palatable by the addition of ghee, or clarified butter, and spices like ground turmeric or cumin.[34] This reconstruction of the modern was, in a way, an attempt at reconstructing the Bengali self. The Bengaliness here encompassed much more than the essence of a region; it was also closely implicated in the self-fashioning of the middle class. In order to be distinct, this middle class did not simply forego all the pleasures emanating from a capitalist modernity; often, new pleasures were imagined to have ancient roots in the Vedic traditions—"pastry," for instance, is a derivative of the Bengali word *pishtak*.[35] Domesticating what came from outside thus made the self essentially hybrid. The point was to cosmopolitanize the domestic and yet keep its tag of "Bengaliness."

34. Bipradas Mukhopadhyay, *Pak-Pranali*, vols. 1–5 (Kolikata, 1335 BS [c. 1928]), 406–407, first published in 1304 BS (c. 1897).

35. Rwitendranath Tagore, *Mudir Dokan* (Kolikata, 1316 BS [c. 1919]), 91.

Practices of food, and imagining the kitchen as the epicenter of the domestic space, have been described as central to a discourse of nationalism.[36] The discourse and debates on these practices and social spaces supposedly aided in conceptualizing an idealized Indian nation. More specifically, "Bengali" and "Indian" have been overlapped in the argument that Bengali nationalism was just the flip side of Indian nationalism. I suggest, instead, that focusing extensively on nationalist ideals of middle-class rhetoric about cuisine tends to rob it of other factors that the cuisine entailed. In fact, the nation-state is increasingly losing its power among many scholars working on the middle class as a significant framework for identity formation. The middle class strived for a refinement of taste and consumption, which in turn would provide the scaffolding to support it. The class that would emerge through this process of material change, and the subsequent discourse of taste, would search for its identity in the region where it was ensconced. In this way Haldar clearly explained why she was interested in writing about Bengali sweets: "In the wide realm of confectionary, Bengal has attained the same unique position with regard to the whole of India as Italy appears to hold on the continent of Europe."[37] She further made the point that in the realm of confectionary, Bengali sweets occupied a superior position when compared with the sweets of the rest of India: "In no other part of this vast peninsula will be found such a wide range of confectionary as are to be met with in this sweet Province flowing with 'milk and honey.'"[38]

A focus on regional identity, however, never stole from the complexity of Bengali cuisine, which can be described as hybrid at the very least. There is no denying the fact that a new gastronomic culture had become part and parcel of middle-class life in the colonial period; however, the response that this new culinary culture received was complex. It was neither a complete disavowal nor a wholehearted reception. The ambivalence of the discourse on middle-class taste nurtured this culture, and the way Bengali cosmopolitanism evolved can be attributed in large part to this complexity. The claim that neither the cosmopolitan nor the vernacular is a given artifact has been convincingly put

36. Jayanta Sengupta, "Nation on a Platter: The Culture and Politics of Food and Cuisine in Colonial Bengal," *Modern Asian Studies* 44, no. 1 (2010): 81–98; Rachel Berger, "Between Digestion and Desire: Genealogies of Food in Nationalist North India," *Modern Asian Studies* 47, no. 5 (2013): 1–22.

37. Haldar, *Bengal Sweets*, 1.

38. Haldar, *Bengal Sweets*, 1.

forth by Sheldon Pollock.[39] By showing that hybridity was an aspect of the cosmopolitanism of the colonial middle class, I can thus also contest those who argue that so-called foreign foods were cooked at home only after liberalization happened in the 1990s in India.[40] These *Mughal*-inspired dishes were not the only products of Bengali cosmopolitanism. To argue that it was only after globalization that the middle class was able to appropriate some kind of cosmopolitanism is to ignore the different layers of hybridity of Bengali cuisine. This hybridity of food was a product of capitalist modernity and would not have been possible without the Columbian exchange. Whatever the degree of heterogeneity, the resulting dishes were presented as the products of an "authentic" cuisine. Bengali cookbooks and recipe columns even discussed such dishes like guava jelly in such terms. In fact, the majority of the British cookbooks written for the British residents in India included recipes from all over Europe. And Indian *soojee* could easily be used in place of semolina. Although there was often an endeavor on the part of the middle class to search for reference points in ancient traditions, this should not be mistaken for indigenism. It was, rather, a means of making new and alien pleasures amenable to themselves.

This quest for indigenizing new pleasures also entailed modifying culinary delights that arrived from other parts of India, which was as much a discursive as a material practice. To try out new experiments, one needed to be adept in the art of cuisine. Indeed, in many cookbooks and recipe columns of the time, cooking and cuisine were increasingly being described in terms of aesthetics and art.

> That confectionary is a living art in Bengal is evinced by the fact that upcountry sweets are assimilated in modified forms, e.g., Laddoos and Hulwas; that novel varieties are from time to time added to the long list e.g., Rajbhog; and that on memorable occasions new sweets are invented and offered for sale, e.g., Delhi Durbar. The nomenclature often is thus an interesting study of contemporary history, to wit, "Lady Canning."[41]

39. Sheldon Pollock, "The Cosmopolitan Vernacular," *Journal of Asian Studies* 57, no. 1 (1998): 6–37.

40. Henrike Donner, "Gendered Bodies, Domestic Work and Perfect Families: New Regimes of Gender and Food in Bengali Middle Class Lifestyles," in *Being Middle Class in India*, ed. Henrike Donner (London: Routledge, 2011), 47–72.

41. Haldar, *Bengal Sweets*, 6.

Haldar was trying to suggest that being a Bengali or finding comfort in a region did not preclude the myriad possibilities of a gastronomic encounter. Rather, the "Bengaliness" of this middle class entailed being open to incorporating elements from other cuisines into its fold. Since Bengali confectionary was already so refined and all-encompassing, Bengali sweetmeat makers could easily bring in sweets from other parts of India or use jams and jellies as fillings for pastries without the fear of losing their identity.

While it is true that the Bengali middle class was reeling under a social, economic, and political crisis that continued even in postcolonial India, it is also true that the aspirations and desires of those from the colonial middle class connected them to middle classes across the world. The former knew that their social standing in colonial society was rather low. In the racially hierarchical social order, they were always placed on a lower rung. But they also knew that their education, their deportment, and, most significantly, their refined taste placed them on a par with the metropolitan middle class.

Thus, Haldar did not shy away from adding innovations or novelties to what she described as a list of "authentic" Bengali sweets. She wrote the recipe for a pudding that she named Bengal Pudding. She insisted that "it is a modification of a European sweet in the light of the confectionary of Bengal."[42] She mixed in *chhana* (cottage cheese) and *khoya* (thickened and solidified milk) with eggs.[43] Haldar made her innovation in a cooker, which was a completely new addition to Bengali kitchens.[44] However, one needs to mention that the specific cooker that Haldar used for steaming the pudding was an Icmic cooker, which was not a colonial introduction to the Bengali kitchen but had been invented by a middle-class Bengali man called Indumadhab Mullick in the early twentieth century. It was a special type of cooker in which rice, pulses, and vegetables could all be cooked together, and quickly. This is evidence of the fact that what was new about this middle class was its close connections to and interactions with the European middle class residing in India.[45]

42. Haldar, *Bengal Sweets*, 128.

43. Food scholars like K. T. Achaya have claimed that the Portuguese brought *chhana*, or cottage cheese, to Bengal. Therefore, *chhana*, which is considered an essential ingredient for making so-called authentic Bengali sweets like *sandesh*, is a much more modern element of Bengali food than is often imagined. The Europeans, of course, would not use either *chhana* or *khoya* in a pudding.

44. Haldar, *Bengal Sweets*, 129.

45. See, for instance, Kris Manjapra, *Age of Entanglement: German and Indian Intellectuals across Empire* (Cambridge, MA: Harvard University Press, 2014).

The Making of a Colonial Middle Class:
A Two-Way Process?

The gastronomic culture of the colonial middle class in Bengal was definitely cosmopolitan. However, "cosmopolitanism" itself is a loaded term, and it can have as many implications for the global as for the regional. In a way, any practice that consciously transgresses the perimeters of the local can be described as cosmopolitan.[46] In the case of cuisine, cosmopolitanism alludes to the openness of cooking for influences from other parts of the world.[47] Examples of such translocal and transregional practices of cosmopolitanism are manifold. In fact, culinary traditions in almost all countries are the result of radical change, of additions of exotic ingredients, and of importations of ideas from all over the world. Today's Mexican food, for instance, bears little resemblance to the almost meatless food of the Aztecs.[48] Colonization, however, was not the only process through which certain areas adapted or changed their culinary habits. What one knows as French cuisine today was not recognizable as distinctly French before the time of the Napoleonic period. It was only after Georges Auguste Escoffier, the famous French restaurateur and culinary writer codified haute cuisine that the modern French cuisine became apparent in the late nineteenth century.[49] In colonial Bengal, a hybrid cuisine came about as a result of the constant interactions of different cuisines and a sense of pleasure in capitalist modernity.

The line between cosmopolitanism and regionalism cannot be drawn clearly with respect to the gastronomic culture of colonial India.[50] The same person adapting to the new gastronomic culture might also cling to what she or he considered to be the essence of Bengal in other respects. However, the onus of being a cosmopolitan certainly did not rest on the shoulders of the colonized

46. Sheldon Pollock, Homi K. Bhabha, Carol A. Breckenridge, and Dipesh Chakrabarty, "Cosmopolitanism," *Public Culture* 12, no. 3 (2000): 577–589.

47. Brian Cowan, "New World, New Tastes: Food Fashions after the Renaissance," in *Food: The History of Taste*, ed. Paul Freedman (Berkeley: University of California Press, 2007), 199–200.

48. Raymond Sokolov, *Why We Eat What We Eat: How the Encounter between the New World and the Old Changed the Way Everyone on the Planet Eats* (New York: Summit Books, 1991).

49. Sokolov, *Why We Eat.*

50. For a discussion on how women of royal households acted as gastronomic entrepreneurs and created a kind of culinary cosmopolitanism in the Indian courtly kitchens during the height of British Empire, see Angma D. Jhala, "Cosmopolitan Kitchens: Cooking for Princely Zenanas in Late Colonial India," in *Curried Cultures: Globalization, Food, and South Asia*, ed. Krishnendu Ray and Tulasi Srinivas (Berkeley: University of California Press, 2012), 49–72.

alone. In fact, the British residing in India could actually be somewhat regional in the sense that they often restricted themselves to their own type of cuisine and steered clear of the native variety.

A change took place in the nature of the English cookbooks written for the British residing in India after 1857. The revolt of 1857 led to the abolition of the rule of the East India Company and direct rule by the crown in India. What followed was an unprecedented degree of racialization of colonial politics. The British residents in India were now expected to keep their distance from the natives. The cookbooks began to advocate a simpler British diet. Most scholars have taken for granted that the British changed their diet after 1857 in order to avoid the earlier Indian variety of foods, which the British now began to consider too native and rich and spicy to be included on their table. Colonel Kinney-Herbert, who wrote under the pseudonym Wyvern, asked his readers to concentrate on simple meals.[51] For Wyvern, simple meals implied reforms in the arena of Anglo-Indian cookery. This reformist cookery meant to do away even with the use of curry powder in Anglo-Indian cooking. But even those among the Anglo-Indian middle class who were in favor of a more "respectful" English cuisine after 1857 could not do away with Indian food altogether.

From *The Indian Cookery Book*, published in 1869, it seems that the so-called reformist endeavors of those who tried to erase whatever "Indianness" was left in British cuisine were not completely successful. In fact, as the name suggests, *The Indian Cookery Book* was basically a compilation of Indian recipes, beginning with rice dishes like *khichri* and *pulao* and moving on to preserves like *kasundi*. *The Indian Cookery Book* was supposedly written by an English woman who had been living in India for thirty-five years. The book is divided into several sections, many of which can hardly be described as containing pure British recipes. Some of the sections are titled "Rice or Chowl," "Pellow or Pooloo," "Burtas or Mashes," and "Indian Pickles, Chutnees, Sauces, etc.," as well as "Indian Preserves, Jams, Jellies, and Marmalades." The author claimed that rice was the staple of many Europeans in India. Surprisingly, the British in India often ridiculed the Bengalis for their eating habits. British officials and many European doctors claimed that the consumption of rice had a debilitating impact on the Bengali body. Rice became the symbol of emasculated Bengalis, as opposed to the "manly" wheat-eating races of northern India. Wheat was the staple food of a number of non-Bengali communities—pejoratively labeled as

---

51. Wyvern [Col. Kinney-Herbert], *Culinary Jottings for Madras* (1878; Madras: n.p., 1879), 220.

Hindustanis—who supposedly ate wheat bread and lentils. But in *The Indian Cookery Book*, rice did not just become the staple of European families in India, the writer also advised the Europeans to closely follow what Indians would eat.

> The best or generally approved qualities of rice for table use are known as the bhaktoolsee, the banafool, the bassmuttee, and cheeneesuckur. In purchasing these, or indeed any other approved quality, care must be taken to avoid *new rice* and what is called *urruah*, which latter has been put through some process of boiling, or damped and then dried. Both are considered unwholesome for general daily consumption, and few Indians will use them.[52]

The book is replete with recipes for indigenous foods like *pulwal*, or green leafy vegetables. For instance, one might consider the recipe for *danta* curry with shrimp, which is a quintessential Bengali food. In fact, in many novels or memoirs, *danta* curry with shrimp was intrinsically associated with the identity of a Bengali. The author took care to explain what a *danta* is to her readers: "The *danta* is a fine, delicate, long, green pod, which the horseradish-tree yields, and contains small peas; these pods are cut into lengths of three or four inches and cooked with shrimps."[53] Eggplant *bhartas* (mashes) or potato *bhartas*, which were mixed with onions and green chilies, became quite popular with the Europeans, and they added them to the existing recipes for such mashes. *The Indian Cookery Book* also carried recipes for *bhartas*/mashes of red herring, cold corned-beef, cold tongue, and cold ham.[54]

Another cookbook, named *A Friend in Need: English-Hindustani Cookery Book*, first published in 1933, adhered to Wyvern's principles about reformist Anglo-Indian cooking. But although the book was replete with recipes for sardine toast, caviar canapés, salmon chowder soup, creamed haddock, and Yorkshire pudding, it also carried one or two recipes for foods like sole pillau.[55] Sole is, of course, not a fish that is usually consumed by Indians, but then again pillau can hardly be called British. Pillau cannot be described as entirely Indian, but nevertheless the European notions of pilaf, or pillau, were formed in the colonies. Lizzy Collingham has argued that the new cookbooks were specifically

---

52. Thirty-Five Years' Resident [pseud.], *The Indian Cookery Book: A Practical Handbook to the Kitchen in India* (1880; Calcutta: Thacker, Spink, 1921), 9.

53. Thirty-Five Years' Resident, *Indian Cookery Book*, 32.

54. Thirty-Five Years' Resident, *Indian Cookery Book*, 35–36.

55. Ladies Committee, F.I.N.S. Women's Workshop, comp., *A Friend in Need: English-Hindustani Cookery Book* (1933; Madras: FINS, 1939).

written for British women in India who wanted to recreate their home environs in the colony. Thus the focus was more on cheese-crumb croquettes, thick kidney soup, and Yorkshire pudding rather than on curries.[56] However, Collingham notes that even after the takeover of India by the British crown and subsequent attempts by the British in India to retain their identity by restraining themselves to a more somber English food, hybridity of cuisine could not be avoided. English women often did not know how to cook. Moreover, Indian kitchens were not prepared for British cooking. As a result, women often had to depend on the *Bawarchis* (Indian Muslim cooks), who incorporated their own knowledge of cooking when making English food.[57]

What needs to be noted here is that often the cookbooks written by the Anglo-Indian writers had an Urdu edition. *A Friend in Need*, just like *The Indian Cookery Book*, was written in two languages. Two recipe columns appear in the second edition of the book, side by side: one was in English and the other was in Urdu.[58] Although *Bawarchis* were not always literate, it was expected that there would be someone in the family who could speak Urdu and be able to explain the recipes in Urdu to the *Bawarchis*. Thus the *Bawarchis* did not necessarily have a problem in understanding what was asked of them. When the Anglo-Indian writers wrote out the recipes, they were reliving their experiences as citizens of the empire, the experience of pleasures they could not totally erase from their memory. This interplay of hybridity that played out so well in the realm of cuisine thus connected the European middle classes with the Indian middle classes in colonial India. Both used cosmopolitan domesticity as a marker of their being part of a middle class where they constantly faced their other.

Epilogue

In his essay on the middle class in Bombay, Prashant Kidambi demonstrates that, despite the economic hardships following the First World War, consumption had become a marker of status, especially in a modernizing urban context.[59] This was more so since caste was no longer a guarantor of social standing for

56. Lizzie Collingham, *Curry: A Tale of Cooks and Conquerors* (New York: Oxford University Press, 2006), 161.

57. Collingham, *Curry*.

58. Ladies Committee, *Friend in Need*, 1939.

59. Prashant Kidambi, "Consumption, Domestic Economy and the Idea of the 'Middle Class' in Late Colonial Bombay," in *Middle Class in Colonial India*, ed. S. Joshi, 108–135.

upper-class Hindus. Thus, what became a matter of concern was fear about the potential threats of unrestrained consumption. Referring to the articles published in Kanara Saraswat community's journals during the 1920s and 1930s, Kidambi brings to our attention the Saraswat Brahmin middle-class endeavor to distinguish between "necessities" and "luxuries." This effort to determine what constituted a necessity also made the Saraswats ponder over what was needed to maintain their upper-caste status as well as their urban middle-class identity. On the one hand, they were expected to perform rituals that would maintain their caste hierarchy. On the other hand, the expenditure incurred from these rituals constrained their ability to engage in the practices of consumption necessary to keep up their middle-class identity. Thus, a number of articles called for reform of the rituals and a reduction in the costs they involved.[60]

My essay also shows that while the aspirations and desires of the colonial middle class were almost at the same level as those of the European middle class, this self-fashioning was also relational. Food was definitely a part of everyday life, but it had to be aestheticized and sanitized in every respect so that it could become a nucleus of the middle-class discourse of taste. The cosmopolitanism of the middle class was fraught with tensions, contradictions, and negotiations. There was certainly a desire on the part of the middle class to embrace many of the new changes that were seeping into colonial society. Its approach to these changes in gastronomic culture and the pleasures beginning to emanate from the "new" food demonstrates the liberal traits inherent in the self-fashioning of the colonial middle class. A constant process of experimentation with new crops and the incorporation of new ingredients is perceptible in the colonial middle-class culture of food. But, of course, this cosmopolitanism can also at best be called only a "hierarchical cosmopolitanism."[61] The middle-class discourse of taste celebrated the universalism of its cosmopolitanism, but this claim was a fantastical one, and, like all cosmopolitanisms, the universalism that the colonial middle class claimed characterized its discourse of taste was incomplete and marred by several particularisms. The cosmopolitanism of the colonial middle class was marked by hierarchy, and the self-fashioning of the colonial middle class was made possible through the construction of various others. Thus, Haldar may have picked up many of her skills in this particular

60. Kidambi, "Consumption," 122–124.

61. Utsa Ray, *Culinary Culture in Colonial India: A Cosmopolitan Platter and the Middle-Class* (New Delhi: Cambridge University Press, 2015).

culinary art from the sweetmeat vendors and confectioners of the city, as she graciously acknowledged, but ultimately *Bengal Sweets* was written for her Anglo-Indian as well as her English-educated colonial middle-class readers. The ingredients she used in her sweets, the language that she wrote in, and the way she aestheticized the labor that went into the making of the confectionary of Bengal, made Haldar the perfect middle-class writer. In this way, Haldar of course did not identify with or relate to the lower orders of colonial society. She was acutely conscious of her class position. But was that not one of the inevitable features of becoming middle class anywhere across the world?[62]

62. Kristin Hoganson, "Cosmopolitan Domesticity: Importing the American Dream, 1865–1920," *American Historical Review* 107 (2002): 55–83.

7

Bureaucratic Civilization

EMANCIPATION AND THE GLOBAL
BRITISH MIDDLE CLASS

Padraic X. Scanlan

E. B. LYON RODE TO BELVIDERE ESTATE, a sugar plantation in Saint-Thomas-in-the-East Parish, Jamaica, in late September 1834. Under the 1833 Slavery Abolition Act (often called the Emancipation Act), enslaved people had been declared "apprentices," legally free from 1 August 1834 but still obliged to work for a term of either four or six years for the people who had once claimed to own them. Lyon, born in the West Indies and of mixed European and African heritage, was a special magistrate, appointed by Parliament and paid a salary to visit estates and resolve disputes between apprentices and former slave owners.[1] From the perspective of the Colonial Office in London, planters were decadent, dissipated, and violent; apprentices were ignorant and impulsive. Apprenticeship would teach planters to act like upright employers and pay wages. Apprentices would learn how to be wage earners and consumers, not only to

---

1. See William A. Green, *British Slave Emancipation: The Sugar Colonies and the Great Experiment, 1830–1865* (Oxford: Clarendon Press, 1991), 136–134; Thomas C. Holt, *The Problem of Freedom: Race, Labor, and Politics in Jamaica and Britain, 1832–1938* (Baltimore: Johns Hopkins University Press, 1992), 57–60; Catherine Hall, *Civilising Subjects: Colony and Metropole in the English Imagination, 1830–1867* (Chicago: University of Chicago Press, 2002), 115; W. L. Burn, *Emancipation and Apprenticeship in the British West Indies* (London: Jonathan Cape, 1937), 196–266; William Law Mathieson, *British Slavery and Its Abolition, 1823–1838* (London: Longmans, Green, 1926), 228–256; and Diana Paton, *No Bond but the Law: Punishment, Race, and Gender in Jamaican State Formation, 1780–1870* (Durham, NC: Duke University Press, 2004), 53–82.

accept wages but also to seek and save them. Lyon had been summoned to Belvidere to negotiate with a group of apprentices who had gone on strike to protest a stoppage in their provisions.[2] Lyon ordered the apprentices back to work. He also ruled that the plantation overseers resume distributing rations, but only after the apprentices returned peacefully to the fields. In protest, the apprentices set fire to a number of buildings on the estate, and the militia was called in to restore order.[3]

In 1833, while the more than eight hundred thousand enslaved people in the British Empire prepared for the transition to freedom, officials in Britain and the Caribbean worried that without slavery, the cane fields would rot or that costs would rise to the point that British colonial sugar would be priced out of the market. The perpetuation of the sugar economy—particularly in the first "crop time" after emancipation—was framed in Parliament, in the Colonial Office, and in the British press as a bellwether for freedom. If plantations kept shipping raw muscovado sugar to British refineries at a competitive price, British politicians opposed to slavery could rest easy. First, wage incentives would be confirmed as the most efficient way of motivating laborers. Second, a good sugar crop would prove that freedpeople understood the putative economic obligations to the British Empire that freedom had imposed upon them. Men like Lyon were charged with protecting this balance between the rights of freedpeople and "the continued cultivation of the soil and good order of society."[4] As the dispute at Belvidere hints, the balance tipped toward the cultivation of sugarcane and would be restored, if necessary, at the end of the barrel of a gun.

2. On labor relations under apprenticeship, see Mary Turner, "Slave Workers, Subsistence and Labour Bargaining: Amity Hall, Jamaica, 1805–1832," in *The Slaves' Economy: Independent Production by Slaves in the Americas*, ed. Ira Berlin and Philip D. Morgan (London: Frank Cass, 1991), 92–106; Mary Turner, "The 11 O'clock Flog: Women, Work and Labour Law in the British Caribbean," *Slavery & Abolition* 20, no. 1 (1999): 38–58; and Mary Turner, "The British Caribbean, 1823–1838: The Transition from Slave to Free Legal Status," in *Masters, Servants, and Magistrates in Britain and the Empire, 1562–1955*, ed. Douglas Hay and Paul Craven (Chapel Hill: University of North Carolina Press, 2004), 303–322.

3. Jamaica Despatch No. 19, Lord Sligo to Thomas Spring Rice, 4 October 1834, *1835 (177) Abolition of Slavery, Papers in Explanation of the Measures Adopted by His Majesty's Government, for Giving Effect to the Act for the Abolition of Slavery throughout the British Colonies. Part I. Jamaica. 1833–1835*, Accounts and Papers (London: Great Britain, House of Commons, 1835), 47.

4. Circular Despatch, Edward Stanley to the Governors of His Majesty's Colonial Possessions Having Local Legislatures, 19 October 1833, *1835 (177) Abolition of Slavery. Papers in Explanation, Part I*, 12.

In Britain, the abolition of the British slave trade in 1807 was widely popular and closely tied to ideas of national virtue and to support for the war effort against Napoleonic France.[5] In comparison, the abolition of slavery in Britain's colonies in 1833–1834 was celebrated as a victory for bourgeois values. Thomas Spring Rice, the colonial secretary when the Emancipation Act came into force, proclaimed that emancipation would result in the "promotion of industry, the consequent creation and accumulation of capital, the possession of property, and the respect for laws which give that property protection . . . those causes of prosperity on which the welfare of nations depends."[6] The law established a £20 million fund to compensate former slave owners. Concomitantly, the law affirmed the obligations of laborers to their employers, reviving apprenticeship for former slaves even as the institution was in its death throes in England.[7] Apprenticeship was a kind of debt. Traditionally, a master offered training in a craft in exchange for a fixed term of obedient labor from an apprentice. In the post-emancipation West Indies, craft apprenticeship was reimagined as an imperial policy, enforced by magistrates and designed to teach former slaves how gratefully to work for wages. Property, obedience, debt, and education: the Emancipation Act was a charter for the global ambitions of the British bourgeoisie.

If Spring Rice's predictions for emancipation reflected the clean lines of ideology, bourgeois liberalism in practice was, for men like E. B. Lyon, footsore and often lonely work. Most of Lyon's working life as a special magistrate was spent traveling and counting. Lyon's visit to Belvidere was just one of thousands made by the special magistrates to sugar and coffee plantations between 1834 and 1838, when apprenticeship was abolished. Lord Sligo, governor of Jamaica in 1834, bragged in a dispatch that the sixty-odd magistrates working in Jamaica

5. Linda Colley, *Britons: Forging the Nation, 1707–1837* (New Haven, CT: Yale University Press, 1992), 350–360.

6. Circular Despatch G: Spring Rice to the West Indian Governors, 30 September 1834, *1835 (278-I) (278-II) Papers Presented to Parliament, by His Majesty's Command, in Explanation of the Measures Adopted by His Majesty's Government, for Giving Effect to the Act for the Abolition of Slavery throughout the British Colonies. Part II. Jamaica (Continued), Barbadoes, British Guiana, and Mauritius. 1833–1835*, Accounts and Papers (London: Great Britain, House of Commons, 1835), 7.

7. Emma Rothschild, *Economic Sentiments: Adam Smith, Condorcet and the Enlightenment* (Cambridge, MA: Harvard University Press, 2001), 87–115.

had, in a single month, travelled 12,341 miles and made visits to 2,922 estates.[8] The handwritten reports of men like Lyon fill a few dozen thick files in the National Archives of the United Kingdom, as well as thousands of pages of printed parliamentary papers. Lyon, typical of his colleagues, rarely sent back to London records of the disputes he arbitrated with either former slave owners or former slaves—we know about the conflict at Belvidere only because the militia was summoned. Moreover, like most magistrates in Britain and the empire, Lyon did not keep records of his summary judgements.[9] Instead, he sent back reports on the rates of work of the nearly twelve thousand apprentices in his district—for example, in spreading manure on the fields and boring cane holes—as well as instances of theft, arson, and "insolence," "an index of the diminution of crime, and the return of industry and cheerfulness."[10] The project of apprenticeship in the West Indies and the transition from slavery to freedom needed to be represented in points of data, aggregated and published to show incremental change.

By observing the changing post-slavery economy of Saint-Thomas-in-the-East, Lyon could *clarify* it, in both senses of the word. With ledgers and work rates, Lyon would make the former slave colonies transparent to readers in London while purifying them of the backwardness of slavery. "Approaching slavery in transactional terms," argue Seth Rockman and Sven Beckert in an essay on the relationship between slavery and capitalism in the nineteenth-century United States, "reveals the institution's fundamental consistency with the emerging business practices and market logic of capitalism, and even its constitutive role."[11] Antislavery was also rooted in the routines and language of business. The faith in free labor expressed in the 1833 Abolition Act is an example of a broader phenomenon that helps to explain the global ambitions of British reformers on the eve of Victoria's coronation: in the 1820s and 1830s, paperwork itself often embodied bourgeois aspirations for a transformed British world.

8. Enclosure A, Jamaica Despatch 140: Lord Sligo to Lord Glenelg, 21 June 1835, *1835 (177) Abolition of Slavery, Papers in Explanation, Part I*, 219.

9. Douglas Hay and Paul Craven, "Introduction," in *Masters, Servants, and Magistrates*, ed. Hay and Craven, 1–58.

10. Report from Edmund B. Lyon, Special Magistrate, Morant Bay, 24 December 1834, Enclosures in Jamaica Despatch 25: Sligo to Thomas Spring Rice, 25 December 1834, *1835 (177) Abolition of Slavery, Papers in Explanation, Part I*, 73.

11. Sven Beckert and Seth Rockman, "Introduction: Slavery's Capitalism," in *Slavery's Capitalism: A New History of American Economic Development*, ed. Sven Beckert and Seth Rockman (Philadelphia: University of Pennsylvania Press, 2016), 1–28, 11.

I call this this phenomenon—liberal reform represented in paperwork—*bureaucratic civilization*. Bureaucratic civilization entailed recording and publicizing information about the lives of non-white British subjects and lower-class Britons to enforce a moral order of bourgeois respectability and an economic order of property and wage labor. This chapter explores the history of emancipation in the British Empire in order to frame the aspirational ideology of work, consumption, and respectability that underwrote bureaucratic civilization and to sketch the practices of paperwork and legwork—of visiting, observing, counting, reporting, and publishing—that put it into practice. Bureaucratic civilization connected antislavery to the wider program of reform. Emancipation was designed both to protect the imperial sugar industry and to transform despotic slave owners into rentiers and bourgeois entrepreneurs, and enslaved people into wage-earning householders. And yet, emancipation is rarely considered in an explicitly imperial perspective by British historians. For historians of domestic British politics, emancipation was a part of the "age of reform" that balanced bourgeois enthusiasm for Evangelical religion and utilitarian social engineering against profound anxiety about popular revolution.[12] For historians of the British Caribbean, the 1830s were defined by the struggle of freedpeople to claim autonomy after the end of slavery.[13] These historiographies—of domestic reform and colonial resistance—are silos. The analytic of bureaucratic civilization, and the granular records of everyday transactions in the West Indies sent by men like E. B. Lyon to men like Thomas Spring Rice, suggest a way to frame the reforms of the 1830s as a global project—to show, for example, how the lives of the London poor were connected to the lives of freedpeople in the West Indies. In 1838, Lord Brougham spoke in the Lords, referring to "the new mass of papers laid on our table from the West Indies."[14] The material history of the "mass of papers" generated by 1830s reform highlights the work of bureaucrats sent across the

12. See, for example, Boyd Hilton, *A Mad, Bad, and Dangerous People?: England, 1783–1846* (Oxford: Clarendon Press, 2006).

13. See, for example, Elsa V. Goveia, *Slave Society in the British Leeward Islands at the End of the Eighteenth Century* (New Haven, CT: Yale University Press, 1965); Holt, *Problem of Freedom*; Hall, *Civilising Subjects*; Natasha Lightfoot, *Troubling Freedom: Antigua and the Aftermath of British Emancipation* (Durham, NC: Duke University Press, 2015).

14. "The Right Honourable Lord Brougham, on the Immediate Emancipation of the Negro Apprentices," in *Speeches of Eminent British Statesmen during the Thirty-Nine Years' Peace: From the Passing of the Reform Bill to the Commencement of the Russian War*, 2nd ser. (London: R. Griffin, 1857), 121.

empire and to the slums and remote countryside of Britain proper to observe and report.

This circuit of paperwork also suggests a way of understanding what the bourgeoisie, or middle class, was in the expanding British world of the long nineteenth century. Britain's empire included the dense industrial cities and long-settled farmland of Britain proper as well as vast frontiers of settler colonial expansion and expropriation. In the Global South, the empire was further divided into informal spheres of economic and political influence and formal colonies ruled directly by powerful British-appointed executives or indirectly by local clients. In this heterogeneous world, form-filling, check-signing, and ledger-writing connected clerks in Kingston-upon-Thames with their counterparts in Kingston, Jamaica, and Kingston, Upper Canada. Moreover, the lives of men like E. B. Lyon show that the global bourgeoisie was more than the merchant-capitalist class. E. B. Lyon was part of a class of clerks and writers sent to enforce bureaucratic civilization and to document a changing British world. In Victorian terms, there were plenty of Ebenezer Scrooges in the British bourgeoisie, middling capitalists with property and wealth, but there were many more Bob Cratchits. Dror Wahrman has argued that the British middle class—and indeed the process of industrialization—was a discourse produced by changing political debate rather than a social reality.[15] Bureaucratic civilization was a discourse, but it was also a real and profound process of social change, driven by industrialization and liberal ideology. Bureaucratic civilization was ideologically a bourgeois project of social reform, put in motion by a hierarchical global middle class that included both well-fed merchants and hand-to-mouth clerks.

This chapter is divided into three sections. The first section limns the relationship between British antislavery, reform, and paperwork. The idea that collecting and publishing information could be a reform in and of itself was associated with the campaign against the slave trade and gained momentum in the wider movement for parliamentary reform in the 1820s. However, the radicalism of exposing corruption in print receded in the face of the fundamental conservatism and gradualism of most British antislavery reformers. The second section expands the ledgers of the West Indies into the wider world of financial paperwork in Britain and its empire. Bureaucratic civilization was intended to inculcate the desire to work for wages among the people upon

15. Dror Wahrman, *Imagining the Middle Class: The Political Representation of Class in Britain, c. 1780–1840* (Cambridge: Cambridge University Press, 2010).

whom it was imposed. Its practices, however, echoed the paperwork of a rapidly consolidating transnational capitalism. For many subjects of bureaucratic civilization, debt was the primary manifestation of this new relationship. Apprentices became visible through the records of the work they did to "repay" Britain for their freedom, while working-class people in Britain were visible to the state in the debts they owed. Finally, in the third section, this chapter returns to the legacy of bureaucratic civilization in the British West Indies. In the 1840s and 1850s, the purported failure of freedpeople to conform to expectations of bourgeois economic and social organization was read by some as a failure of emancipation, and the failure of emancipation was incorporated into critiques of the British bourgeoisie.

Antislavery, Paperwork, and Reform

Antislavery was a quintessential middle-class campaign of the late eighteenth century. The end of the British slave trade was a source of patriotic pride and one of the first social-reform campaigns with its own merchandise. Opponents of the slave trade signed petitions, but they also bought plates and prints and other bric-a-brac to put their patriotism on display.[16] As many historians have noted, the momentum and energy of the campaign against the slave trade carried over to other projects, including anti-vice campaigns and missionary work.[17] Bureaucratic civilization also had early success in the campaign against the slave trade, which began in earnest with efforts to gather and publish information on British slave traders, an exhausting, often dangerous investigation. Victorian writers memorialized the hard work of early antislavery activists with particular brio. Samuel Smiles, in Self-Help, an 1860s bestseller, praised the activist and orator Thomas Clarkson for suffering a nervous breakdown brought on by "travelling more than thirty-five thousand miles" in the 1790s in pursuit of the testimony and records of slave traders.[18]

16. See the discussion in John Brewer, "Commercialization and Politics," in *The Birth of a Consumer Society: The Commercialization of Eighteenth-Century England*, ed. Neil McKendrick, John Brewer, and J. H. Plumb (Bloomington: Indiana University Press, 1982), 197–264.

17. For a recent discussion, see Alan Lester and Fae Dussart, *Colonization and the Origins of Humanitarian Governance: Protecting Aborigines across the Nineteenth-Century British Empire* (Cambridge: Cambridge University Press, 2014).

18. Samuel Smiles, *Self-Help; With Illustrations of Character, Conduct, and Perseverance by Samuel Smiles* (London: John Murray, 1868), 259–260.

Reform by investigation and publication was rehearsed in the campaign against the slave trade and taken up by advocates for the reform of Parliament. In his *The Black Book; Or Corruption Unmasked!*, which was revised and updated almost continuously until the mid-1830s, John Wade published lists exposing patronage, "placemen," and aristocratic privilege, the hallmarks of the "old corruption."[19] The title was a play on the elegant, red-bound books printed to illustrate the family trees of the English peerage. "The aristocracy," Wade wrote, playing on this point, "may be considered only one family, plundering, deluding, and fattening on the people."[20] Drawing on the patriotic and moral prestige of the practices of the campaign against the slave trade and its mass publicity, Wade conjured morality out of a clear account of bureaucracy.

Wade's and other radical Parliamentary reformers' sense of the moral valence of transparency and publicity borrowed from antislavery; however, at the higher levels of the British government, the radical urgency of reform was blunted by another feature of white British antislavery: its gradualism and racism.[21] Parliamentary antislavery formally reignited in 1823 with a series of resolutions proposed by George Canning in favor of gradual emancipation. As Philip Curtin writes, Canning's resolutions were "the unmistakable writing on the wall" for slavery in the British Empire.[22] Tellingly, a year later, in another major speech to Parliament on antislavery, Canning compared black freedom to Frankenstein's monster: "the splendid fiction of a recent romance," a creature "possessing the form and strength of a man, but the intellect only of a child."[23] Canning then presented an early solution to the imaginary problem of preparing enslaved

19. See Philip Harling, *The Waning of "Old Corruption": The Politics of Economical Reform in Britain, 1779–1846* (Oxford: Clarendon Press, 1996).

20. John Wade, *The Black Book; Or, Corruption Unmasked!*, vol. 1 (London, 1828), 94.

21. On early British antislavery and the transatlantic character of gradual emancipation in the late eighteenth century, see Christopher L. Brown, "Empire without Slaves: British Concepts of Emancipation in the Age of the American Revolution," *William and Mary Quarterly*, 3rd ser., 56, no. 2 (1999): 273–306; Paul J. Polgar, "'To Raise Them to an Equal Participation': Early National Abolitionism, Gradual Emancipation, and the Promise of African American Citizenship," *Journal of the Early Republic* 31, no. 2 (2011): 229–258; James J. Gigantino, *The Ragged Road to Abolition: Slavery and Freedom in New Jersey, 1775–1865* (Philadelphia: University of Pennsylvania Press, 2014); and Arthur Zilversmit, *The First Emancipation: The Abolition of Slavery in the North* (Chicago: University of Chicago Press, 1969).

22. Philip D. Curtin, *Two Jamaicas: The Role of Ideas in a Tropical Colony, 1830–1865* (Cambridge, MA: Harvard University Press, 1955), 61.

23. "Amelioration of the Slave Population in the West Indies," Parliamentary Debates, House of Commons, 15 March 1824, *Parliamentary Debates: Forming a Continuation of the Work Entitled*

people for freedom—the policy of "amelioration," of gradually increasing the legal rights of enslaved people in order to prepare a path for abolition.[24] Canning's position was decidedly imperial—amelioration and abolition were projects designed in London and imposed in the slave-holding colonies.

As Canning framed an imperial antislavery position in the House of Commons, the permanent staff of the Colonial Office hastened to design mechanisms for incremental amelioration and gradual emancipation. After his 1825 appointment, the Colonial Office of the 1820s and 1830s was anchored by James Stephen, the son of the leading antislavery jurist James Stephen. Stephen fils was both a committed antislavery advocate and a path-breaking bureaucrat. The Blue Books, blank workbooks meant to be filled in with statistics and reports, were first sent out by the Colonial Office to the British Empire's colonial officials in about 1828.[25] Stephen and his colleagues hoped to obtain a complete picture of the empire and to use that information to effect reform. In 1826, amelioration took an imperial turn, as London imposed new regulations on the colonies, restricting corporal punishment and work hours, expanding property rights for enslaved people, and requiring that planters keep the Sabbath by sending their slaves to church instead of the cane fields. In concert with Canning's imperial vision, the amelioration policy's most radical feature was the right it seemed to claim for London to impose new kinds of legislation on the West Indian colonies, with or without consent. In some colonies, a new office, the protector of slaves, was established to hear the complaints of enslaved people. The protector of slaves represented new rights for enslaved people and new protections from planter violence—but the office's fundamentally gradual, case-by-case character was also designed to protect the overall integrity of the slave colonies and the sugar industry.

When, in the House of Commons on 14 May 1833, Edward Stanley famously called emancipation in the British Empire "the mighty experiment," he referred not only to the abolitionist legislation he had tabled, but also to the data

---

the *Parliamentary History of England from the Earliest Period to the Year 1803*, vol. 10 (London, 1824), cc. 1103.

24. On amelioration see, for example J. R. Ward, *British West Indian Slavery, 1750–1834: The Process of Amelioration* (Oxford: Clarendon Press, 1988); Christa Dierksheide, *Amelioration and Empire: Progress and Slavery in the Plantation Americas* (Charlottesville: University of Virginia Press, 2014); Caroline Quarrier Spence, "Ameliorating Empire: Slavery and Protection in the British Colonies, 1783–1865" (PhD diss., Harvard University, 2014).

25. Robert Montgomery Martin, *Statistics of the Colonies of the British Empire . . . : From the Official Records of the Colonial Office* (London: W. H. Allen, 1839), iii.

collected under amelioration policies.[26] Stanley was firm: more legal freedom would be necessary to augment amelioration. "Do you think," Stanley asked the House, "[enslaved people] can be made fit for freedom, till freedom has exercised its influence upon their minds and upon their moral character?"[27] Stanley described a case published in the parliamentary papers of an Antiguan planter who had been placed in charge of over four hundred former slaves whom the planter had "maintained and regulated according to the manners of the inhabitants of civilised countries."[28] Among these former slaves, Stanley declared, there had been evidence of "remarkable" industry and desire for property ownership and only a single case of petty larceny. Stanley drew a few conclusions. First, it was possible to measure civilization—through criminal statistics, accounts of land ownership, and indices of productivity. Second, although free trade and free labor were natural, former slaves would still need to be taught how to behave naturally. "To throw the slave suddenly into freedom," Stanley told the House, "would be to destroy all his inclinations to industry."[29]

Recent histories of paperwork in the antebellum South, as well as work on the history of archives and bureaucracies show that methods of recordkeeping in businesses and governments both shape, and are shaped by, policy.[30] Many reformers saw sugar planters as primitive and boorish; an influential argument against plantation slavery in the Caribbean was that it seemed to discourage innovation and improvement. This was caricature; planters were deeply interested in quantifying the labor of enslaved people and in improving both agricultural techniques and methods of violent coercion to increase yields. Planters

26. "The Right Honourable E. G. Stanley (Now Earl of Derby), on the Emancipation of the Slavers," in *Speeches of Eminent British Statesmen*, 23–82, 24; see also Seymour Drescher, *The Mighty Experiment: Free Labor vs. Slavery in British Emancipation* (New York: Oxford University Press, 2002).

27. "Right Honourable E. G. Stanley," 60.

28. "Right Honourable E. G. Stanley," 61.

29. "Right Honourable E. G. Stanley," 71–72.

30. Caitlin Rosenthal, *Accounting for Slavery: Masters and Management*. Cambridge, MA: Harvard University Press, 2018; Caitlin Rosenthal, "Slavery's Scientific Management: Masters and Managers," in *Slavery's Capitalism*, ed. Beckert and Rockman, 62–86; Caitlin C. Rosenthal, "From Memory to Mastery: Accounting for Control in America, 1750–1880," *Enterprise and Society* 14, no. 4 (2013): 732–748; Michael Zakim, "Paperwork," *Raritan* 33, no. 4 (2014): 34–56; Michael Zakim, "Producing Capitalism: The Clerk at Work," in *Capitalism Takes Command: The Social Transformation of Nineteenth-Century America*, ed. Michael Zakim and Gary John Kornblith (Chicago: University of Chicago Press, 2012), 223–248.

were also innovators in recordkeeping. The kinds of measurements—rates for boring cane holes, clearing fields, stoking boilers, and the like—taken by the special magistrates to measure apprentices' productivity had been devised by the planters themselves.[31] Consequently, when special magistrates sought to "prove" that apprenticeship was more effective than slavery as a way of organizing labor, they relied on statistics and statistical categories devised under slavery. Managerial practices made by slavery became managerial practices for measuring freedom.

Bureaucracy, Debt, and Capitalism

The special magistrates produced a vast archive of paperwork to illustrate the gradual improvement promised by the 1833 Abolition Act, as though paperwork itself could be emancipatory. However, the magistrates' archive, voluminous as it was, was tiny in comparison with the printed world of hypothecated plantation records, deeds, securities, and insurance policies that connected the plantations to Britain. The practices of paperwork meant to reform the British world cross-pollinated with the practices of British capitalism. For example, the ownership of Belvidere, the estate E. B. Lyon visited barely a month after emancipation, was spread between the heirs of the planter John Cope Freeman and was divided into annuities. The Freemans—who had been close to Jane Austen and her family—were absentees, bound by insurance, income, credit, and family to slavery but resident in Abbots Langley, Hertfordshire. The estate was managed by George Cuthbert, a Scot and a member of Saint John's College, Cambridge, and Lincoln's Inn, who managed at least three other estates and also owned land in Scotland.[32] Land, credit, securities, and money connected

---

31. Justin Roberts, *Slavery and the Enlightenment in the British Atlantic, 1750–1807* (Cambridge: Cambridge University Press, 2013); B. W. Higman, *Plantation Jamaica, 1750–1850: Capital and Control in a Colonial Economy* (Kingston, Jamaica: University of the West Indies Press, 2006), 94–112.

32. On the ownership of Belvidere, see "Philip Dormer Stanhope," and "George Cuthbert," in *Legacies of British Slave-Ownership Database*; Catherine Hall, Nicholas Draper, Keith McClelland, Katie Donington, and Rachel Lang, *Legacies of British Slave-Ownership: Colonial Slavery and the Formation of Victorian Britain* (Cambridge: Cambridge University Press, 2014), 38; and John Venn and J. A. Venn, eds., *Alumni Cantabrigienses: A Biographical List of All Known Students, Graduates and Holders of Office at the University of Cambridge, from the Earliest Times to 1900,* 1944 ed., vol. 2, part 2 (Cambridge University Press, 2011), 135. On Cuthbert, see "Jamaica St Thomas-in-the-East, Surrey 508 (Belvidere Estate)," in *Legacies of British Slave-ownership*

Belvidere's owners to British economic life. E. B. Lyon was a petty jurist and clerk sent to resolve a colonial dispute that was, in fact, imbricated into a global network of credit and landownership. The planters were compensated using ultramodern financial instruments in order to guarantee that their right to "property" would be honored.[33]

By 1841, in his sketch of "The Capitalist," published in *Heads of the People*, a popular collection of pithy satirical essays, F. G. Tomlins described a cipher, plainly but expensively dressed, whose politics were "the wonder and the sphynx's riddle to the vulgar and uninitiated."[34] The "Capitalist" might vote one day for "equality and cheap bread" but might stump for "high prices and despotism" the next. In all things, though, "the Capitalist" remained "consistent to one principle, and that is his own principal."[35] Tomlins hazarded that the capitalist "breed" had been growing in fits and starts throughout the eighteenth century, but that it did not come into its own until Pitt the Younger's ascendance in the 1780s and 1790s, when on "the vast hot-bed of his financial arrangements, numerous splendid specimens were produced," fattened on government loans. "Like everything else in the nineteenth century," Tomlins concluded, "that took to progressing at all," the rise of the capitalists "went on at a quadruple pace. Taxes, profits, population, inventions, gases, steam, legislation, learning, lying."[36]

Historians of the United States in the long nineteenth century have, in the past decade, made the relationship between slavery and capitalism a central analytic in their field.[37] And yet, the abolition of slavery in the British Empire—a tectonic shift in colonial policy and the single largest single financial bailout in

---

Database, ; Douglas Hamilton, *Scotland, The Caribbean and the Atlantic World, 1750–1820* (Manchester: Manchester University Press, 2005), 204–207; *The Scottish Jurist: Containing Reports of Cases Decided in the House of Lords, Courts of Session, Teinds, and Exchequer, and the Jury and Justiciary Courts*, vol. 5 (Edinburgh: Michael Anderson, 1833), 204–207.

33. See the recent work of the *Legacies of British Slave-Ownership* project, Nicholas Draper, *The Price of Emancipation: Slave-Ownership, Compensation and British Society at the End of Slavery* (Cambridge: Cambridge University Press, 2013); and Hall et al., *Legacies of British Slave-Ownership*.

34. William Makepeace Thackeray et al., *Heads of the People; Or, Portraits of the English* (London, 1841), 213.

35. Thackeray et al., *Heads of the People*, 214.

36. Thackeray et al., *Heads of the People*, 209.

37. See, notably, Sven Beckert, *Empire of Cotton: A Global History* (New York: Knopf, 2014); Walter Johnson, *River of Dark Dreams: Slavery and Empire in the Cotton Kingdom* (Cambridge, MA: Belknap, 2013); Edward E. Baptist, *The Half Has Never Been Told: Slavery and the Making*

British history—barely disturbs the surface of histories of the British world in the nineteenth century. As Catherine Hall observed, "Distance insulated metropolitan Britain from the physical realities of slavery . . . and has continued to shelter British history from them since."[38] Historians of the British Empire risk ceding the history of the British Empire in the Caribbean to historians of the United States, who have "discovered" it, weaving it into American histories of capitalism, slavery, and antislavery.[39] Since Eric Williams, historians of Britain have debated the extent to which the rise of industrial capitalism in Britain affected slavery in the West Indies. The common denominator for the debate has been that slavery and capitalism were indelibly connected; the debate has hinged, for the most part, on whether slavery was abolished *because* or *in spite* of its relationship to industrial capitalism.[40] The preoccupation with the causal relationship between capitalism and British emancipation has obscured the importance of emancipation to imperial history, not only in the Caribbean, but also in the wider empire, and in Britain itself. However, whether slavery was economically vigorous in the British Empire of the early 1830s or not, it was abolished as free trade and reform ascended in prestige and as the industrial production of cotton finally outstripped the plantation production of sugar in terms of overall importance to the imperial economy. Free trade and official antislavery insulated Britain from American slavery, even as Britain's industrial revolution subsisted on slave-grown cotton. Paper itself was a product of the world of this "empire of cotton." In 1837, Britain exported roughly £100,000 a year

of American Capitalism (New York: Basic Books, 2014); and the chapters in *Slavery's Capitalism*, ed. Beckert and Rockman.

38. Hall et al., *Legacies of British Slave-Ownership*, 250.

39. See Edward Bartlett Rugemer, *The Problem of Emancipation: The Caribbean Roots of the American Civil War* (Baton Rouge: Louisiana State University Press, 2009); Matthew Karp, "King Cotton, Emperor Slavery: Antebellum Slaveholders and the World Economy," in *The Civil War as Global Conflict: Transnational Meanings of the American Civil War*, ed. David T. Gleeson and Simon Lewis (Columbia: University of South Carolina Press, 2014), 36–55; and Matthew Karp, *This Vast Southern Empire: Slaveholders at the Helm of American Foreign Policy* (Cambridge, MA: Harvard University Press, 2016).

40. Eric Williams, *Capitalism & Slavery* (New York: Russell and Russell, 1961); Seymour Drescher, *Econocide: British Slavery in the Era of Abolition* (Pittsburgh: University of Pittsburgh Press, 1977); and James Walvin, "Why Did the British Abolish the Slave Trade? Econocide Revisited," *Slavery & Abolition* 32, no. 4 (2011): 583–588. Economic histories of the British Caribbean, needless to say, also preponderate toward assessments of the sugar economy. See, for example, Douglas Hall, *Free Jamaica, 1838–1865: An Economic History* (New Haven, CT: Yale University Press, 1959).

worth of books and produced reams of paper worth between £1.2 and £1.3 million. Grimy cotton sweepings, cleaned in new steam-powered machines, were recycled into pulp, making Manchester the center of paper production as well as the seat of cotton refining, cotton financing, and cotton credit.[41]

Cotton made paper and paper made cotton. The empire of cotton, as Sven Beckert has shown, existed not only in fields and factories but also in the letters, ledgers, and calculations of the agents, merchants, and clerks who recorded the millions of individual transactions that bound enslaved laborers and factory workers together in a transnational network substantially unmoored from any particular political jurisdiction.[42] Credit and debt were the blood of the system, pushing it forward, shaping its demands. For most Britons in the 1830s, the ethic of debt that made capitalism possible meant perpetual insecurity and the always-present fear of insolvency. "A debtor," one writer noted in 1833, "is a man of mark. Many eyes are fixed upon him . . . his name is upon many books. . . . The man who pays his way is unknown in his neighbourhood."[43] When well-meaning middle-class Britons wanted to know the lives of the laboring poor, petty debts were the most substantial traces left in the records.

Debt had its own moral valence. If poorer Britons were stalked by debt, freedpeople in the West Indies found that their relation to British middle-class reformers was defined by it. Emancipation was an "experiment." Reformers also emphasized that it had been granted, on sufferance (perhaps on layaway) to apprentices, and would need to be paid for. The logic of debt repayment was not only confined to the idea that apprentices, having once been considered property, would need to reimburse their former "owners" for the value of their labor. Debt became a moral expectation that apprentices would be grateful for receiving freedom subject to the restrictions devised and imposed by Britain. With the apparatus of bureaucratic civilization, cultural practices as well as money could be weighed against the costs of emancipation to Britain. In turn, West Indian planters were condemned for their imprudence. "It is a most calamitous circumstance in the situation of these unfortunate beings," James

41. *Statistical Account of the British Empire: 2* (London, 1837), 127.

42. Beckert, *Empire of Cotton*; see also Sven Beckert, "Emancipation and Empire: Reconstructing the Worldwide Web of Cotton Production in the Age of the American Civil War," *American Historical Review* 109, no. 5 (2004): 1405–1438; and Sven Beckert, "From Tuskegee to Togo: The Problem of Freedom in the Empire of Cotton," *Journal of American History* 92, no. 2 (2005): 498–526.

43. *The Museum of Foreign Literature, Science and Art*, vol. 22 (London, 1833), 450.

Stephen (the elder) wrote, "that the master who exacts their labours, and on whom alone they depend for subsistence, is almost always a mortgagor in possession."[44] Credit and debt made industrial capitalism possible; techniques for recording and representing what was owed and to whom became instruments with which reformers reckoned with both the British poor and the former slaves.

The similarities between slavery and debt preceded the abolition of the slavery. In the 1810s, after the end of the British slave trade, debt imprisonment was framed as "truly a *Trade of Slavery*, a *Slave-trade* indeed."[45] Lower-middle-class fears of debt also mapped onto objections to paper currency. William Cobbett, a great foe of paper money, opined, "Yes: we talk about *dearness;* we talk of *high prices;* we talk of things *rising in value;* but, the fact is, that the change has been in the *money* . . . the money, from its abundance, has *fallen in value*."[46] Even proponents of paper currency worried that trade built on debt was not real trade, describing the British North Sea possession of Heligoland as a trash heap of "salted sugar and rotten coffee" left to decay while "trade flourishes to such a degree, that the name of a bankrupt in the Gazette, is as rare as a nightingale in Scotland, or a guinea in circulation."[47] Debts were recorded by the lower-middle-class clerks, overseers, and bookkeepers, and debt menaced these global Bob Cratchits. Neither the clerks nor the people they reduced to numbers had much capital, whether financial, social, or political. Bureaucratic civilization aligned neatly with the managerial techniques, the logic of debt, and the mounting insecurity and alienation of a rising industrial capitalism. The basic instruments of British middle-class retailing, credit, and paperwork, the pieties of British middle-class life, the self-regard of British middle-class civilization, and the anxieties of precarious British middle-class comfort were embodied in a global program of reform.

44. James Stephen, *The Slavery of the British West India Colonies Delineated: Being a Delineation of the State in Point of Law* (London: J. Butterworth and Son, 1824), 87.

45. Walter J. Baldwin, *English Slave Trade! Petition on the Injustice . . . of Imprisonment for Debt, and on the Grievances of the King's Bench Prison Presented by Lord Holland and Samuel Whitbread . . . to the Houses of Lords and Commons . . . with Remarks* (London, 1813), 1.

46. William Cobbett, *Paper against Gold and Glory against Prosperity. Or, an Account of the Rise, Progress, Extent and Present State of the Funds and of the Papermoney of Great-Britain Etc* (London: J. M'Creery, 1815), 322.

47. Philip Francis, *Reflections on the Abundance of Paper in Circulation, and the Scarcity of Specie* (London, 1810), 15.

The Limits of Reform

Ironically, the end of apprenticeship was abetted by an overstretched bureau-cratic civilization. The data gathered by observers from missionary organ-izations showed that even under apprenticeship, women were still being flogged by both planters and, worse, special magistrates. In response, a move-ment of middle-class women, augmented by broader petitioning campaigns, called for vigorous reforms to apprenticeship. However, the Jamaican Assem-bly, resentful of imperial interference, opted to end apprenticeship early, be-ginning a constitutional crisis that not only left the apprentices free but also reaffirmed the power of the white planter minority to impose legislation on the free black majority. In 1838, eliding the rupture in the imperial constitution, Lord Brougham declared the experiment over. "The slave has shown," he said, "by four years' blameless behaviour, and devotion to the pursuits of peaceful industry, that he is as fit for his freedom as any English peasant."[48] According to the metrics of the Emancipation Act, emancipation had "failed." Brougham indicated this himself, subtly comparing freedpeople to the English peasantry, a class quickly disappearing in England, driven into tenancy by the enclosure of common land and into an expanding industrial proletariat by a changing econ-omy. Emancipation was designed to reproduce modern middle-class values and desires in freedpeople. Instead, Brougham admitted, it seemed to have revived a class of medieval farmers. Freedpeople and former slave owners, and by exten-sion the West Indian colonies they inhabited, were temporally out of step with the rest of the British world. The West Indies had been the objective of intense, jealous interest in the eighteenth century. After the end of slavery, the sugar colo-nies were an afterthought in London. Meanwhile, missionaries and the mission-ary press came to the forefront as a source of information about the West Indies in Britain. Missionary organizations had their own bureaucracies, their own ways of measuring the success or failure of their projects, and their own vision of how to disseminate bourgeois values into the empire.

As industrialization intensified in Britain, uprooting more and more people from rural areas and pulling them toward crowded slums, some working-class Britons began to resent emancipation. From the 1790s, working-class radicals rejected what they took to be the narrow focus of elite reformers like William Wilberforce on the suffering of enslaved people in the colonies and demanded reform of Britain's institutions in order to improve the lot of poor Britons.

48. "Right Honourable Lord Brougham," 129.

William Cobbett, for example, was a strident critic of elite antislavery as a shallow cover for predatory class politics.[49] Mrs. Jellyby, in Dickens' *Bleak House*, is a high-Victorian caricature of a "telescopic philanthropist," more interested in humanitarian projects far from Britain than in the suffering of the poor in the London streets, or indeed the welfare of her own children. Mrs. Jellyby's eyes see "nothing nearer than Africa," where she dreams of "the general cultivation of the coffee berry—*and* the natives—and the happy settlement, on the banks of the African rivers, of our superabundant home population."[50] Mrs. Jellyby is a comic figure, but her belief in the transforming imperial power of commerce and in the idea that the solution to British poverty could be found in imperial reform is consistent with bureaucratic civilization. Middle-class reformers promoted economic freedom as a transformative, uplifting force in London as much as in the post-emancipation West Indies. Turning former slaves into wage laborers was of a piece with turning former farmers into factory workers.

In *Civilising Subjects*, Catherine Hall uses Thomas Carlyle's work as a bellwether for the moment when the British middle-class public grew disenchanted with emancipation. Where tens of thousands of bourgeois Britons had signaled their virtue in the 1820s and early 1830s by signing petitions for emancipation, by the 1840s, many saw the West Indies as a failed British project and emancipation as an error.[51] It is telling, then, that part of Carlyle's chiliastic critique of emancipation was a critique of paperwork itself. In his history of the French Revolution, Carlyle described the years before the outbreak of the revolution as "The Paper Age," a period defined by "Bank-paper, wherewith you can still buy when there is no gold left; Book-paper . . . so beautifully hiding from us the want of Thought!"[52] Carlyle's critique of banknotes and the empty platitudes

49. See James Epstein, "Taking Class Notes on Empire," in *At Home with the Empire: Metropolitan Culture and the Imperial World*, ed. Catherine Hall and Sonya O. Rose (Cambridge: Cambridge University Press, 2006), 251–274; Susan Thorne, "'The Conversion of Englishmen and the Conversion of the World Inseparable': Missionary Imperialism and the Language of Class in Early Industrial Britain," in *Tensions of Empire: Colonial Cultures in a Bourgeois World*, ed. Frederick Cooper and Ann Laura Stoler (Berkeley: University of California Press, 1997), 238–262.

50. Charles Dickens, *Bleak House* (2 vols.), vol. 18 of *Works of Charles Dickens* (Boston: Ticknor and Fields; London: Chapman and Hall, 1868), 1: 24.

51. See Hall, *Civilising Subjects*; Catherine Hall, "'From Greenland's Icy Mountains . . . to Afric's Golden Sand': Ethnicity, Race and Nation in Mid-Nineteenth-Century England," *Gender & History* 5, no. 2 (1993): 212–230.

52. Thomas Carlyle, *The French Revolution: The Bastille*, Thomas Carlyle's Collected Works (London: Chapman and Hall, 1872), 39. See also the gloss in Mary Poovey, *Genres of the Credit*

of the philosophes became more acidic when directed toward the industrial bourgeoisie of the 1840s and 1850s. Carlyle grasped the centrality of paperwork to reform and capital and condemned them both. The empire, as governed by the well-meaning Colonial Office, had become "a world-wide jungle of redtape, inhabited by doleful creatures, deaf or nearly so to human reason."[53] In Carlyle's essays, "Bobus Higgins," "with his cash-accounts and larders dropping fatness, with his respectabilities, warm garnitures, and pony-chaise" was a grotesque caricature of the complacent wealthy British bourgeois swell.[54] Bourgeois posturing disgusted Carlyle; so did emancipation. "West-Indian Blacks," he wrote, "are emancipated, and it appears refuse to work; Irish Whites have long been entirely emancipated; and nobody asks them to work."[55] The trust in progress of the 1830s acquired a dark afterimage: "Nearly all the men that speak," Carlyle wrote, "instruct us, saying, 'Have you quite done your interesting Negroes in the Sugar Islands? Rush to the Jails, then, O ye reformers. . . . But except this whitewashing of the scoundrel-population, one sees little 'reform' going on."[56] The paperwork that middle-class reformers believed could clarify the empire of the 1830s became, in Carlyle's bestselling books, the obfuscating red tape and pompous cant of the 1840s and 1850s.

As the nineteenth century wore on, paperwork lost some of its moral luster, but it remained the cutting edge of global capitalism. Bureaucracy remained a defining feature of middle-class life: from lowly clerks to high-paid lawyers, the global bourgeoisies of the British Empire worked with paper and bought, sold, and traded multiplying paper instruments of wealth. Emancipation, in Lord John Russell's view in 1841, had ushered freedpeople into "practical freedom, of means of education and of physical comfort to a very high degree."[57] That "practical freedom" was shaped by bureaucratic civilization—a chimera of paperwork, capitalism, and bourgeois morality.

Economy: Mediating Value in Eighteenth- and Nineteenth-Century Britain (Chicago: University of Chicago Press, 2008), 153–169.

53. Thomas Carlyle, "Downing Street," in *Latter-Day Pamphlets [1850]*, Thomas Carlyle's Collected Works (London: Chapman and Hall, 1870), 107–154, 107.

54. Thomas Carlyle, *Past and Present [1843]*, Thomas Carlyle's Collected Works (London: Chapman and Hall, 1870), 25.

55. Thomas Carlyle, "The Present Time," in *Latter-Day Pamphlets [1850]*, 3–58, 32–33.

56. Thomas Carlyle, "Model Prisons," in *Latter-Day Pamphlets [1850]*, 59–106, 83.

57. Guiana Despatch No. 136, Lord John Russell to Governor J. Jeremie, 20 March 1841, *1841 (321) Papers Relative to the West Indies, 1841, British Guiana*, Accounts and Papers (London: Great Britain, House of Commons, 1841), 262.

Conclusions

Emancipation was an emblematic project of reform in the British world of the 1830s. However, as Carlyle's bilious critiques suggest, by the mid-Victorian era, many middle-class Britons had become skeptical of emancipation. And yet, the project of reproducing bourgeois values and "civilization" was repeated again and again during the long nineteenth century, both in Britain itself and in the wider empire in the form of slum-visiting, temperance campaigns, the industrial schools movement, campaigns against prostitution, missionary work among colonized people, residential schools in settler colonies, and many other programs. Printed and manuscript archives overflow with high-minded magazines, printed parliamentary reports full of tables of statistics and excerpted letters, vast troves of missionary papers and publications, and endless ephemera. Meanwhile, the instruments of financial paperwork proliferated and grew in sophistication, knitting together the global financial marketplace. Formerly enslaved people were seen through the lens of a British mentality that conflated freedom with participation in the market and civilization with a desire to integrate into that market, to internalize and inhabit its values. The British global bourgeoisie is difficult to define in detail, but its bureaucratic civilization is a bridgehead from which to begin the work.

PART III

Capitalism and Class

8

Modern Business and the Rise of the Japanese Middle Classes

Janet Hunter

THE EMERGENCE OF A WESTERN-STYLE MIDDLE CLASS in Japan has been dated to the interwar years. The First World War economic boom and the rapid expansion of urbanization that followed led to the appearance of new patterns of consumer culture that were often associated with the appearance of "modern" youth.[1] How far the constraints of the 1930s and the wartime years marked a hiatus in this development has been subject to debate, but as economic growth began to gather pace from the early 1950s, scholars began to identify what one seminal work termed "Japan's new middle class," which consisted predominantly of the army of salarymen (*sarariiman*) employed by the large companies spearheading the growth.[2] By the late 1970s, surveys showed that a high proportion of all Japanese self-identified as "middle class." The emergence of the middle class in Japan is therefore regarded mainly as a twentieth century phenomenon.[3]

---

1. See, for example, Barbara Hamill Satō, "The *Moga* Sensation: Perceptions of the *Modan Gāru* in Japanese Intellectual Circles during the 1920s," *Gender and History* 5, no. 3 (1993): 361–381; Barbara Hamill Satō, *The New Japanese Woman: Modernity, Media and Women in Interwar Japan* (Durham, NC: Duke University Press, 2003).

2. Ezra F. Vogel, *Japan's New Middle Class: the Salary Man and his Family in a Tokyo Suburb* (Berkeley: University of California Press, 1963).

3. David Chiavacci, "From Class Struggle to General Middle Class Society to Divided Society: Societal Models of Inequality in Postwar Japan," *Social Science Japan Journal* 11, no. 1 (2008): 5–27.

The emergent middle class of the interwar and postwar years was popularly perceived as marking a significant discontinuity with earlier forms of class and social stratification, but more recent research has cast doubt on the extent to which such a discontinuity exists. Such debates are, of course, highly contingent on definitions of "middle class," but if we think of a middle class as defined by its income, lifestyle, and aspirations, then early modern Japan would seem to have been conducive to its appearance. Accelerating urbanization in the Tokugawa (Edo) period (c. 1600–1868) supported the growth of a market economy in which a significant proportion of the population no longer engaged in agriculture. By the eighteenth century, access to disposable income extended well beyond a small wealthy elite. Research has demonstrated the rise of a consumer culture and the existence of a very substantial commercial elite who, together with officials of the samurai ruling class, highly skilled artisans, scholars, and wealthy farmers, could be viewed as constituting a kind of middle class, or at least providing the pool from which a kind of middle class might appear. Estimates suggest that by the mid-nineteenth century, this group comprised up to a quarter of Japan's total population, which, at over thirty million, was already large by European standards.

Considering the emergence of a global bourgeoisie and the rise of the middle classes during the long nineteenth century therefore requires us in the Japanese case to think seriously about the relationship between economic and social developments in the latter part of the Edo period and those of the 1920s, the time by which scholars tend to agree that a "new middle class" was emerging. These transitional decades from the mid-nineteenth century to the 1920s were characterized by dramatic political change starting with the Meiji Restoration of 1868, and the no-less-dramatic social, intellectual, economic, and cultural transformations through the Meiji period (1868–1912) and beyond. The country also moved rapidly from relative isolation to growing international integration, a transition closely associated with the increasing transfer of goods, technology, and ideas between Japan and other countries in Asia and between Japan and the West. Japan's integration into the global and imperialist world of the age of empire was not marked by the unequivocal colonial, subordinate relationship with the West that was the lot of most other countries in Asia and Africa. Like China and other powers in Asia, Japan was from the 1850s bound by "unequal" treaties with the US and European powers, but no Japanese territory was conceded to the control of a Western power. Revision of the unequal treaties was secured in the early 1890s, and full tariff autonomy by the end of the first decade of the twentieth century. An alliance based on equal partnership was concluded with Britain in 1902. Japan therefore retained more independence in its interactions with the West than was the case with most other "periphery" territories. These realities of Japan's nineteenth-century development were fundamental both to the changing shape of class and social relations and to the discourse surrounding them.

It is not possible within the constraints of this chapter to offer a full analysis of the emergence of a "middle class" in Japan in the long nineteenth century. My objective is rather to discuss some of the key issues raised by previous scholarship on the emergence of a middle class in Japan that can help us better understand how far developments in Japan may have been part of the appearance of a broader global bourgeoisie. My main focus will be on business and economic transformation. In Japan, as elsewhere, economic processes played a crucial role in the emergence of social distinctions and social groupings and in any discourse relating to them. Considerations of income, occupation, and consumption can help to shed light on Japan's changing social structures in the late nineteenth and early twentieth centuries and to locate them in a longer-term and more global context.

The next section considers previous analyses of the emerging middle class of twentieth-century Japan and the extent to which it can be traced back to pre-restoration economic, social, and intellectual antecedents. It will be shown that defining what constitutes the middle class in Japan has proved distinctly challenging, and the use of the term, and the discourse relating to it, remains often ambiguous. I will then consider two issues that feed into these debates. One is the emergence of the new commercial and business elites of the late nineteenth century who, along with bureaucrats and professionals, are often identified as the core of Japan's new middle class. It will be shown that members of this group had their origins in earlier elites and more traditional forms of economic and occupational activity. The other is the evolution of patterns of material consumption across the transitional period from the early nineteenth century, which can illuminate the extent to which Japan had a social group that exhibited material values or attitudes that might be associated with a middle class.

The Making of the Japanese Middle Class

Interpretations of class formation in early modern and modern Japan were for much of the twentieth century largely shaped by the frameworks of Marxism, which in the initial decades became a major vehicle of political dissent and of intellectual heterodoxy in the face of an increasingly dominant nationalist state. Marxism-Leninism remained fundamental to the thinking of most historians through the early post-1945 decades, if only as the source of basic frameworks and nomenclatures and as a stimulus to develop particular foci of study. The bourgeoisie (*burujoaji*) figured prominently in much of this scholarship, but its composition and role were not clear-cut. Ambiguity was compounded by fundamental disagreements over how Japan's path of capitalist development might accord with any Marxist-Leninist scenario. Was the Meiji Restoration a bourgeois revolution, or was it not? How could the existence of seemingly feudal characteristics in the countryside be explained? What were the drivers behind Japanese imperialism at a time when it seemed that the country had a long way to go before achieving the highest stage of capitalism?[4] Class became a widely used category and generated a rich historical scholarship, but the core factors behind class formation and the characteristics of class identity often remained the subject of disagreement.

We therefore find that in much of the Japanese literature the terms "bourgeois" and "bourgeoisie" tend to be used to refer to the capitalist class (haute bourgeoisie) who owned or controlled most of society's capital and means of production, those identified by McCloskey as "captains of industry."[5] These were the very rich of prewar Japan and included the owners of the largest *zaibatsu* (financial conglomerates) and other big businesses. Earlier estimates suggested that this group comprised no more than a few thousand families, a figure supported by recent analyses of Japan's highly unequal pattern of income and wealth distribution in the prewar period.[6] Despite its relatively small size, this elite was highly fragmented in the late nineteenth century, consisting of

4. For analysis of the prewar debates and their significance in economic history, see, for example, Germaine A. Hoston, *Marxism and the Crisis of Development in Prewar Japan* (Princeton, NJ: Princeton University Press, 1986); Kaoru Sugihara, "The Japanese Capitalism Debate, 1927–1937," in *Agrarian Structure and Economic Development* ed. R. Datta, P. Robb, and K. Sugihara, Occasional Papers in Third World Economic History 4 (London: School of Oriental and African Studies, 1992), 34–60.

5. Deirdre McCloskey, *Bourgeois Dignity: Why Economics Can't Explain the Modern World* (Chicago: University of Chicago Press, 2010), 3. McCloskey herself uses the term "bourgeois" in a far broader sense.

6. For income distribution, see Hirotake Yazawa, *Kindai Nihon no Shotoku Bunpu to Kazoku Keizai* [Income distribution and the family economy in modern Japan] (Tokyo: Ajia Insatsu, 2004). For the very rich, see Shunsuke Nakaoka, "The Making of Modern Riches: The Social Origins of the Economic Elite in the Early 20th Century," *Social Science Japan Journal* 9, no. 2 (2006): 221–241.

diverse elements including former domain lords (*daimyō*), merchants who had benefited from political patronage (*seishō*), and provincial businessmen. It also included some wealthy landlords; the agricultural sector remained dominant, though most landlords owned only small amounts of land. Each group retained its own interests, and together they failed to cohere into a formal bourgeoisie class. This fragmentation, scholars have argued, was a product of Japan's late development; Japan's immature capitalism was compelled to try and compensate for the absence of a coherent formal bourgeoisie class in the context of the global division of labor. The state had had to become the key agent in coping with the problems raised by the immaturity of Japan's capitalism.[7] The overall result, Nakamura and others have suggested, was a distinctive Japanese typology of bourgeoisie, with its higher echelons concentrated in the country's largest urban areas.[8]

This historiography did not ignore the existence in Japan of a petite bourgeoisie consisting of retailers, artisans, and the self-employed and professionals who might in more recent discourse be viewed as the core of a middle class, but their form was also seen as a manifestation of the immaturity of Japanese capitalism. However, there was little engagement with any concept of a middle class comprising professional and educated individuals, as well as those who hired or owned labor and capital. Even less was this scholarship concerned with middle-class identity in terms of materialistic values or conventional attitudes.

Other approaches to the analysis of class began to appear after the Second World War, complementing and building on these existing analytical foundations while also being shaped by them. One was the American-influenced "modernization" school, which, seeking explicitly to offer a non-Marxist and supposedly value-free yardstick for analyzing Japan's history, posited the existence of a universal "modernity" toward which Japan had been progressing since the nineteenth century, albeit temporarily losing its way in the decades immediately prior to 1945. Historians increasingly questioned, though, the extent to which the modernization yardstick was genuinely value-free and also suggested that it was powerless to explain the history of society and culture. The concept,

---

7. One of the best known analyses of the Japanese bourgeoisie can be found in Masanori Nakamura, "Kaikyū Kōsei" [Class structure], in *Nihon Sangyō Kakumei no Kenkyū (Ka)* [Research on Japan's industrial revolution, 2 vols.], ed. Kà'ichirō Ōishi (Tokyo: Tokyo University Press, 1975), 65–128.

8. Nakamura, "Kaikyū Kōsei," 108–127.

some argued, was both culturally determined (Western-centric) and time-bound.[9]

Japan itself witnessed the emergence of "people's history" (*minshūshi*), which sought to escape some of the assumptions behind both Marxist and modernist interpretations and to create a distinctive Japan-based historical approach. The *minshūshi* scholars focused on issues of intellectual history and popular consciousness, somewhat equivalent to the study of *mentalités* in the West, but their ethnographic studies embraced some individuals of the middling sort and had echoes of the social history and history from below that had emerged in Western scholarship at around the same time.[10] It remained the case, though, that most scholars writing within the frameworks of modernization theory and people's history rarely explicitly tackled the issue of class, in particular the position of a middle class. Their definitions of class identity, and their interpretations of social identity formation, were highly diverse. Like their Marxist-influenced counterparts, argues Mark Jones, they are open to the criticism of using the term "middle class" in an inadequately historicized way.[11]

More recent research has responded to this perceived lack of historicization of class in Japan and drawn on the arguments of scholars elsewhere who have identified class as at least in part a social and cultural construction. Our current understanding of the emergence of the middle class in early twentieth-century Japan stems from research that has sought to escape the confines and assumptions of earlier approaches and to inject a greater understanding of the historical contexts and processes behind the evolution of social distinctions. There is agreement that the measures taken during the early 1870s to dismantle the old hereditary caste system—which consisted of four main groups: *bushi* (samurai), peasants, artisans, and merchants[12]—was a key generator of social change, even though it took decades for the change to fully take effect. The difficult transitional decades after the Meiji Restoration of 1868 were marked by a "shift

9. T.R.H. Havens, "Beyond Modernization: Society, Culture and the Underside of Japanese History"; and Ardath W. Burks, "Beyond Modern," both in *Japan Examined: Perspectives on Modern Japanese History*, ed. Harry Wray and Hilary Conroy (Honolulu: University of Hawai'i Press, 1983), 45–54.

10. For an analysis of the *minshūshi* scholarship, see Carol Gluck, "The People in History: Recent Trends in Japanese Historiography," *Journal of Asian Studies* 38, no. 1 (1978): 25–50.

11. Mark A. Jones, *Children as Treasures: Childhood and the Middle Class in Early Twentieth Century Japan* (Cambridge, MA: Harvard University Press, 2010), 325n8.

12. Other social groups included the imperial family and "undergroups" (*burakumin, hinin*), but these four were the core of the status system.

from status to class, from aristocracy to meritocracy, from a society where birth determined social position to one where merit determined social place."[13] Taking account of this transition, it is argued, is fundamental to any appropriately historicized analysis of class formation in modern Japan that allows us to go beyond economic determinants and to better understand the characteristics and material preferences that have come to be identified with being middle class.

How large the Japanese middle class was by the 1920s is debatable, although there is agreement that in the interwar years it remained relatively small and that its high concentration in urban areas gave it a profile in excess of its actual numbers. But numbers are contingent on definition, and, as Andrew Gordon has noted, the middle class in Japan "has been a shifting cultural construct as well as a shifting set of social behaviors."[14] There is some agreement, though, that a potentially useful distinction can be drawn between "old" and "new" middle classes, a distinction analogous to that discussed by Houchang Chehabi's chapter in this volume. The old middle classes comprised small-scale business owners, manufacturers, and landowners (perhaps equivalent to the petite bourgeoisie), most of whom were engaged in traditional and long-standing occupations and activities. By contrast, the new middle class consisted of professionals and intellectuals associated with the growth of white-collar employment, with the proliferation of public and private networks of city services, and with the expansion of urban commerce and culture industries. This group is estimated to have grown from 4 percent of the total population in 1915 to 12 percent by 1925.[15] The emergence of this new middle class was integral to the rise of the modern economy, the spread of education and knowledge, and a move toward meritocracy. It was these intellectual and white-collar workers who were the forerunners of the *sarariiman* of the postwar decades.[16]

This important distinction, which initially appeared in the Japanese scholarly literature, in part resonates with the earlier distinction between the petite

13. Jones, *Children as Treasures*, 13.

14. Andrew Gordon, "The Short Happy Life of the Japanese Middle Class," in *Social Contracts under Stress: The Middle Classes of America, Europe, and Japan at the Turn of the Century*, ed. Oliver Zunz, Leonard Schoppa, and Nobuhiro Watari (New York: Russell Sage Foundation, 2002), 108–129, 110.

15. Louise Young, *Beyond the Metropolis: Second Cities and Modern Life in Interwar Japan* (Berkeley: University of California Press, 2013), 5.

16. For comment on the distinction, see David Ambaras, "Social Knowledge, Cultural Capital, and the New Middle Class in Japan, 1895–1912," *Journal of Japanese Studies* 24, no. 1 (1998): 1–33.

and haute bourgeoisie, but it would also seem to offer an important starting point for comparing the Japanese middle class with its counterparts elsewhere, particularly those in similarly "immature" capitalist economies. I will return to this point below, but two comments are in order here. One is simply that the reference to an old middle class implies the existence in Japan of a middle class prior to the early twentieth century, a middle class based on occupations that predated the economic transformation of the late nineteenth century. The second is that it underlines the extent to which discussions on the middle class can get both hijacked and confused by terminology. As Jones notes, Japanese historians using the distinction between the new and old middle classes refer to the new middle class as *shinchūkansō* and do not employ the more literal *chūtō kaikyū* used to translate the Western term "middle class" into Japanese from the latter part of the nineteenth century.[17] This term (*shinchūkansō*) also avoids the standard word for "class" used by scholars writing in the Marxist tradition. In contrast, interwar writers referred to *chūryū* when thinking about what might be meant by "middle class."[18] Writing about a slightly later period, Earl Kinmonth uses the term "old middle class" as the equivalent of the Japanese *puchiburu* (petit bourgeois),[19] retranslated in most dictionaries as "*lower* middle class." Kunio Odaka notes that in the early 1960s at least three terms were used interchangeably in debates about the Japanese middle class, raising significant questions about middle-class identification and impeding rigorous analysis.[20] The term now normally used to refer to middle class in Japanese—*chūsan kaikyū*—did not exist in the late nineteenth century. Throughout these transitional decades and beyond, there was no single agreed-upon wording for referring to the middling elements in society. In the absence of one accepted vernacular term, the Japanese articulation of what was middle class was up for grabs not just until the 1920s but well after.

Notwithstanding these ambiguities, the evidence suggests that in the early twentieth century, Japan witnessed the emergence of a social stratum that can be defined as middle class in terms of its materialist values and its attitudes and

17. Jones, *Children as Treasures*, 315n8.

18. Jordan Sand references use of this term by the architectural historian Itō Chūta in 1915, Jordan Sand, *House and Home in Modern Japan: Architecture, Domestic Space, and Bourgeois Culture 1880–1930* (Cambridge, MA: Harvard University Press, 2003), 166.

19. Earl H. Kinmonth, "The Impact of Military Procurements on the Old Middle Classes in Japan, 1931–1941," *Japan Forum* 4, no. 2 (1992); 247–265, 260n1.

20. Kunio Odaka, "The Middle Classes in Japan," *Sociological Review* 10 (1962 suppl.): 25–43, 28–29.

aspirations. We therefore need to ask where being perceived as middle class in early twentieth-century Japan came from and what it consisted of. David Ambaras has argued that the removal of many of the old social certainties in the early 1870s initiated a fluid and uncertain period in which a new group of white-collar workers (who were to form the core of the new middle class) emerged with an aspiration to address the country's social problems. These so-called new middle class reformers increasingly "articulated a vision of society in which they functioned as principal promoters of national progress"[21] and looked to influence state policies toward the identification of social problems and the organization of everyday life. The group was not a homogeneous one, but it achieved a growing hegemony over social discourse and practice that by the 1900s generated a coherent representation of what it might mean to be middle class.[22] These white-collar groups were joined by a cohort from Japan's growing business sector (both old and new), underlining the importance of economic factors in the appearance of the emerging middle class.

So what did being middle class in 1920s Japan consist of? Gordon has emphasized how the rise of the urban middle classes was closely associated with the rise of mass consumer society and the spread of commercialized leisure, suggesting that Japan was sharing in aspects of twentieth-century modernity.[23] Certainly being middle class was essentially an urban phenomenon associated with the growth of the service economy. "Urban expansion," writes one scholar, "became a vehicle for middle class hegemony. What was good for the city was good for the middle class."[24] Aspiring to be middle class brought with it a whole set of prescriptions relating to housing, dress, food, and other aspects of daily life.[25] Such aspiration was contingent on income and occupation. While a growing number of urban residents aimed for middle-class status and values in the 1920s and 1930s, it was conceived as a hierarchical ladder on which families could go up and down, and there remained many for whom it was an unrealizable proposition. Louise Young has noted how in one provincial city, Sapporo, the emerging middle class juxtaposed its identity not against that of

21. Ambaras, "Social Knowledge," 1.

22. Ambaras, "Social Knowledge," 30–33.

23. Andrew Gordon, "Consumption, Leisure and the Middle Class in Transwar Japan," *Social Science Japan Journal* 10, no. 1 (2007): 1–21, 1.

24. Young, *Beyond the Metropolis*, 189.

25. Elise Tipton, "How to Manage a Household: Creating Middle Class Housewives in Modern Japan," *Japanese Studies* 29, no. 1 (2009): 95–110.

the working class but against the marginalized underclass consisting of workers such as street sweepers and garbage collectors.[26] The identification of the middle class as merit based and its self-representation as the standard bearer of progress made it not just a social foundation but also one closely associated with national identity. This meant that it could never be accessible to the country's minorities, even when they achieved affluence. Middle-class discourse was silent on the *burakumin*, the descendants of old discriminated castes. Successful Korean immigrants, who enjoyed equality of suffrage with their Japanese counterparts from 1925 and who often internalized Japanese values, might see themselves as middle class, but they could never become "middle class Japanese" in the way that this identity was constructed.[27]

What is perhaps very distinct about the Japanese case is that the middle class was perceived "neither as a political force nor as an economic engine of growth but as a social foundation for national strength." Its "foundation and fountainhead" was the family.[28] This formulation of middle-class image and reality based on the family had significant implications for gender roles, as the movement to reform daily lives and construct a middle-class culture around what Jordan Sand has appositely called "House and Home" led to the "creation" of middle-class housewives and to middle-class women becoming the vanguard of new modes of consumption and leisure.[29] Over the decades up to 1900, women's education levels had risen considerably, but they nevertheless were increasingly subject to formal exclusion from participation in the institutions of the state and the ownership of property, pushed into "domestication," and constrained by the concept of separate spheres for men and women. Their education was shaped around this "good wife, wise mother" precept, which spread downward from the elite to those who could afford the luxury of nonworking adult women in the household.[30] Educators of women believed that it was the way in which women ran their households that situated them as members of

26. Young, *Beyond the Metropolis*, 8.

27. Jeffrey P. Bayliss, "Minority Success, Assimilation and Identity in Prewar Japan: Pak Chungŭm and the Korean Middle Class," *Journal of Japanese Studies* 34, no. 1 (2006): 33–68.

28. Jones, *Children as Treasures*, 2 and 7.

29. Sand, *House and Home in Modern Japan*.

30. Marnie S. Anderson, *A Place in Public: Women's Rights in Meiji Japan* (Cambridge, MA: Harvard University Press, 2011). The luxury of "idle" women did not extent to the majority of the Japanese population in the interwar years; most families needed the labor of both male and female members for survival, hence restricting the size of any middle class.

the modern middle class. Their consumption patterns were symbolic of class membership, as was their adherence to values such as hard work and frugality.[31] With the feminist movement small and constrained, women's political and social rights tightly curtailed, and women's status as legal minors, aspirant middle-class housewives were offered an opportunity to contribute in a way that was commensurate with their mobilization on behalf of the objectives of the state.[32] At the same time, economic circumstances also shaped women's position in the construction of the Japanese middle class, through their ability to consume and by facilitating a focus on family rather than just the family economy. It was through confirmation of their domestic role that women were the key to the reproduction of the middle class.

But if this was the identity of Japan's new middle class, to what extent was its composition the natural evolution of preexisting social groups, particularly of the one increasingly referred to as the "old" middle class? The evolving discourse on the new middle class in the early twentieth century argued that it needed to combine the best characteristics of all the pre-restoration status groups, thereby removing it from close identification with any single status group of the early modern period. However, this assumption that the new middle class was a product of social fusion raises further questions about the extent to which preexisting groups in society, even if not middle class in name or identity, laid the foundations for its emergence. That the former ruling class, the samurai at the apex of the Tokugawa structure, played a key role in the transitional decades is indisputable. Unsurprisingly in view of their former leadership status and relatively high levels of education, it was they who took the lion's share of most professional occupations up to the turn of the century, as well as government employment. The cachet of former warrior status had declined by the early twentieth century, however, and modern business as well as the bureaucracy was increasingly employing the beneficiaries of the new education system and economic change. We know much less, however, about the commercial classes engaged in traditional production and retail, mostly through small family businesses, and the richer farmers. They are the subject of the next section.

31. Tipton, "How to Manage a Household."
32. See, for example, Sheldon Garon, *Molding Japanese Minds: The State in Everyday Life* (Princeton, NJ: Princeton University Press, 1998).

New Business Elites and the Old Commercial Classes

While the new middle class of the twentieth century was powerfully identified with education and meritocracy and the white-collar and professional workers of the public sector, it also included a new cohort of educated professional managers and administrators in business and commerce who shared the same educational background, cultural interests, and societal aspirations. This modern economic elite, however, remained throughout the prewar period very small in comparison with its counterpart in more traditional forms of economic activity, what had come to be seen as the old middle class. Here the distinction that can be drawn between the Japanese equivalent of the *Wirtschaftbürgertum* and the *Bildungsbürgertum* was a stark one. Many of those engaged in traditional commercial pursuits had limited contact with new influences, practices, and goods. The ways in which they located themselves in society remained strongly influenced by older concepts and ways of doing things. We therefore need a more nuanced understanding of the role of business and commerce in becoming middle class.

The social origins of modern businessmen in late nineteenth-century Japan have been much debated. Although decades old, these debates have been in many respects inconclusive, and the search for political, economic, and social links between old and new business regimes in nineteenth-century Japan is ongoing.[33] Recent work has underlined the diverse social origins of post-restoration commercial actors, demonstrating that a range of social groups contributed to post-restoration business prosperity. The rural industrialization process that occurred in Japan from the eighteenth century had produced across the nation myriad small businesses in production and retailing catering to local niche markets and a diversity of tastes, many of which survived and prospered in the second half of the nineteenth century. The Hiromi fertilizer business founded near Osaka in the early 1800s, for example, has been cited as an example of how traditional forces banded together in exclusive and continuing trading relationships to withstand the rise of more modern companies.[34] Small and

33. The classics of these debates include J. Hirschmeier, *The Origins of Entrepreneurship in Meiji Japan* (Cambridge, MA: Harvard University Press, 1964); K. Yamamura, *A Study of Samurai Income and Entrepreneurship* (Cambridge, MA: Harvard University Press, 1974); and J. Hirschmeier and T. Yui, *The Development of Japanese Business, 1600–1973* (London: Allen and Unwin, 1975).

34. Satoru Nakanishi, "Vertical Integration and Commercial Accumulation in the Management of a Merchant Business," *Japanese Research on Business History* 23 (2006): 11–33. See also

medium businesses remained conspicuously important in Japan through the twentieth century, but despite their categorization as "old" middle class, they were also part of the "new" economy. Small became big, and old became new. At the other end of the scale, by the early twentieth century many of Japan's richest families, of both samurai and non-samurai origins, were engaged in business, and this "upper bourgeoisie," as it were, appears to have shared with its European counterparts a number of common features, including a high rate of self-recruitment and the importance of family background.[35]

But this diversity of origins cannot be mapped neatly onto the pre-restoration social hierarchy. The "new" and "old" middle class dichotomy may be helpful in understanding the twentieth century, but it is less so when applied to the transitional decades. The Tokugawa period witnessed the emergence of socio-economic groups who transcended the formal status boundaries and could be seen as potentially middle class, most of them associated with rural and local interests. Rich farmers (*gōnō*) often served as village leaders after the restoration, representing local interests and investing in local businesses. One Meiji period journalist and intellectual, Tokutomi Sohō, identified the *gōnō* as the locus of the values of the middle class, equating them to the English gentry, before later criticizing them for decadence.[36] Some regions of Japan saw the emergence of country samurai (*gōshi*), who took the part of local leaders, to some extent bridging the formal gap between samurai and farmer. Some dictionaries translate *gōshi* as "squire." These groups were distinct from any urban bourgeoisie, but given that in the late nineteenth century some 70 percent of Japan's population still resided in rural areas and relied partly or wholly on land cultivation, the rural dimension of any emergent middle class cannot be ignored. Recent scholarship on the *meibōka*, a term often translated as "local notables," has shown the importance of village headmen, merchants, and rich farmers who took local leadership roles from the eighteenth century onward. While assets and hereditary leadership roles were important for their activities, they were also characterized by a concern for the public interest. Before the restoration, *meibōka* were key actors in the provision of local public goods, and afterward

Kanji Ishii and Satoru Nakanishi, *Sangyōka to Shōka Keiei* [Industrialization and the management of merchant houses] (Nagoya: Nagoya University Press, 2006).

35. Nakaoka, "Making of Modern Riches."

36. Earl H. Kinmonth, *The Self Made Man in Meiji Japanese Thought* (Berkeley: University of California Press, 1981), 106–110. For the *gōnō*, see Edward Pratt, *Japan's Protoindustrial Elite: The Economic Foundations of the Gōnō* (Cambridge, MA: Harvard University Press, 1999).

they were major players in supporting and developing local economies.[37] A number of historians have highlighted the role of regional society in shaping the whole pattern of Japan's modern development, and the locality, including the middle class in that locality, is now firmly integrated into any analysis of late nineteenth-century social and economic change.[38] What frames the emergence of the "new" middle class groups in the early twentieth century, however, is that increased information flows, in conjunction with universal primary education, became ever more important in shaping social norms. In the process, discourse was characterized by a movement away from the strictly local in the direction of the national, and discourse relating to the middle class and its lifestyle was no exception to this rule. As noted earlier, consumption was at the heart of the image of modern national life associated with Japanese middle-class identity, and the consumption patterns of Japan's "middling" population will be considered in the final section.

Consumption in the Making of the Middle Class

"By the interwar years," Penelope Francks states, "household consumer goods were becoming a key element in defining the respectable, modern, middle class," and Sand's work shows how these goods were in large part focused on the home, in line with the emphasis on the new modern household as the foundation of

37. See, for example, Masayuki Tanimoto, "Capital Accumulation and the Local Economy: Brewers and Local Notables," in *The Role of Tradition in Japan's Industrialisation: Another Path to Industrialisation*, ed. Masayuki Tanimoto (Oxford: Oxford University Press, 2006), 301–322; Masayuki Tanimoto, "Zairai Keizai Hattenron no Shatei: 'Zairai' 'Kindai' no Nigenron o Koete" [Perspectives on indigenous economic development: Beyond the dichotomy of "tradition" and "modernity"], in *Nihon Shigaku no Furontia: Rekishi no Jikū o Toinaosu* [Frontiers in the study of Japanese history: Questioning time and space in history], ed. Ken'ichirō Aratake, Mitsuo Kinoshita, and Mitsutoshi Ōta (Tokyo: Hōsei University Press, 2015), 73–110.

38. See, for example, Masayuki Tanimoto and Takeshi Abe, "Kigyō Bokkō to Kindai Keiei, Zairai Keiei" [Enterprise boom and modern management, traditional management], in *Nihon Keiei Shi* [History of management in Japan], vol. 2: *Keiei Kakushin to Kōgyōka* [Management renovation and industrialization], ed. Matao Miyamoto and Takeshi Abe (Tokyo: Iwanami, 1995), 91–138; Naofumi Nakamura, *Chihō kara no Sangyō Kakumei: Nihon ni okeru Kigyō Bokkō to Gendōryoku* [An industrial revolution from the regions: The driving force of the enterprise boom in Japan] (Nagoya: Nagoya University Press, 2010); Masayuki Tanimoto and R. Bin Wong, eds., *Public Goods Provision in the Early Modern Economy. Comparative Perspectives from Japan, China, and Europe* (Berkeley: University of California Press, 2019), chapters 2–4.

national life.[39] The connection between patterns of consumption and political or social status was not, of course, new or in any way unique to Japan, but the way in which premodern patterns of consumption evolved had major implications for the consumption practices of the twentieth-century Japanese middle class.

The hereditary, ascribed status system of early modern Japan was paralleled by detailed sumptuary regulations prescribing the forms of consumption deemed appropriate for each social group. Over the course of time, however, it became increasingly difficult to maintain such limitations on consumption, and significant disparities emerged between wealth, formal status, and consumption patterns. The "alternate attendance" system (*sankin kōtai*) located much of the country's ruling class in Edo (present day Tokyo), concentrating much of the demand for goods and services in a small geographical area. Edo, along with the two other major cities of Osaka and Kyoto, spearheaded a growth in urban consumption that spread to the many provincial cities and towns across the Japanese islands.[40] Many of the goods purchased by urban residents were supplied by regions beyond the city limits, stimulating the growth of market-oriented production and exchange over an ever-wider area. Prosperous merchants and artisans were able to make purchases well outside the traditionally prescribed parameters.

In the process of rural industrialization stimulated by this growing market-based demand, the production of many goods shifted to the countryside to take advantage of lower labor costs and farmers' ability to combine part-time manufacturing production with the demands of wet-rice agriculture. To what extent this rural industrialization was equivalent to any kind of proto-industrialization in Europe continues to be debated, but all the evidence suggests that consumption levels in rural areas also rose considerably. While there were many who did not necessarily benefit from these changing circumstances, it is clear that the growth in rural consumption was not restricted just to a wealthy elite. There is evidence of some kind of "industrious revolution" in eighteenth- and early nineteenth-century Japan, in which major changes in time allocation facilitated

39. Penelope Francks, *The Japanese Consumer: An Alternative Economic History of Modern Japan* (Cambridge: Cambridge University Press, 2009), 135–136; Sand, *House and Home in Modern Japan*.

40. Much of this overview draws on Francks, *Japanese Consumer*, chapters 2 and 3. For early modern Osaka, see James L. McClain and Osamu Wakita, eds., *Osaka: The Merchants' Capital of Early Modern Japan* (Ithaca, NY: Cornell University Press, 1999).

the purchase of goods through the market in a way analogous to that identified by Jan de Vries in the case of Europe.[41] The term "consumer revolution" has not really been applied to Japan in the early modern period, but consumption there was, in many forms, and on a very large scale. With it came greater potential for social stratification. Gradations within the status groups were often shifted or modified by income availability, and hence the ability to consume. Traditional elites might find that those who had conventionally been their social inferiors now had the ability to consume goods that they themselves had regarded as their prerogative. The scale of market-based consumption of individual families in the provinces was often extensive.[42]

Might this increasing consumption, then, be associated with anything approximating a middle class? Clearly, many urban artisans and merchants who were equivalent to some kind of bourgeoisie at the start of the long nineteenth century could engage in new and opulent forms of consumption that could be increasingly identified with some kind of bourgeois lifestyle. As noted earlier, the economic changes also produced new candidate groups for the appellation of middle class, who also enjoyed consumer lifestyles analogous to what might be expected of the middling groups within society. However, the Japanese case raises one very particular issue regarding consumption as part of middle-class identity. Because Japan's international exchanges had been severely limited since the mid-seventeenth century, patterns of consumption were largely based on domestically evolved goods and services. Exposure to most Western consumer goods and practices was relatively rare, even at the very highest levels of society.[43] Increased consumption in the transitional decades therefore took place

41. See Osamu Saito, "An Industrious Revolution in an East Asian Market Economy?," *Australian Economic History Review* 50, no. 3 (2010): 240–261; Jan de Vries, "The Industrious Peasant in East and West: Markets, Technology and Family Structure in Japanese and Western European Agriculture," *Australian Economic History Review* 51, no. 2 (2011): 107–119.

42. See, for example, Satoru Nakanishi and Tomoko Futaya, "Japanese Modernisation and the Changing Everyday Life of the Consumer: Evidence from Household Accounts," in *The Historical Consumer: Consumption and Everyday Life in Japan*, ed. Penelope Francks and Janet Hunter (Basingstoke: Palgrave, 2012), 107–126; Satoru Nakanishi, "Bunmei Kaika to Minshū Seikatsu" [Civilization and enlightenment and people's daily lives], in *Nihon Keizaishi*, vol. 1: *Bakumatsu Ishinki* [Economic history of Japan, vol. 1: Bakumatsu and Restoration Period], ed. Kanji Ishii, Haruhito Takeda, and Akira Hara (Tokyo: University of Tokyo Press, 2000), 217–281.

43. There is now agreement that Japan's interaction with other countries during the "seclusion" period was significantly greater than originally thought, but the extent to which exposure to foreign goods and practices permeated beyond a small minority remained minimal.

in the context of what were later termed "traditional" or "Japanese" goods and services, in contrast to the "Western," or "modern," goods associated with Japan's opening up to external trade. Through to at least the 1890s, consumption of "traditional" goods was the major part of consumption growth, and their production was the main driver of economic growth. Even after that, the lifestyles of most Japanese changed only slowly.

This parallel existence of indigenous and imported patterns of consumption complicates any consideration of consumption as integral to middle-class identity. It raises questions about whether it is possible to identify universal ideas and practices that supported the rise of a global middle class, and to ask about the ways in which non-Western middle classes modified Western ideas and practices and merged them with indigenous practices. Clearly, in Japan the emergence of an identifiable middle class in the years from the First World War was associated with imported (mostly Western) influences, but this was primarily true only of the "new" middle class, and only up to a certain point. Particularly in rural areas, housing continued to conform to older practices, and urban middle-class homes manifested a hybridity that was seen to achieve a desired modern rationality while retaining the best of Japanese tradition. Food consumption was still largely based around rice and its accompaniments, but there was more of it, and it was better. Women in particular continued to wear traditional forms of dress rather than Western ones into the 1940s and 1950s. Department stores took on a notably Japanese twist that persists to this day.[44] Many scholars have used the word "double life" (*nijū seikatsu*) to refer to the way in which imported and indigenous elements coexisted in the lives of most Japanese through much of the twentieth century. If even the new middle class offered strong evidence of hybridity when it came to consumption, how much more did the old middle class, whose activities and lifestyles could be more easily traced back to earlier generations.

Conclusion

To what extent, then, was this emerging middle class in Japan global in its construction and outlook? Certainly Japan had close links with European countries in the late nineteenth century, welcoming a shared identity as an "old" nation. The influence of the United States was also strong, and the international

44. See, for example, Louise Young, "Marketing the Modern," *International Labor and Working Class History* 55 (1999): 52–70.

interactions of the bourgeoisie and the new middle class went well beyond Europe. At the same time, Japan, and perhaps especially its new elites and middle class, distanced itself from other Asian countries, concerned that China and Korea, for example, were failing to adapt to the new global realities of Western domination, hence rendering Japan itself vulnerable. In that context, the Japanese middle class and elites saw a degree of Western emulation as the key to survival. The construction of the Japanese middle class thus reflected some of the Western ideas that had increasingly entered Japan from the 1860s, and an increasing number of the Japanese elite were able to travel abroad and see for themselves manifestations of the lifestyles of the upper and middle classes elsewhere. Translations of Western texts on self-help and advancement, including Samuel Smiles's *Self Help*, were enormously influential on the thinking of many intellectuals, although there was something of a backlash against imported views in the 1890s.[45] The influence of Western ideas of bourgeois lifestyles and identities certainly mattered, but they were worked out in a particular Japanese context, and continuities in terms of lifestyles and consumption patterns remained conspicuous. Learning from the West did not mean abandoning Japanese materialist values or traditional attitudes but, rather, trying to define them more clearly in an Asian context and adopting a pragmatic and eclectic approach to the introduction of Western institutions, Western techniques, and Western lifestyles. The uncertainties caused by rapid change promoted the search for a middle-class-based national identity that embraced the reassertion of an often "created" tradition. In this context, Japan's middle class, as Jones comments, shared certain values with its counterparts in other countries, including a commitment to moral living, employment of scientific knowledge within daily life, and educational achievement based on merit, but it was also distinctive in the extent to which that quest for educational achievement was based on the family.[46]

The country's emulation of the West was viewed externally as relatively successful, and Japan was perceived as advancing up the ladder of civilization. By the early twentieth century, the middle classes elsewhere could expect to find a degree of common ground with their counterparts in Japan. Contemporaries in Britain and the United States welcomed evidence of the parallel growth of capitalism and democracy that would later be lauded by modernization

45. Kinmonth notes that we cannot assume that the Japanese translation of Samuel Smiles's book was identical in nuancing or interpretation to the Western original (*Self Made Man*, 330).

46. Jones, *Children as Treasures*, 16.

theorists. At the same time, however, a sense of otherness persisted. Racial stereotypes often trumped the potential for shared global values favored by Japan's capitalist elite and much of the still-small middle class, and in Japan itself the emergence of the middle class was in large part the outcome of shared ideas on the need to retain Japanese autonomy in a globalizing world and to make Japan "modern" as part of that objective.[47]

As elsewhere, the emergence of the Japanese middle class in the long nineteenth century was closely tied to global links of commerce and communication and to the international exchange of goods and norms. That its evolution was in substantial part the consequence of the growing global influence of the West is indisputable, although it was also strongly shaped by Asian connections. However, Japan's avoidance of Western colonization meant that Western values were never imposed on Japan by outsiders, although they were to some extent diffused by the state. Up until World War I, and in some cases even later, the daily lives of many Japanese remained largely untouched by knowledge of Western customs and practices. The consequence was the existence of a fragmented middle class characterized by unresolved tensions between transnational bourgeois values, indigenous traditions, and commitment to the national challenges posed by global power politics and new-found imperialist status. When in the 1930s a combination of global and national economic problems put the interests of the middle class increasingly at odds with those of other groups in society, these tensions allowed Japan's new middle class to be drawn into support of new and more dangerous state objectives.

47. In commercial ethics, for example, the Japanese were considered to be at the bottom of the global hierarchy, "below even the Chinese" (see Janet Hunter, *"Deficient in Commercial Morality?" Japan in Global Debates on Business Ethics in the Late 19th–Early 20th Centuries* (Basingstoke: Palgrave, 2016).

9

The Semiperipheral Hand

MIDDLE-CLASS SERVICE PROFESSIONALS
OF IMPERIAL CAPITALISM

Kris Manjapra

THIS CHAPTER CONSIDERS an important fraction of the global bourgeoisie
that developed as service providers in an emerging global regime of imperial
capitalism, and it examines the sociology of knowledge production associated
with this substratum of the emerging middle class. By the late eighteenth
century, a new racial and imperial phase of global capitalism flourished with the
rise of Liberalism. It operated through the supposed working of the invisible
hand and discourses of free markets and abolition. As scholars have recently
argued, this phase of capitalism depended upon the simultaneous integration
of different modes of accumulation: the continuous forcible accumulation of
life and resources from parts of the earth, and levels of society, inhabited by racialized subjects (primitive accumulation); the skilled and increasingly highly
technologized combination of those inputs in metropolitan centers (capitalist
accumulation); and huge outlays of financial and knowledgeable services to co-
ordinate the logistics and distribution networks of the emerging world
system.[1]

By the late eighteenth century, an unprecedented dependence on information
characterized this emergent phase in global capitalism's life.[2] As imperial

1. Kalyan Sanyal, *Rethinking Capitalist Development* (New Delhi: Routledge, 2014).
2. C. A. Bayly, *Empire and Information* (Cambridge: Cambridge University Press, 1996).

capitalism came into full bloom, it was a planetary military-fiscal-scientific-agricultural-industrial complex and required vast inputs of commodified and exchangeable knowledge in order to organize, supervise, and *manage* the global economic order.

In this era, a management revolution was taking place within empire. It relied on gentlemanly capital, which was anchored in imperial metropolitan centers, and on managerial and information capital that maintained webs of connection and communication between metropolitan centers and the imperial peripheries. This connective tissue was spun by the semiperipheral hand. If the world system was marked by an unprecedented acceleration of communication, exchange, and circulation in the nineteenth century, then the semiperipheral hand played the functional role making goods, labor, ideas, and services move faster—faster accumulation of land and labor products, faster ships and distribution technologies, faster transfers of credit, faster transfers of information.

Imperial capitalism relied on the intense investment in industrial mining and industrial agriculture and on a global division of labor to acquire, distribute, and process these primary inputs. Cash crops from colonial peripheries, especially sugar and cotton, supplied the fundamental calorific and clothing needs of the crowds of laborers working in imperial metropolitan factories in places such as Liverpool, Manchester, and London. And, as Sidney Mintz famously described, these same cash crops were the most important primary inputs for the origins of industrial production itself.[3] Cotton spinning, sugar refining, and the processing of ores supplied the lifeblood of the Industrial Revolution. Imperial capitalism depended on vast frontiers of primitive accumulation, whether in the coal and iron belts of northern England or across the vast plantation frontiers of the Caribbean, the American South and West, and the Indian Ocean Rim. With roots in the fifteenth century, the great expansion and consolidation of the imperial capitalist system took place from the late eighteenth century onward—what Sven Beckert, drawing on the work of Eric Williams and Sidney Mintz, terms the transformation from "war capitalism" to "industrial capitalism" around the 1780s.[4]

This economic transformation was dependent on new management and knowledge services. The imperial capitalist complex that engulfed the earth after

3. Sidney Mintz, *Sweetness and Power: The Place of Sugar in Modern History* (New York: Viking, 1985).

4. Sven Beckert, *Empire of Cotton* (New York: Knopf, 2014), 220.

the Haitian Revolution of 1791 depended on a globally mobile echelon of service professionals. Actuarial sciences, accounting sciences, legal services,
intelligence services, statistical services, surveying services, utilities services,
operations and logistics services, engineering services, and various other ancil-
lary services of colonial capitalist governmentality all came of age at the very
time when free markets were supposedly rising triumphant. This essay is concerned with the new circulating managerial manpower that emerged in this era,
because it constituted an important fraction of the emerging nineteenth-century
global middle classes.

My discussion draws, in parts, on Immanuel Wallerstein's schematic conception of three geopolitical divisions of world capitalism—core, semiperiphery, and
periphery. From Wallerstein's original definition, "core areas" are "economically
advanced" places where "industries [are] born"; "peripheries" are economically
underdeveloped areas where "forced labor (slavery and coerced cash-crop
labor)" is exploited; and "semiperipheries" are "an in between form . . . and
[do] not become the total satellites into which peripheral areas develop."[5] These
semiperipheries are marked by the "complexity of economic activities, strength
of the state machinery, cultural integrity, etc." More than a mere residual category, the semiperiphery plays a systematic role in the world economy, as
Wallerstein notes:

> The semiperiphery is a necessary structural element in a world-economy.
> These areas play a role parallel to that played by middle trading groups in an
> empire. They are collection points of vital skills that are often politically
> unpopular. These middle areas (like middle groups in an empire) partially
> deflect the political pressures which groups primarily located in peripheral
> areas might otherwise direct against core-states.[6]

If the core regions comprise the areas of capital intensity, then the semiperipheries are areas of *skill intensity* and *knowledgeable resources*, rich in managerial, technical, and strategic services. Meanwhile, the peripheries of the earth
are the sites of primary accumulation and are forced to supply captive or disposable labor and ecological inputs.

Wallerstein's model emphasizes the geographic logic of these three substruc-
tures. Indeed, there was a very rough geographic organization of imperial

---

5. Immanuel Wallerstein, *The Modern World System*, vol. 1 (New York: Academic Press, 1974),
101–107.

6. Wallerstein, *Modern World System*, 349.

capitalist activity from the 1500s to 1900s, which saw the establishment of "cores" in the imperial cities and banking centers of Western Europe, "semiper-ipheries" in the principalities of Northern, Central, Southern and Eastern Europe, and "peripheries" in overseas colonies.

But geographic essentialism obscures our understanding of the complex function of the emerging global system. Scholars have long pointed out that core, semiperiphery, and periphery are best understood not as geographic *places* but rather as economic *functions*. Furthermore, these disparate functions were not only distributed across globe-straddling terrains but also tangled up in the very same locations. Aihwa Ong and Doreen Massey, for example, explore how the logics of gender, race, and colonialism help to orchestrate the interweaving of different functions of global capitalism in a single city or societal context.[7] Indeed, one might say the quintessential Dickensian plot, from *Oliver Twist* to *Great Expectations*, is spun from the friction between the three functional strata of core, semiperiphery, and periphery within a single city, as the lives of convicts, hawkers, clerks, lawyers, shopkeepers, bankers, and others are woven together. In my usage here, the term "semiperiphery" is not a geographic designator but a theoretically reconstructed concept that seeks to place the spotlight on forms of connectivity that stretched across the emerging accumulation centers, on the one hand, and extractive zones of the modern capitalist world economy, on the other.

Christof Dejung, David Motadel, and Jürgen Osterhammel, in their introduction to this volume, provide a valuable and multidimensional definition of the "global bourgeois" in sociological and cultural terms. And they observe that "at [the] core [of bourgeois middle classes] was the economic or entrepreneurial bourgeoisie . . . as well as the educated or professional bourgeoisie, comprising lawyers, judges, teachers, medical doctors, scholars, architects, apothecaries, engineers, master artisans, and others." In this chapter, I am interested in those "economic and entrepreneurial" and "educated or professional" middle classes particularly involved in circuits of distribution and communication across colonial divides. I propose that these groups may be thought of as "semiperipheral" in terms of their function. The semiperiphery, here, is not a place but a set of multisited functions, and those functions were historically provided by attorneys, mercenaries, army officers, surveyors, engineers, travel writers, Man

7. Aihwa Ong, "The Gender and Labor Politics of Postmodernity," *Annual Review of Anthropology* 20 (1991): 279–309; Doreen Massey, *Spatial Divisions of Labour* (London: Macmillan, 1984).

Fridays, secretaries, translators, and scientific advisors who helped produce and manage colonial frontiers of difference and helped create pathways of circulation and appropriation across those frontiers. These agents, who constituted a new and important fraction of the emerging global bourgeoisie in the eighteenth and nineteenth century, were enlisted by imperial states and by private enterprises to know, conquer, and integrate "the wastelands," both near and far, for the expansion of global capitalism.

Dale Tomich, in his important work *Through the Prism of Slavery*, insists that the domains of capitalist world economy—production, exchange, distribution, and consumption—must not be studied as reified, static, and separate arenas. Rather, these categories "may be understood as relations that presuppose, condition, and are formative of one another as distinct parts of a whole."[8] The interrelation of production, exchange, distribution, and consumption means that each of these moments is a condition and constitutive element of the others. Following on Tomich's fundamental observation and its implication for rethinking class stratification within such an interrelated, multisited, and dynamically expanding capitalist world economic system, I wish to draw attention here to that particular subset of middle-class professionals and experts who oversaw and directed the expanding *distribution* channels of finance, commodities, services, knowledge, and cultural norms across colonial divides. These functions of distribution were never separate from the realms of colonial production, exchange, and consumption, but intrinsic to and embedded within all of them. This chapter seeks a clearer picture of these semiperipheral middle classes as they contributed to the emergent connectivities of imperial capitalism.

A Management Revolution in Empire

During the shift from a mercantile order of exploitation to a global industrial order around the flexion point of the late eighteenth century, a key function of the imperial state was to subject colonial "peripheries" to imperial categories of control and management and to embed these subjugated domains within arteries of capitalist mobility. Imperial statecraft forcibly placed its colonies *in relation to* other colonies, ports, hinterlands, and metropolises around the world. The logic of measuring, routinizing, classifying, benchmarking, auditing, containerizing, and coordinating the transfer of labor power and commodities

8. Dale Tomich, *Through the Prism of Slavery: Labor, Capital, and World Economy* (Lanham, MD: Rowman and Littlefield, 2004), 44–48.

between distant colonial locations and across cultural and political borders was one of the imperial state's basic imperative.[9] Military practices, seaway engineering, railroad operations, canal construction, environmental sciences, ethnographic surveillance, and actuarial services were among the most important new sectors of the global economy. Drawing on the insight of Alfred Chandler, we might say that imperial states, by the eighteenth century, were not just an occupying and extracting force, but also a *vast managerial* force. Hence, imperial states called forth a new kind of manpower—the manpower of the scientific advisor and the middle manager.

In *The Visible Hand*, Alfred Chandler described the rise of professional management services, instead of free markets, as the defining characteristic of modern capitalism. He claimed that a "management revolution" occurred in the USA during the nineteenth century.[10] On his account, this management revolution occurred after the 1840s and was marked by the transition from personal to impersonal forms of commerce and by the expansion of utilities, reconnaissance, and civil engineering services. In the case of the USA, according to Chandler's classic argument, new economic operations emerged from the 1870s onward that allowed enterprises to "vertically integrate" vast amounts of knowledge and extend increased control over the production process.

I apply Chandler's argument to the subject of this chapter by pointing out that the archetype of the knowledge-rich enterprise, characterized by the combination of semiautonomous units, each with its own manager and hierarchy, first arose in the imperial joint-stock companies of the 1600s, such as the British East India Company (EIC) and Dutch East India Company (VOC)—a point that Chandler himself makes.[11] Indeed, as scholars such as Philip Stern and David Hancock have argued, the colonial "Company-State," as well as networks of imperial families, had long been involved in coordinating complex managerial tasks over global distances.[12] By the late eighteenth century, colonial joint-stock companies, especially the EIC and the VOC, became exponentially more dependent on middle managers as they embarked on new quasi-state projects

9. H. V. Bowen, *The Business of Empire: The East India Company and Imperial Britain, 1756–1833* (Cambridge: Cambridge University Press, 2006), 159.

10. Alfred Chandler, *The Visible Hand* (Cambridge, MA: Belknap Press, 1977).

11. Chandler, *Visible Hand*, 40, 41.

12. Philip Stern, *The Company-State* (Oxford: Oxford University Press, 2011); David Hancock, *Citizens of the World: London Merchants and the Integration of the British Atlantic Community, 1735–1785* (Cambridge: Cambridge University Press, 1995).

of tax collection, population resettlement, and opening of frontiers for industrial agriculture and mining. As this occurred, colonial statecraft became increasingly knowledge hungry and management intensive. In the British case, the East India College at Haileybury was established in 1809 to train professional bureaucrats for the empire, while the Institution of Civil Engineers emerged in 1818 and served to professionalize the technical knowhow long associated with the military's Royal Corps of Engineers.[13] Linda Colley notes that in the late eighteenth century, Scottish institutions were especially important for producing the ships' engineers, colonial administrators, and spies of the empire. The semiperipheral institutions of Scotland were "not England's peer," Colley notes, but "its superior" in the development of expertise.[14] Andrew MacKillop's work specifically explores the central contribution of Scottish expertise to the rise of the British Empire across Asia.[15] Thus, the iconic forms of the middle manager and scientific adviser first developed not in American big businesses of the 1870s but in the colonial capitalist enterprises of the preceding centuries, and especially in the colonial lakes of the Caribbean Sea and the Indian Ocean.

This emerging global cohort of service providers and managers operated across national and imperial boundaries. These managers were hired to strategically transfer knowledge between imperial states, for example, between Spanish and Dutch, British, and American or between French and Portuguese colonies. These managers worked across different state systems in order to carry out the replicative logic of imperial capitalism, which was the drive toward modular reproduction, standardization, routinization, benchmarking, and the commodification of land, labor, and services.

So, the function of the semiperipheral hand, embodied in imperial middle management, was to make previously incommensurable terrains and cultures increasing translatable, and increasingly exchangeable, one for the other. Service providers were hired to help convert autonomous and incongruous territories into integrated, replicating, exploitable capitalist spaces. The project itself was replete with failure, since juxtapositions, contestations, rebellions, and

---

13. A. R. Buchanan, "The Diaspora of British Engineering," *Technology and Culture* 27 (1986): 501–524.

14. Linda Colley, *Britons* (New Haven, CT: Yale University Press, 1992), 124, 132.

15. Andrew Mackillop, "A Union of Empire? Scotland, the English East India Company and the British Union," in *The Union of 1707: New Dimensions*, ed. Stewart J. Brown and Christopher A. Whatley (Edinburgh: Edinburgh University Press, 2008), 116–134.

"polyrhythms" inevitably resulted.[16] But, despite the ongoing unevenness and conflicts, the semiperipheral hand was bent on making the earth flat.

Imperial knowledge workers employed post-Enlightenment universalist scientific practice, applying universalistic categories and methods to the production of records on human and animal life, and ecological matter, in the effort to dominate and manage them.[17] Following Partha Chatterjee and Frederick Cooper, I use "post-Enlightenment" to denote a shift in knowledge production that began around the turn of the nineteenth century, through which theoretical innovations of the Enlightenment came to be contested and elaborated in sociological and political practices.[18] Post-Enlightenment keywords, such as "bourgeois equality," "liberalism," "national history," "imperialism," "improvement," "modernity," and "culture" all represent vexed imperialist engagements with the conceptual legacy of selfhood, nation-statehood, and scientific universality that developed during the Enlightenment period, circa 1650–1815. This essay is concerned with that emerging multiethnic and international class of professionals that wielded methods of post-Enlightenment sciences through the skein of expanding empires.

Practices of the Semiperipheral Hand

One of the boldest expressions of post-Enlightenment science and imperial praxis came at the cusp of the nineteenth century with Napoleon Bonaparte's Egypt expedition of 1798–1801. As an army commander during the French Revolution, Napoleon propelled his Egyptian campaign with the ethos of spreading universal science and rationality to the "Orient." Napoleon summoned around 170 French mineralogists, engineers, philologists, linguists, biologists, and other scholars to participate in his invasion of Egypt. The Napoleonic forces in Egypt and Syria had the largest complement of scientists and savants ever deployed in a European military campaign. Napoleon intended to conquer by armed might and by the muscularity of universalist knowledge. As Edward Said observed, "[Napoleon's] idea was to build a sort of living archive for the

16. On polyrhythm, see Antonio Benitz-Rojo, *The Repeating Island: The Caribbean and the Postmodern Perspective* (Durham, NC: Duke, 1992).

17. Thomas Metcalf, *Imperial Connections* (Berkeley: University of California Press, 2007), 10–15.

18. On the post-Enlightenment, see Partha Chatterjee, "Transferring a Political Theory," *Economic and Political Weekly* 21 (1986): 120–128; and Frederick Cooper, *Colonialism in Question: Theory, Knowledge, History* (Berkeley: University of California Press, 2005), 4.

expedition" that would help lay the groundwork for French domination of the whole "Orient" and upstage the British imperial competitor. [19]

Scores of knowledge French knowledge professionals collected and categorized zoological, ethnographic, architectural, and literary artifacts, and these were collated and published in twenty-three enormous volumes between 1809 and 1828, in the encyclopedic *Description de l'Égypte*. The massive scale of such weaponized knowledge production was matched by the "information empire" of the British in India around this same time.[20] And the deployment of post-Enlightenment science also targeted the Caribbean and South America in the early nineteenth century. For example, the young Alexander von Humboldt had initially hoped to join Napoleon's Egyptian expedition but was prevented from doing so by the British naval blockade. He eventually decided to make his own name as a traveling savant and obtained an authorization from the king of Spain to undertake a significant scientific survey of the Spanish Caribbean and Americas, from Cuba to Mexico.[21]

We will return to Humboldt in the Americas later, but for now, let us observe that the Indian Ocean zone and the circum-Caribbean arena were the two main overseas theaters for the European imperial deployment of post-Enlightenment science at the turn of the nineteenth century. Across these interregional nexuses, the semiperipheral hand aided the surveillance, categorization, confiscation, occupation, and transformation of land and the forcible resettlement of human populations and plant biota on an unprecedented scale.

But long before the arrival of knowledge-hungry imperialism in the context of the Enlightenment, European beneficiaries of the transatlantic slave trade, from the late 1400s onward, ravenously produced and devoured huge amounts of racialized, colonizing, and commodifying knowledge about the wider world. Slave ships carried not just slavers and the enslaved but also secretaries, ship surgeons, traders, soldiers, and preachers.[22] By the seventeenth century, ethnographic reports about West Africa were often published by those surgeons, army officers, and pastors, and their writings helped legitimate the ravages of kidnapping and torture that transformed African persons into slave chattel.

19. Edward Said, *Orientalism* (New York: Pantheon Books, 1978), 84.

20. Bayly, *Empire and Information*.

21. Myron Echenberg, *Humboldt's Mexico: In the Footsteps of the Illustrious German Scientific Traveller* (Montreal: McGill University Press, 2017), xxxvii.

22. S. P. L'honoré Naber, ed., *Reisebeschreibungen von Deutschen Beamten und Kriegsleuten im Dienst der Niederländischen West- und Ost-Indischen Kompagnien 1602–1797* (Haag: Martinus Nijhoff, 1930).

Racialized travel accounts about the "blacks" and "negroes" of West African society were translated, reproduced, and circulated across Europe, and helped to discursively and falsely transform persons into expendable cargo in the white imperial mind.[23]

In the decades of Abolition from the 1790s to the 1840s, which culminated in the demise of slavery in the British Empire, an advancing cotton frontier pushed inland along the Mississippi and westward into the Indian country of Alabama and Oklahoma. Propelled by the cotton gin and the cruelty of slavery, the American South emerged across the northern littoral of the Caribbean Sea. Meanwhile, sugar and coffee frontiers opened up across Trinidad, Guyana, Cuba, and Brazil in the same period and also depended on slavery in some cases and on indentured labor in others. Eventually, from the 1880s onward, a frontier of banana cultivation arose across the Caribbean and Central America—across Honduras, Costa Rica, and Jamaica—under the pressure of Boston and New York financial capital. Whether it was cotton in the north, sugar in the middle, or bananas in the south, plantation frontiers expanded across the circum-Caribbean region during the nineteenth century. This expansion called forth biopolitical transformations that involved the transfer of whole populations of workers and vast amounts of biota and the completion of monumental logistics projects: for example, major railroad expansion beginning in the 1840s, the damming of the Mississippi River in 1881, and the Panama Canal in 1913.

The engineering of nature was always a counterpoint to the engineering of machines and travel technologies. An extensive triangular transfer and circulation of biota took place among imperial research gardens, such as Kew in London, and the two main nineteenth-century plantation zones of the earth (the Caribbean Sea and the Indian Ocean) and locales of European settler colonialism in southern Africa and Asia Pacific.[24] Over the course of the eighteenth and nineteenth century, imperial capitalism pursued the commodification and engineering of plant life.

Take the example of the expanding cotton frontier along the northern Caribbean. The amount of cotton grown in the United States greatly expanded as a result of the Louisiana Purchase. But the quality of American cotton was dependent on the variety of seeds planted. Desirable qualities, such as pest resistance, high crop yield, and silky fiber were all dependent on the selection of

23. For example, Willem Bosman's famous *A New and Accurate Description of the Coast of Guinea* (London: James Knapton, 1704).

24. Richard Drayton, *Nature's Government* (New Haven, CT: Yale University Press, 2000).

cotton seed, and American planters questioned how to engineer the best cultivars. Knowledge was at the crux of the expanding industrial agricultural regime.

As scholars have shown, the origins of the American "cotton kingdom" can be traced to the West Indies, where cotton had long been cultivated for the world market. It was the mobility of planters, attorneys, managers, and enslaved people between places such as Antigua and Haiti, on one hand, and Louisiana and the Mississippi Delta, on the other, that stimulated the improvement of American cotton at the turn of the nineteenth century. But cotton scientists also sought knowledge from far-distant places. For example, Frank Levett had long been involved in the cotton mart of Izmir, Anatolia, and was purportedly the first to start growing a new kind of cotton seed in Georgia known as Sea Island cotton, which was prized for its silky fibers.[25] The transfer of Egyptian and Anatolian cotton seeds helped to bring about America's cotton boom.[26] With the propagation of new varietals of cotton around the 1790s, the introduction of Whitney's cotton gin, and the forcible confiscation and occupation of Native American lands across the Southwest in the early 1800s, the American South became the iconic world center for cotton production up until the Civil War.[27]

By the 1820s, when the plantation frontier opened up in India, the colonial government developed plans to make India a producer of the cotton cash crop based on the American model. By the early 1840s, East India Company officials made efforts to transfer an American varietal of cotton seed, known as New Orleans seed, to the Bombay Presidency in order to stimulate industrial production. The company also tried to cultivate modern plantation techniques, hiring ten American planters to set up experimental farms in India. These knowledgeable service providers spent two years in India, in places such as Bombay, Dharwar, and Dhaka, training aspiring planters in India in the American Method.[28]

The transfer of biota, and the modeling of best practices for agricultural production in one colonial periphery or another, was a pursuit in genetic engineering, biopolitical management, and intellectual property. Similar examples

25. Beckert, *Empire of Cotton*, 102.

26. Delmar Hayter, "Expanding the Cotton Kingdom," *Agricultural History* 62 (1998): 226.

27. Walter Johnson, *River of Dark Dreams* (Cambridge, MA: Belknap Press, 2013), 30.

28. K. L. Tuteja, "American Planters and the Cotton Improvement Programme in Bombay Presidency in the Nineteenth Century," *Indian Journal of American Studies* 28 (1998): 103–108; Tarasankar Bannerjee, "American Cotton Experiments in India and the American Civil War," *Journal of Indian History* 47 (1969): 425–432.

of colonial states recruiting scientific experts to help open up new plantation frontiers occurred throughout the nineteenth century. Andrew Zimmerman studied how, during the time of Reconstruction, Black American cotton experts from the Tuskegee Institute of Alabama were hired by German colonial officials to set up cotton farms in Togo.[29] During the same period, similar processes in the modular transfer of crop science and plant life took place between Cuba and Java.[30]

Cuba and Java became the two most important sugar-production economies in the world in the latter half of the nineteenth century. By the 1840s, as Ulbe Bosma and Jonathan Machado-Curry point out, the sugar industry was highly technologized, due especially to the advent of the steam-powered sugar mill. Engineers were needed to manage the technological revolution taking place on the plantations. The Dutch East India Company recruited large amounts of foreign engineering talent; for example, the largest contingent of foreign experts in Java in the 1840s was composed of Germans.[31] In Cuba, we also observe a similarly large reliance on foreign engineers for the sugar industry, as steam came to the cane fields in the same period. Meanwhile, agricultural scientists, such as Alvaro Reynoso, of Cuba, developed scientific standards for sowing, tilling, salting, and irrigating sugar cane, which were translated into Dutch and widely circulated as the template of "best practices" in Java.[32] So whether we speak of American cotton cultivation techniques being used in India, or Cuban techniques being employed for Javanese sugar, or Brazilian rubber being grown in Malaya, or similar kinds of transfers of expertise and biota that led to the expansion of tea, coffee, and cocoa, we observe how commodified, modular, knowledge science was circulating between the circum-Caribbean and Asia. The colonial capitalist system created a need for globe-entangling knowledge, which generated commodified and modular types of scientific and management services. These established the conditions of the possibility for the rise of an important fraction of the new global middle classes.

Indeed, if the circum-Caribbean was one major arena for the advancing frontiers of imperial capitalism in the nineteenth century, so too was the Indian

29. Andrew Zimmerman, *Alabama in Africa* (Princeton, NJ: Princeton University Press, 2010).

30. Ulbe Bosma and Jonathan Machado-Curry, "Two Islands, One Commodity: Cuba, Java, and the Global Sugar Trade (1790–1930)," *New West Indian Guide* 86 (2012): 237–262.

31. Ulbe Bosma, "Het Cultuurstelsel en zijn buitenlandse Ondernemers," *Tijdschrift voor Sociale en Economische Geschiedenis* 2 (2005): 2–28.

32. Bosma and Machado-Curry, "Two Islands, One Commodity," 245.

Ocean. British colonial capital pressed opium, sugar, and indigo production onto Bihar and Bengal from the 1820s onward. These cash crops were soon superseded by the onslaught of the tea and jute frontiers moving into Assam and Ceylon. In Java, we see the aggressive advance of the coffee and cocoa frontiers with the inauguration of the Cultivation System (Java) in the 1830s.[33] And, by the 1890s, came the rise of the rubber frontier in Malaya, just as the automobile industry in America and Europe began its ascent.[34] As in the Caribbean, these advancing Asian plantation frontiers were dependent on military force, the confiscation and occupation of lands, and the destruction of indigenous sovereignties. These projects also required intensive inputs of scientific knowledge by experts, consultants, and managers who claimed the ability to scientifically understand, represent, and manage "the wastelands." Plantation complexes developed not in isolation from each other but in interregional relation. Transfers of production models, techniques, life and labor power, and capital were in continuous circulation among centers of imperial capitalist production. And during the nineteenth century, middle managers and their colonial lords even envisioned a project of re-creating the Caribbean in Asia.[35]

Knowledgeable Services

The expansion of industrial agrarian frontiers also required new credit instruments and new agencies to manage the access to capital. It is well known that the actuarial sciences and the insurance industry were revolutionized in the eighteenth century. "Fire, life, and marine insurance emerged in their modern forms" during this period, notes Robin Pearson, and marine insurance, especially, was developed primarily thanks to the Atlantic slave trade.[36] Actuarial science and underwriting was professionalized and standardized, attaining "technical certainty" by the 1840s.[37]

33. R. E. Elson, *Village Java under the Cultivation System* (Sydney: Allen and Unwin, 1994), xix.

34. David Nonini, *British Colonial Rule and the Resistance of the Malay Peasantry* (New Haven, CT: Yale University Southeast Asian Studies, 1992), 68.

35. Meanwhile, Dutch planters imposed what they called West Indian–style coffee production on Java in the 1830s. Elson, *Village Java*, 67.

36. Ian Baucom, *Specters of the Atlantic* (Durham: Duke University Press, 2005).

37. Robin Pearson, "Towards an Historical Model of Services Innovation," *Economic History Review* 50 (1997): 235–256; W. D. Rubinstein, *Capitalism, Culture and Decline in Britain, 1750–1990* (London: Routledge, 1993).

Meanwhile, agency houses, financial institutions that had long been active in the Caribbean, began operating in India by the 1780s with the crackdown on private trading. Instead of EIC men-on-the-spot engaging in private and personal commerce in the Indian subcontinent, agency houses emerged as new corporate institutions through which company officials could invest private money and continue to skim wealth from the vibrant India trade. Agency houses were hubs of patronage and paternalism and provided another site for the emergence of a new fraction of the imperial middle classes. Young British men with some social capital but with limited opportunities for advancement often vied for entry-level positions in colonial agency houses, which offered the prospect of rapid class mobility. John Palmer was one such young imperial Briton in India, and he represents the heightened case of a general social phenomenon. Palmer, born in Calcutta to an army officer in the 1770s, entered the Royal Navy as a teenager. After his decommission from the navy due to redundancy, he failed to secure a cadetship with the East India Company. Fortunately, Palmer obtained a clerking position in one of the fifteen agency houses in Calcutta, and he soon rose to the position of partner in that firm. Leveraging his advantageous position in an extensive patronage network, he then started his own agency house, John Palmer & Company, and eventually became known as the "prince of merchants" in Calcutta by the 1820s. Palmer, like so many inexperienced, desperate, and redundant youth of the Old Regime, found his footing in the emerging New Order by mastering the gestures of the semiperipheral hand in the colonies.[38]

Agency houses, such as Palmer & Company, were normally composed of a small number of partners, an Indian commercial agent (the *bania*), and a large and multiethnic corps of clerks. That staff, composed of middle managers, was responsible for information collection. Agency houses produced a new set of management professionals, of both European and Asian origin, within empire.[39] Indian translators, informants, and clerks were hired to provide detailed information about village production and upcountry marts, especially in the context of the expanding indigo, rice, opium, tea, coffee, and sugar frontiers in

38. Anthony Webster, "An Early Global Business in a Colonial Context: The Strategies, Management, and Failure of John Palmer and Company of Calcutta, 1780–1830," *Enterprise and Society* 6 (2005): 98–133; Anthony Webster, *The Richest East Indian Merchant: The Life and Business of John Palmer of Calcutta, 1767–1836* (Woodbridge: Boydell Press, 2007), 25–27.

39. Christof Dejung, "Bridges to the East: European Merchants and Business Practices in India and China," in *Commerce and Culture, Nineteenth-Century Business Elites*, ed. Robert Lee (Farnham: Ashgate, 2011), 93–116.

which Palmer & Company held major interests. Meanwhile, the agency houses' attorneys managed trusts and wills, and other staff members managed shipping lines and the purchase of freightage. Agency houses in Calcutta even invested in Caribbean markets. For example, Gillanders, Arbuthnot & Company of Calcutta was one of the main companies to finance the shipment of "hill coolies," the first Indian indentured laborers, from the port of Calcutta to sugar estates in British Guyana in the 1830s.

Finance capital was the keystone of the advancing plantation frontiers, and the raison d'être of the agency house. But more important to the argument being made in this essay, finance capital was intensely hungry for knowledge and specialized managerial skills. It relied upon indigenous and commercial informants, upon scientific advisors, and upon the professional know-how of attorneys, accountants, and engineers. Here, in the very specific example of the agency house, we glimpse a major dynamic at work that determined the rise of a fraction of the global bourgeoisie: the recruitment of knowledge experts in order to service the needs of imperial capitalist enterprises as they transformed the "wastelands" into legible, calculable, and fungible productive zones for the financial outlook of imperial capitalism.

A revolution in British investment took place in the 1820s, after the defeat of Napoleon at Waterloo and the downfall of the Spanish American empire and the rise of Creole nationalisms. The Napoleonic and Bolivarian Wars, respectively, spelled the political, fiscal, and industrial ascent of nineteenth-century British world supremacy. As the Spanish Empire crumbled in Latin America under the pressure of the juntas, new opportunities for British investment in economies such as Mexico, Venezuela, and Argentina, opened up. For example, as Michael Costeloe shows, in the 1820s, large numbers of English petty investors—schoolteachers, pastors, bureaucrats, and policemen—bought into joint-stock companies involved in Mexico-based enterprise.[40] Costeloe makes the important point that the fall of the Spanish Empire and the rise of the Creole republics spurred a huge investment boom in Latin America and dominated by British capital. He also shows that these investments, made by thousands of amateur investors and not by a small number of investment tycoons, were highly reliant on the commodified knowledge services of outside experts.

As mentioned earlier, Alexander von Humboldt was inspired by the ideal of the enlightened Napoleonic savant in the service of empire. He traveled as

40. Michael Costeloe, *Bubbles and Bonanzas: British Investors and Investment in Mexico* (Lanham, MD: Lexington Books, 2011), xi.

an entrepreneurial scientist—and as a function of the semiperipheral hand—across the tangled interimperial arena of the circum-Caribbean in the early nineteenth century. The dozens of volumes he published on his travels to the Spanish-speaking Americas made him into one of empire's most iconic outside experts. Humboldt's "pure" scientific contribution certainly had consequences for imperial capitalist designs: he assessed mining prospects and provided forecasts on South American economic productivity.[41] Humboldt published on the ethnographic make-up of the societies he encountered. His writings were quickly translated into English and circulated widely in British society during the 1810s and 1820s. Costeloe informs us, for example, that British speculators relied on Humboldt's voluminous demonstration of scientific mastery over the landscapes, animal life, and political cultures of New Spain in planning their investment bonanza in Mexico.[42] By representing the "periphery" scientifically, the reproductions of Alexander von Humboldt's writings satiated the pangs of knowledge hunger among the British imperial speculating classes.

We might consider Humboldt as less of an icon and more of a heightened exemplar of a vast family relation of empire's scientific service providers that emerged in the early nineteenth century. In 1829, Humboldt would later undertake a reconnaissance expedition, sponsored by the Russian tsar, deep into Russia to the Eurasian Steppe and Central Asia. Humboldt became a patron of imperial scientific professionals, including the French botanist, Aimé Bonpland; the Swiss-American biologist, Louis Agassiz; and the German surveyors, Adolf, Hermann, and Robert Schlagintweit. These decades also saw famous imperial travels by Allan Cunningham through Australia, Alexander Cunningham through northern India, Alexander Burnes through Central Asia, George Everest across the Himalayas, and, of course, Charles Darwin to South America and the South Pacific. If imperial capitalism insisted on the conquest of territory, scientific travelers were advancing the complementary conquest of Enlightenment science, as they sought to measure, map, and, ultimately, control the hidden order inherent in material, botanical, and cultural systems around the world. And the institution of the university itself was being transformed at this very time. By the late eighteenth century, it had emerged increasingly as a body of researching scholars charged with producing knowledge that both served to prepare prospective terrains for imperial conquest and to manage and

41. Alexander von Humboldt, *Political Essay on the Kingdom of New Spain* (London: Longman, Hurst, Rees, Orme, and Brown, 1811).

42. Costeloe, *Bubbles and Bonanzas*, xiii.

contain the messy outcomes of conquest after the fact.[43] Knowledge and militarism were inextricably interwoven in modern liberal empire.

Mobility and Dispossession

As already mentioned, imperial capitalism required the forcible resettlements of peoples and depended on the expertise of ethnographers, port officials, doctors, scientists, and statisticians, all of whom envisioned human communities as moveable, removable, and exploitable populations. The 1840s saw the beginning of one of the greatest eras of human mobility in modern times. With the end of slavery in the British Caribbean, and the flight of black freed people away from the plantations and into the hinterlands, came a great demand for new sources of labor and a need for knowledgeable techniques of managing laborers on a population-wide level. Racial calculations were at play as colonial officials in the Caribbean discussed projects, first, to settle the hinterlands with white "industrious" peasants in order to restrain and contain black flight; and, second, to populate the abandoned plantations with cheap Indian and Chinese workers.

Colonial governments initially looked to Europe—namely, Ireland, Scotland, Portugal, and Germany—for white labor. The first experiments to bring "model" peasants from Germany into the countryside began in Jamaica and Brazil in the 1830s. In Jamaica, two German emigrants, Solomon Myer, a coffee planter, and Wilhelm Lemonius, a former militiaman of the British colonial army, collaborated on their plans to bring German peasants to the Jamaican hill country.[44] The hope was to eventually establish a white heartland secured against "indolent" black ex-slaves. The pursuit was organized by the Colonial Office in London and by the Jamaican Assembly.

The Jamaican government paid the cost for the sea voyage, made provisions for the immigrant townships, and granted land plots to the immigrants. The experiment of bringing white labor to Jamaica was writ large in Brazil, where the colonial state directed over two hundred thousand German and Swiss

43. Rainer Christoph Schwinges, ed., *Humboldt International: Der Export des deutschen Universitätsmodells im 19. und 20. Jahrhundert* (Basel: Schwabe, 2001); Tamson Pietsch, *Empire of Scholars: Universities, Networks and the British Academic World, 1850–1939* (Manchester: Manchester University Press, 2013; see also Andrew Zimmerman, *Anthropology and Antihumanism in Imperial Germany* (Chicago: University of Chicago Press, 2011).

44. Douglas Hall, "Bountied European Immigration with Special Reference to the German Settlement at Seaford Town up to 1850," *Jamaica Journal* 9 (1977): 2–9.

migrants to the southern Brazilian hinterlands over the course of the nineteenth century.[45] These were eugenic and biopolitical projects to claim the Caribbean hinterlands as white lands and required vast amounts of state intervention and managerial capital.

The transfer and organization of racialized Asian populations was taking
place on a global scale beginning at this same time. As new plantation frontiers
were being opened up across South Asia and Southeast Asia, forcibly displaced
people were channeled across the oceans to work on the old plantations of the
Caribbean and on new plantation sites across the Indian Ocean and the Pacific.
The British colonial administration expanded greatly after the 1850s, especially
in the aftermath of the 1857 rebellion. The Indian Civil Service, established in
1858, was manned mostly by white managers. The ICS aimed to administer the
diverse communities in India as "populations" and to control and register the
commodified populations sent outside of India as indentured laborers. Given
the almost 1.5 million persons who migrated out of India from the 1840s to 1860s
as indentured laborers, and the complaints about an emerging new system of
slavery, the colonial state decided to expand its bureaucratic oversight and to
invest greater managerial capital. In 1871, a new unit was created within the Department for Agriculture, Revenue and Commerce of the Government of
India specifically devoted to Indian labor emigration. Meanwhile the protector
of immigrants, a new middle-management position, was established in all British colonies to oversee the dealings of indentured laborers.[46]

The expansion of logistics networks also facilitated the expansion of imperial capitalism. Here, the role of scientists in India and the Caribbean is obvious. For example, the forestry expert, Dietrich Brandis, born in Bonn in 1824,
was hired by the British government in 1856. He served as superintendent of
the forest of Burma and was named the inaugural inspector of forests in India
in 1864. Inspired greatly by Alexander von Humboldt, Brandis provided clear
proposals and plans for the colonial state about how to manage the forestry

45. Reinhardt Wagner, *Deutsche als Ersatz für Sklaven* (Frankfurt: Vervuert, 1995); Gisela
Büttner Lermen, *Deutsche Auswanderinnen in Südbrasilien* (Heidelberg: Verlag Regionalkultur,
2006); Sebastian Conrad, *Globalisation and the Nation in Imperial Germany* (Cambridge: Cambridge University Press, 2010), 285; Beatrice Ziegler, *Schweizer statt Sklaven: Schweizerische
Auswanderer in den Kaffee-Plantagen von Sao-Paulo (1852–1866)* (Stuttgart: Steiner, 1985).

46. Martin Moir, "The Examiner's Office: The Emergence of an Administrative Elite in the
East India House (1804–1858)," in *India Office Library and Records Report for 1977* (London:
British Library, 1979), 25–42; Hugh Tinker, *A New System of Slavery* (London: Oxford Univer-
sity Press, 1974), 236–287.

resources of British India—a crucial question in the time of railroad construction.[47] While superintendent of Pegu forests, Brandis asserted the right of the colonial state to confiscate native lands and helped to promulgate the policy of Crown Prerogative.

We note the recurring theme of Brandis as a traveling service provider and as a German expert doing managerial work for someone else's empire. His allegiance to the British Indian state was secured through the wage mechanism, not through customary or courtly allegiance. He was a foreign salaryman of the East India Company. And Brandis's managerial and engineering skills were crucial to resolving the logistics challenges facing the Raj as it sought to forcibly acquire indigenous lands for timber production.[48]

Brandis hired a group of young German-speaking foresters as his assistants, including Gustav Mann, Bertolt Ribbentrop, Wilhelm Schlich, and Carl Schenk. Gustav Mann had worked at Kew Gardens and had led expeditions to West Africa before coming to serve in India. Meanwhile, Schenk was soon hired by the Vanderbilts to start a forestry school in North Carolina. The Biltmore School, founded by Schenk, became a major provider of know-how in lumber harvesting just at the time when the railroad boom of the American Gilded Age and Westward Expansion were taking place, as Native lands were aggressively overtaken for settlement and resource exploitation.[49] Meanwhile, Albert Fink, trained at Darmstadt University as a civil engineer, became the superintendent of the Louisville and Nashville Railroad in 1865 and was renowned for developing a method of cost accounting to facilitate large-scale logistics projects.[50]

The botanists' work of knowing and managing the "wastelands" so as to incorporate them into logistics networks of industrial agriculture led the British Indian government to hire Frederick Stolizka from Vienna University in 1864 to lead the botanical survey. Fritz Noelte, also a student at the University of Vienna, was hired around the same time to man the geological survey. August Heinrich Petermann, a cartographer trained in Berlin in the 1830s, was hired for projects in Edinburgh and London beginning in 1842. He became the leading developer of new methods for representing meteorological, hydrological,

47. Kris Manjapra, *Age of Entanglement* (Cambridge, MA: Harvard University Press, 2014); Ramachandra Guha, *Environmentalism: A Global History* (New York: Longman, 2000).

48. Manjapra, *Age of Entanglement*, 69.

49. Ned Blackhawk, *Violence over the Land: Indians and Empires in the Early American West* (Cambridge, MA: Harvard University Press, 2006); Jodi Byrd, *Transit of Empire: Indigenous Critiques of Colonialism* (Minneapolis: University of Minnesota Press, 2011), 117–146.

50. Chandler, *Visible Hand*, 116.

geological, and ethnographic information on maps and thus helped to feed the insatiable knowledge hunger of British colonial expansion. The colonial state ravenously needed to "see" in new ways, and the semiperipheral hand supplied the lenses. These scientists produced the concept of the "wastelands" and made it useful for imperial designs. Geologists, foresters, and cartographers were elemental to the establishment of infrastructures and logistics networks for the advancing regime of industrial agricultural capitalism.

A Global Semiperiphery

Empire depended on its semiperipheral functionaries. From London bookkeepers to German doctors, travel writers, and scientists to lettered clerks from Scottish and Irish traditional society to caste communities of Asian scribes and translators, the semiperiphery was nearby and far away at the same time. In the circum-Caribbean, the white and colored Creoles, as well as a stratum of the enslaved Africans, served as knowledgeable experts, engineers, and planners in the expanding regime of industrial agriculture.[51] Likewise, in South Asia, particular castes, such as the Brahmins of Madras or the Brahmins, Kayasthas, and Kshatriyas of Bengal, dovetailed easily into the British colonial administration as knowledge professionals.[52] A stratum of Indians was thus turned into the middle managers of the very regime that dominated them.

The techniques of knowledge associated with priestly and business castes, and rooted in a segmentary social system of caste domination, were highly prized by the colonial state. Traditional techniques of knowledge production, including taking testimonials, making validations, computation, cataloguing, and other scribal activities, were part of the Indian semiperiphery and were incorporated into the designs of the British Empire. This strata of high-caste, high-status Indians became the indigenous middle classes of colonial society and represent a subfraction of the global bourgeoisie, always demarcated from the white middle classes by the colonial rule of racial difference.

As this chapter has argued by considering service providers involved in finance, crop science, population management, and logistics planning, the very value of these knowledgeable professionals derived from their ability to

---

51. Olaudah Equiano, *The Interesting Narrative of the Life of Olaudah Equiano* (1789; Chicago: Lakeside Press, 2004).

52. Tithi Bhattacharya, *The Sentinels of Culture* (New Delhi: Oxford University Press, 2005); Bhavani Raman, *Document Raj* (Chicago: University of Chicago Press, 2012).

accumulate and distribute knowledge at the behest of imperial states and from their ability to move across imperial boundaries. This multiethnic corps of knowledge professionals of empire brought cores into volatile contact with peripheries.

The semiperipheral hand connected metropolitan boardrooms, research offices, salons, ballrooms, and clubhouses to the appropriative edges of empire, where dispossession and colonial militarization took place. The world economy of the nineteenth-century economy was dependent on the spread of frontiers of primitive accumulation. One fraction of the global middle class—a multiethnic, tradition-bound, world-traveling, salary-loyal fraction—was produced out of this crucible. Members of this stratum offered their knowledge to the highest bidder, and the knowledge they offered was often rooted in old modes of discipline and authority but now oriented by globally replicating imperatives of industrial capitalism. These professionals fed the insatiable knowledge and management cravings of colonial states. They made the "wastelands" legible; they provided the justification for invasion and conquest; they legitimated the grand narrative of progress and the civilizing mission. They contributed an Old-World charm, a certain scientific enchantment and managerial finesse, to the spread of instrumental rationality and techniques of appropriation across colonial frontiers.[53] We thus grasp a clearer understanding of the function of the semiperipheral hand as it strove to suture together the social, political, and ecological ruptures caused by imperial expansion with the post-Enlightenment fabric of texts, tabulations, and scientific representations.

---

53. Theodor Adorno and Max Horkheimer, *Dialectic of Enlightenment* (New York: Continuum, 1987); Max Weber, "Science as a Vocation," in *From Max Weber: Essays in Sociology*, ed. H. H. Gerth and C. Wright Mills (New York: Routledge, 2009), 129–158.

PART IV

Religion and the Betterment of the World

10

The Muslim Bourgeoisie and Philanthropy in the Late Ottoman Empire

Adam Mestyan

DESPITE LOSING TERRITORIES, the Ottoman Empire experienced a three-fold growth in population, a tenfold growth in trade value, and a significant but yet unknown expansion of taxable urban and agricultural land surface during the long nineteenth century.[1] Interventions of European Christian empires and an international debt regime weakened the government's control over trade while state centralization produced uneven results. How did such spectacular economic change and Christian dominance impact the structure of society in a diverse Muslim empire?

The main effect of economic change was growing inequality and new ways of expressing distinctions between urban groups and the rural society. This chapter assumes that a networked urban, elite culture emerged among absentee landowners, government employees, and urban professionals in the Ottoman Empire in the nineteenth century. Importantly, as with all imperial

1. For the purpose of this article, the Ottoman Empire means all tax- and tribute-paying provinces (thus including Egypt) until 1914. The population grew from about eleven million to about thirty-three million inhabitants during the long nineteenth century; trade value increased form below £10 million to over £100 million. Roger Owen, *The Middle East in the World Economy, 1800–1914* (1981; London: I. B. Tauris, 2009), 287–291. I wish to thank Bruce Hall, Frances Hasso, Anna Krylova, Jehangir Melaghem, Mustafa Tuna, Avner Wishnitzer, Kim Greenwell, and the reviewers and the editors of this volume for their help.

bourgeoisies, the Ottoman one had a diasporic dimension: merchants still traded in the Mediterranean and Persia; statesmen and grandees inhabited the European pleasure zones; students studied in European capitals; and many Ottoman subjects lived from Paris to New York to Buenos Aires. The Ottoman imperial bourgeoisie became a global, urban, and fragmented yet networked society with political, economic, and sexual ties to the other European bourgeoisies by 1914. This explains the "internationalism" and ability of wealthy individuals to easily form political and cultural organizations across borders before and after the First World War. However, they were rarely interested in advancing social equality.[2]

This essay focuses on wealthy Muslims with international connections among the Ottoman bourgeoisie. In the first half of this essay, I formulate the problem of the Muslim bourgeoisie in historiography and I propose a loose taxonomy of the Ottoman urban prestige groups: the Muslim bourgeois-aristocracy and the urban professionals. Inevitably, this is a sketch and I pay some attention also to Ottoman Christians and Jews, who have been the usual focus of the Ottoman bourgeoisie narratives. In the second half, I focus on philanthropic events in order to contrast the old and new elements of urbanity and show "Islam" as a principle of group-ness. As has been done for nineteenth-century Britain, by studying philanthropic sociability we can understand how Ottoman urban groups practiced new social rituals, claimed honor and prestige, preserved religious compartmentalization, exhibited solidarity, and disciplined the less fortunate. Scholars have already highlighted the identification function of philanthropy in smaller ethno-religious communities, such as the Ottoman Greeks, and traced benevolent societies in Egypt as nationalist organizations on which the government relied until the 1940s.[3] This essay inserts Ottoman Muslims into the global history of the bourgeoisie and thus historicizes the "Islamic sociability" so often described as a middle-class

2. Andrew Arsan, "'This Age Is the Age of Associations': Committees, Petitions, and the Roots of Interwar Middle Eastern Internationalism," *Journal of Global History* 7 (2012): 166–188.

3. Efi Kanner, "From the 'Sick', 'the Blind', and 'the Crippled' to the Nation of 'Toiling People': Visions of the Poor in the Late Ottoman Empire and the Early Turkish Republic," in *Wealth in the Ottoman and Post-Ottoman Balkans: A Socio-Economic History*, ed. Evguenia Davidova (London: I. B. Tauris, 2016), 117–138; the latest work on Egypt is Lisa Pollard, "Egyptian by Association: Charitable States and Service Societies, circa 1850–1945," *International Journal of Middle East Studies* 46 (2014): 239–257.

phenomenon today.[4] Charitable events and organizations were general phenomena for helping the poor and stood in striking contrast with the persistent lack of actual social equality policy.

There is a vocabulary problem. Scholars often use the categories "bourgeois" and "middle class" to analyze urban groups, such as merchants, artisans, and muftis in seventeenth-century Istanbul and eighteenth-century Cairo.[5] Here I use the borrowed French term "bourgeoisie" to denote wealthy groups who engaged in new forms of urban consumption and exhibited a distinct social habitus associated with Europe in the Ottoman cities of the nineteenth century. This is not to deny earlier forms of urbanity but, rather, to recognize that from the 1840s many Ottoman urban groups developed a new awareness of the world by critically comparing themselves and others to what they termed "Europe" and the "West." Their central notion was competition. In this sense, being bourgeois was an inherently subjective, transcultural comparative act in the long nineteenth century, and it remains so in state-engineered processes to create "entitled patriots" in contemporary Muslim societies.[6]

In order to understand the late Ottoman Empire on its own terms, one has to note that Islam had a different existence then than it does today. I use "Ottoman Muslim" here not as a theological-legal identity affiliation but as a personal religio-social administrative position and a principle of public solidarity within a modernizing caliphate-empire. New nation states retroactively framed religion-based groupings in the late Ottoman Empire as backward and antimodern formations. We should not appropriate these categories, which served specific goals in the interwar period. True, the first global Muslim entrepreneursheiks, such as the Egyptian Muhammad 'Abduh (1849–1905) and the Syrian Rashid Rida (1865–1935), also appear among the Ottoman Muslim bourgeoisie. They mobilized the Islamic textual tradition as a grouping principle against

4. Charles Tripp, *Islam and the Moral Economy: The Challenge of Capitalism* (Cambridge: Cambridge University Press, 2006), 97–102.

5. Cemal Kafadar, "How Dark Is the History of the Night, How Black the Story of Coffee, How Bitter the Tale of Love: The Changing Measure of Leisure and Pleasure in Early Modern Istanbul," in *Medieval and Early Modern Performance in the Eastern Mediterranean*, ed. Arzu Öztürkmen and Evelyn Birge Vitz (Turnhout: Brepols, 2014), 243–269; Nelly Hanna, *In Praise of Books: A Cultural History of Cairo's Middle Class, Sixteenth to Eighteenth Century* (Cairo: American University of Cairo Press, 2004).

6. Calvert W. Jones, *Bedouins into Bourgeois: Remaking Citizens for Globalization* (Cambridge: Cambridge University Press, 2017).

absolute government and targeted culturally middle-class groups. Thus the Ottoman bourgeoisie also carried the roots of twentieth-century Islamic organizations.

The Muslim Bourgeoisie as a Problem of Empire

Research on the bourgeoisie often retains nation state frames. I attempt here to think in terms of empire. How was social inequality different in the Ottoman imperial formation from other large systems of power in the late nineteenth century?

There is no Ottoman counterpart to study "the *ashraf* (descendants of the Prophet) to middle classes" model, so important in British Delhi.[7] There is not yet an explicit study showing an "*ashraf* to bourgeoisie" path in the Ottoman provincial capitals—Tirana, Damascus, Jerusalem, Bagdad, Cairo, and not even in the often-analyzed Beirut—in the long nineteenth century. There are several reasons for this gap: less available quantitative data, lack of interest in elite social history, the paradigm of colonization, nation-state frames, and the focus on non-Muslims as agents of modernity.

Is there anything common among the diverse late Ottoman cities? An earlier scholarly solution was to restrict the academic use of "Ottoman bourgeoisie" to non-Muslim commercial groups, especially in Istanbul. According to this "bifurcated" theory, a state-related Muslim bureaucracy existed next to a non-Muslim commercial bourgeoisie.[8] Another version of this solution was the division between an agrarian and "small" (internal) commercial Muslim class and a typically urban non-Muslim international commercial one.[9] These attempts took Istanbul or port cities as master examples and privileged non-Muslims, who were often associated with the European colonial empires.[10]

---

7. Margrit Pernau, *Ashraf into Middle Classes: Muslims in Nineteenth-Century Delhi* (Oxford: Oxford University Press, 2013).

8. Fatma Müge Göçek, *Rise of the Bourgeoisie, Demise of Empire: Ottoman Westernization and Social Change* (New York: Oxford University Press, 1996), 16, 81; Keith David Watenpaugh, *Being Modern in the Middle East: Revolution, Nationalism, Colonialism, and the Arab Middle Class* (Princeton, NJ: Princeton University Press, 2006), 8, 38.

9. Kemal H. Karpat, *Studies on Ottoman Social and Political History: Selected Articles and Essays* (Leiden: Brill, 2002), 48–49.

10. Representative works are Bernard Lewis, *The Emergence of Modern Turkey*, 2nd ed. (London: Oxford University Press, 1968), 448–463; Niyazi Berkes, *The Development of Secularism in Turkey* (Montreal: McGill University Press, 1964); Reşat Kasaba, *The Ottoman Empire*

Historians have recently challenged the bifurcated models based on new evidence about imperial schooling, the Muslim control of inland trade, and the lack of uniform ethno-religious identities.[11] Some criticize the analogy of British India with the Ottoman Empire, and historians describe social change even in the Egyptian province without using the colonial paradigm.[12] Others have questioned whether "modernity" should be seen as the perfect execution of European manners. Some authors suggest understanding "imperfection" as a form of resistance.[13] The challenge is to find a theoretical framework that describes social change without direct European rule and accommodates the agency of local Muslim elites while paying equal attention to the domination of the European empires along the shores.

The question of how globalization impacted the Muslim landlords and urban professionals and how it enabled some agrarian groups to join them is

and the World Economy: The Nineteenth Century (Albany: State University of New York, 1988); Malak Zaaluk, Power, Class, and Foreign Capital in Egypt: The Rise of the New Bourgeoisie (London: Zed Books, 1989), 2–6; and the essays in Halil İnalcik and Donald Quatert, eds., An Economic and Social History of the Ottoman Empire, 1300–1914 (Cambridge: Cambridge University Press, 1994).

11. Carter Vaughn Findley, Turkey, Islam, Nationalism, and Modernity: A History, 1789–2007 (New Haven, CT: Yale University Press, 2010), 119–123.

12. Christine Philliou, "Nationalism, Internationalism, and Cosmopolitanism: Comparison and Commensurability," Comparative Studies of South Asia, Africa and the Middle East 36, no. 3 (2016): 455–464; Adam Mestyan, Arab Patriotism: The Ideology and Culture of Power in Late Ottoman Egypt (Princeton, NJ: Princeton University Press, 2017); Daniel Stolz, The Lighthouse and the Observatory: Islam, Science, and Empire in Late Ottoman Egypt (Cambridge: Cambridge University Press, 2018).

13. Jens Hanssen, Fin De Siècle Beirut: The Making of an Ottoman Provincial Capital (Oxford: Oxford University Press, 2005); Johann Büssow, Hamidian Palestine: Politics and Society in the District of Jerusalem 1872–1908 (Leiden: Brill, 2011); Sibel Zandi-Sayek, Ottoman Izmir: The Rise of a Cosmopolitan Port, 1840–1880 (Minneapolis: University of Minnesota Press, 2012); On Barak, On Time: Technology and Temporality in Modern Egypt (Berkeley: University of California Press, 2013); Till Grallert, "To Whom Belong the Streets?: Property, Propriety, and Appropriation: the Production of Public Space in Late Ottoman Damascus, 1875–1914" (PhD diss., Freie University, 2014); Avner Wishnitzer, Reading Clocks, Alla Turca: Time and Society in the Late Ottoman Empire (Chicago: Chicago University Press, 2015); Toufoul Abou-Hodeib, A Taste for Home: The Modern Middle Class in Ottoman Beirut (Stanford, CA: Stanford University Press, 2017); Adam Mestyan, "Upgrade? Power and Sound during Ramadan and 'Id al-Fitr in the Nineteenth-Century Ottoman Arab Provinces," Comparative Studies of South Asia, Africa, and the Middle East 37, no. 2 (2017): 262–279; and the following notes in this chapter.

important because after the Congress of Berlin in 1878, the majority population became Sunni Muslim in the remaining Ottoman territories due to migration.[14] The late Ottoman military elite was predominantly Muslim.[15] Scholars have been slowly exploring the social life of Muslim merchants who controlled inland trade.[16] For instance, in 1840 in Damascus, sixty-six Muslim, twenty-nine Christian, and twenty-four Jewish large merchant houses specialized in European trade and had considerable wealth.[17] Internal trade is important since, for instance, in 1870 external trade was still only about 8 percent of the total Ottoman production.[18] Furthermore, since state education was a system of mixed Islamic and Western elements,[19] scholars argue that "the Ottoman state . . . had the Islamic credentials to co-opt the new classes"[20] and that "the central authorities rebuilt the state as an Islamic state."[21] Thinking about empire through Islam may have further consequences. For instance, some argue that Islamic law hindered Ottoman capitalism, and thus, the economic foundations of the bourgeoisie were missing, or at least were different than in Christian societies.[22] Historical evidence challenges such generalizations. There was a spectacular variety of Muslim

14. Justin McCarthy, "Muslims in Ottoman Europe: Population from 1800 to 1912," *Nationalities Papers* 28, no. 1 (2000): 29–43, 36.

15. Michael Provence, *The Last Ottoman Generation and the Making of the Modern Middle East* (Cambridge: Cambridge University Press, 2017), 14–17.

16. Pascal Ghazaleh, *Fortunes urbaines et stratégies sociales: généalogies patrimoniales au Caire, 1780–1830*, 2 vols. (Cairo: L'Institut français d'archéologie orientale, 2010); Omar Cheta, "Rule of Merchants: The Practice of Commerce and Law in Late Ottoman Egypt, 1841–1876" (PhD diss., New York University 2014); Emre Erol, *The Ottoman Crisis in Western Anatolia: Turkey's Belle Époque and the Transition to a Modern Nation State* (London: I. B. Tauris, 2016), 18.

17. Abdul-Karim Rafeq, "A Fractured Society: Ottoman Damascus in the Mid-19th Century," in *Histoire, archéologies, et littératures du monde musulman: Mélanges en l'honneur d'André Raymond*, ed. Ghislaine Alleamue, Sylvie Denoix, and Michel Tuchscherer (Cairo: L'Institut français d'archéologie orientale, 2009), 193–204.

18. Erik J. Zürcher, *Turkey: A Modern History* (1993; London: I. B. Tauris, 2004), 48.

19. Benjamin Fortna, *The Imperial Classroom* (Oxford: Oxford University Press, 2002), 13, 22–24.

20. Kemal H. Karpat, *The Politicization of Islam: Reconstructing Identity, State, Faith, and Community in the Late Ottoman State* (Oxford: Oxford University Press, 2001), 89–116, 90.

21. Frederick Anscombe, *State, Faith, and Nation in Ottoman and Post-Ottoman Lands* (New York: Cambridge University Press, 2014), 90.

22. Timur Kuran, *The Long Divergence: How Islamic Law Held Back the Middle East* (Princeton, NJ: Princeton University Press, 2010).

family-property devolution practices even in relatively close cities such as Nablus and Tripoli.[23]

The inclusion of Muslims in bourgeois practices opens the way to rethink the category of "bourgeois" as a claim on prestige, to restate the role of religion as an administrative approach and solidarity principle, and to assume "a cluster of Ottoman bourgeoisies."[24] The idea of a Muslim bourgeoisie sharing with non-Muslims a new life also prompts a wide definition of the Ottoman imperial public sphere. I consider four structural elements: the old and new public spaces—mosques, churches, squares, markets, hotels, salons, coffeehouses, theaters, casinos, gardens, promenades; the press in various Ottoman languages (Turkish, Arabic, Greek, Ladino, Armenian, Italian, and French); associations and their activities—charitable societies, literary, musical, and athletic clubs, religious organizations; and public performances of old and new entertainment genres in various languages. By the late nineteenth century, as elsewhere, the Ottoman public sphere was no longer a virtual domain of textual exchange between notable intellectuals, because capitalist urbanism allowed new, temporary, gendered spatial forms of public "group-ness." The transition from public sphere to public space also embodied networks of information, wealth, and sexual politics between cities by the 1900s. These spaces, exchanges, and technologies were policed by the wealthy groups.[25]

Geographically, to accommodate diversity at an imperial scale, Cem Emrence suggests a theory of three distinct regional trajectories in the Ottoman Empire: coastal, inland, and borderland. Each type has a particular political and socioeconomic structure.[26] Regionalism in general is more useful than the coastal/inland dichotomy for linking economic factors to social change.[27] The coastal

23. Beshara B. Doumani, *Family Life in the Ottoman Mediterranean: A Social History* (Cambridge: Cambridge University Press, 2017), 16–17.

24. Christoph Herzog, "Review of *Rise of the Bourgeoisie, Demise of Empire. Ottoman Westernization and Social Change* by Fatma Müge Göçek," *Die Welt des Islams* 42, no. 1 (2002): 127–129, 129.

25. Göçek, *Rise of the Bourgeoisie*; Watenpaugh, *Being Modern*, 61–64; Serdar Öztürk, "Osmanlı İmparatorluğu'nda Kamusal Alanın Dinamikleri" [The dynamics of the public sphere in the Ottoman Empire], *İletişim* 21 (2005): 95–124; Cânâ Bilsel, "L'espace public existait-il dans la ville ottomane? Des espaces libres au domaine public à Istanbul (XVIIe–XIXe siècles)," *Études balkaniques* 14 (2007): 73–104; see later notes for specific studies.

26. Cem Emrence, "Imperial Paths, Big Comparisons: The Late Ottoman Empire," *Journal of Global History* 3, no. 3 (2008): 289–311, 291.

27. Doumani, *Family Life*, 31.

forms of new sociability may have prompted inland Muslim urban ruling groups, who often circulated between port cities and the hinterland, to synchronize.[28] New social practices appeared first in the coastal trajectory due to market relations and the discourse on (Western) modernity.[29] Also, although there are arguments for coastal primacy, we should not see the spread of modernity in a schematic path from the ports to the Ottoman interior.

I propose two, loose large layers in the upper strata of Ottoman society, including Egypt's: the bourgeoisie-aristocracy and the urban professionals. One can observe a type of Muslim aristocratization simultaneous to the emergence of new professionals in the second half of the nineteenth century. The bourgeois aristocracy is a category I employ to include the wealthiest Muslims who were often affiliated with the government. I call them bourgeois-aristocracy because they typically claim a type of hereditary prestige. These prestige groups had multiple faces. While "middle class" was translated as *orta sınıf* in Turkish and as *al-tabaqa al-wusta* in Arabic, just to mention two imperial languages, "bourgeoisie" has been used as a loan word: *burjuvazi* in Turkish, *burjuwaziyya* in Arabic. At the same time, in Ottoman Arabic journalism a number of older words (*a'yan*, "notables"; *zevat*, "Turkish-speaking aristocrats"; *umara'*, "princes"; *khassa*, "the elite"; *ashraf*, "descendants of the Prophet") remained in use to denote these prestige groups.

We can distinguish three layers within this high bourgeois-aristocracy. The first comprises the branches of the Ottoman sultanic households and high administration, including the khedivial family of Egypt and the sharifian families from Mecca. They directed the government and had immense income from land, endowments, and taxes. They lived in palaces and newly built downtown apartments and became multilingual by the fin de siècle. They are the Ottoman aristocracy whose members masked themselves as haute bourgeoisie, as others had done in Europe. In many cases, they used their positions for private capitalist enterprises.

Second is the crucial group of the Muslim provincial notables, the *a'yan*, who combined social prestige and landownership with service in the administration. They were rooted in religious lineages, wealth, tax-collecting, or control of local forces. Scholarship has focused on them as the major players after the eighteenth-century rearrangement of Ottoman property relations. Those in the Anatolian

28. Adam Mestyan, "Music and Power in Cairo: Azbakiyya," *Urban History* 40, no. 4 (2013): 681–704.

29. Emrence, "Imperial Paths," 300–301.

and Balkan provinces are described as representing a "proto-modernity" who established an uninstitutionalized "partnership" with the sultanic adminis-tration, but this partnership failed in 1808.[30] The *a'yan* also went through an "Ottomanization" process, balanced by "localization," in which Ottoman Turkic elites became assimilated into local urban societies,[31] though Ottoman-ization/localization were not exclusively elite processes.[32] The Tanzimat, the imperial reforms from the 1820s, aimed at neutralizing the *a'yan* so that the politics of notables "dissolved into the integrated administrative structure of the empire."[33] In the Syrian provinces, *urban* notables were the subjects of Ottomanization.[34] In the Egyptian province, the *rural* village headmen cooper-ated with the governor in order to create a proto-national sub-Ottoman mon-archy. One local effect of global change was that village headmen became in-creasingly nationalist *a'yan* in the Egyptian province.[35] Even in the Balkans, among the Christian notables such as the Wallachian boyars, property became inscribed "into a logic of legitimating identity."[36] The precondition of *a'yan em-bourgeoisement* was secure landholding, which was practically guaranteed by the 1858 Land Law (though tax farming remained the norm until the end of the empire).[37] Groups of the dominantly Muslim elites in the Arabic-speaking provinces practiced new bourgeois urban rituals by the fin de siècle, but post-1908 Young Turk administrators viewed them as obstacles of "progress."[38] The

30. Karen Barkey, *Empire of Difference: The Ottomans in Comparative Perspective* (Cambridge: Cambridge University Press, 2008); Anscombe, *State, Faith, and Nation*; Ali Yaycioglu, *Partners of the Empire: Crisis of the Ottoman Order in the Age of Revolutions* (Stanford, CA: Stanford University Press, 2016).

31. Ehud Toledano, "The Emergence of Ottoman-Local Elites (1700–1900): A Framework for Research," in *Middle Eastern Politics and Ideas: A History from Within*, ed. Ilan Pappé and Moshe Ma'oz (London: Tauris, 1997), 145–162.

32. Hanna, *In Praise of Books*, 85.

33. Hanssen, *Fin de Siècle Beirut*, 15.

34. Albert Hourani, "Ottoman Reform and the Politics of Notables," in *The Emergence of the Modern Middle East* (Berkeley: University of California Press, 1981), 36–66.

35. Adam Mestyan, "Domestic Sovereignty, A'yan Developmentalism, and Global Microhis-tory in Modern Egypt," *Comparative Studies in Society and History* 60, no. 2 (2018): 415–445.

36. Andrea-Roxana Iamcu, "Defining the Patrimony: Name, Lineage and Inheritance Prac-tices (Wallachia at the Beginning of the Nineteenth Century)," in *Wealth in the Ottoman and Post-Ottoman Balkans*, ed. Davidova, 50–69.

37. Quatert suggests thinking about the Land Law as a legal instrument to promote agricul-tural development. İnalcik and Quatert, *Economic and Social History*, 855–861.

38. Watenpaugh, *Being Modern*, 99–100.

politics of the Muslim *a'yan* bourgeoisie is crucial to understanding even the interwar period.

Finally, imperial high bureaucrats, wealthy merchants, commanding army officers, bankers, and rich doctors belonged to the Ottoman bourgeois-aristocracy, too. It is in this third subgroup that we encounter extreme diversity, since non-Muslims, especially Greek, Armenian, and Syrian Christian traders, attained unprecedented domination in commerce and banking with foreigners. This third, mostly coastal group can be defined by either capital earned by trade, investment in land, administrative service, or professional work. Muslim grandees and merchants transformed their strategies to preserve wealth (instead of establishing religious endowments, they also started to invest in bonds and property).[39] Wealth was produced through migration, too.[40] Today's nostalgia for the cosmopolitan coastal society is for the privileged lifestyle of these wealthy groups.[41]

The urban layer I call middle groups includes smaller lawyers, doctors, educated craftsmen in guilds (*esnaf*), smaller merchants, middle-ranking soldiers, teachers, and lesser scholars of religion. Their shared characteristic is that they owned one or few properties, and some engaged in urban agriculture, too. These urban groups composed approximately one-third of the population in eighteenth-century Cairo,[42] where there were 177 guilds in 1801.[43] Guilds were important. In Salonica, there were 116 guilds in the 1860s, and 287 in 1887 in Istanbul.[44] Religious differences within the guilds apparently did not matter.[45]

---

39. Ibrahim al-Bayyumi Ghanim, *Al-Awqaf wa-l-Siyasa fi Misr* [Religious endowments and politics in Egypt] (1968; Cairo: Dar al-Shuruq, 1998), 161; Edhem Eldem, "(A Quest for) the Bourgeoisie of Istanbul: Identities, Roles and Conflicts," in *Urban Governance under the Ottomans: Between Cosmopolitanism and Conflict*, ed. Ulrike Freitag and Nora Lafi (London: Routledge, 2014), 159–186, 174.

40. Akram Fouad Khater, *Inventing Home: Emigration, Gender, and the Middle Class in Lebanon, 1870–1920* (Berkeley: University of California Press, 2001), 108–110.

41. Will Hanley, "Grieving Cosmopolitanism in Middle East Studies," *History Compass 6*, no. 5 (2008): 1346–1367.

42. Hanna, *In Praise of Books*, 6.

43. Quoted in Pascale Ghazaleh, "Organising Labour: Professional Classifications in Late Eighteenth to Early Nineteenth Century Cairo," in *Crafts and Craftsmen of the Middle East*, ed. Suraiya Faroqhi and Randi Deguilhem (London: I. B. Tauris, 2005), 235–260.

44. İnalcik and Quatert, *Economic and Social History*, 894.

45. Randi Deguilhem, "Shared Space or Contested Space: Religious Mixity, Infrastructural Hierarchy, and the Builder's Guild in Mid-Nineteenth Century Damascus," in *Crafts and Craftsmen*, ed. Faroqhi and Deguilhem, 261–282.

In Istanbul, the relationship between guilds and centralization was far from negative in the early 1800s, and despite losing monopolies in the 1860s, guilds were abolished only in 1910–12.[46] In Egypt, guilds still had their own subsystems in the mid-nineteenth century. They worked relatively undisturbed until the 1880s, when they were adapted to the new economy within the British imperial system.[47]

The most discussed middle group comprises the educated professionals with modest income: lesser bureaucrats in the provincial administrations, shopkeepers, journalists, and teachers in cities. By the interwar period, they were the Muslim efendi masses. It is this modernizing middle group that historians have found so hard to define with economic markers that they suggest viewing this category as a cultural construction. Middle-classness has been defined as a social strategy, an awareness of the industrializing world, a vocabulary of and a claim on "civilization," a mentality, a public sartorial and behavioral code, and a mode of self-measurement to Western European urbanity. Importantly, not everyone, such as those in the professions, accepted or switched permanently to the new codes of middle-classness.[48]

However, middle-classness was not the construction of the middle groups only. The bourgeois-aristocrats claimed fluency in middle-class Western practices, too. They and the middle groups shared disciplining visions. One such new vision was about gender. The matrix of honor, public presence, domesticity, and productivity became a feature of gendered bourgeois discourses.[49] The female body and mind became a symbolic battleground of civilization in public discourse and rendered gendered, particular freedoms to socioeconomic position. At the same time, new notions of the male body emerged and the

46. İnalcık and Quatert, *Economic and Social History*, 897; Suraiya Faroqhi, "Introduction," in *Bread from the Lion's Mouth: Artisans Struggling for a Livelihood in Ottoman Cities*, ed. Suraiya Faroqhi (New York: Berghahn Books, 2015), 1–47, 19.

47. John Chalcraft, "The End of Guilds in Egypt: Restructuring Textiles in the Long Nineteenth Century," in *Crafts and Craftsmen*, ed. Faroqhi and Deguilhem, 338–367.

48. Eldem, "(A Quest for) the Bourgeoisie," 159, 174; Watenpaugh, *Being Modern*; Lucie Ryzova, *The Age of the Efendiyya: Passages to Modernity in National-Colonial Egypt* (Oxford: Oxford University Press, 2014); Abou-Hodeib, *Taste for Home*.

49. Holly A. Schissler, "The Harem as the Seat of Middle-Class Industry," in *Harem Histories: Envisioning Places and Living Spaces*, ed. Marilyn Booth (Durham, NC: Duke University Press, 2010), 319–341; Beth Baron, *Egypt as a Woman: Nationalism, Gender, and Politics* (Cairo: American University in Cairo Press, 2005); Hanan Kholoussi, *For Better, For Worse: The Marriage Crisis That Made Modern Egypt, 1898–1936* (Stanford, CA: Stanford University Press, 2010); Abou-Hodeib, *Taste for Home*, 5–6, 18–19.

standard of Ottoman male beauty was transformed.[50] Middle-classness became a male efendi quality in interwar Egypt.[51] The discourses of gender were
connected not only to secularism but also to class. Working women's "public-
ness" meant further exploitation.[52]

Another shared discursive strategy of social distinction was the invention
of the "peasant." Arab intellectuals formulated the *fellah* as "an archetypal narrative other for the cosmopolitan, urban subject."[53] The new use of "taste" in
Arabic became a feature of difference: "a move toward recasting class
difference."[54] Similarly, among Ottoman Greeks "the poor" and "laziness" became tropes opposed to the respectable groups.[55]

Finally, some intellectuals viewed religion as an obstacle to unity in the patriotic middle class. For instance, an Egyptian writer in 1902 thought that education would provide the nonreligious solidarity needed to unite the middle
of society and this would help Egypt to become similar to Western countries.[56]
Even in the domain of Ottoman temporal culture, standardized clock time became "a weapon in the hands of much more radical groups that sought to
transform the political order in the name of (their vision of) modernity" although the radical Westernization was only one of the options available.[57]

The new codes did not go unchallenged. There was public criticism of "super-
westernization," and Ottoman Turkish novels and short stories often ridiculed
the new consumption habits.[58] The first printed, serialized Arabic novel

50. Murat Yıldız, "'What Is a Beautiful Body?' Late Ottoman 'Sportsman' Photographs and
New Notions of Male Corporeal Beauty," *Middle East Journal of Culture and Communication* 8
(2015): 192–214.

51. Wilson Chacko Jacob, *Working Out Egypt: Effendi Masculinity and Subject Formation in Colonial Modernity, 1870–1940* (Durham, NC: Duke University Press, 2011); Ryzova, *Age of Efendiya.*

52. Duygu Köksal and Anastasia Falierou, eds., *A Social History of Late Ottoman Women: New
Perspectives* (Leiden: Brill, 2016), 14.

53. Samah Selim, *The Novel and the Rural Imaginary in Egypt, 1880–1985* (London: Routledge-
Curzon, 2004), 5.

54. Toufoul Abou-Hodeib, "Taste and Class in Late Ottoman Beirut," *International Journal
of Middle East Studies* 43, no. 3 (2011): 475–492, 477.

55. Kanner, "From the 'Sick,'" 121.

56. Muhammad 'Umar, *Hadir al-Misriyyin aw Sirr Ta'akhkhurihim* [The present condition
of Egyptians, or, the secret of why they are late] (Cairo: Matba'at al-Muqtataf, 1902), 188.

57. Wishnitzer, *Reading Clocks*, 10, 22.

58. Şerif Mardin, "Super-Westernization in Urban Life in the Ottoman Empire in the Last
Quarter of the Nineteenth Century," in *Religion, Society, and Modernity in Turkey* (1974; Syracuse, NY: Syracuse University Press, 2006), 135–163.

("Shame, then I am not a European!") also offered the first critique of the changes in 1858 in Beirut.[59] In post-1908 Aleppo, even a male Christian Arab journalist demanded intellectual sacrifice (intellectual work to find new solutions to the empire's survival) for the Ottoman nation through a critique of European civilization.[60]

Charity as a Social Site of the Muslim Bourgeoisie

One specific domain in which the Ottoman bourgeoisies practiced new social codes was charity events. Studies about the Ottoman public sphere, with some exceptions, has been restricted to the press and the theater, typically from a post-Ottoman nation-state or "Middle East" point of view.[61] The inclusion of public *spaces* in the public sphere highlights the physical aspect of performative togetherness. In these urban spaces—theaters, clubs, coffeehouses, casinos, salons, public gardens—events organized for charity exhibited new habitus. We can categorize the spaces according to wealth, gender, religion, and status: not everyone could enter the opera houses in Izmir, Istanbul, and Cairo; and vice versa, the Alexandria, Haifa, or Izmir *café-chantan* was a dangerous place for bourgeois-aristocrat ladies.[62] I focus on gatherings, which were organized and prompted by the discourse of charity, occurring in the bourgeois-aristocrat versions of these spaces. It is here that we can find the Muslim bourgeois also in action.

The idea of charity in the form of a public association was new in the Ottoman Empire. The old Muslim practice of *zakat* was a duty performed

59. Matti Moosa, *The Origins of Modern Arabic Fiction*, 2nd ed. (Boulder, CO: Lynne Rienner Publishers, 1997), 157.

60. Watenpaugh, *Being Modern*, 88.

61. Metin And, *Tanzimat ve İstibdat Döneminde Türk Tiyatrosu, 1839–1908* [Turkish theater in the periods of Tanzimat and Opression, 1839–1908] (Ankara: Türkiye İş Bankası Yayınları, 1972); Ami Ayalon, *The Press in the Arab Middle East: A History* (New York: Oxford University Press, 1995); Olga Borovaia, *Modern Ladino Culture: Press, Belles Lettres, and Theatre in the Late Ottoman Empire* (Bloomington: Indiana University Press, 2012); Murat Şiviloğlu, *The Emergence of Public Opinion in the Ottoman Empire, 1826–1876* (Cambridge: Cambridge University Press, 2018).

62. Malter Fuhrmann, "Down and Out on the Quays of İzmir: 'European' Musicians, Innkeepers, and Prostitutes in the Ottoman Port-Cities," *Mediterranean Historical Review* 2, no. 24 (2009): 169–185; Avner Wishnitzer, "Eyes in the Dark: Nightlife and Visual Regimes in Late Ottoman Istanbul," *Comparative Studies of South Asia, Africa and the Middle East* 2, no. 37 (2017): 245–261.

individually. The other form of institutionalized philanthropy, the inalienable endowment by private individuals (*vakıf* in Turkish, *waqf* in Arabic), designed the family future; protected wealth from the rulers while providing funding for the family, the poor, basic urban services (water, street maintenance, education); and emanated symbolic prestige. Both male and female Muslims could establish, inherit, and govern *waqf*.[63]

Compared to the above, the charitable society (*cem'iyet-i hayriyye* in Ottoman Turkish, *al-jam'iyya al-khayriyya* in Arabic, *société de bienfaisance* in French) was a new bourgeois format for claiming social and group solidarity. Article 13 of the 1876 constitution allowed associations, and the 1885 Egyptian Civil Code also provided freedom for charitable associations.[64] The main goal of the philanthropic ("service") organizations was to help public education and health care by collecting money. They operated in the environment of hundreds of other clubs and associations. In Egypt, the land they possessed on which they built schools was tax free. To some extent, these associations and even the government services competed with Catholic and Protestant missionary establishments.[65]

The charitable society was a global uniform type of solidarity practice. Ottoman charity shared structural similarities with European middle-class philanthropy: the discourse on poverty, the understanding of agency as a moral quality, the transferability between male urban power and philanthropic positions, and the simultaneous thematization (domesticity, hygiene) and silencing of women.[66]

The Ottoman societies typically displayed subgroup solidarity without actively proselytizing. The European high bourgeoisies also practiced social rituals of charity that were often based on religious belonging. But there are two important differences: first, in the Ottoman case it is very rare to find

63. Doumani, *Family Life*, 59–64; Amy Singer, *Charity in Islamic Societies* (Cambridge: Cambridge University Press, 2008).

64. A. H. Hourani, D. A. Rustow, A.K.S. Lambton, A. Demeerseman, and Aziz Ahmad, "Djam'iyya," in *Encyclopaedia of Islam*, 2nd ed., ed. P. Bearman, Th. Bianquis, C. E. Bosworth, E. van Donzel, and W. P. Heinrichs, online (Leiden: Brill, 2019); Pollard, "Egyptian by Association," 245.

65. Mine Ener, *Managing Egypt's Poor and the Politics of Benevolence, 1800–1952* (Princeton, NJ: Princeton University Press, 2003), 100–105.

66. Alison Twells, *The Civilizing Mission and the English Middle Class, 1792–1850: The Heathen at Home and Overseas* (Basingstoke: Palgrave Macmillan, 2009).

non-religion-based charitable occasions (usually these were state-related gatherings such as fundraising for Ottoman soldiers through aid committees) and, second, the societies worked in a contested religious universe in which the government also claimed Islamic legitimacy. Old and new forms of charity were always the domain of rulers, too: charity provided the sultan with the image of a modern pastor who cares for his flock (even the first Ottoman steamship company was named *Şirket-i Hayriyye*, the "charitable company").[67] For Muslim elites, engagement in philanthropy meant political visibility and a claim to prestige.

Charitable societies in Ottoman cities emerged first as ethno-religious associations of Christian and Jewish communities, sometimes with some missionary involvement, chaired by the leaders of the respective communities.[68] In Istanbul, Muslim bureaucrats from the 1840s also established semiofficial societies with educational aims. From the midcentury, Ottoman lodges of European freemasonry emerged, which were smaller, elite male political groupings. Then, from around the early 1870s, somewhat earlier than in Russia, Ottoman Muslim charitable societies started to proliferate. [69]

In Ottoman Beirut, Muslim bourgeoisies established a society in 1875 whose first investment was a printing press and the publication of a journal. This was the nucleus of the Muslim Society of Benevolent Intentions, established in 1878, which aimed at both modern education (including female education) *and* upholding Islamic morality. The organization also helped students to study medicine in Cairo and Istanbul. By the 1880s, this society was absorbed by the Ottoman administration, but its properties were transformed into *waqf* and thus could further support modern schooling.[70] A similar organization, the Society for the Foundation of Schools, was established in Damascus in 1878, which opened new primary schools in *waqf* buildings and

67. Singer, *Charity in Islamic Societies*, 196; Nadir Özbek, *Osmanlı İmparatorluğu'nda Sosyal Devlet: Siyaset, İktidar Ve Meşrutiyet, 1876–1914* [The social state in the Ottoman Empire: Politics, power and reform, 1876–1914] (Istanbul: İletişim, 2002).

68. A society helped the Christians of Aleppo already in the eighteenth century: Yaron Ayalon, *Natural Disasters in the Ottoman Empire: Plague, Famine, and Other Misfortunes* (New York: Cambridge University Press, 2015), 130.

69. Mustafa Özgür Tuna, *Imperial Russia's Muslims: Islam, Empire and European Modernity, 1788–1914* (Cambridge: Cambridge University Press, 2015), 141.

70. *Jam'iyyat al-Maqasid al-Khayriyya al-Islamiyya* [The Muslim Society of Charitable Intentions], Hanssen, *Fin de Siècle Beirut*, 169–171.

the famous al-Zahiriyya public library. Later, this society was also absorbed into the imperial administration.[71] These flourishing Muslim educational societies involved significantly the local *a'yan* and progressive *'ulama'* in the Ottoman Syrian provinces and were often connected to the brief period of constitutional rule and to the reformer Midhat Pasha's governorship in the region.[72]

In late Ottoman Egypt in the 1860s and 1870s, there were approximately six Muslim charitable societies, although some might have been ephemeral.[73] There were some other societies with aims mixed between philanthropy and profit making. The largest and most enduring Christian charitable societies in Egypt were Ottoman Syrian Christian organizations, such as the Syrian Orthodox Society, established in 1875 or 1876 in Alexandria. This organization attracted thirty-four thousand subscribers by 1880. In 1881, Armenians in Egypt also established their own charitable society.[74]

In the imperial capital, charitable societies could be directly connected to imperial politics. The Military Donations Society, established by the famous reformer Midhat Pasha in 1876 at the time of the Bosnian war, was effectively transformed into a political, Muslim paramilitary organization that played a role in forcing the new sultan to proclaim the Ottoman Constitution in December 1876.[75] This is a good example that not every society was "private" or "civil" but rather a political tool of imperial elites. Statesmen and powerful officials participated in the "civil" societies that established a semipolitical sphere. In this way, these bourgeois forms of civil society could threaten the government by an alternative elite network.

The societies served as means to establish an unofficial, "private" welfare system by asking for donations from the bourgeois-aristocracy, and in the case of Ottoman Christians and Jews, donations from Europe. Low state investment

71. Stefan Weber, *Damascus: Ottoman Modernity and Urban Transformation*, vol. 1: *Text* (Damascus: Proceedings of the Danish Institute, 2009), 154–155; and Grallert, "To Whom Belong the Streets?," 85.

72. Donald Cieota, "Islamic Benevolent Societies and Public Education in Ottoman Syria, 1875–1882," *Islamic Quarterly* 26 (1982): 42–53; and Grallert, "To Whom Belong the Streets?," 403.

73. Anouar Abdel-Malek, *L'Égypte moderne: Idéologie et renaissance nationale* (1975; Paris: L'Harmattan, 2004), 285–286.

74. *Al-Ahram*, 17 May 1881, 2.

75. Şerif Mardin, *The Genesis of Young Ottoman Thought: A Study in the Modernization of Turkish Political Ideas* (Princeton, NJ: Princeton University Press, 1962), 75.

in civil education and health care and community resistance to imperial measures were the main causes behind the needs.[76]

Primary schools were abundant. Yet there were only fifty-one preparatory state schools in the entire empire in 1892,[77] and in British-occupied Ottoman Egypt, for instance, the literacy rate was only 4.8 percent in 1897 (Koran schools usually taught the Koran by heart).[78] Civil middle schools were often expensive but military schools were free.[79] Even in a large city such as Damascus in 1880, there were only twelve government schools, which typically educated Muslim children.[80] In Baghdad, the civil high school had only 96 students but the military school enrolled 846 boys in 1900.[81] Extragovernmental institutions were thus in need. The flip side of this "need" was a form of resistance by communities to the centralizing imperial government.

Similarly, hospitals, especially in provincial towns, were funded through private donations and were often affiliated with a religious community. Was this, again, a reaction to the negligence of government or a sign of distrust in government-owned medical facilities? In Istanbul, the earliest private, "modern" hospital was actually bestowed through an older form of charity, the *waqf*, by, ironically, Zeynep Hanım—the daughter of Mehmed Ali Pasha, the governor of Egypt—and her husband Yusuf Kamil Pasha in 1875.[82] In Cairo, societies had built eleven hospitals and nine clinics by 1912.[83]

Muslim scholars of religion made use of the charitable societies and their events to propagate their political views. They saw a duty of the government to help the Muslim societies. The young Muhammad 'Abduh (1849–1905), later to be famous as a Muslim reformer, underlined the usefulness of associations for Muslim Egyptians and asked for government support in the 1870s.[84] 'Abduh

76. It needs further research as to whether philanthropy was limited to urban environments only or it extended to the rural poor.

77. Fortna, *Imperial Classroom*, 124.

78. Ziad Fahmy, *Ordinary Egyptians: Creating the Modern Nation through Popular Culture* (Stanford, CA: Stanford University Press, 2011), 33.

79. Provence, *Last Ottoman Generation*, 21.

80. Randi Deguilhem, "Damas au XIXe siècle, un cosmopolitisme de l'esprit? Les nouvelles écoles laïques de l'état ottoman," *Cahiers de la Méditerranée* 67 (2003): 165–176.

81. Provence, *Last Ottoman Generation*, 24.

82. Feza Günergun and Şeref Etker, "Medicine," in *The Encyclopedia of the Ottoman Empire*, ed. Gabor Agoston and Bruce Masters (New York: Facts on File, 2009), 357–362, 360.

83. Pollard, "Egyptian by Association," 245.

84. Republished in Muhamad 'Abduh, *al-A'mal al-Kamila* [Complete works], vol. 2 (Cairo: Dar al-Shuruq, 1993), 5–7.

gave a long speech at an evening of the Society of Benevolent Intentions in the winter of 1880.[85] In the same year, 'Abd Allah Nadim (1845–1896), the famous poet and founder of the Muslim Charitable Society wrote a play, *Al-Watan* (The homeland), in which the character 'Izzat makes a very clear distinction between the rich in Europe who "[are] in industrial, in educational, in commercial societies and [who] necessarily increase their [nation's] strength and the strength of their wealth" and the rich in Egypt, who "exploit the poor and the cleaners, and eat and drink, and if they get together, they boast about cooks, slaves, servants, and houses."[86] At the end of the play, the charitable society is the social institution that 'Izzat deems appropriate to establish a school for educating the poor, just as the author Nadim had established his real charitable society and school in 1879.[87]

During the British occupation of Egypt, the most important Muslim charity society was the Egyptian Muslim Charitable Society, established in September 1892 and chaired by the young Khedive Abbas Hilmi II himself (r. 1892–1914). This society, undoubtedly with political aims, brought together Egyptian Muslim notables. It is characteristic that at their first meeting, whose income was for the poor, a European artist's show, fireworks, and local acrobats were staged in the Azbakiyya Garden Theater.[88] The social form of non-Muslim entertainment did not obstruct the gathering of Muslim bourgeoisies at all since Islam here only served as a grouping, a "commonality," for attaining solidarity.[89] Between 1908 and 1918, an immense number of secret clubs and organizations, many with explicit political aims, popped up in the imperial capital and the provinces. The Greater Syrians living in Egypt, such as Rashid Rida and the rich Lotfallah family, especially claimed leadership through associations and committees until the 1930s.

85. *Al-Waqt*, 6, 7, 8, 10, 11, and 12 December 1880.

86. 'Abd Allah al-Nadim, "Shadhra min Riwayat al-Watan wa-Hiya Riwaya Tashkhisiyya al-Gharad min-ha al-Hithth 'ala al-Ta'awun (li-Insha' al-Madaris al-'Ilmiyya wa-l-Sina'iyya)" [Fragments from the play "The Homeland": It is a theatrical story whose aim is to urge for cooperation (to establish scientific and industrial schools)], in *Sulafat al-Nadim*, ed. 'Abd al-Fattah al-Nadim, vol. 2 (Cairo: Matba'a Hindiyya, 1901), 33–63, 49.

87. Philip Sadgrove, *The Egyptian Theatre in the Nineteenth Century, 1799–1882* (1996; Cairo: AUC Press, 2007), 145.

88. Ahmad Shafiq, *Mudhakkirati Fi Nisf Qarn* [My memories about half a century], vol. 2 (1934; [Cairo]: Al-Hay'a al-Misiriyya al-'Amma li-l-Kitab, 1994), 50.

89. Frederick Cooper, *Colonialism in Question* (Berkeley: University of California Press, 2005), 75–76.

These associations organized events—performances, dinners, and balls (in the Arabic of the time: *balu, hafla, walima*)—that were important public occasions for fund-raising. These could occur also outside of the charity sphere, of course, but especially between the 1850s and 1890s there was a strong connection between performances, balls, community charity, and the press.

Balls, receptions, and soirées took place in Cairo, Alexandria, Beirut, Izmir, and Istanbul in theaters, hotels, palaces, embassies, and gardens. The prime season was the period from January to March every year. This season was central to the marriage strategies of the Ottoman bourgeoisies. The ball was essential in the symbolic repertoire: to be invited—or worse, not invited—was deeply meaningful and consequential. If the theater was supposedly open to everyone, the ball was strictly exclusive.

There was a strong European-Mediterranean dimension of Ottoman ball culture. The first balls in Ottoman Alexandria were given by Western European diplomats such as the French consul. In Izmir, the Greek community organized charitable balls in new casinos and the Euterpe Theater.[90] From 1869 in Cairo, charity balls were held regularly in the Khedivial Opera House.[91] In Istanbul, embassies were regular venues for balls and receptions, and local Christians had already used the Naum Theatre in the 1850s for balls.[92]

The emerging local societies competed with Italian, French, and Greek organizations. In the spring of 1881 alone, the French Charitable Society and the Roman Catholics advertised their charitable balls, and a masquerade was organized for the Free Italian Schools in the Opera of Cairo, but Arab societies were also holding charitable events in Cairo and Alexandria.[93] Such moments reveal the way in which non-Ottoman (Christian) societies opened up new forms of sociability for Ottoman (Christian) Arabs. For instance, despite the expectations of the French, the ball of the Charitable Society of Roman Catholics in 1881 was mostly attended not by the French or Italian residents but by Syrian Catholic Arab families—and Khedive Tevfik.[94]

90. Zandi-Sayek, *Ottoman Izmir*, 32–33.

91. The earliest society ball I could locate in the Khedivial Opera House was on 3 April 1872, by the Société de Secours Italienne. Table of expenses and incomes dated 16 April 1872, box 80, collection "The Reign of Ismail," Dar al-Watha'iq al-Qawmiyya (DWQ) [The National Archives of Egypt], Cairo.

92. For instance, Emre Aracı, *Naum Tiyatrosu: 19. Yüzyıl İstanbul'unun İtalyan Operası* [Naum Theater: An Italian opera in 19th-century Istanbul] (Istanbul: Yapı Kredi Yayınları, 2010), 207.

93. *Al-Ahram*, January, February, and March 1881.

94. *Al-Ahram*, 16 March 1881, 3.

Ottoman Muslim notables and intellectuals instrumentalized public balls as a form of informal politics, too. For instance, in February–March 1882, 'Abd Allah Nadim, Muhammad 'Abduh, and (the Christian) Adib Ishaq (all related to the activist Jamal al-Din al-Afghani) were the star speakers at the gatherings of charitable associations and balls. Nadim and 'Abduh both demanded a constitution during these gatherings.[95] On these occasions, politics converged with new habitus in new arenas of the public sphere.

In Istanbul, the Pera (Beyoğlu) spaces (theaters, hotels, embassies, and casinos) were highly desirable venues, because they embodied "Europe." For instance, the Palais de Cristal (usually called "the French theater") was magnificently decorated; the gaslit central ballroom had eighteen columns that held the balconies that were so ideal for chatting and gossiping.[96] Some institutions in Pera hosted balls every Saturday night, though surely not all of these were charity occasions per se.[97] Concerts and balls were organized for the Pera public and for the Ottoman elite, sometimes even with the participation of the Sultan Abdülmecid himself, already in the 1850s.[98]

Charitable theater performances, supported by the local press, were the main examples where group solidarity and the cultural capital of the Ottoman bourgeoisies were connected in the new public sphere. In Beirut in 1858, perhaps the very first occasion of an Arab subgroup expressing itself in the new public forms of the Ottoman imperial society was a performance staged for the local staff of the Ottoman Bank and some notables of the city and that was, in turn, advertised by the very first private Arabic (Christian) newspaper.[99] In Damascus, Christian Arabic plays were put on in missionary schools from the 1860s, and soon Muslim entertainers created new musical theater troops.[100]

95. 'Abd al-Rahman al-Rafi'i, *Al-Thawra al-'Urabiyya wa-l-Ihtilal al-Injilizi* [The 'Urabi revolution and the English occupation] (Cairo: Maktabat al-Nahda al-Misriyya, 1949), 227–234.

96. *Journal de Constantinople*, 17 January 1862.

97. *La Turquie*, 10 February 1876, 1.

98. Seren Akyoldaş, "The Teutonia: A Case Study of the German cultural presence in the Ottoman Empire" (MA thesis, Boğazici University, 2009); on Greek communal music, see Merih Erol, *Greek Orthodox Music in Ottoman Istanbul: Nation and Community in the Era of Reform* (Bloomington: Indiana University Press, 2015); Mrs. Edmund Hornby, *In and Around Stamboul* (Philadelphia: James Challen and Son, [1858]), 216–218.

99. Anonymous, *Hadiqat al-Akhbar*, 19 June 1858, 3–4.

100. Philip Sadgrove, "The Syrian Arab Theatre after Marun Naqqash (the 1850s and the 1860s)," *Archív Orientálni* 55 (1987): 271–283, 280.

From the 1870s, charity performances became standard parts of bourgeois life in late Ottoman cities.

The balls and performances as laboratories of habitus embodied an intersection between education, religiosity, patriotism, and new social codes. The bourgeois and middle-class practices threatened to undermine the Ottoman system since the constitution was suspended. The 1908 military coup d'état served the interests of Ottoman imperial civil society and restored the constitution. The real power struggle, however, then started with this immense change: which bourgeois group would control the government and the army? Or, would the army control the empire and the bourgeoisies?

Conclusion

This essay has suggested a loose taxonomy for the cluster of Ottoman bourgeoisies: the bourgeois-aristocracy and the middle groups. My experiment has used an imperial framework instead of one of nation-states, and I have highlighted wealthy Muslims among the Ottoman imperial bourgeoisie.

The underlying mosaic of religious solidarity below the public discourse of patriotism encompassed subtle forms of cultural resistance against centralization and facilitated activities for building parallel communal systems to buttress insufficient state welfare services. Muslims also had to organize themselves since the governments, despite their Islamic character, did not supply enough institutions to compete with global challenges and the missionaries. New community techniques thus did not demolish faith-based solidarity; on the contrary, religion was a principle of public grouping. The Ottoman Empire in this regard is similar to the civic structure in the United States but without the latter's republican and full capitalist conditions.

Two further observations can be made. The first is that Ottoman civil society was unable to claim effective control over the government, partly due to the extreme geographical range. However, since members of the bourgeois-aristocracy were culturally integrated into global consumption and social practices, the transition to national elite publics after the First World War was a relatively easy social process. Political transition, on the other hand, was obstructed under the mandate system in the 1920s.

The second point is that some charitable societies were political playgrounds of the Muslim bourgeoisies. This is why we find pashas as presidents and such legendary figures as al-Afghani and 'Abduh occasionally attending a social event. Societies have been crucial ever since. Even the Muslim Brotherhood is a "society" (their official name is the Society of the Muslim Brothers) that, in the 1930s, had its own theater troupe. This suggests that, instead of being anomalies, today's Islamic charity foundations, which claim extremely pious credentials, continue the bourgeois associations of late Ottoman social transformation.

11

Worlds of a Muslim Bourgeoisie

THE SOCIOCULTURAL MILIEU OF
THE ISLAMIC MINORITY IN
INTERWAR GERMANY

David Motadel

A GROUP PHOTOGRAPH, printed in 1929 in the *Moslemische Revue*, a magazine of the Islamic community in Berlin, shows a group of Muslims who have gathered in front of the mosque at the Fehrbelliner Platz to celebrate their highest religious holiday, the Feast of Sacrifice, 'Id al-Adha (Fig. 11.1).[1] There are thirty-six women and forty-six men in total. Of the women, twenty-seven have their head covered. Whether this was as a sign of their faith cannot be said with any certainty; in any case, almost every one has covered her hair with an elegant hat, which reflects the fashion worn by German bourgeois ladies of the 1920s. Only one wears a scarf, chicly wound around her head. Nearly all of the men wear a smart European brimmed hats, although some of them instead wear a turban or fez; and all of them are dressed in trousers, shirts, and jackets, and a few also wear ties. The clothing of the Berlin Muslims was an expression of a hybrid

---

1. This chapter is based on the article "Islamische Bürgerlichkeit: Das soziokulturelle Milieu der muslimischen Minderheit in Berlin 1918–1939," *Tel Aviver Jahrbuch für Deutsche Geschichte* 37 (2009): 103–121. *Islamische Bürgerlichkeit* is translated as "Islamic bourgeois culture." *Bürgertum* and *Bürgerlichkeit* are translated as "bourgeoisie" and "bourgeois culture" or "middle-class culture," respectively, following David Blackbourn and Richard J. Evans, eds., *The German Bourgeoisie: Essays on the Social History of the German Middle Classes from the Late Eighteenth to Early Twentieth Century* (London: Routledge, 1991).

FIGURE 11. Photograph of the 'Id al-Adha celebration in Berlin. From the *Moslemische Revue* 2 (1929), inner jacket cover; photographer unknown.

culture that combined elements of Islamic tradition with modern bourgeois fashion.

The group photograph is fairly representative of the pictures taken of (mostly male) Muslims in Berlin during the 1920s and 1930s.[2] Their fashion was characterized by restrained, fine clothing, particularly the black or gray suits usually donned by contemporaneous bourgeois gentlemen.[3] Their headgear was also remarkable. In the above-mentioned photograph, most of the men are shown with a European-style brimmed hat, which had become an identifiable sign of bourgeois affluence in Europe since the nineteenth century.[4] Although in the photograph only ten men wear a turban or fez, the red felt hat and the cloth wound around the head appear in a number of other photographs that were taken of the Berlin community in the interwar period. Both types of head covering, which allowed for the forehead to touch the ground during prayers, had, since the late nineteenth century, become explicit symbols of Islam, which was one of the reasons for the promulgation of the "hat laws" in Turkey (November 1925) and Iran (August 1927; July 1935).[5] In Berlin, moreover, many Muslims from India wore the turban, which had been a symbol of the Indian Muslim middle class since the nineteenth century, even though Muslims in India had also been wearing the fez as a sign of a pan-Islamic solidarity with the Ottoman Caliphate since the late nineteenth century.[6]

2. Numerous photographs were printed in the editions of the *Moslemische Revue* (hereafter *MR*).

3. Sabina Brändli, *"Der herrlich biedere Mann": Vom Siegeszug des bürgerlichen Herrenanzugs im 19. Jahrhundert* (Zurich: Chronos, 1998).

4. Hermann Bausinger, "Bürgerlichkeit und Kultur," in *Bürger und Bürgerlichkeit im 19. Jahrhundert*, ed. Jürgen Kocka (Göttingen: Vandenhoeck und Ruprecht, 1987), 121–142, 123–127, on the history of the hat in bourgeois culture.

5. Houchang E. Chehabi, "Dress Codes for Men in Turkey and Iran," in *Men of Order: Authoritarian Modernization under Atatürk and Reza Shah*, ed. Touraj Atabaki and Erik J. Zürcher (London: I. B. Tauris, 2004), 209–237; Patricia L. Baker, "The Fez in Turkey: A Symbol of Modernization?," *Costume* 20 (1986): 72–85; Bianca Devos, *Kleidungspolitik in Iran* (Würzburg: Ergon, 2006); and the contributions to Nancy Lindisfarne-Tapper and Bruce Ingham, eds., *Languages of Dress in the Middle East* (London: Curzon, 1997).

6. Chehabi, "Dress Codes," 210–211; and Margrit Pernau, "Shifting Globalities—Changing Headgear: The Indian Muslims between Turban, Hat and Fez," in *Translocality: The Study of Globalising Processes from a Southern Perspective*, ed. Ulrike Freitag and Achim von Oppen (Leiden: Brill, 2010), 249–267.

Muslim life in Berlin was institutionalized in the interwar years.[7] For the first time in German history, Muslims, followers of various Islamic groups and sects, organized themselves in associations, founded their own publications, and constructed their own buildings. The Berlin mosque—today known as the Wilmersdorf Mosque—opened in 1925. Overall, at the time some eighteen hundred to three thousand Muslims (the number varies in the interwar period) from more than forty countries—India, Central Asia, the Arab world, Turkey, and beyond—were living in the German capital.[8]

Across Western Europe, new, organized Muslim communities emerged during the interwar years.[9] Many thousands of Muslims were living in Britain,

7. An overview of the history of the Muslim community in interwar Germany is provided by Gerhard Höpp, "Zwischen Moschee und Demonstration: Muslime in Berlin, 1920–1930," parts I–III: MR 3 (1990): 135–146; 4 (1990): 230–238; 1 (1991): 13–19; Gerhard Höpp, Muslime in der Mark: Als Kriegsgefangene und Internierte in Wünsdorf und Zossen, 1914–1924 (Berlin: Das Arabische Buch, 1997); Gerhard Höpp, "Muslime unterm Hakenkreuz: Zur Entstehung des Islamischen Zentralinstituts zu Berlin e.V.," MR 1 (1994): 16–27; Britta Richter, "Islam im Deutschland der Zwischenkriegsjahre," Zeitschrift für Türkeistudien 2 (1996): 257–266; and Bernd Bauknecht, Muslime in Deutschland von 1920 bis 1945 (Cologne: Teiresias, 2001). Broader overviews of the history of the Muslim community in Germany are M. S. Abdullah, Die Geschichte des Islams in Deutschland (Graz: Styria, 1981); M. S. Abdullah, Und gab ihnen sein Königswort: Berlin-Preußen-Bundesrepublik: Ein Abriß der Geschichte der islamischen Minderheit in Deutschland (Altenberge: Cis, 1987); and Nasir Ahmad, A Brief History of the Berlin Muslim Mission and the Berlin Mosque (Berlin: Wilmersdorf Mosque, 2006).

8. Höpp, "Zwischen Moschee und Demonstration," I, 136, on the 1920s; and Muhammad S. Abdullah, "Zwischen Anbiederung und Friedenspredigt," MR 3 (1999): 129–138, 137, on the 1930s. The ethnic and national structure of the group varied in the interwar years. Generally, the history of this minority during this period can be characterized by mobility, by a constant flow of people (especially students, merchants, and diplomats) who intended only to stay for a limited time in Germany but nevertheless long enough to organize themselves. Even if religion stood at the center of activities of Muslim associations, it was possible for both national and Islamic identities (which also overlapped) to coexist. In addition, a number of national associations were set up in Berlin alongside the Islamic organizations. Occasionally the tension between nationalist and religious groups also led to conflicts, particularly between the Islamic community and Egyptian nationalists and Turkish Kemalists.

9. Previous scholarship has analyzed Muslims mostly under national or ethnic (for instance Algerians in France or Indians in England), rather than under religious, categories. For this reason there are only a few analytic studies on the history of Muslim minorities in Western Europe: Humayun Ansari, The Infidel Within: Muslims in Britain since 1800 (London: Hurst, 2004); Sadek Sellam, La France et ses Musulmans: Un Siècle de Politique Musulmane (1895–2005) (Paris: Fayard, 2006); the contributions in Mohammed Arkoun, ed., Histoire de l'Islam et des Musulmans en France du Moyen Age à nos Jours (Paris: Albin Michel, 2006); and, for a

particularly in Manchester, Liverpool, South Shields, Cardiff, and London; most of them had a South Asian background, but many also came from the Arab world and sub-Saharan Africa. At the same time, tens of thousands of Muslims, mostly from North Africa, were living in France, especially in Marseilles, Fréjus, and Paris. Just as in Germany, these Muslims began to organize themselves, setting up institutions from mosques and schools to cemeteries and publications.

To be sure, there had been a Muslim presence in the heartlands of Western Europe in the late nineteenth and early twentieth centuries. But the Muslim presence in the region was highly atomized, and the first clusters and networks of individuals emerged only after 1918. The arrival of Muslim migrants was the result of structural changes and events. Structurally, Muslim immigration was connected to the increasing globalization of Europe, especially of the labor market, and to European imperialism. Moreover, major events, most importantly the First World War and, to a lesser extent, the Russian Revolution and the collapse of the Ottoman Empire, led to increasing migration and to a period of formal organization and institutionalization of Muslim life in western Europe in the interwar years. More generally, the making of these early Muslim communities was part of the much wider historical phenomenon of migration and the emergence of new minorities in the global age, ranging from Chinatowns in New York to Lebanese communities in Senegal.[10]

The social composition of these new minorities could vary significantly. The emerging Muslim minorities in Western Europe were socially heterogeneous. In Britain, for example, they included a substantial Muslim working class of industrial workers and seafarers, like the legendary Yemeni and Somali sailors of Cardiff and South Shields. In a metropolis like London, on the other hand, the Islamic community was far more bourgeois, being dominated by students, merchants, and Islamic missionaries. In France, too, Muslims from various social backgrounds mingled, ranging from the impoverished colonial veterans in places like Fréjus to the middle class Muslims of Paris, comprising students,

---

comparative perspective, David Motadel, "The Making of Muslim Communities in Western Europe, 1914–1939," in *Transnational Islam in Interwar Europe: Muslim Activists and Thinkers*, ed. Umar Ryad and Götz Nordbruch (New York: Palgrave Macmillan, 2014), 13–43.

10. Dirk Hoerder, "Migrations and Belongings 1870–1945," in *A World Connecting: 1870–1945*, ed. Emily S. Rosenberg (Cambridge, MA: Harvard University Press, 2012), 435–589; and, more generally, Michael H. Fisher, *Migration: A World History* (Oxford: Oxford University Press, 2013), provide good overviews.

merchants, diplomats, and political activists. In comparison, the German Muslim community was socially more homogenous.

This chapter examines the sociocultural milieu of the Muslim community in Berlin. It focuses on those Muslims who organized themselves in groups and associations. Although the following pages only provide a rough overview, they will demonstrate that interwar Berlin saw the emergence of a specific sociocultural milieu that can be described as *Islamic bourgeois*. I will start, however, with some more basic and fundamental reflections on the relationship between class and religious diaspora in the age of globalization.

Religious Diaspora and the Global Bourgeoisie

Scholars have long examined the bourgeois middle class as a social formation in terms of Marx or Weber.[11] Over the last decades, however, cultural historians and anthropologists have increasingly described the bourgeoisie in cultural terms, as a social group characterized by specific lifestyles, forms of habitus and patterns of behavior, and values and norms.[12] In short, they have looked at the specific cultural distinctions by which the members of this class have marked their social field.[13] There is a direct connection between class and

11. Hans Mommsen, "Die Auflösung des Bürgertums seit dem späten 19. Jahrhundert," in *Bürger und Bürgerlichkeit*, ed. Kocka, 288–315, provides an overview of the process of dissolution of the classical bourgeoisie as social formation since the turn of the century.

12. M. Rainer Lepsius, "Zur Soziologie des Bürgertums und der Bürgerlichkeit," in *Bürger und Bürgerlichkeit*, ed. Kocka, 79–100. A cultural understanding of social formations was most notably advocated by the Bielefeld research project "Sozialgeschichte des neuzeitlichen Bürgertums"; see Hans-Jürgen Puhle, "Introduction," in *Bürger in der Gesellschaft der Neuzeit: Wirtschaft—Politik—Kultur*, ed. Hans-Jürgen Puhle (Göttingen: Vandenhoeck und Ruprecht, 1991), 7–13, 9. On the cultural formation of social difference, see Jürgen Kocka, "Bürgertum und Bürgerlichkeit als Probleme der deutschen Geschichte vom späten 18. zum frühen 20. Jahrhundert," in *Bürger und Bürgerlichkeit*, ed. Kocka, 21–63; and, in the same volume, Bausinger, "Bürgerlichkeit und Kultur," 121–142 and Thomas Nipperdey's commentary: "'Bürgerlich' als Kultur," 143–148; Jürgen Kocka, "Bürgertum und bürgerliche Gesellschaft im 19. Jh. Europäische Entwicklungen und deutsche Eigenarten," in *Bürgertum im 19. Jahrhundert*, vol. 1: *Deutschland im europäischen Vergleich*, ed. Jürgen Kocka (Göttingen: Vandenhoeck und Ruprecht, 1988), 11–76; and, more generally, Linda Young, *Middle-Class Culture in the Nineteenth Century* (New York: Palgrave, 2003); and Jerrold Seigel, *Modernity and Bourgeois Life: Society, Politics, and Culture in England, France, and Germany since 1750* (Cambridge: Cambridge University Press, 2012).

13. Pierre Bourdieu, *Distinction: A Social Critique of the Judgement of Taste* (Cambridge, MA: Harvard University Press, 1987).

culture, even though, in practice, bourgeois culture was often heterogeneous and not always congruent with the social formation of the bourgeois middle class.[14]

Scholars have, moreover, examined all kinds of variations and hybridizations of bourgeois culture.[15] Thus, religion (in this case, Islam) could become an important part of bourgeois culture. Although the notion of an incompatibility between bourgeois culture and piety has long informed scholarship on the history of the bourgeois middle class, during the last years historians have repeatedly demonstrated that religious and bourgeois lifestyles and value systems in fact regularly merged.[16]

Particularly well researched in this respect is the bourgeois milieu of the Jewish minority in nineteenth-century Germany. Jewish identities and lifestyles did not necessarily need to be abandoned during the process of Jewish emancipation. In fact, when integrating into German society, members of the Jewish minority were often not guided by cultures perceived as national (e.g., German) or religious (e.g., Christian); rather, they acculturated within a specific social milieu.[17] Bourgeois society offered Jews the opportunity to retain

14. Manfred Hettling, "Bürgerliche Kultur: Bürgerlichkeit als kulturelles System," in *Sozial- und Kulturgeschichte des Bürgertums: Eine Bilanz des Bielefelder Sonderforschungsbereichs (1986–1997)*, ed. Peter Lundgreen (Göttingen: Vandenhoeck und Ruprecht, 2000), 319–339.

15. Homi K. Bhabha, *The Location of Culture* (London: Routledge, 1994) was one of the first to draw attention to the hybridity and coalescing of identities and cultures, which are often understood as homogenous. Bhabha argues that mixed forms of cultural patterns of behavior and thinking as well as identities create a "third space"; on cultural hybridity, see also the works of Stuart Hall, Paul Gilroy, Gayatri Spivak, and Néstor García Canclini.

16. Frank-Michael Kuhlemann, "Bürgertum und Religion," in *Sozial- und Kulturgeschichte*, ed. Lundgreen, 293–318, provides an overview.

17. Simone Lässig, *Jüdische Wege ins Bürgertum: Kulturelles Kapital und sozialer Aufstieg im 19. Jahrhundert* (Göttingen: Vandenhoeck und Ruprecht, 2004), is the most comprehensive study. As early as 1935 Jacob Katz already drew attention to the fact that Jews had not "assimilated" within the "German nation" but only within one part of it, the bourgeois middle class, see Jacob Katz, *Die Entstehung der Judenassimilation in Deutschland und deren Ideologie* (Frankfurt: Droller, 1935), 32. Shulamit Volkov pointed out in 1988 that bourgeois culture was not the consequence but instead a vehicle of Jewish emancipation, see Shulamit Volkov, "Die Verbürgerlichung der Juden in Deutschland: Eigenart und Paradigma," in *Bürgertum im 19. Jahrhundert*, vol. 2: *Wirtschaftsbürger und Bildungsbürger*, ed. Kocka, 343–371. Similar arguments have been put forward by Marion Kaplan, *Jüdisches Bürgertum: Frau, Familie und Identität im Kaiserreich* (Hamburg: Dölling und Galitz, 1997); Jacob Toury, "Der Eintritt der Juden ins deutsche Bürgertum," in *Das Judentum in der deutschen Umwelt 1800–1850*, ed. Hans Liebeschütz and Arnold Paucker (Tübingen: Mohr Siebeck, 1977), 139–242; Michael Meyer, *The Origins of the*

their Jewish cultures and to combine them with a bourgeois middle-class life.[18] In a similar way, Muslims who organized themselves during the 1920s and 1930s in Berlin also combined Islamic and bourgeois lifestyles and values into a hybrid form of Islamic bourgeois culture. However, in contrast to the Jewish minority, which over the course of the nineteenth century gradually made the bourgeois culture of the German non-Jewish middle class its own, the Muslims of Berlin did not have to learn and adapt to bourgeois norms and patterns of behavior in Germany (the period of their stay in Germany would have been too short for this in any case) but brought them with them from their home countries, where the majority of these Muslims had belonged to the nonaristocratic elites.

In fact, bourgeois culture had spread among urban elites throughout the world since the late nineteenth century. One simple explanation of this phenomenon is the global spread of (Western) bourgeois cultural norms and lifestyles among economically and socially independent, privileged groups at that time. This can be observed in cases of cultural ideals (such as gender roles) or aesthetics (such as fashion) as much as in concrete patterns of behavior (such as table manners) and institutional standards (such as academic titles). Generally, these transfer processes were fueled by European imperialism and by a more general increase in global mobility. In the non-European world, the new bourgeois patterns of living and thinking often melded with indigenous culture.[19]

Another explanation (which does not, however, exclude transfer processes) derives from the global transformation of social structures throughout the nineteenth century—to some extent powered by global capitalism and European imperialism—which in societies across the world produced modern (urban) middle classes whose members shared common values and lifestyles. Part of

---

Modern Jew: Jewish Identity and European Culture in Germany, 1749–1824 (Detroit, MI: Wayne State University Press, 1967); and Till van Rahden, *Juden und andere Breslauer: Die Beziehungen zwischen Juden, Protestanten und Katholiken in einer deutschen Großstadt von 1860 bis 1925* (Göttingen: Vandenhoeck und Ruprecht, 2000). On minorities in general, Stefi Jersch-Wenzel, "Minderheiten in der bürgerlichen Gesellschaft," in *Bürgertum im 19. Jahrhundert*, vol. 2, ed. Kocka, 392–420.

18. Lässig, *Jüdische Wege*, 20.

19. Since the late nineteenth century, the creation of hybrid forms of culture have been undoubtedly fueled by processes of globalization, see Marwan M. Kraidy, *Hybridity: Or the Cultural Logic of Globalization* (Philadelphia: Temple University Press, 2005); and Jan Nederveen Pieterse, *Globalization and Culture: Global Mélange* (London: Rowman and Littlefield, 2003).

these new middle classes were businessmen and entrepreneurs, physicians, administrative elites, and academics, who distinguished themselves from both the lower classes and the aristocracy. The global differentiation of societies—which was also influenced by colonialism—and the making of the global middle class can be seen as a part of the "birth of the modern world."[20] To be sure, a study of the emergence of bourgeois middle classes across the world is methodically not unproblematic. These problems arise not just from the often very different social and cultural contexts in which the new middle classes emerged but also from semantic heterogeneity.[21]

Although historians have long studied the history of the bourgeois middle classes mainly as a European and American phenomenon, more recently an increasing number of studies have looked at bourgeois classes and cultures outside the West.[22] Muslim majority societies were no exception. Lands from the Ottoman Empire to Persia to British India saw the emergence of middle classes.[23] In an age of increasing global mobility, members of these classes

20. C. A. Bayly, *The Birth of the Modern World, 1780–1914: Global Connections and Comparisons* (Oxford: Blackwell, 2004). David Cannadine has referred to the importance of class and social status with regard to the interaction between members of European and non-European elites within the British Empire, see David Cannadine, *Ornamentalism: How the British Saw Their Empire* (London: Penguin, 2001).

21. Reinhart Koselleck, Ulrike Spree, and Wilhelm Steinmetz, "Drei bürgerliche Welten: Zur vergleichenden Semantik der bürgerlichen Gesellschaft in Deutschland, England und Frankreich," in *Bürger in der Gesellschaft*, ed. Puhle, 14–58; and the contributions in *Bürgertum im 19. Jahrhundert*, ed. Kocka, problematize these differences within Europe.

22. Jürgen Osterhammel, *The Transformation of the World* (Princeton, NJ: Princeton University Press, 2014), 761–778; and Jürgen Osterhammel, "Hierarchies and Connections: Aspects of a Global Social History," in *An Emerging Modern World, 1750–1870*, ed. Sebastian Conrad and Jürgen Osterhammel (Cambridge, MA: Harvard University Press, 2018), 661–888, provide general accounts on the middle class in global history. Moreover, see the contributions in A. Ricardo López and Barbara Weinstein, eds., *The Making of the Middle Class: Toward a Transnational History* (Durham, NC: Duke University Press, 2012); and in this volume.

23. Important case studies on the development of bourgeois classes and culture in the Arab world are Ulrike Freitag, "Gibt es eine arabische Gesellschaftsgeschichte?," in *Wege der Gesellschaftsgeschichte*, ed. Jürgen Osterhammel, Dieter Langewiesche, and Paul Nolte (Göttingen: Vandenhoeck und Ruprecht, 2006), 161–177; Ulrike Freitag, "Arabische Buddenbrooks in Singapur," *Historische Anthropologie* 2 (2003): 208–223; Keith David Watenpaugh, *Being Modern in the Middle East: Revolution, Nationalism, Colonialism, and the Arab Middle Class* (Princeton, NJ: Princeton University Press, 2006); Lucie Ryzova, *The Age of the Efendiyya: Passages to Modernity in National-Colonial Egypt* (Oxford: Oxford University Press, 2014); Toufoul Abou-Hodeib, *A Taste for Home: The Modern Middle Class in Ottoman Beirut* (Stanford, CA: Stanford University

would move to other countries in search of opportunities and personal improvement. Cosmopolitanism became a central characteristic of the bourgeois middle classes, allowing its members to expand the territorial boundaries of their social worlds.[24] In the diaspora, they would form bourgeois exile milieus and interact with members of the bourgeois middle class of the majority societies.

The assumption that bourgeois middle-class lifestyles and ideals existed beyond Europe's borders serves as the starting point for the following discussion of the Muslim community in Berlin. In the German diaspora, Muslims, who often had very diverse national backgrounds, were able to interact and organize themselves on the basis of two commonalities: Islamic and bourgeois lifestyles and values.

Press, 2017); and Adam Mestyan's chapter in this volume. On the Ottoman bourgeoisie, see Fatma Müge Göçek, *Rise of the Bourgeoisie, Demise of Empire: Ottoman Westernization and Social Change* (New York: Oxford University Press, 1996); and Edhem Eldem, "(A Quest for) the Bourgeoisie of Istanbul: Identities, Roles and Conflicts," in *Urban Governance under the Ottomans: Between Cosmopolitanism and Conflict*, ed. Ulrike Freitag and Nora Lafi (London: Routledge, 2014), 159–186. On the Iranian bourgeois middle class, see the chapter of Houchang Chehabi in this volume. And on India, see Margrit Pernau, *Ashraf into Middle Classes: Muslims in Nineteenth-Century Delhi* (Oxford: Oxford University Press, 2013); Sanjay Joshi, *Fractured Modernity: The Making of a Middle Class in Colonial North India* (Oxford: Oxford University Press, 2001); and Utsa Ray's chapter in this volume.

24. There is a remarkable body of literature on cosmopolitanism in history. Bernhard Gißibl and Isabella Löhr, eds., *Bessere Welten: Kosmopolitismus in den Geschichtswissenschaften* (Frankfurt: Campus, 2017) provides an overview. On the history of cosmopolitanism as an idea, from antiquity to the enlightenment and beyond, see Albert Mathiez, *La Révolution et les étrangers: Cosmopolitisme et défense nationale* (Paris: La Renaissance du Livre, 1918); Thomas J. Schlereth, *The Cosmopolitan Ideal in Enlightenment Thought: Its Form and Function in the Ideas of Franklin, Hume, and Voltaire, 1694–1790* (Notre Dame, IN: University of Notre Dame Press, 1977); and Pauline Kleingeld, "Six Varieties of Cosmopolitanism in Late Eighteenth-Century Germany," *Journal of the History of Ideas* 60, no. 3 (1999): 505–524. A good source collection on the history of ideas of cosmopolitanism is Garrett Wallace Brown and David Held, eds., *The Cosmopolitanism Reader* (Cambridge: Polity Press, 2010). On the history of cosmopolitanism as a practice, see the chapters in Sugata Bose and Kris Manjapra, eds., *Cosmopolitan Thought Zones: South Asia and the Global Circulation of Ideas* (New York: Palgrave Macmillan, 2010); Seema Alavi, *Muslim Cosmopolitanism in the Age of Empire* (Cambridge, MA: Harvard University Press, 2015); and Su Lin Lewis, *Cities in Motion: Urban Life and Cosmopolitanism in Southeast Asia, 1920–1940* (Cambridge: Cambridge University Press, 2016).

Islamic-Bourgeois Lifestyles

With a few exceptions, the members of the Muslim community in Berlin were financially independent and highly educated. Most of them came from the upper middle classes of their home countries. In fact, the majority of Berlin's Muslims were part of the educated bourgeoisie (the *Bildungsbürgertum* in the German context): persons who made a living through special knowledge and who strongly believed in the value of education.

The community included businessmen and merchants alongside writers and journalists, like Habibur Rahman, born in India in 1901, who for some time also served as the general secretary of the Islamic community.[25] Moreover, there were also a number of physicians among them, such as the editor of the Islamic journal *Liwa al-Islam*, Ilias Bragon, a veterinarian who had come from Turkey in 1920; and the Syrian Wassil Rasslan, a general practitioner who had moved to Berlin in 1924, graduated from university in 1933, and practiced in a Berlin hospital before earning his doctorate in 1934.[26]

The core of the community was formed by members of Berlin universities, in particular students. Many of the students had been sent officially to study in Germany by the governments of their home countries, which also funded their stays. Such students included, for example, the Iranian A. Rahman Saif, who edited the journal *Azadi-yi Sharq*, the Iraqi Abbud al-Ibrahim, who was a council member of the Deutsch-Moslemische Gesellschaft (German-Muslim Society), and the Egyptian Ahmad Wali, who was the deputy chairman of the group and who had already been sent to Germany before the First World War by the Egyptian government and concluded his medical studies there in 1929.[27] Wali also worked as a lector in Arabic at the oriental studies faculty in Berlin, much like the Egyptian medical student Mohammed Jahia Haschimi, who lived in Germany from 1923 to 1937.[28] Similarly, the founder and imam of the Islamische Gemeinde zu Berlin (Islamic Community in Berlin), Abdul Jabbar Kheiri, had come from Delhi to Berlin in 1919 to study history and economics.[29] Supervised by Werner Sombart, he completed his doctorate in 1927.

25. Höpp, "Muslime unterm Hakenkreuz," 19.
26. Höpp, "Muslime unterm Hakenkreuz," 19, 25; and Bauknecht, *Muslime in Deutschland*, 45.
27. Höpp, "Muslime unterm Hakenkreuz," 27; Höpp, "Zwischen Moschee und Demonstration," I, 136, and III, 13–14; and Bauknecht, *Muslime in Deutschland*, 96.
28. Höpp, "Muslime unterm Hakenkreuz," 19, 25.
29. Höpp, "Zwischen Moschee und Demonstration," I, 136, and III, 13.

Another significant group in the community that should not be overlooked were the diplomats from Muslim countries. In the early 1920s, for example, the Turkish embassy imam Hafiz Schükrü served as deputy chairman of the Islamische Gemeinde zu Berlin.[30] During the mid-1920s, envoys of various Muslim states had attempted to organize Berlin's Muslims within the Gesellschaft für Islamische Gottesverehrung (Society for Islamic Worship). In the end, however, all of these associations fused with the Deutsch-Moslemische Gesellschaft, the society that ran the mosque. Members of the embassies were regularly involved in the activities of the mosque, and sometimes even led the Friday prayers.

Last, German converts to Islam should be mentioned, since they exercised significant influence in Berlin's Muslim community. Islam was well respected in the circles of Berlin's bourgeois avant-garde. The prominent writer from Baku Lev Nussimbaum, alias Mohammed Essad Bey, even converted to Islam while living in Berlin in an effort to further his career in the literary circles of the Weimar Republic.[31] The converts came almost exclusively from the educated middle class and had a particularly strong influence on bourgeois Muslim journalism in Berlin.

In the Muslim community life of Berlin, Islamic culture and bourgeois forms of sociability merged.[32] In the early 1920s, the fashionable Orient Club in the Kalckreuthstraße was a popular meeting place for Muslims.[33] Islam provided the official framework of the club, an attempt to overcome ethnic differences between Arabs, Persians, Turks, Tartars, Indians, and Afghans. Indeed, in the early years of the Weimar Republic, a kind of bourgeois-Islamic club culture emerged in the rooms of Berlin's Orient Club.

30. Höpp, "Zwischen Moschee und Demonstration," I, 136.

31. Tom Reiss, *The Orientalist: Solving the Mystery of a Strange and Dangerous Life* (New York: Random House, 2005).

32. The ideal type of a bourgeois association was characterized by its independence from the state, voluntary membership, specific and limited purpose, and equality of members, see Christian Eisenberg, "Arbeiter, Bürger und der 'bürgerliche Verein' 1820–1870: Deutschland und England im Vergleich," in *Bürgertum im 19. Jahrhundert*, vol. 2, ed. Kocka, 187–219, 189–192; Thomas Nipperdey, "Verein als soziale Struktur in Deutschland im späten 18. und frühen 19. Jahrhundert," in *Gesellschaft, Kultur, Theorie: Gesammelte Aufsätze zur neueren Geschichte* (Göttingen: Vandenhoeck und Ruprecht, 1976), 174–205; and the contributions to Otto von Dann, ed., *Vereinswesen und bürgerliche Gesellschaft in Deutschland* (Munich: Oldenbourg, 1984).

33. Bauknecht, *Muslime in Deutschland*, 44–45.

The three largest Islamic organizations established in the interwar period, which united the majority of Berlin's Muslims, were the Islamic Community in Berlin, founded in 1922; the Society for Islamic Worship, founded in 1924, and, finally, from 1925, the German-Muslim Society and its mosque in Wilmersdorf, which was established by representatives of the Lahore Ahmadiyya movement. In these organizations, and especially in the mosque, members of various religious groups and sects—such as followers of the Ahmadiyya movement from India, Sunnis from Syria, or Shi'ites from Iran—came together, forming a kind of ecumenical community. The meetings in the associations and the mosque were of a social, cultural and, of course, religious nature; they were not intended to serve as a forum for political debate and organization. The celebration of the festivals in the Islamic calendar, particularly the breaking of the fast at the end of Ramadan and the birthday of the Prophet, were strictly organized and frequently accompanied by academic lectures that were intended to attract an educated audience.

Events of the Muslim community were also regularly held in German educational institutions, particularly secondary schools. For instance, lectures were often organized in the assembly hall of the Gymnasium on the Georgstraße, near the Friedrichstraße station, or in the assembly hall of the Fürstin Bismarck School, on Sybelstraße in the bourgeois Charlottenburg neighborhood.[34] Humboldt House, in Fasanenstraße in Charlottenburg which was established by the Alexander von Humboldt Foundation in 1927 and served primarily as a facility for foreign student associations, was also used as a meeting place.

Humboldt House was in particular used by Muslim academic associations in Berlin. As early as 1918, the Central Asian Muslim Alimjan Idris had founded the Verein zu Unterstützung Russisch-Mohammedanischer Studenten (Association for the Support of Russian Muhammadan Students).[35] In 1924, members of the Islamic Community in Berlin established the Islamia student association, along with its official journal *Der Islamische Student*.[36] Another Islamic academic institution, the Islam Institute, was founded in 1927 at a general

---

34. Höpp, "Zwischen Moschee und Demonstration," I, 139, and II, 232.

35. Ursula Spuler-Stegemann, *Muslime in Deutschland: Nebeneinander oder Miteinander* (Freiburg: Herder, 1999), 35.

36. Nafi Tschelebi, "Die Bildungsbestrebungen der Akademisch-Islamischen Vereinigung 'Islamia,'" *Hochschule und Ausland* 6–8 (1927): 103; and Höpp, "Zwischen Moschee und Demonstration," II, 234.

meeting of Islamia in Humboldt House.[37] The chairman of the foundation council, Mohammed Abdul Nafi Tschelebi, declared that the institute was primarily intended to give the Muslim students living in the Germany "spiritual and moral support," to supplement their specialist training "in the spirit of a general European education," and, at the same time, to preserve their "native cultural character."[38] Among it sections, the institute comprised an Islamic library, an Islamic archive, and an Islamic publishing house.[39] The directors of the institute sought close contacts with German academics and political elites. At the opening ceremony, guest speakers included both the orientalist Georg Kampffmeyer, who was also directly involved in the establishment of the institute, and Julius Bachem, a member of the Prussian parliament. The German Honorary Committee of the Islam Institute was chaired by Franz von Papen. Its members included the artist Bruno Richter, the former minister of state Albert Südekum, and the director of Berlin Technical University, Professor Krencher, as well as numerous German scholars of Islamic studies.

It is not possible to make generalized statements about the closeness or nature of relations between the Muslims and the German majority society in Berlin. It seems clear, however, that sustained acculturation within the German educated middle class hardly took place. Yet, the sociocultural background of the Muslims in Berlin and the nature of their associational life meant that they mainly came into contact with educated Germans, particularly academics, students, diplomats, and businessmen. In a way, their education and their bourgeois associations served as cultural capital in the Muslims' relations with the bourgeois circles of the majority society.

Apart from the Islam Institute, with its illustrious Honorary Committee, representatives from the other Islamic associations also sought to involve German personalities from business, academia, and politics in their institutions. The council of the German-Muslim Society, for example, also included non-Muslim representatives, such as the land secretary Fritz Beyer and Hans Klopp vom Hofe.[40]

The most important opportunities for contact between the Muslims and members of the German bourgeois middle class were the numerous educational

---

37. Höpp, "Zwischen Moschee und Demonstration," II, 234; Höpp, "Muslime unterm Hakenkreuz," 18; and also Der Islamische Student 1 (1927): 1.

38. Quoted in Höpp, "Zwischen Moschee und Demonstration," II, 235.

39. Höpp, "Muslime unterm Hakenkreuz," 16–17.

40. Bauknecht, Muslime in Deutschland, 96.

lectures organized by the Muslim societies. Occasionally, the speakers were not Muslims themselves but professors from Berlin's universities. The German guests at these events often had professional links to Muslim countries. In 1933, the *Deutsche Allgemeine Zeitung* discovered among the guests attending the celebration of the birthday of the Prophet

His Excellency V. Davidoff, Prof. Tara Chand Roy, lector at the Indo-Germanic Seminar, Dr. Goeppel from the Alexander Humboldt Foundation, Dr. Bruno from the Buddhist House in Frohnau, Dr. Wollmann from the Humboldt College, and the traveler of India, Dr. Ing. Achenbach.[41]

The *Moslemische Revue*, the official organ of the German-Muslim Society, prided itself on the fact that both Albert Schweitzer and the famous orientalist, minister of state Carl Heinrich Becker, had referred to the magazine in their public speeches.[42] Even Albert Einstein, Martin Buber, Martin Niemöller, Thomas Mann, and Hermann Hesse are said to have attended events at the mosque.[43]

Last, it should be mentioned that interactions between Muslims and members of the German middle class also frequently took place in non-Muslim organizations. Particularly important in this respect were a number of German academic associations, most notably the Deutsche Gesellschaft für Islamkunde (German Society for Islamic Studies). Many German non-Muslim academics also published in the Muslim journals, particularly the *Moslemische Revue*, whose editors were at pains to make the journal appeal to the educated bourgeoisie.

Islamic-Bourgeois Values

The members of Berlin's Muslim associations defined themselves through Islam and bourgeois lifestyles and values. This was reflected in the nature of their associations, in the type of locations they chose for meetings and lectures, and, not least, in the style of dress many chose to wear. The nature of this Islamic bourgeois culture became most evident, however, in the Muslim publications

41. "Die Berliner Islambekenner feiern Mohammeds Geburtstag," *Deutsche Allgemeine Zeitung*, quoted in "Das Echo unserer Arbeit," *MR* 1–2 (1935): 45.

42. "An unsere Freunde!," *MR* 2/3 (1931): 33–37, 36.

43. Peter Schütt, "Preußens Gloria und die Grüne Fahne des Propheten," *Mut: Forum für Kultur, Politik und Geschichte* 362 (1997): 40–51, 50.

of the interwar period, as will be discussed in the following, focusing on articles that appeared in the *Moslemische Revue*.[44]

The *Moslemische Revue*, which was published from 1924 to 1941, is the longest-lived and undoubtedly also the most bourgeois journal among the Islamic periodicals published during the interwar years. The German-Muslim Society endeavored to make it the official organ of all Muslims living in Berlin. As a result, members of various Islamic groups and sects can be found among its authors. German converts in particular wrote regularly for the *Moslemische Revue*, a phenomenon that may be explained by the fact that the magazine appeared in German and that it also had the purpose to demonstrate the success of Islamic missionary work, a central goal of the society.[45]

Remarkable first of all is the elaborate style of German in which the articles in the *Moslemische Revue* were written. In content they were intellectually sophisticated and at times even intended to be academic in nature. This is not least reflected in the repeated citations of academic titles, starting with the editor, Imam Muhammad Abdullah, who was introduced on the frontispiece as "professor." The academic degree, a symbol of institutionally recognized education, was thus deliberately used as cultural capital to represent the journal in bourgeois society. At the same time, this practice reveals that the authors were almost exclusively academically educated.

In order to connect Islamic and bourgeois values, the authors frequently attempted to demonstrate that bourgeois values were ideals (allegedly) already inherent in Islam. They thereby emphasized the entire spectrum of values conventionally identified as bourgeois: education and scholarship, self-reflection, diligence and hard work, cleanliness and morality, modesty, restraint, and frugality were all characterized as genuinely Islamic.

The efforts made to characterize these ideals as Islamic might also be explained as an attempt to confront orientalist stereotypes prevalent in Europe. After all, the European bourgeois middle class had traditionally projected their taboos, such as fanaticism, fatalism, laziness, and a lack of punctuality onto

44. Gerhard Höpp, *Arabische und islamische Periodika in Berlin und Brandenburg 1915–1945: Geschichtlicher Abriß und Bibliographie* (Berlin: Das Arabische Buch, 1994) provides an overview of Islamic journalism in Berlin. More than a dozen periodicals explicitly labelled "Islamic" arose between 1918 and 1945 in Germany, though most of them were rather short-lived. The majority of publications appeared in German, the lingua franca of Muslims in interwar Berlin, but a number also appeared in other languages, some in several languages.

45. Ahmad, *Brief History of the Berlin Muslim Mission*.

Muslims and the Islamic world.[46] Undoubtedly the texts in the *Moslemische Revue* had a representative function, since one of its central aims was to influence the relationship between Berlin's Muslims and the majority society. And in this respect, the importance of bourgeois ideals to the Islamic minority shows parallels with the social importance of these ideals for German Jews in the process of the Jewish emancipation in Germany, as first pointed out by George Mosse.[47]

In the following pages, four bourgeois-Islamic themes that predominated in the content of the *Moslemische Revue* will be discussed. One of the motifs that recurred most frequently was that of independence and free will. The "freedom to act and of opinion" was part of the "Muslim nature," explained Muhammad Abdullah, for example in his essay "Die Willensfreiheit im Quran" (Free will in the Qur'an) published in the *Moslemishe Revue* in 1931. Abdullah appealed to his readers: "Be your own master. You create your own fortune."[48]

The ideal of independence was often directly linked to the belief in reason, which was to replace religious dogmas and collective rules in regulating human action. The affinity between rational reason and Islam was summed up by the author Mohammed Syed Abd-Elaal with the words: "Muhammad did not reach for the sword. His weapons were logic and reason."[49] And the Jewish convert Hamid Marcus, who was briefly chairman of the German-Muslim Society, characterized Islam in his contributions as being "simple, reasonable, rational."[50] Almost no contributor to the *Moslemische Revue* elaborated theologically on this connection more than the student M. T. Ahmad. Ahmad explained the ideal of freedom of action and rational reason using the theological concept of ijtihad, the process of reaching a legal judgement by an independent interpretation of the Qur'an and Sunna.[51]

---

46. Edward W. Said, *Orientalism* (New York: Pantheon, 1978).

47. George L. Mosse, "Jewish Emancipation: Between Bildung and Respectability," in *The Jewish Response to German Culture: From the Enlightenment to the Second World War*, ed. Jehuda Reinharz and Walter Schatzberg (Hanover, NH: University Press of New England, 1985), 1–16.

48. S. M. Abdullah, "Die Willensfreiheit im Quran," *MR* 2/3 (1931): 51–53, 53.

49. Mohammed Syed Abd Elaal, "Mohammed und das Schwert," *MR* 1/2 (1932): 34–39, 34.

50. Hugo Marcus, "Hans Ellenbergs Orientbuch," *MR* 2/3 (1931): 60–63, 61. On Marcus, see Marc David Baer, "Muslim Encounters with Nazism and the Holocaust: The Ahmadi of Berlin and Jewish Convert to Islam Hugo Marcus," *American Historical Review* 120, no. 1 (2015): 140–171.

51. M. T. Ahmad, "Die Grundbegriffe des islamischen Gesetzes," *MR* 3/4 (1933): 69–84.

The authors of the *Moslemische Revue* repeatedly referred to various virtues, above all a strong work ethic and the ideal of restraint. "All work," the convert Omar Schubert wrote, "that allows a person to live an honorable existence is respected." Laziness, on the other hand, was "branded a sin."[52] Muhammad Abdullah even used the idea of an Islamic work ethic to represent Islam as being particularly progressive in comparison to other religions. Whereas Jews and Christians reserved one day of the week exclusively for religious veneration and prohibited any other activity on this day, in Islam, Friday was set as the day for common prayer, but the faithful were by no means prohibited from working on this day.[53] Finally, he combined the idea of special striving with the ideal of the happy medium: the "middle path between the two extremes of a complete day of rest and an uninterrupted work day."[54] In a contribution by the other editor of the *Moslemische Revue*, Maulana Sadr-ud-Din, such a work ethic was associated with the liberal justification of private property and economic inequality, for "those who are more talented than others," he wrote, "should also be allowed to earn more."[55] At the same time, however, these earnings should be used to help others, and not for profligacy. Restraint, moderation, and modesty were also repeatedly occurring topoi. Often, the life of the Prophet Muhammad was held up as a shining example in this respect; for example, in the writings of Azeez Mirza, who earned his doctorate in Berlin and worked for a short time as imam in the mosque, or Hamid Marcus, who in a speech given on the occasion of the birthday of the Prophet in 1931 spoke about his "wisdom, restraint, and courage."[56]

Alongside references to traditional values, the articles in the *Moslemische Revue* also cultivated a belief in modern scholarship. Both the "natural sciences" and "modern European Islamic studies," with its "most recent research results," were emphasized to assert the contemporary relevance of Islam.[57] Bourgeois belief in the profane (natural) sciences in this case did not therefore become a substitute for religion but a means to underpin the Islamic faith. Once again

---

52. Omar W. A. Schubert, "Der Wert des Islam," *MR* 2/3 (1931): 39–46, 46.

53. S. M. Abdullah, "Die Bedeutung des Freitag-Gebets," *MR* 1 (1931): 1–3.

54. Abdullah, "Freitag-Gebets," 3.

55. Maulana Sadr-ud-Din, "Eigentum und Arbeit in Koranischer Beleuchtung," *MR* 2 (1937): 65–67, 65.

56. Azeez Mirza, "Mohammed als Mensch," *MR* 1 (1938): 3–8, 3–5; and, on Hamid Marcus's speech, "An unsere Freunde!," 34.

57. Omar Rolf Ehrenfels, "Die Symbolik im Islam I," *MR* 1/2 (1933): 15–21, 15; and Omar Rolf Ehrenfels, "Islam als Lebensform," *MR* 1 (1936): 2–6, 2.

the authors made use of a comparison with other religions: "No Muslim will feel insulted in his faith by the modern natural sciences, such as is the case with many Christians," claimed the convert Omar Rolf Ehrenfels.[58] References were repeatedly made to the flowering of Islamic science in the Middle Ages, which had made modern European science possible. An Islamic history was thereby constructed that was congruent with the ideals of progress and education. The argument that the ideals of progressive scholarship and education were traditionally inherent in Islam paralleled the rhetoric of Jewish and Christian bourgeois authors of the time, who also interpreted their religions as inherently progressive and scientific. At the Ramadan celebration in 1939, for instance, the Egyptian Ahmad Galwash noted:

> All of us know that the reflection on things represents the start and content of all scientific research; for science is merely knowledge that has been acquired through systematic observation, through experiments and thought. The Qur'an therefore recommends to insightful people the awareness of God and the utilization of science in that it combines moral stature with material progress. For this reason Islam drove learning and scholarship forward like no other religion. I hardly need to mention the examples from Islamic and Arabic history. Islam represents a middle path in comparison to other religions in that it seeks to unite the veneration of the one God with the practical command of nature.[59]

Moreover, the belief in modern scholarship and the sciences was supplemented by the themes of classical education. In 1931, the *Moslemische Revue* made the following comment on the Ramadan lecture by Rauf Malik: "The extent to which he called on the whole apparatus of European thought to support his subject was astonishing."[60] The recognition of classical education and the appreciation of high culture in general shone through the majority of the essays. Recurring themes were art, music, literature, history, and philosophy— themes that were repeatedly connected to Islam.

In the European context, a bourgeois education meant above all the study of classical texts and classical antiquity. The texts in the *Moslemische Revue* drew on this pattern but went on to replace and supplement references to ancient Rome and classical Greece with those to classical Islam. Instead of Homer,

---

58. Ehrenfels, "Lebensform," 5.
59. "Id-Ul-Fitr in Berlin," *MR* 3 (1939): 73–76, 75.
60. "An unsere Freunde!," 33.

Aristotle, Ovid, or Virgil, Ibn Khaldun, Omar Khayyam, or Muhammad Rumi became the subject of discussion, thus filling the bourgeois ideal of classical knowledge with Islamic content.[61]

But references to Islamic high culture did not always replace references to Western classicism. In fact, numerous essays and speeches sought to directly engage with the classical intellectual world of Rome and Greece. One author declared: "Christianity and Islam are rooted in the same religious and cultural soil, namely Hellenism."[62] Greek classicism only found its direct continuation, according a 1938 article by Muhammad Abdullah, in the revelation of Muhammad.[63] Similar lines of argument and comparisons could be found in the essay "Der Islam und die Stoa" (Islam and the stoa).[64]

Finally, the works of modern European thinkers who had expressed sympathy for Islam, such as Edward Gibbon, Thomas Carlyle, and Bernard Shaw, also served as reference points.[65] Quotations from European cultural authorities were used to communicate Islam to a bourgeois European public. For the Muslims in Berlin, German classicism and idealism were thereby of particular importance; striking were the references to Goethe, which reoccur in the works of many of Berlin's Muslim writers—for example, in M. T. Ahmad's 1933 essay "Hervorragende Europäer über den Islam" (Outstanding Europeans on Islam).[66]

Other authors who referred to Goethe were the German converts, particularly Omar Rolf Ehrenfels and Hamid Marcus. Both men emerged as the main representatives of bourgeois Islam in interwar Berlin. In 1932, Ehrenfels praised the "manifold connections between Goethe's metaphysical world view and that

---

61. *MR*, passim.

62. Bruno Hiller, "Islam und Abendland vor Tausend Jahren," *MR* 1 (1937): 22–32, 29. The idea of Hellenism as a common foundation had been discussed by German orientalists for some time. The debate was started by the eminent orientalist Carl Heinrich Becker, see Carl Heinrich Becker, *Das Erbe der Antike in Orient und Okzident* (Leipzig: Quelle und Meyer, 1931); and Carl Heinrich Becker, "Der Islam im Rahmen einer allgemeinen Kulturgeschichte," *Zeitschrift der Deutschen Morgenländischen Gesellschaft* 76 (1922): 18–35; see also Alexander Haridi, *Das Paradigma der "islamischen Zivilisation"—oder die Begründung der deutschen Islamwissenschaft durch Carl Heinrich Becker (1876–1933): Eine wissenschaftsgeschichtliche Untersuchung* (Würzburg: Ergon, 2005). My thanks to Ursula Wokoeck for the reference.

63. S. M. Abdullah, "Der Islam und das Naturwissenschaftliche Zeitalter," *MR* 3 (1938): 68–73.

64. Werner Benndorf, "Der Islam und die Stoa," *MR* 1/2 (1932): 26–29.

65. Ahmad, "Die Grundbegriffe," 69.

66. M. T. Ahmad, "Hervorragende Europäer über den Islam," *MR* 1/2 (1933): 46–47.

of the Muslims" in his article "Goethe und der deutsche Islam" (Goethe and German Islam).[67] Hamid Marcus, more than anybody else, frequently set up parallels between Islam and European philosophy.[68] In his "Der Islam und die Philosophie Europas" (Islam and European philosophy), he linked Islam with the philosophy of Kant, Nietzsche, and Leibniz, and in the essay "Spinoza und der Islam" (Spinoza and Islam), he noted not only philosophical but also biographical similarities between the Dutch thinker and the Prophet.[69]

From 1933 onward, the words of Hamid Hugo Marcus, the German Muslim of Jewish origin, like the writings of other representatives of Berlin's bourgeois Islam, including the coeditor of the *Moslemische Revue*, Sadr-ud-Din himself, were no longer or only very infrequently printed. Here, the question of the antibourgeois moments in the essays of the magazine arises: the limits of Islamic bourgeois culture in an era of extremes. The bourgeois values, which evidently shaped the content of the *Moslemische Revue* so strongly in the 1920s and 1930s, cannot hide the fact that the contributions to the paper increasingly articulated a sense of crisis and cultural criticism. Ultimately, some authors even welcomed National Socialism as a solution to this crisis.[70] The history of the relationship between Berlin's Muslims and National Socialism requires undoubtedly more detailed study, as do many of the other issues raised above.[71] The history of the emergence of the Muslim minority in Germany in the interwar years remains

67. Omar Rolf Ehrenfels, "Goethe und der deutsche Islam," *MR* 1/2 (1932): 10–16, 15; see also Omar Rolf Ehrenfels, "Der Islam und die junge Generation in Europa," *MR* 4 (1931): 81–91, 82.

68. Hugo Marcus, "Das Wesen der Religion," *MR* 2 (1924): 79–84; Hugo Marcus, "Der Islam und die Philosophie Europas," *MR* 2 (1924): 84–88; Hugo Marcus, "Mohammeds Gestalt," *MR* 3 (1924): 120–128; Hugo Marcus, "Christus, Tolstoi und Marx," *MR* 3 (1924): 153–157; Hugo Marcus, "Das Leben ist des Lebens Sinn," *MR* 1 (1925): 13–18; Hugo Marcus, "Islam und Protestantismus," *MR* 2 (1925): 17–22; Hugo Marcus, "Naturgesetz, Rechtsgesetz und Sittengesetz," *MR* 3–4 (1925): 49; Hugo Marcus, "Spinoza und der Islam," *MR* 1 (1929): 8–25; Hugo Marcus, "Hans Ellenbergs Orientbuch;" and Hugo Marcus, "Der Geistige Gehalt der Ramadanzeit," *MR* 1/2 (1933): 8–12.

69. Marcus, "Der Islam und die Philosophie Europas"; and Marcus, "Spinoza und der Islam."

70. The latter can be found in Muhammad Ali, "Der Beitrag des Islams zur Zivilisation," *MR* 2/3 (1934): 44–46; and Faruq H. Fischer, "Ist der Islam 'unmodern'?: Eine Parallele zwischen der alten Religion und dem heutigen Europa," *MR* 2/3 (1934): 62–73. On the impact of the Nazi takeover on the community, see Bauknecht, *Muslime in Deutschland*, 82–90; and Abdullah, "Anbiederung und Friedenspredigt," 129–138.

71. David Motadel, *Islam and Nazi Germany's War* (Cambridge, MA: Harvard University Press, 2014), provides general insights into the complex histories of Muslims under Nazi rule.

neglected. The contribution here cannot, therefore, be any more than a tile in the mosaic.

To conclude, the previous pages have demonstrated that both class and religion played a crucial part in the history of the Muslim minority in interwar Germany. Shared religious and social cultures enabled Muslims from diverse ethnic, national, and linguistic backgrounds to forge a community. Bourgeois values and lifestyles shaped not only the milieu of the community but also its relations with German majority society. Berlin's Muslims accommodated themselves remarkably well into the German bourgeois worlds of the city. Further, the case has demonstrated that the history of Muslim communities in Europe cannot simply be reduced to a culturalist, essentialist, and binary "East and West" or "Islam and Europe" narrative.[72]

More generally, the chapter has shed some light on the complex intersection of class, religion, and diaspora in the global age. It has shown that the emergence of middle classes and bourgeois cultures across the Muslim world had a direct impact on Muslim migrant communities and their relationship to non-Muslim majority societies. At the heart of these new minorities was a remarkable cosmopolitanism that was part of both their religious and social worlds.

72. Said, *Orientalism*; and Samuel P. Huntington, *The Clash of Civilizations and the Remaking of World Order* (New York: Simon and Schuster, 1996) are prominent examples of studies that assume the existence of such cultural boundaries.

12

From Global Civilizing Missions
to Racial Warfare

CLASS CONFLICTS AND THE
REPRESENTATION OF THE
COLONIAL WORLD IN EUROPEAN
MIDDLE-CLASS THOUGHT

Christof Dejung

IN DECEMBER 1831, the French writer Saint-Marc Girardin, who later became an eminent professor of history at the Sorbonne, published an article on the major revolt of the Lyon silk workers some weeks earlier, which had cost 169 lives and was among the first workers' uprisings in the industrial age.[1] Girardin was convinced that the revolt had been the inevitable consequence of the antagonism between "the class that owns and the one that does not own" in industrial society and saw it as a given that the have-nots would continue to assault the bourgeoisie because "they are the ones that are stronger and more numerous." Without any effort he then went on to compare the social conditions within Europe with those in Haiti before the slave rebellion of 1791:

> Each manufacturer lives in his factory like the colonial planter in the middle of their slaves at the ratio of one to hundred; and the Lyon riots are related to the insurgency of Santo Domingo. . . . Today, the barbarians that menace society are no longer living in the Caucasus nor in the Tartar steppes; they are in the outskirts of our industrial cities. . . . This is where the danger

---

1. Fernand Rude, *La Révolte des canuts, 1831–1834* (Paris: La Découverte, 2001).

251

for modern society is located. . . . In this situation, it is necessary for the middle class to understand their interests and the duty it has to discharge.[2]

Girardin was by no means the only one to resort to the colonial world in order to comprehend the challenges the middle class would face in the upcoming class conflict. In the nineteenth and early twentieth centuries, observers regularly drew parallels between metropole and colonial world. Whereas supporters of the working classes compared the oppression of colonized peoples to the exploitation of the European proletariat in order to denounce bourgeois profit seeking home and abroad, advocates of the middle classes argued that it was only by spreading middle-class values such as the quest for education, cleanliness, and work discipline that social order and development could be established in both metropoles and colonies.[3] Girardin himself considered the implementation of social change according to the bourgeois role model "beneficial for modern society" and warned that without such measures there would be nothing than "ferocity and barbarianism."[4]

The ways in which metropole and colony were related to each other by contemporaries has been explored in recent years in a number of studies from the fields of new imperial history. These studies stand in striking contrast to older social historical accounts, which interpreted both the emergence of the middle classes and subsequent class conflicts as consequences of intra-European modernization processes and which generally disregarded the relations between Europe and the wider world. Even studies in social imperialism, which examined the ways the European bourgeoisie aimed to relieve social tensions by using colonial imaginaries, stemmed from the assumption that the middle classes had already established themselves as a social group as a consequence of internal transformations, such as industrialization.[5] The extent to which the European middle classes were shaped by the imperial world order, or came into being as a result of global entanglements in the first place, was not an issue that historians bothered with before the late 1990s. Challenges to such a restricted

2. Saint-Marc Girardin, "L'aimable faubourien," *Journal des Débats*, 8 December 1831.

3. Rebekka Habermas, "Lost in Translation: Transfer and Nontransfer in the Atakpame Colonial Scandal," *Journal of Modern History* 86 (2014): 47–80, provides a case study for Germany.

4. Girardin, "L'aimable faubourien."

5. Hans-Ulrich Wehler, *Bismarck und der Imperialismus* (Cologne: Kiepenheuer und Witsch, 1969); John M. MacKenzie, *Propaganda and Empire: The Manipulation of British Public Opinion, 1880–1960* (Manchester: Manchester University Press, 1984).

Eurocentric scope, such as Eric Williams's *Capitalism and Slavery* (first published in 1944), which linked the sugar plantations of the Caribbean to the riches of businessmen who were at the core of the emerging European bourgeoisie, were studiously ignored.[6]

During the last decade and a half, historians began to challenge the notion that we can understand the history of the European middle classes by merely considering intra-European processes.[7] They have argued that fundamental aspects of what Europe saw as tokens of its modernity, such as the Enlightenment, the establishing of modern science or the breakthrough of capitalism, were in fact the result of global interaction.[8] Others have pointed out that the "dual revolution" of the late eighteenth century that paved the way for the emergence of the middle classes—the Industrial and the French Revolutions—cannot be explained without being set within a global historical framework.[9] The middle classes that established themselves in the wake of the dual revolution in turn can be considered the stratum that was more interested than any other in intellectual and economic globalization. As early as the 1840s, Karl Marx and Friedrich Engels argued that it was not least this global outlook that sustained the bourgeois claim to be the social avant-garde in a rapidly changing world:

> The discovery of America, the rounding of the Cape, opened up fresh ground for the rising bourgeoisie. The . . . increase in the means of exchange and in commodities . . . gave to commerce, to navigation, to industry, an impulse

6. Eric Williams, *Capitalism and Slavery* (Chapel Hill: University of North Carolina Press, 1944).

7. Frederick Cooper and Ann Laura Stoler, eds., *Tensions of Empire: Colonial Cultures in a Bourgeois World* (Berkeley: University of California Press, 1997); John Phillip Short, *Magic Lantern Empire: Colonialism and Society in Germany* (Ithaca, NY: Cornell University Press, 2012).

8. Sebastian Conrad, "Enlightenment in Global History: A Historiographical Critique," *American Historical Review* 117 (2012): 999–1027; Jane Gleeson-White, *Double Entry: How the Merchants of Venice Created Modern Finance* (London: Allen and Unwin, 2012), chapter 1; Sven Beckert, *Empire of Cotton. A Global History* (New York: Knopf, 2015).

9. Maxine Berg, "In Pursuit of Luxury: Global Origins of British Consumer Goods in the Eighteenth Century," *Past and Present* 182 (2004): 85–142; Giorgio Riello, *Cotton: The Fabric That Made the Modern World* (Cambridge: Cambridge University Press, 2013), 211–237; C. A. Bayly, *The Birth of the Modern World, 1780–1914: Global Connections and Comparisons* (Malden, MA: Blackwell, 2004), 86; Suzanne Desan, Lynn Hunt, and William Max Nelson, eds., *The French Revolution in Global Perspective* (Ithaca, NY: Cornell University Press, 2013).

never before known, and thereby, to the revolutionary element in the tot-
tering feudal society, a rapid development.[10]

Obviously, not all members of the middle classes were engaged in such global
endeavors. In fact, only a small number of members of the upper middle class,
such as businessmen and scholars, actually acted regularly on a global level. Those
who can be ranked among the lower middle classes, be they schoolteachers, accountants, public servants, shopkeepers, doctors, or lawyers, were seldom involved in activities beyond their immediate orbit (even though the establishing
of overseas colonies offered some of them the opportunity to go abroad to make
their career). This different scope is quite characteristic of the heterogeneity
of the European middle classes. Yet despite the huge discrepancies in terms of
income, social status, political orientation, or ability to influence political
decision-making according to country of origin, one thing that characterized
the middle classes and justifies their classification as a discernible social group
was a particular cultural orientation—the way of living, development of an
individual personality, work ethic, dichotomic gender order, and belief in progress—that was meant to serve as a common moral base throughout Western
Europe.[11]

This cultural canon was definitely shaped by the globalized world of the nineteenth century and actually mirrored the global context in which the European
bourgeoisie came into being. Bourgeois culture was not only characterized by
the consumption of commodities imported from colonial possessions, such as
sugar, tea, cocoa, coffee, and tobacco (commodities that members of the lower
strata could often not afford on a regular basis until the turn of the twentieth
century) but also by viewing exotic plants and animals by visiting zoological
and botanical gardens.[12] What is more, the bourgeois claim to be the spearhead

10. Karl Marx and Friedrich Engels, *Das kommunistische Manifest* (1848; London: German
Cooperative Publishing Co., 1890), 2.

11. Jan Bank and Maarten van Buuren, *1900: The Age of Bourgeois Culture* (Houndmills: Pal-
grave, 2004); Manfred Hettling and Stefan-Ludwig Hoffmann, "Der bürgerliche Wertehimmel:
Zum Problem individueller Lebensführung im 19. Jahrhundert," *Geschichte und Gesellschaft* 23
(1997): 333–359; Jürgen Kocka, "The Middle Classes in Europe," in *The European Way: European
Societies during the Nineteenth and Twentieth Centuries*, ed. Hartmut Kaelble (London: Berghahn
Books, 2004), 15–43; Jerrold Seigel, *Modernity and Bourgeois Life: Society, Politics, and Culture in
England, France, and Germany since 1750* (Cambridge: Cambridge University Press, 2012).

12. Sidney Mintz, *Sweetness and Power: The Place of Sugar in Modern History* (New York:
Viking-Penguin, 1985); Catherine Hall and Sonya O. Rose, eds., *At Home with the Empire: Metropolitan Culture and the Imperial World* (Cambridge: Cambridge University Press, 2006).

of worldwide development and civilizational progress involved distinct boundary work and a demarcation between them and social groups that were deemed to be uncivilized or barbaric, such as the European underclasses or the inhabitants of colonial peripheries. These ideas were not merely superficial, they also influenced political decision-making and attitudes toward these "primitives" at home and abroad.[13]

From this perspective, several historians have examined the civilizing missions of the philanthropic societies that were implemented after the late eighteenth century in both the slums of European metropoles and colonial peripheries.[14] These endeavors may suggest that the urban middle classes of that period did not perceive social developments in European and non-European regions as distinct phenomena as such but instead considered them as aspects of worldwide modernization. Yet many of these studies on these civilizing missions do start from the premise that there was bourgeois hegemony and postulate that the middle classes were assured of their social position to such an extent that they felt obliged to raise other social groups to attain their standard of civilization. This, however, is only part of the story, as this chapter aims to show. There is reason to believe that the self-perception of the European middle classes was rather ambiguous and at least partly characterized by uncertainty about the sustainability of their social position, in particular after the late nineteenth century. The fact that middle-class universalism was always in tension with colonial projects as well as metropolitan power struggles shows "the fundamental contradictions inherent in the bourgeois projects and the way universal claims were bound up in particularistic assertions," as Ann Laura Stoler and Frederick Cooper point out.[15]

13. See Michael Adas, "Contested Hegemony: The Great War and the Afro-Asian Assault on the Civilizing Mission Ideology," *Journal of World History* 15 (2004), 31–63; and Jürgen Osterhammel, "'The Great Work of Uplifting Mankind': Zivilisierungsmission und Moderne," in *Zivilisierungsmissionen: Imperiale Weltverbesserung seit dem 18. Jahrhundert*, ed. Boris Barth and Jürgen Osterhammel (Konstanz: UVK, 2005), 363–425, for the history of the civilizing missions.

14. See, among others, Susan Thorne, "'The Conversion of Englishmen and the Conversion of the World Inseparable': Missionary Imperialism and the Language of Class in Early Industrial Britain," in *Tensions of Empire*, ed. Cooper and Stoler, 238–262; Sebastian Conrad, "'Education for Work' in Colony and Metropole: The Case of Imperial Germany, c. 1880–1914," in *Empires and Boundaries: Rethinking Race, Class, and Gender in Colonial Settings*, ed. Harald Fischer-Tiné and Susanne Gehrmann (London: Routledge, 2009), 23–40.

15. Ann Laura Stoler and Frederick Cooper, "Between Metropole and Colony: Rethinking a Research Agenda," in *Tensions of Empire*, ed. Cooper and Stoler, 1–56, 3.

In this chapter, I explore what it means to examine European bourgeois culture in a global historical context. In the first section, I will refer to the activities of the home missionary movement in many Western European countries and identify the extent to which the yardstick of civilization and development was the culture of the European middle classes in this philanthropic discourse. The fact that analogies between European and colonial "savages" could be established with such ease may be evidence of the fact that they were an integral part of the middle-class utopia of development and progress. Section two highlights the repugnancy of this discourse. The question of whether it could be justified to implement Western civilization by force if it was rejected by the inhabitants of the colonies was contested among contemporaries. What is more, the fact that Europeans time and again encountered exponents of colonial middle classes could not challenge the contemporary stereotype of a clear-cut distinction between Western modernity and colonial backwardness, and such encounters were obviously not considered evidence for the existence of such a thing as a global bourgeoisie. Section three explains that the intensification of the class conflict and the emergence and intensification of social-Darwinist and racial theories after the mid-nineteenth century challenged the liberal optimism that had shaped the civilizing missions. However, at the same time, those warning about a decline of Western civilization and the outbreak of global racial warfare also regularly expressed caution about the European underclasses. By showing that ideas of both the rise and the decline of bourgeois society involved comparisons between European underclasses and colonial subjects, this chapter aims to reveal the globalized cultural horizon of the European middle classes in the long nineteenth century.

Civilizing Missions Home and Abroad

The missionary philanthropic movements that emerged after the late eighteenth century all over Western Europe are among the most striking examples of how colony and metropole could be connected to each other in middle-class thought. On the one hand, they were combating drunkenness among the metropolitan underclasses and improving the sanitary conditions in the slums, essentially hoping to transform European workers into decent and industrious subjects. On the other hand, the missionaries intended to "civilize" colonial subjects in faraway places such as sub-Saharan Africa and the Indian subcontinent. The ubiquity of these Protestant and (to a lesser extent) Catholic missionary organizations reveals that religion remained an important aspect of the European lifestyle despite the critique of religious institutions since the Enlightenment. While the missionaries themselves often came from artisanal or lower-middle-class families, the promoters of the missionary organizations were members of the emerging urban middle classes such as merchants, industrialists, medical doctors, lawyers, and writers. Even though ideologically the missionary organizations were critical of the damaging consequences of social progress, such as urbanization, industrialization, secularization, and consumerism, they seemed not to have been at odds with the middle classes as the promoters of this very process. These movements were influenced by both Enlightenment notions of education and social progress and the emphasis on social action as a fundamental marker of Christian lay religious practice and middle-class identity. Participation in philanthropy allowed them "the development of a shared identity, defined by a participation in a progressive project which was both national and global in its reach," as Alison Twells has explained.[16]

Time and again, missionaries compared colonial "savages" to the underclasses of the European slums. One of the most remarkable examples of such a comparison was the one made by William Booth in his book *From Darkest England and the Way Out*. The book was published in 1890 and became a huge success, selling over three hundred thousand copies. Booth, who came from a working-class family, was the founder of the East London Christian Mission, which in 1878 became the Salvation Army.[17] The title, *From Darkest England*, was clearly an allusion to Henry Morton Stanley's accounts of his expeditions *In Darkest Africa*. Consequently, Booth maintained in the introduction:

> Darkest England like Darkest Africa reeks with malaria. The foul and fetid breath of our slums is almost as poisonous as that of the African Swamp. . . . Just as Darkest Africa . . . much of the misery of those whose lot we are considering arises from their own habits. Drunkenness and all manner of uncleanness, moral and physical abound. . . . A population sodden with drink, steeped in vice eaten up by every social and physical malady, these are the denizens of Darkest England among whom my life has been spent and to

16. Alison Twells, *The Civilising Mission and the English Middle Class, 1792–1850* (Basingstoke: Palgrave, 2009), 5.

17. For the engagement of the Salvation Army in colonial and metropolitan civilizing missions in more detail, see Harald Fischer-Tiné, "Reclaiming Savages in 'Darkest England' and 'Darkest India': The Salvation Army as Transnational Agents of the Civilizing Mission," in *Civilizing Missions in Colonial and Postcolonial South Asia: From Improvement to Development*, ed. Carey A. Watt and Michael Mann (London: Anthem Press, 2011), 125–164.

whose rescue I would now summon all that is best in the manhood and woman-hood of our land.[18]

Such analogies can be found in many contemporary texts all over Europe and may be considered evidence for the close transnational networks between the missionary movements in different countries.[19] Colonial concepts of race could be transferred to metropolitan situations in order to interpret class-political con-flicts, and vice versa. Even though race and class, due to their different origins, never became completely interchangeable, they could be mapped onto each other and serve as discursive tools to examine the relations between colonial subjects and European underclasses to middle-class modernity.[20]

The aim of the home mission movement was to prevent the working classes from abandoning their religious faith due to the massive social transformations that took place in the nineteenth century. Yet besides spreading the Gospel, the missionaries also attempted to implement a certain way of life that involved work discipline, housekeeping, and sobriety. Their goal, in other words, was to put into effect a "'middle of the road Christianity', whose middle-class values could be adapted lower on the social scale," as Harald Fischer-Tiné explains.[21] Thus a Salvationist observed with obvious relief in the 1890s that "conversion has a wonderful effect on a man; he is very soon decently clothed; his home becomes better, and although he remains a working man, outwardly he might pass with the clerks."[22]

The missionaries were not the only ones who were bothered by urban pov-erty. In the second part of the nineteenth century, secular reform movements emerged that made no reference to the civilizing of colonial peoples and were solely interested in raising the living standards of domestic workers.[23] In Brit-ain, secular social reformers such as Charles Booth (not related to William

---

18. William Booth, *In Darkest England and the Way Out* (London: International Headquar-ters, 1890), 14–15.

19. Rebekka Habermas, "Mission im 19. Jahrhundert. Globale Netze des Religiösen," *Histo-rische Zeitschrift* 287 (2008): 629–679.

20. For this aspect, see, among others, Etienne Balibar and Immanuel Wallerstein, *Race, Nation, Class: Ambiguous Identities* (London: Verso, 1991).

21. Fischer-Tiné, "Reclaiming Savages," 128.

22. Quoted in Victor Bailey, "In Darkest England and the Way Out: The Salvation Army, Social Reform and the Labour Movement, 1885–1910," *International Review of Social History* 29 (1984): 133–171, 139.

23. Twells, *Civilising Mission*, 215–216.

Booth) and Benjamin Seebohm Rowntree published detailed surveys on poverty within British cities without mentioning overseas peoples as a possible benchmark for the degree of civilization of the domestic poor.[24] The quite global approach of the missionary movement was thus rivaled by the distinctly nationally oriented perspective of secular philanthropists. This difference can be considered evidence for the wide variety of approaches to dealing with social problems among the European middle classes. However, until the late nineteenth century, when social reforms such as the implementation of the welfare state by Bismarck in the German *Kaiserreich*, and the early twentieth century, when Liberal reforms in Britain were set in motion by governments, the urban missionaries often composed the most important bourgeois organizations active in certain workers' housing areas and can be considered an example of the middle-class desire to self-organize and shape society. They passed on their impressions of the lives of the urban poor to the middle classes, who supported the missionary movement. A similar case can be made for the colonial peripheries, where missionaries were often among the most important actors for gathering ethnographic, geographical, botanical, or zoological knowledge and propagating this information through Europe in missionary publications, exhibitions, and, due to their networks with metropolitan scholars, scientific journals.[25]

The civilizing missions at home and abroad were often described as two fronts, however geographically separated, of the same war against savagery. This analogy did occasionally provoke some resistance among the European public. The German pastor Friedrich von Bodelschwingh, who established both *Arbeiterkolonien* in Germany and missionary stations in Africa, was repeatedly criticized for his notion that "the frontiers between the *Heimat* and the world of the heathen did merge" and "that the German protectorates [in Africa] were put on a par with the German hinterland."[26] However, given the success of the missionary movement all over Europe and the constant support they got from local middle classes, this critique did not seem to have been especially detrimental.

24. Charles Booth, *Life and Labour of the People*, 2 vols. (London: Macmillan, 1889/91); Benjamin Seebohm Rowntree, *Poverty: A Study of Town Life* (London: Macmillan, 1901).

25. Patrick Harries, *Butterflies & Barbarians: Swiss Missionaries in South-East Africa* (Oxford: James Currey, 2007).

26. Gustav von Bodelschwingh, *Friedrich von Bodelschwingh: Ein Lebensbild* (Bielefeld: Pfennigverein Bethel, 1922), 273.

In any case, imperial technologies of knowledge production, such as the cartographical mapping of spaces of disease and disorder or the anthropological classification of human types, could easily be adopted by the emerging metropolitan discipline of urban social studies.[27] The frequent comparisons of urban slums with overseas peripheries encouraged the metropolitan public to reflect on relations between domestic and colonial subalterns and arguably widened the gap between European middle classes and the urban poor.[28] Friedrich Engels (the son of a wealthy German cotton-textile manufacturer and thus the offspring of the very bourgeoisie he so vehemently critiqued) noted in his *Condition of the Working Classes in England*, published in 1845, that the suffering of the miserable in the London West End was as mysterious to many observers as the living conditions of "the savages in Australia or on the South-sea islands."[29] As a matter of fact, contemporary authors following agendas as diverse as evangelical Christianity and socialism tried to conceptualize an understanding of the social order within Europe by drawing analogies with the non-European world. In terms of middle-class ideology, this was logically rather consequent. If the processes of social development and modernization were taken seriously then without any doubt they had to be applicable worldwide. The alleged savagery of both the metropolitan underclasses and colonial subjects, as well as the promise of acquiring a certain stage of development when following the directions of their bourgeois instructors, was thus quite characteristic of the way the European middle classes perceived the world in the mid-nineteenth century.[30]

This discourse, however, was rather ambiguous. It had to deal with the fact that colonial peoples and European proletarians stood in a different relation to the project of modernity. Whereas the social problems of the European slums were a direct consequence of urbanization and industrialization—and thus of the dramatic transformation of European societies after the turn of the nineteenth century—the alleged savagery of non-European societies was interpreted as the result of a lack of progress. Why the negative impact of progress and a

27. Mariana Valverde, "The Dialectic of the Familiar and the Unfamiliar: 'The Jungle' in Early Slum Travel Writing," *Sociology* 30 (1996): 493–509.

28. Alexandra Przyrembel, *Verbote und Geheimnisse: Das Tabu und die Genese der europäischen Moderne* (Frankfurt: Campus, 2011), 18.

29. Friedrich Engels, *Die Lage der arbeitenden Klasse in England* (Leipzig: Otto Wiegand, 1845), 34.

30. Similar arguments have been put forth in studies on liberal imperialism. For an overview, see Matthew P. Fitzpatrick, ed., *Liberal Imperialism in Europe* (London: Palgrave, 2012).

lack of progress could both lead to social conditions that were considered similar, and what that meant for the civilizing mission and the project of modernity as a whole, was never discussed in the writings of the propagators of the civilizing missions. At the same time, it was not always clear which of the two groups—the urban poor and the inhabitants of colonial possessions—were to be considered more civilized. In fact, most members of the middle classes were of the opinion that the European workers had reached a higher stage of development, since they lived in houses, carried out paid labor, and had been christened. However, this assessment was not shared by all observers. A Swiss ethnographer who had been engaged in missionary work, for instance, maintained in 1885 that his "organ of smell had never been offended in a Negro hut by the unqualifiable and infernal air that so often wafts against us in the homes of our proletariat."[31] This uncertainty about how to assess the respective relation of urban and colonial savagery to middle-class modernity can be considered evidence for the difficulties the European middle classes encountered when they attempted to reduce the worldwide social transformations of the nineteenth century to a common denominator.

Metropolitan Hypocrisy and Blindness to Colonial Violence

That the promoters of the civilizing missions pursued what they considered worthy goals should not belie the fact that their ambitions involved a good deal of hypocrisy and a tendency to ignore the oppressive character of colonial rule. An exemplary case of such tendencies is Gustave Moynier, a Geneva lawyer coming from a well-off family who was not only a co-founder of the Red Cross but also the president of the Société Genevoise d'utilité publique, a philanthropic society established by the Geneva bourgeoisie to support the local working class by providing education, ameliorating sanitary conditions, and fighting alcoholism, activities that were meant to marshal the workers to achieve "true civilization."[32] Interestingly enough, this civilizing mission was not restricted to Switzerland. Moynier also became an advocate of the development

31. E. Mähly, "Zur Geographie und Ethnographie der Goldküste," *Verhandlungen der Naturforschenden Gesellschaft in Basel* 7 (1885): 809–852, 843.

32. Gustave Moynier, *De l'abus des boissons envirantes dans le canton de Genève* (Genève: J.-G. Fick, 1863), 49; Gustave Moynier, *Les institutions ouvrières de la Suisse. Mémoire rédigé à la demande de la commission centrale de la confédération suisse pour l'exposition de Paris et présenté au*

and civilizing of Africa.[33] His involvement confirms that colonialism was an issue that did not bother just actors coming from imperial powers but also those coming from European countries without colonies.[34] In 1876, Moynier attended a meeting in Brussels, organized by King Léopold II to discuss the exploration of Africa. A year later, he was the driving force behind the foundation of the Swiss national committee for the exploration and civilizing of Central Africa and became a joint editor of the journal *L'Afrique explorée et civilisé* after 1879. The journal published, among others, reports of explorers and missionaries and led a campaign against slavery in sub-Saharan Africa. A treatise that Moynier wrote in 1883 and sent to all European governments was at least partly responsible for the recognition of the Congo Free State, which was proclaimed by King Léopold at the Berlin Congo Conference in 1885. In 1890, Léopold nominated Moynier as a consul general of the Congo.

Considering Moynier's engagement in international law and philanthropy, it is striking how eagerly he supported the annexation of the Congo to become the personal property of King Léopold, an action that was not covered by international law and was a unique case in the history of colonialism.[35] An important motive might have been precisely his aim to promote what he considered modern civilization. He and his fellow campaigners were convinced that every aspect of African culture that seemed incompatible with European customs should be erased. This obviously involved superstition and fetishism. In addition, the civilizing of Africa should be promoted by the adoption of a middle-class sexual morality; polygamy, nakedness, and homosexuality were especially to be combated. Generally, the articles in *L'Afrique explorée et civilise* emphasized the inferiority of the Africans, even though the remarkable state of their dwellings and the capacity of their agricultural production was pointed out in some articles.[36] The natives were indeed considered capable of

---

jury international institué par le décret impérial du 9 juin 1866 (Genève: Librairie Cherbuliez, 1867), 43.

33. Albert Wirz, "Die humanitäre Schweiz im Spannungsfeld zwischen Philanthropie und Kolonialismus: Gustave Moynier, Afrika und das IKRK," *Traverse: Zeitschrift für Geschichte* 2 (1998): 95–110.

34. For the case of Switzerland, see Patricia Purtschert and Harald Fischer-Tiné, eds., *Colonial Switzerland: Rethinking Colonialism from the Margins* (Houndmills: Palgrave, 2015).

35. For the violent annexation of the Congo, see Adam Hochschild, *King Leopold's Ghost: A Story of Greed, Terror, and Heroism in Colonial Africa* (London: Pan Macmillan, 1998).

36. "Un exemple de l'influence des arabes dans l'Afrique centrale," *L'Afrique explorée et civilisé* 9, no. 9 (1888): 272–277, 275.

development to a high degree by the missionaries, though only under the condition that they were instructed by Europeans.[37] However, if the Africans resisted embracing the benefits of European civilization, the Europeans were to bear down on the natives. Moynier was convinced that the Europeans could legitimately use force in the Congo to defend themselves against rebellious "savages" and gain respect from their African subjects.[38] To fulfil the civilizing mission, he was even inclined to turn a blind eye to colonial atrocities. As late as 1907, and thus nearly a decade after the mass murders in the Congo Free State began to provoke a public outcry all over Europe, Moynier maintained that "to allow the black race to participate in the means of modern civilization in order to better their fate" was one of the most attractive tasks the white race might undertake.[39]

Because of their disdain, many promoters of overseas civilizing missions also failed to register one of the most striking effects of their activities, the emergence of a non-European middle class. One of the few metropolitan observers who did so was the German anthropologist Georg Thilenius. In 1925, he described the rise of an "educated upper crust . . . of lawyers, medical doctors, wholesalers, great land owners and artisans" among "Indians, Negroes and Polynesians." According to Thilenius, the reason why their emergence was mostly ignored in the metropoles was the very fact that (admittedly due to the influence of "European civilization" in the colonies) they had been able to reach, within a few generations, a similar stage of development as the European middle classes. To accept this fact would mean nothing less than to blur the boundary "that made for and intensified the self-confidence of the Europeans."[40]

Even though the civilizing projects were never explicitly designed to establish a local middle class in colonial possessions, in practice they often did precisely that. In sub-Saharan Africa, for example, this happened in South Africa and Rhodesia. Initially, neither the Christian missionaries, in whose schools Africans received a Western-style education, nor the colonial administration had an interest in creating literate indigenous elites in the British settler

---

37. "La mission du Congo," *L'Afrique explorée et civilisé* 2, no. 1 (1880): 15–18, 16; "Le cannibalisme en Afrique," *L'Afrique explorée et civilisé* 2, no. 5 (1880): 99–102, 99.

38. Gustave Moynier, *La question du Congo: Lettre circulaire à messieurs les membres et associés de l'Institute de droit international* (Genève: Imprimerie Charles Schuchardt, 1883), 21.

39. Gustave Moynier, *Mes heures de travail* (Genève: Société Générale de l'Imprimerie, 1907), 72–73.

40. Georg Thilenius, *Völkerkunde und Schule: Einführung in die Ausstellung des Museums für Völkerkunde Hamburg 1.–7. Juni 1925* (Munich: J. F. Lehmanns, 1925), 5.

colonies. Yet colonial aspirations could not be realized without such elites. The missionary schools needed African teachers, and both the colonial bureaucracy and Western businesses wanted indigenous clerks. By and by, African medical doctors, nurses, and welfare workers also became important for maintaining social order, which made for an ever-growing African middle class after the turn of the century.[41]

Such processes, however, are barely mentioned in writings of missionaries, nor do they figure very prominently in the accounts of colonial administrations. Both of them were concerned with their respective civilizing missions—and both needed the notion of colonial savagery to legitimize their endeavors—to such an extent that they were not able to recognize the fact that non-European elites were able to adopt Western middle-class features much more easily than the colonial discourse would make us assume. What is more, the emerging middle classes in the Middle East and South Asia became engaged in civilizing missions of their own. They planned to educate and improve the conditions of life of the local poor in a manner quite similar to that of the European home missionary movement.[42] In some cases this could make for bourgeois networks that overcame ethnic barriers, despite the colonial context. The Salvation Army, for instance, had established a branch in India as early as the 1880s. Even though their most important partner was the colonial administration, the Salvationists had also established close ties to the rulers of Indian princely states and Indian industrialists, the latter being very interested in the engagement of the Salvation Army to propagate temperance among factory workers. Among the most important supporters of the Salvation Army on the subcontinent was the Tata dynasty, which ran a widespread conglomerate and was among the most eminent promoters of Indian industrialization. In return for financial support, Frederick Booth Tucker, the commissioner of the Indian Salvation Army, established contacts between Jamsetji Tata and some steel tycoons from Pittsburgh

---

41. Leo Kuper, *An African Bourgeoisie: Race, Class, and Politics in South Africa* (New Haven, CT: Yale University Press, 1965); Michael O. West, *The Rise of the African Middle Class. Colonial Zimbabwe, 1898–1965* (Bloomington: Indiana University Press, 2002).

42. Prashant Kidambi, "Becoming Middle Class: The Local History of a Global Story—Colonial Bombay, 1890–1940," in *The Making of the Middle Class: Toward a Transnational History*, ed. A. Ricardo López and Barbara Weinstein (Durham, NC: Duke University Press, 2012), 141–160; Keith David Watenpaugh, *Being Modern in the Middle East: Revolution, Nationalism, Colonialism, and the Arab Middle Class* (Princeton, NJ: Princeton University Press, 2006), 81–93.

whom he knew from an earlier trip to the United States.[43] Again, such cooperation was barely acknowledged in colonial discourses; however, it reveals that
social and economic elites from different parts of the world could indeed act
as part of a global bourgeoisie without ever using this term explicitly.

Fears of the Decline of Western Civilization

Even though the middle classes had acquired a hegemonic position in several
Western European countries by the late nineteenth century, they saw the bourgeois world order as being under constant threat. The fear of civilizational
downfall seems to have been closely associated with the middle-class ideology
of progress and development. In Europe, the rise of the working-class movement explicitly challenged the social status of the bourgeoisie. What is more,
the constant antagonism of the local population in colonial possessions toward
colonial rule also made many observers doubt the legitimacy and the prospect
of success of the colonial project. Thus, the constant fear of being overthrown
by the rise of "barbaric" underclasses in both colonial peripheries and the slums
of European metropoles became a topos in middle-class thought after the mid-
nineteenth century. This fear was the downside of the unprecedented rise of
the European middle classes to cultural hegemony. As the middle-class realm
of ideas had not least been shaped by the experience of permanent sociopolitical change and economic transformation, it seemed to be not far-fetched to
believe that ultimately the bourgeois revolution might also "devour its children"
(a phrase coined by Jacques Mallet du Pan in reference to the French
Revolution).[44]

Many conservative writers of the late nineteenth century considered the uncivilized masses of the European metropoles a serious danger to middle-class
society. As did the missionaries before them—but with much less optimism
in regard to the possibility of civilizing the urban poor—they argued that the
European underclasses were at a similar stage of civilization as the colonial "savages." Gustav Le Bon was one who, in his successful study *The Psychology of
Peoples*, compared the underclasses of European industrial countries with the
inhabitants of Tierra del Fuego, who were supposedly still living in conditions

43. Fischer-Tiné, "Reclaiming Savages," 145.

44. Jacques Mallet du Pan, *Considerations sur la nature de la révolution de France* (London:
Flon, 1793), 80.

similar to that of the European Stone Age.[45] And Sigmund Freud maintained in his work on group psychology, which was influenced by Le Bon's study on crowd psychology, that any member of a crowd would behave like "a passionate, not supervised savage in a situation that is new to him."[46]

Non-European intellectual elites, such as members of Egypt's middle classes, could use Le Bon's argument that social progress depended on the activities of the upper crust to sustain their own projects of social modernization and nation building. The translation of Le Bon's scientific study of the crowd into Arabic thus became immensely popular among the Egyptian middle classes in the early twentieth century.[47] That success shows that European and non-European middle classes shared a similar way of distinguishing themselves from their respective underclasses; however, the lessons they drew from Le Bon's analogies between European and non-European societies were rather different. Whereas non-European middle classes could use them for self-empowerment, many members of the European middle classes interpreted them as a warning sign of a decline of both Western society and the social position of the bourgeoisie.

The Swiss anthropologist Otto Stoll specifically argued that there was no clear distinction between European civilization and the colonial *Naturvölker*—in other words, those colonial primitives whose fate was primarily shaped by their natural environment—because within European societies "the largest part of the populace consisted of a *Naturvolk*." Only a minority of Europeans were able "to rise above their level to a higher grade of intellectual freedom."[48] This minority belonged obviously to the "enlightened, educated" urban middle classes.[49] In particular, the peasantry cultivated a belief in sorcery and magic in a manner "we are used to reading about only in the case of African, Siberian, or American peoples."[50] As long as the seductiveness of the populace concerned only

45. Gustave Le Bon, *Les lois psychologiques de l'évolution des peuples* (Paris: Félix Alcan, 1894), 30.

46. Sigmund Freud, *Massenpsychologie und Ich-Analyse* (Vienna: Internationaler Psychoanalytischer Verlag, 1921), 33.

47. Timothy Mitchell, *Colonising Egypt* (Cambridge: Cambridge University Press, 1988), 122–123. For the resonance of Western scientific texts among Arabic readers and the ways they were linked to domestic ideas, see Marwa Elshakry, *Darwin in Arabic, 1860–1950* (Chicago: University of Chicago Press, 2013).

48. Otto Stoll, *Suggestion und Hypnotismus in der Völkerpsychologie* (Leipzig: Veit, 1904), 15.

49. Otto Stoll, "Zur Kenntnis des Zauberglaubens, der Volksmagie und Volksmedizin in der Schweiz," *Jahresbericht der Geographisch-Ethnographischen Gesellschaft in Zürich* (1908/9): 37–208, 200.

50. Stoll, "Zur Kenntnis des Zauberglaubens," 199.

the inhabitants of rural peripheries, this was not a major problem for middle-class society. According to Stoll, it was much more dangerous if the urban poor were to be seduced by the "dangerous suggestive force" of socialism.[51] The intensification of class conflict rendered it possible for scholars from the newly established discipline of anthropology to offer their expertise in how to dissolve social tensions.[52] For example, Adolf Bastian, the founding father of German anthropology, was convinced that anthropological research was fit to do this, because the European underclasses were living on a "similar level (in the stratification of culture and non-culture)" as the peoples of colonial possessions. In a text of 1893, he claimed that "those who are interested in the constitution of our civilization . . . will be well advised [to look] at the sublayers (in Folklore and anthropology)." This would allow for insight into the thinking of both European and colonial primitives and then help to compel them "(while still small and weak) . . . into mastery . . . —for the advantage of culture and of its blessings."[53]

Both Stoll and Bastian were advocates of liberalism and hoped that social tensions could finally be eased by a mix of education and governmentality. Yet this belief in the triumphal procession of the bourgeois world order came under ever greater pressure after the late nineteenth century. The similarity between colonial and European "savages" was no major problem as long as the European middle classes could rely on the belief that sooner or later all social problems could be solved due to technological, cultural, and social progress. This assumption, however, was challenged more and more at the end of the nineteenth century. Joseph-Arthur de Gobineau was convinced that European society had been dominated by an Aryan aristocracy until the French Revolution and had been subsequently subverted from within by a revolution of commoners led by ethnically mixed middle classes. The rule of the middle classes in turn was threatened by the rebellion of racially inferior lower orders, according to Gobineau. In such a weakened state, Europe was considered a vulnerable prey

51. Stoll, *Suggestion*, 581.

52. See Henrika Kuklick, *The Savage Within: The Social History of British Anthropology, 1885–1945* (Cambridge: Cambridge University Press, 1991) for the adaption of anthropology to social problems within Europe; and George W. Stocking, ed., *Volksgeist as Method and Ethic: Essays on Ethnography and the German Anthropological Tradition* (Madison: University of Wisconsin Press, 1996); and Henrika Kuklick, ed., *A New History of Anthropology* (Malden: Blackwell, 2008) for an overview of the history of anthropology.

53. Adolf Bastian, *Controversen in der Ethnologie. I: Die Geographischen Provinzen in ihren culturgeschichtlichen Berührungspunkten* (Berlin: Weidmann'sche Buchhandlung, 1893), 74.

to the "yellow" hordes ascending in the East.[54] Such ideas seemed ever more plausible after the turn of century. Gustave Le Bon claimed that the European social elites had been weakened by the social transformations of the nineteenth century and soon would be unable to control the mob.[55] At the same time, the liberal utopia was also challenged by the constant antagonism of non-European peoples toward the Eurocentric world order in the age of empire. In particular, the rise of Japan and the victory of Japanese troops in the war against Russia in 1905 had shocked many European observers, because it was the first occasion since early modern times that an Asian country had gained a victory in a military conflict against a European empire. Many authors thus warned against the Yellow Peril and assumed that the days of European world dominance might be numbered.[56]

Such challenges to liberal middle-class society from internal and external pressures resulted in increasing fear of degeneration and discontent with modern civilization after the turn of the twentieth century.[57] Oswald Spengler predicted the decline of the west in his book of that title, which he had begun to write in 1911 and whose German original was published right after the First World War.[58] Another author, the Catholic, conservative Swiss writer and historian Gonzague de Reynold, who was vexed by the fact that Europe had lost its global leadership role to the United States and to the Soviet Union after 1918, propagated the picture of a European continent that was "wounded, sick, bleeding and tantalized by pain."[59] In his eyes, the moral condition of Europe had been weakened by modern civilization, and it was only by a return to its roots

54. Gregory Blue, "Gobineau on China: Race Theory, the 'Yellow Peril,' and the Critique of Modernity," *Journal of World History* 10 (1999): 93–139.

55. Gustave Le Bon, *Les opinions et les croyances* (Paris: Ernest Flammarion, 1911), 178.

56. Wolfgang Schwentker, "The 'Yellow Peril' Revisited: Western Perceptions of Asia in the Age of Imperialism," in *Cultural Negotiations: Sichtweise des Anderen*, ed. Cedric Brown and Therese Fischer-Seidel (Tübingen: Francke, 1998), 33–47; Cemil Aydin, "A Global Anti-Western Movement? The Russo-Japanese War, Decolonization, and Asian Modernity," in *Competing Visions of World Order: Global Moments and Movements, 1880s–1930s*, ed. Sebastian Conrad and Dominic Sachsenmaier (New York: Palgrave, 2007), 213–236.

57. Daniel Pic, *Faces of Degeneration: A European Disorder* (Cambridge: Cambridge University Press, 1989).

58. Oswald Spengler, *Der Untergang des Abendlandes*, 2 vols. (Munich: Beck, 1922/1923).

59. Gonzague De Reynold, "Der geistig-moralische Zustand des Europa von heute," *Schönere Zukunft*, October 13, 1929. For an in-depth analysis of de Reynold's thinking, see Aram Mattioli, "Denkstil 'christliches Abendland': Eine Fallstudie zu Gonzague de Reynold," in *Der Wert "Europa" und die Geschichte: Auf dem Weg zu einem europäischen Geschichtsbewusstsein*, ed.

in Christianity and antiquity that Europe could hope to get back to its global mission: "Europe is the continent that does need to project itself out of itself, the continent of expansion and conquest, of discovery and colonization. Europe is born imperial. It has been created to be the globe." And if Europe did not want to become a "colony of underdeveloped peoples," it had better return to its true roots.[60]

For the prophets foretelling the crisis of Western civilization, liberalism seemed to have become a luxury that European elites no longer could afford. Consequently, they called for strong leaders and authoritarian governments. Spengler, for instance, was convinced that a new era of "Caesarism" was about to rise.[61] Democracy was considered dangerous, because it was feared that it would only reinforce the power of the mob and ultimately lead to socialism. Philanthropy, which for nineteenth century social reformers (and the middle classes who supported them) was an integral part of bourgeois culture, was described as utterly foolish, because it only strengthened the "savages" at home and abroad. The conservative American writer Madison Grant expressed it in his book *The Passing of the Great Race* like this:

> Throughout history it is only the race of the leaders that has counted and the most vigorous have been in control and will remain in mastery in one form or another until such time as democracy and its illegitimate offspring, socialism, definitely establish cacocracy and the rule of the worst and put an end to progress. . . . The stoppage of famines and wars and the abolition of the slave trade, while dictated by the noblest impulses of humanity, are suicidal to the white man.[62]

In his dystopian account, Grant floated the idea of an upcoming global racial war and argued that liberalism, in the long run, would be suicidal for both the bourgeois elite in particular and Western civilization in general, a concept that again underscores how closely the perception of social problems in Europe and the colonies could be interlinked in early twentieth-century thought.[63]

Kerstin Armborst and Wolf-Friedrich Schäufele (Mainz: Veröffentlichungen des Instituts für Europäische Geschichte Mainz, Beiheft online 2, 2007), paragraphs 60–75.

60. Gonzague De Reynold, *La Formation de l'Europe*, vol. 1 (Fribourg: LUF, 1944), 75.

61. Spengler, *Untergang des Abendlandes*, vol. 2, 635.

62. Madison Grant, *The Passing of the Great Race or the Racial Basis of European History* (1916; London: G. Bell and Sons, 1921), 79.

63. For a similar argument, see Lothrop Stoddard, *The Revolt against Civilization: The Menace of the Under Man* (New York: Charles Scribner's Sons, 1922).

Such theses found strong resonance among European conservatives and re-actionaries, especially after the Russian Revolution and the end of the First World War. Eugen Bircher, a right-wing Swiss politician and medical doctor, pointed out in an enthusiastic review of Grant's *Passing of the Great Race* that modern society, with its factories, cities, and democracies would, "from a racial point of view," result in the "survival of the unfittest."[64] Urbanization, which had been the sine qua non of the emergence of the middle classes as a social group, was considered the reason for their decline by many right-wing thinkers after the turn of the twentieth century. In 1940, Bircher reviewed Richard Korherr's *Volk und Raum* in a Swiss military journal (in 1943, Korherr would be tasked to work out a statistical report on the solution of the "Jewish ques-tion" by Heinrich Himmler). In this review, Bircher wrote:

> The introduction of this great and exceptional . . . study addresses a problem which . . . concerns all of humankind: the problem of population. It points out that we white people have the greatest interest to unite; otherwise we will be overrun and destroyed by the colored races sooner or later; that the increase of the colored races has become a colored flood and that the war of the races from a colored point of view has come into immediate reach. . . . In addition to that it is revealed that it is urbanization throughout the world, in Europe and most particularly in Germany that leads to the decline . . . of the white people.[65]

In a similar vein Oswald Spengler claimed in his *Hour of Decision*, published in 1933:

> If the white proletariat breaks loose in the United States, the Negro will be on the spot, and behind him the American Indian and the Japanese will wait until their turn has come. . . . And would the white leaders of the class con-flict be at a loss if colored riots would pave the way for them? They have never been selective in regards of their means.[66]

All the writers, scholars, and doctors mentioned in this chapter were mem-bers of the European middle classes. The fact that right-wing authors regularly

---

64. Eugen Bircher, "Zur Rassenfrage in der Schweiz," *Schweizerische Monatshefte* (1925): 671–677.

65. Eugen Bircher, "Review of Richard Korherr, Volk und Raum, Würzburg 1938," *Allgemeine Schweizerische Militärzeitung* 86, no. 3 (1940): 175–176.

66. Oswald Spengler, *Jahre der Entscheidung. Deutschland und die weltgeschichtliche Entwick-lung* (Munich: Beck, 1933), 164.

linked their anti-socialist notions with a caution about peoples of the Global South may be considered evidence of the remarkable global vision of the world order many of these thinkers had. As had the nineteenth-century missionary movement and their middle-class supporters, the "reactionary avant-garde"[67] of the early twentieth century established their ideas by constantly relating domestic sociopolitical processes to an assessment of processes in the non-European periphery.[68]

After 1945, such notions of comparing colonial subjects to European underclasses obviously became less convincing due to the ostracism of fascism and racism after the Second World War, decolonization, the establishment of welfare states, and the incorporation of the labor movement into the political mainstream in many Western European countries. The frequent analogies between European and non-European "savages," however, may be considered as ways in which the European middle classes coped with the rapid transformation of the world between the late eighteenth century and the early twentieth century and as evidence for the truly global horizon of the European middle classes in the age of empire.

67. Hans Ulrich Jost, *Die reaktionäre Avantgarde: Die Geburt der neuen Rechten in der Schweiz um 1900* (Zurich: Chronos, 1992).

68. Conversely, middle classes in other parts of the world were also disappointed by liberalism at that time. For instance, Fascist ideas and practices became popular among Middle Eastern middle classes after the 1920s and were used as means to fight for political influence. Watenpaugh, *Being Modern*, 255–278.

PART V
Failures and Fringes

13

Asymmetric Globality and South American Narratives of Bourgeois Failure

David S. Parker

IN THE LATE NINETEENTH AND EARLY TWENTIETH CENTURIES, arguably the high-water mark of European technological progress, imperial expansion, and cultural influence, South American intellectuals lamented that their countries' upper and middle classes had failed to duplicate the historical revolution they attributed to Europe's bourgeoisie. Pessimistic autodiagnoses evolved from a mid-1800s focus on the Spanish cultural inheritance to evolutionary biological theories at century's turn and to nationalist, Marxist, and anti-imperialist critiques by the 1920s. Diverse as these explanations were, the specific shortcomings they identified—lack of entrepreneurial drive, obsession with status, conspicuous consumption, and overdependence on state patronage—were remarkably stable and persistent. Some echo still today in conventional theories of Latin American underdevelopment. To the extent that those critiques had any basis in reality, they reflected South America's role in the world economy as an exporter of primary products and an importer of manufactures. Yet the narrative of bourgeois failure also drew on a mythic view of Europe, in particular the "bourgeois revolution" paradigm that few historians today accept

The author wishes to thank Ezequiel Adamovsky, Gonzalo Cáceres, Gabriela Castillo, Amitava Chowdhury, Richard Drayton, Enrique Garguín, Dennis Gilbert, Rebecca Manley, Claudia Stern, Sergio Visacovsky, the volume editors, and Princeton University Press's readers for their comments to earlier drafts.

uncritically. The belief that their nations lacked a true bourgeoisie arose from a commonplace but erroneous vision of Europe's history, which was assumed to be the template for all history.

The Tale of the "Missing" Latin American Bourgeoisie

The same transformational global forces that gave birth to the Manchester mill-owner or London financier in the age of empire begat the *estanciero* (rancher) of the Argentine pampas, the cotton or sugar baron of coastal Peru, and the nitrate mineowner of the Chilean Atacama. With family fortunes as likely to be derived from agriculture as from finance, urban real estate, or the perks of public office, South America's wealthy entrepreneurs did not wage political battle against a hereditary aristocracy—more often families intermarried—and rarely if ever did they self-identify as bourgeois.[1] Political radicals called them oligarchs, aristocrats, or *burgueses* interchangeably, while they thought of themselves simply as *gente decente*, respectable people, a designation they extended also to the lawyers, bureaucrats, merchants, intellectuals, and clerks that composed a middle class in their flourishing but mostly nonindustrial import-export economies.[2]

Did South America's diversified landowning business elite constitute a bourgeoisie? Was their worldview capitalist and liberal, as opposed to feudal? Those who answer affirmatively point to their science-driven, risk-taking entrepreneurship in developing new export products, adopting new technologies, and finding new markets.[3] Those who disagree depict a ruling caste whose power resided in quasi-colonial relations of domination and whose liberalism was but a thin veneer, a desire to feel "modern" while perpetuating caste privileges that enabled rent seeking.[4] Arnold Bauer, quoting a period observer,

1. Dennis Gilbert, *The Oligarchy and the Old Regime in Latin America, 1880–1970* (Lanham, MD: Rowman and Littlefield, 2017), chapter 1.

2. "Mostly nonindustrial" does not signify a total absence of factory production but does describe economies in which manufacturing for the internal market was at best a complement to more dynamic import-export sectors. See Fernando Rocchi, *Chimneys in the Desert: Industrialization in Argentina during the Export Boom Years, 1870–1930* (Stanford, CA: Stanford University Press, 2006).

3. Roy Hora, "Landowning Bourgeoisie or Business Bourgeoisie? On the Peculiarities of the Argentine Economic Elite, 1880–1945," *Journal of Latin American Studies* 34 (2002): 587–623, 598.

4. Michael Johns, "The Antinomies of Ruling Class Culture: The Buenos Aires Elite, 1880–1910," *Journal of Historical Sociology* 6 (1993): 74–101, 74.

called Chilean entrepreneurs "primitive producers, civilized consumers" who were fascinated with the technology, goods, and fashion created by Europe for a new global bourgeoisie but ill-equipped to bring about the economic, social, or political changes that would allow a genuinely bourgeois society to flourish.[5]

If not the landowning business elite, did the clerks, professionals, merchants, and intellectuals perhaps embody a true bourgeois sensibility? This, too, is a debate that has divided scholars. Products of rapid urbanization, booming commercial economies, expanding public and private bureaucracies, and intergenerational mobility via education, they were fast growing in numbers, political weight, and awareness of their distinct interests, whether they called themselves middle-class or not.[6] At the same time, naysayers highlight the ties of kinship and patronage that bound so many of them to the rich landowning families, accuse them of emulating aristocratic lifestyles by spending beyond their means, and decry their alleged lack of entrepreneurial creativity or national vision.[7] Narratives of inadequacy thus indict the rich investor class and the urban mesocracy alike: neither, critics contend, was genuinely bourgeois and neither was revolutionary.

In exploring the genesis and history of this "missing bourgeoisie" paradigm, we need to keep two points in mind. First, that essential concepts such as "feudal" and "bourgeois" were European imports, inherently problematic in their application to Latin America yet significant shapers of Latin Americans' own self-image. Second, that positivist and later Marxist theories of historical stages contributed to Latin Americans' mistaken belief that changes occurring on their continent in 1880 or 1920 were analogues to processes that Britain and France

5. Arnold J. Bauer, "Industry and the Missing Bourgeoisie: Consumption and Development in Chile, 1850–1950," *Hispanic American Historical Review* 70 (1990): 227–253, 246.

6. Ezequiel Adamovsky, *Historia de la clase media argentina* (Buenos Aires: Planeta, 2009); Patrick Barr-Melej, *Reforming Chile: Cultural Politics, Nationalism, and the Rise of the Middle Class* (Chapel Hill: University of North Carolina Press, 2001); D. S. Parker, *The Idea of the Middle Class: White-Collar Workers and Peruvian Society, 1900–1950* (University Park, PA: Penn State University Press, 1998). Also Brian P. Owensby, *Intimate Ironies: Modernity and the Making of Middle-Class Lives in Brazil* (Stanford, CA: Stanford University Press, 1999); and David S. Parker and Louise E. Walker, eds., *Latin America's Middle Class: Unsettled Debates and New Histories* (Lanham, MD: Lexington Books, 2013).

7. Fredrick B. Pike, "Aspects of Class Relations in Chile, 1850–1960," *Hispanic American Historical Review* 43 (1963): 14–33; also J. Pablo Silva, "Rethinking Aspects of Class Relations in Twentieth-Century Chile," in *Latin America's Middle Class*, ed. Parker and Walker, 171–196.

had undergone at some earlier point in their history. Stageism made it impossible to imagine global simultaneity—to see Peruvian cotton haciendas and British textile factories as interconnected cogs in a single world economy. Instead, stageism led Latin Americans to see only backwardness at home and to perceive modernity only in industrial Europe and the United States.[8]

Bauer had a point that urban Latin Americans were immersed in a mental world where Europe provided the omnipresent frame of reference, though not because they were ruled—as has sometimes been argued—by a culturally colonized, *déraciné* elite inhabiting a faux French fantasyland. Cities and ports around the world were essential nodes of late nineteenth-century globalization, making South American capitals as much a part of the bourgeois West as Lisbon, Madrid, or perhaps even Paris itself. European letters, news, fashions, architecture, technology, politics, and people impinged insistently upon the consciousness of ordinary Latin Americans. Read any early twentieth-century university thesis, expert treatise, professional journal, or government report, and no matter the topic one finds French and English authors copiously cited and their ideas fully assimilated. Newspapers published French poetry and serialized novels and sent correspondents to or hired freelancers in most major European capitals. Transoceanic telegraph cables, ever-cheapening steamship travel, international scientific conferences, a robust Paris-based Spanish-language publishing industry, and mass immigration all contributed strands to a thick web of European-Latin American entanglements, as people and ideas traveled back and forth with unprecedented speed and frequency.

Although the region's most successful intellectuals also wrote for French and Italian journals (Uruguayan Eugenio Garzón, for example, was an editor at *Le Figaro*), in general Parisian newspapers had no reciprocal interest in sending reporters to Santiago or Lima.[9] Latin American diplomatic legations made monumental efforts to boost their countries' reputations and attract immigrants and investors, complaining when Europeans showed no comprehension of the difference between one country and the next.[10] Benjamin Vicuña Subercaseaux believed the only way to convince Europeans of Chile's virtues was to

8. Michael Adas, *Machines as the Measure of Men: Science, Technology, and the Ideologies of Western Dominance* (Ithaca, NY: Cornell University Press, 1989).

9. *L'Amérique latine et "Le Figaro" en l'honneur d'Eugenio Garzón* (Paris: Imprimerie Cabasson, 1909).

10. Ingrid Fey, "First Tango in Paris: Latin Americans in Turn-of-the-Century France, 1880 to 1920" (PhD diss., University of California, 1996), chapter 2 and 378–379.

publish, in Paris, a guidebook written in the voice of a Frenchman pretending to have just returned from an extended stay and prefaced by a French notable.[11]

We may interpret this "asymmetric ignorance," to use Dipesh Chakrabarty's noteworthy phrase, as a product of European arrogance, or we may blame Latin Americans for their failure to impress the world by defeating a major power in war (as Japan did in 1905) or by producing and exporting high-value-added manufactures.[12] Either way, it created a feedback loop reinforcing the perception that no South American country could match the progress and glitter that rich Chileans saw on their visits to Paris or New York, that Peruvian middle classes read about in their weekly magazines, or that Argentine sociologists debated with great insight in Spanish, French, Italian, or English. Fin de siècle South Americans' growing sense of national identity could not but be soured by this feeling that their nations were marginal players on the new bourgeois globe. Since they were not as marginal as Africa, Asia, or the Islamic world (the idea of a Third World or Global South would not form for several decades more), Latin Americans were just as likely as their European counterparts to traffic in orientalist stereotypes of African savagery, Muslim laziness and fatalism, and Chinese despotism or vice. But always in the back of urban South Americans' collective mind was a certain deficit of self-esteem, born of being ignored by the Europeans whose progress they sought to replicate. In this climate of self-doubt that internalized the asymmetries of late nineteenth-century globality, Latin American intellectuals compared their own upper and middle classes to the imagined European bourgeoisie and found them wanting.

The cases of Argentina, Chile, and Peru provide a useful and generalizable comparison set.[13] Argentina after 1880 was by every account the most successful of Latin American nations, with a rich, diverse pastoral economy and a thriving capital described as the Paris of South America. "Rich as an Argentine" became a common expression as the country attracted some four million European immigrants between 1870 and 1920. Peru, in contrast, seemed irreparably backward following her defeat in the 1879–83 War of the Pacific.

11. Benjamín Vicuña Subercaseaux, *Un país nuevo (cartas sobre Chile)* (Paris: Imprimerie André Eyméoud, 1903), vii–viii.

12. Dipesh Chakrabarty, *Provincializing Europe: Postcolonial Thought and Historical Difference* (Princeton, NJ: Princeton University Press, 2000), 28–29.

13. Generalizable at least to most of South America: for Mexico, Central America, and the Caribbean, proximity to an increasingly imperialist United States is a complicating factor.

Comparatively few Europeans chose Peru as a destination, and despite a modest early twentieth-century economic recovery, pessimism reigned. Chile, victorious in war, had gained the nitrate fields that Peru lost, and Chilean capitalists invested their new wealth in banks, vineyards, and Santiago mansions. Yet relative prosperity did not spare Chile from deep social and political tensions, which were often expressed in terms of national crisis and decline. Given the differences between these countries, what captures the attention is how universal the lament of bourgeois deficiency was in all three. The critique went through multiple and diverse iterations but common threads ran throughout.

From Colonial Backwardness to Biological Inferiority

In the early postindependence years it had still been possible to assume that the new nations of Latin America could unlock the engine of progress as soon as they broke from the fetters of Spain's mercantilist order, drafted enlightened constitutions and commercial codes, and destroyed the stultifying influence of the Church, the guilds, and the privileged colonial elite. But by midcentury, as the region's instability, dictators, wars, and economic problems persisted and as the United States demonstrated that a colonized past was no obstacle to economic advancement, the critique turned inward, taking on not just archaic Spanish laws and entrenched interests but the very culture that Spain had implanted in its domains. Latin American liberals came to believe they needed a "mental emancipation."[14] "Spain educated us to be vassals and serfs," wrote Argentine Esteban Echeverría in 1846. "We are independent but not free."[15]

Juan Bautista Alberdi similarly sought Argentina's mental emancipation from the Spain of Philip II and the Inquisition, advocating a practical education, taught in English, "the language of liberty, industry, and order."[16] But for Alberdi even more important than education was the "living action of modern Europe, exercised through free trade, through immigration, and through

14. Jorge Larraín, *Identity and Modernity in Latin America* (Malden, MA: Polity Press, 2000), 77, citing Mexican Gabino Barreda.

15. Esteban Echeverría, *Dogma socialista*, 2nd ed., Grandes Escritores Argentinos 60 (Buenos Aires: W. M. Jackson, 1944), 188–193.

16. Juan Bautista Alberdi, *Bases y puntos de partida para la organización política de la República Argentina*, 2nd ed., Grandes Escritores Argentinos 68 (Buenos Aires: W. M. Jackson, 1944), 62–63.

industry."[17] Alberdi famously contrasted coastal and interior Latin America as separate worlds living centuries apart. The interior, absent the influence of Britain and France, was "the product of sixteenth-century Europe, of Europe at the time of the conquest, . . . preserved intact as if in a jar."[18] A jump to English time, Alberdi believed, required that European "habits of industry and practices of civilization" be grafted onto American rootstock, "like you do with grapevines," a process he believed was beginning to occur in immigrant-filled port cities such as Valparaíso, Chile.[19]

It is understandable why South Americans would compare themselves to Britain, Germany, France, or the United States and come to the conclusion that large swathes of their countries were still caught "upstream" on the "stream of time."[20] The idea of each society evolving through historical stages, and its implication that Latin American nations needed only to duplicate the steps that the "advanced countries" had taken in *their* pasts, was a powerful one. It offered hope that Latin America's comparative backwardness was not a sign of defeat in capitalism's global footrace but merely the result of a later start.

But the evolution-through-stages paradigm, which presumably inspired hope in Alberdi and Echeverría, could just as easily bring despair when progress came too slowly. By the turn of the twentieth century, Latin America's obvious failure to keep pace with the marvels showcased at the universal expositions of Paris and Chicago led intellectuals to seek new answers in positivist social psychology and biological science. Steeped in racial essentialism—Hippolyte Taine's environmental determinism, Herbert Spencer's social Darwinism, the concept of degeneration—these biological theories pointed in the same anti-Spanish direction as Echeverría or Alberdi, but with a greater sense of scientific inescapability.

Influential texts of the era introduced metaphors of congenital illness: Agustín Alvarez, *Manual de patología política* (Argentina, 1899), César Zumeta, *Continente enfermo* (Venezuela, 1899), Manuel Ugarte, *Enfermedades sociales* (Argentina, 1905), Alcides Arguedas, *Pueblo enfermo* (Bolivia, 1909).[21] Although

17. Alberdi, *Bases y puntos*, 69–70.

18. Alberdi, *Bases y puntos*, 70.

19. Alberdi, *Bases y puntos*, 70, 77–78.

20. Johannes Fabian, *Time and the Other: How Anthropology Makes Its Object* (New York: Columbia University Press, 1983), 17.

21. Michael Aronna, *"Pueblos Enfermos": The Discourse of Illness in the Turn-of-the-Century Spanish and Latin American Essay* (Chapel Hill: University of North Carolina, Department of Romance Languages, 1999), 27.

modern scholars tend to focus on these authors' racism against South America's native and mestizo masses, the texts also focused on the flaws of the white upper and middle classes, many offering versions of the narrative of the absent or deficient bourgeoisie.

Typical was Carlos Octavio Bunge's *Nuestra América*, first published in Argentina in 1903. Starting from what he described as the axiomatic principle "that each nation possesses a collective psychology" not entirely immutable but capable only of gradual change, Bunge argued that the Latin American, as a hybrid derived from Spanish, native, and African stock, had all the negative qualities of that unfortunate mix. Looking at Latin America's ruling and middle classes, Bunge described the dominant trait as laziness, both physical and psychic, which had been inherited from the arrogant Spaniard's degeneration in the American environment.[22]

> The psychological poverty of the rich class, which doesn't found progressive institutes or endow universities, schools, libraries, or museums . . . is a product of ignorance, which is the child of apathy. . . .
>
> Look to [our directing classes] for great financial, political or literary ideas; . . . I fear that you won't even find the ability to *imagine wealth*, which is the greatest of the virtues of the Anglo-Americans. We Hispano-Americans don't even recognize this virtue, which we consider venality. Venality, oh, critics, is the passion of a property-owner who, with a million pesos of capital, only thinks about enjoying himself abroad; venality is the avaricious sentiment of a hacienda owner who is incapable of risking even a cent in any forward-looking enterprise and only aspires to hold on to as much of his rents as he can. But the action of the capitalist who, with 500 thousand dollars tries to earn 20 or 30 million—even if it be in the commerce of shoe leather or pork bellies— . . . this is not the venality of the hot-dog seller, this is the imagination of riches![23]

The idea that Latin America's bourgeoisie lacked business imagination and suffered from risk aversion, a habit of consuming beyond their means, and a

22. Carlos Octavio Bunge, *Nuestra América (Ensayo de psicología social)*, 6th ed. (Buenos Aires: Vaccaro, 1918), 51, 141, 171. A 1905 printing of the first edition (Valerio Abeledo, editor) is available at archive.org. It may be worth noting that Bunge does not reference the identically titled and now famous 1891 essay by José Martí.

23. Bunge, *Nuestra América*, 173–174, 208–209.

tendency to depend on the state rather than on their own devices was not unique to Bunge—nor was the belief that Latin America's technological backwardness and recurring economic crises were attributable to that deficient national psychology. The Bolivian Alcides Arguedas in *Pueblo enfermo* zeroed in on the phenomenon he called *funcionarismo* (public-sector bloating), administrative corruption, and the white-collar tendency to sit around the office talking rather than efficiently and courteously making a sale, as the foreign merchants did.[24] His critique was nothing new; the term *empleomanía* was already in use as early as 1866, when Luis Benjamin Cisneros used it to illustrate Peru's need to create new industries rather than relying on expanding government employment paid from customs revenues.[25] The main difference between 1866 and the 1900s was that Cisneros had identified a problem for which he offered policy solutions, while Bunge and Arguedas saw *empleomanía*, inefficiency, and prodigality as national character traits.

The ubiquity of the biological metaphor did not mean, however, that all authors coincided in their diagnoses. Evolutionary science provided a grammar, but within that idiom multiple causal arguments were possible. To explain *empleomanía* in Peru, for example, Manuel Vicente Villarán pointed in 1900 to an educational system dominated by classicism and universities that produced only lawyers.[26] Emilio Rodríguez Mendoza, describing the identical phenomenon in Chile, focused on how that nation's nitrate export boom had created "an enormously rich treasury in the midst of a poor country," thus making it natural, even inevitable, for educated professional men to turn to government for employment and for vote-hungry politicians to oblige them.[27]

José Ingenieros, reviewing Bunge's *Nuestra América*, critiqued his exclusive focus on biology as opposed to environment.[28] Drawing on Taine, Ingenieros

24. Alcides Arguedas, "Pueblo Enfermo," in *Obras completas*, vol. 1 (Mexico City: Aguilar, 1959), 393–616, 463–467.

25. Luis Benjamin Cisneros, *Obras completas*, vol. 3 (Lima: Librería e Imprenta Gil, 1939), 34–37.

26. Manuel Vicente Villarán, "Las profesiones liberales en el Perú" (1900), in *Páginas escogidas* (Lima: P. L. Villanueva, 1962), 309–310.

27. Emilio Rodríguez Mendoza, *Ante la decadencia*, quoted in Cristián Gazmuri R., *El Chile del Centenario: Los ensayistas de la crisis* (Santiago: Instituto de Historia, Pontificia Universidad Católica, 2001), 23.

28. José Ingenieros, "'Nuestra America', de Bunge," *Revista de Derecho, Historia y Letras* 16 (1903): 203–225.

explained that laziness was typical of peoples who inhabit regions of tropical abundance, while diligence was characteristic of peoples in cold northern climes for whom the Darwinian struggle requires greater industriousness. Environmentalism had the added benefit of forecasting a rosy future for Argentina, as temperate-climate European whites immigrating to the temperate pampas would not have the defects that Mediterranean races developed in tropical places.[29] But perhaps most fascinating was Ingenieros's synthesis of environmental determinism with a theory of historical stages rooted in a reading of Marx:

> Passing from the feudal to the agro-export phase, [Argentina's] political future . . . has changed because of the incorporation of a great mass of immigrants of the white race; its descendants, now enriched, are being brought into the capitalist class in formation and they will be rather hostile to the feudal oligarchies, aiming to take away their political power: it will be the struggle of the capitalist bourgeoisie against feudal privileges.[30]

In other words, Ingenieros believed that European immigration would provide the preconditions for Argentina's bourgeois revolution soon to come, a revolution that would in turn play a crucial part in a Darwinian evolutionary struggle that the remnants of the feudal Spanish race would lose. Understanding this argument, we should not be as surprised as the young Peruvian radical Eudocio Ravines was when meeting Ingenieros in Buenos Aires in 1924–25. When Ravines asked the venerable social scientist what Peru needed to solve its perpetual problems of dictators and poverty, Ingenieros reportedly answered: "White race, my son! White race."[31]

From Darwinism to Nationalism

Ravines recalled not being impressed. Unlike Argentina, Peru was a majority-indigenous country whose colonial glory had long faded and whose principal source of immigrant labor was East Asia. It should be no surprise that Peruvian intellectuals found themselves attracted instead to theories that allowed for education to overcome blood. One original early challenge to biological

29. Ingenieros, "'Nuestra America', de Bunge."

30. José Ingenieros, *Ensayos escogidos* (Buenos Aires: Centro Editor de América Latina, 1980), 62.

31. Eudocio Ravines, *The Yenan Way* (New York: Charles Scribner's Sons, 1951), 16.

determinism came from the most radical of Peru's turn-of-the-century thinkers, Manuel González Prada. On the one hand, González Prada frequently cited European race theorists like Herbert Spencer and Gustave LeBon and, like Bunge and Arguedas, drew on metaphors of pathology: he famously described Peru as a nation so sick that "wherever you poke your finger, pus erupts."[32] On the other hand, one of his later essays, "Our Indians" (1904), openly attacked "the division of humanity into superior and inferior races" and ridiculed a Eurocentric construction of Western history that belittled Latin America:

> Not one of the Spanish American nations exhibits today the political and social misery that reigned in Europe under feudalism; but Europe's feudal epoch is now regarded as an evolutionary stage, while the period of Spanish American revolutions is viewed as an irreparable, terminal condition. . . . Are there two sociological laws, one for the Latins of America and another for the Latins of Europe?[33]

González Prada was ahead of his time in denouncing the imperialist logic of European science. But little by little, other South American thinkers also began to jettison ideas of evolutionary destiny, and their critiques of the bourgeoisie were increasingly tinged with nationalism.

In Chile in particular, a literature of biting social criticism dominated the early twentieth century, spawning such titles as *Ante la decadencia* (Emilio Rodríguez Mendoza, 1899), *La crisis moral de la república* (Enrique Mac-Iver, 1900), *La decadencia de Chile* (Florentino Abarca, 1904), *Nuestra inferioridad económica* (Francisco Antonio Encina, 1912), and *Cómo se hunde el país* (How the country sinks; Carlos Pinto Durán, 1917).[34] Many of these works employed an idiom of race and national psychology just as Bunge and Arguedas did, but Chilean writers faced a unique problem. For much of the nineteenth century Chile had been hailed as an island of stability amid the chaos of her neighbors. With her victory over Peru in the War of the Pacific, patriotic propaganda exalted Chilean courage, virility, abnegation, ingenuity, and united purpose. The idea that

, 32. Manuel González Prada, "Propaganda and Attack," in *Free Pages and Hard Times,* ed. David Sobrevilla (New York: Oxford University Press, 2003), 93–104, 99.

33. Manuel González Prada, "Our Indians," in *Free Pages and Hard Times,* ed. Sobrevilla, 181–194, 182, 184–185. This text was originally drafted in 1904 but published posthumously, leaving open the possibility of post-1904 revisions.

34. Bernardo Subercaseaux, *Historia de las ideas y de la cultura en Chile,* vol. 4: *Nacionalismo y cultura* (Santiago: Editorial Universitaria, 2007), appendix. See also Gazmuri, *Chile del Centenario.*

Chileans were racially *superior*, popularized in Nicolás Palacios' *Raza chilena* (1904), had been heard at least since the 1881 occupation of Lima.[35]

So how were Chileans to account for their growing sense of crisis and decline two decades later? Wary of attributing their fate to biology or environment, Chilean intellectuals blamed their ruling class. Four critiques stand out: the bourgeoisie's incapacity as entrepreneurs and their dependence on government favor, their Frenchified culture, consumption beyond their means, and their inadequate solidarity with the nation in response to the social question. These failings had allegedly opened the door for foreign interests to exploit opportunities that Chileans left untapped. The master criticism that unified it all was the "decadence of the spirit of nationality." Francisco A. Encina, in *Nuestra inferioridad económica*, provided the clearest exposition of these themes. His indictment of the educational system and its production of parasitic liberal professionals was almost identical to Villarán's. His denunciation of Hispanic indolence, prodigality, and ostentation was an attenuated version of Bunge's. But rather than seeing emulation of Europe as a solution to, or exit from, Chile's fateful Iberian heritage, Encina argued that it only made things worse:

> Our fathers believed—and almost all our intellectuals continue believing—that in intimate contact with the European people our society would harmoniously assimilate all of its civilization; ... that with refinement, we would also obtain the necessary economic aptitudes to meet the new demands created by progress.
>
> Unfortunately that did not happen.
>
> As always occurs when an inferior people is placed in intimate contact with other more developed ones, we assimilate the refinements and capacity for consumption typical of the superior civilizations but none of the great economic or moral forces that comprise its core. We learned cleanliness and hygiene, to dress elegantly, to live in comfort, to listen to music, to appreciate the beauty of sculpture and painting, to read verse and attend the theater; but we did not acquire at the same time their practical sense, their constant application, their precision, their capacity for association, their sense of honor, ... their technical competence.[36]

35. Hugo Maureira, "'Valiant Race, Tenacious Race, Heroic, Indomitable and Implacable': The War of the Pacific (1879–1984) and the Role of Racial Ideas in the Construction of Chilean Identity" (MA thesis, Queen's University, 2002).

36. Francisco A. Encina, *Nuestra inferioridad económica*, 6th ed. (Santiago: Editorial Universitaria, 1986), 180.

He did not believe that Chileans who traveled to Europe truly assimilated its "intellectual and moral influence,"[37] nor did he agree that European immigrants transferred their skills to Chileans; rather, foreigners displaced locals in textbook Darwinian fashion. The sad result could be seen in Chile's trade deficits, failure to protect national industries, concessions to foreign mining firms, and excessive government spending, but according to Encina, the illness of superficial cosmopolitanism and admiration for foreigners went deeper, robbing Chileans of "the vitality of our own organism."[38] He argued that what Chile *should* learn from the European was self-confidence:

> In England a young man would not be considered educated if, upon leaving school, he doubted for an instant that an abyss separates his race from all others in the world, or if he hesitated to believe that everything English, for the sole fact of being English, is superior to all things foreign.[39]

Encina sustained the long-standing critique that Latin societies needed to do more to foster the practical, entrepreneurial values of a genuine bourgeoisie, but contrary to Alberdi, he believed that the path to that mental revolution was via nationalism, not emulation.

The Argentine Ricardo Rojas's *La restauración nacionalista* (1909) was equally eloquent in its denunciation of cosmopolitanism, making the case that the emulation of France and Britain was not the antidote to Argentina's Spanish backwardness but a return to the mental habits of colonialism:

> Beneath the façade of shining progress, we continue spiritually as if we were in the times of the colony. . . . We live waiting for the ship from overseas, which back then came every three months with news from Cádiz and now arrives daily with news of France and England.[40]

After blaming an educational system dominated by foreign- or immigrant-run private schools of dubious quality, Rojas went on to skewer an alienated, vacuous press for destroying the sentiment of nationality—filling its pages with column after column of news about "events in Russian and Italian villages so trivial and unimportant that even over there the stories barely make the local

---

37. Encina, *Nuestra inferioridad económica*, 141–142.

38. Encina, *Nuestra inferioridad económica*, 143–144.

39. Encina, *Nuestra inferioridad económica*, 212.

40. Ricardo Rojas, *La restauracíon nacionalista*, 2nd ed., *Obras completas*, vol. 4 (Buenos Aires: Juan Roldán y Cía, Librería La Facultad, 1922), 118.

papers," obituaries of the "Bishop of Bordeaux or some nephew or brother of the Emperor of Austria," and other international news of no civic value to Argentines.[41]

The 1920s: Marxism, Anti-imperialism, Vanguardism

In the aftermath of the First World War, three intellectual developments further invigorated the failed bourgeoisie narrative while again transforming it: the spread of materialist languages of class, Marxist theories of imperialism as an economic stage of capitalism, and the vanguardist idea of the declining West. Illustrative of the first is a conference given in 1918 by the Chilean academic, politician, and worker's-housing advocate Juan Enrique Concha Subercaseaux. Concha had no patience for ideas of class struggle, yet his speech repeatedly used terms such as *burguesía* and *proletariado*, *clase obrera* and *clase media*, as he argued that Chile's upper classes needed to better orient workers and attend to their well-being. Central to his argument was that Chile had, among all world nations, an unusually large chasm between rich and poor that was exacerbated by the congenital weakness of her middle class.

> There exists in our social organization, as in all the countries of the world, an intermediate class that is habitually given the name of bourgeoisie or middle class. . . . This bourgeoisie, in other countries like the United States, France, and Germany, is the industrial class par excellence and a great element of progress and social peace, because the industrialist is by nature a man who loves order. . . .
>
> [But] our bourgeoisie or middle class does not have the social consistency of a class that it has in other countries, where it constitutes a genuine stratum, respected by those who are a little bit above and by those who are below on the scale of real social inequalities.[42]

The specific critique Concha makes—the predominance of liberal professions in the making of Chile's middle class, the class's lack of unity, its aping of an elite that it silently resents—had all been heard before. What was noteworthy, especially given Concha's conservatism, was its explicit vocabulary of class. The First World War and its global aftermath of strikes and revolutions

41. Rojas, "La restauracíon nacionalista," 189.

42. Juan Enrique Concha Subercaseaux, *Conferencias sobre economía social dictadas en la Universidad Católica de Santiago de Chile* (Santiago: Imprenta Chile, 1918), 122–124.

was the watershed here: whereas before the war only a tiny percentage of Latin American writings had sounded remotely Marxist in their language, after 1918 class terminology became the norm, spilling beyond the community of militants and into everyday discourse.[43]

The other two trends, economic theories of imperialism and the idea of the West in crisis, find illustration in the debate between Peruvians Víctor Raúl Haya de la Torre and José Carlos Mariátegui. With Haya de la Torre, the founder of a pan-Latin American anti-imperialist movement he called APRA,[44] we see the conceit of stageism evolve into a full-blown theoretical model—Haya called it his "theory of historical space-time"—to contrast the process of class formation in South America with Europe's experience:

> There has not occurred in our nations the evolution that can be observed in the British, French, or German bourgeoisies, who, having been strengthened as economic classes over a long period of growth, ultimately capture political power and more or less violently wrest it from the classes that represent feudalism. In Indo-America we have not had time to create a powerful and autonomous national bourgeoisie, sufficiently strong to displace the plantation-owning classes—a prolongation of Spanish feudalism. [45]

Haya argued that neither peasants nor workers could lead Latin America's nationalist struggle because the peasant was mired in feudal ignorance and the working class, whose life initially improved under the impulse of well-paying foreign firms, was "new, young, weak, [and] fascinated by the temporary advantages."[46] All this led Haya to conclude that only the middle class was capable of directing a "united front of manual and intellectual workers," similar to Sun-Yat Sen's Guomindang.[47] Tracing a thread from the racial or climatic determinism of Bunge or Ingenieros though the nationalism of Encina and Rojas to the Lenin-influenced anti-imperialism of Haya de la Torre might seem challenging, but the elements of purported bourgeois failure remained very much the same. Bunge and Encina decried the Latin middle class's congenital inability to compete against the more diligent, efficient, practical, precise,

---

43. David S. Parker, "Peruvian Politics and the Eight-Hour Day: Rethinking the 1919 General Strike," *Canadian Journal of History* 30 (1995): 417–438, 422–426.

44. *Alianza Popular Revolucionaria Americana* (American people's revolutionary alliance).

45. Haya de la Torre, *El anti-imperialismo y el APRA* (Lima: Fondo Editorial del Congreso del Perú, 2010), 114.

46. Haya de la Torre, *Anti-imperialismo y el APRA*, 126.

47. Haya de la Torre, *Anti-imperialismo y el APRA*, 131–132.

honorable, and competent foreign merchant. In writing that "imperialism economically subjugates or destroys the middle classes in the backward countries it penetrates," Haya de la Torre spoke a radically different language but made the identical point.[48]

The Peruvian journalist and independent Marxist José Carlos Mariátegui seemed at first glance to agree with Haya de la Torre: few ideas were more central to Mariátegui's thought than the concept of bourgeois failure, and Haya's portrait of a feeble national bourgeoisie easily marginalized by foreign interests accorded with Mariátegui's picture of "semi-feudal" Peru.[49] But to Haya's proposal of an anti-imperialist front guided by the middle class, Mariátegui countered that the diagnosis contradicted the prescription. If Peru had no true bourgeoisie, no nationalistic middle class, how could that class possibly lead the new society? In an often-cited 1928 polemic against Haya, Mariátegui contrasted Peru's bourgeoisie with that of China:

> The Chinese nobleman or bourgeois feels intimately Chinese. When whites express contempt for their stratified and decrepit culture, they respond with [equal] contempt and with pride in their thousand-year traditions. . . . The circumstances are not the same in Indo-America. . . . In Peru the white aristocrat and bourgeois despise all that is plebeian, national. They feel, first and foremost, white. The petty bourgeois mestizo imitates this example. The Lima bourgeoisie fraternizes with Yankee capitalists, and even with their mere employees, at the country club, the tennis club, and in the streets. The Yankee can marry a criollo elite girl without race or religion being an obstacle; she, in turn, has no qualms about nationality or culture in preferring matrimony with an individual of the invading race. Nor does a middle-class girl feel such scruples. The *huachafita* who can catch a Yankee employee of

48. Haya de la Torre, *Anti-imperialismo y el APRA*, 128.

49. Of the vast secondary literature on Mariátegui, I have found the following sources most useful: in English, Harry E. Vanden, *National Marxism in Latin America: José Carlos Mariátegui's Thought and Politics* (Boulder, CO: Lynne Rienner, 1986); Jesús Chavarría, *José Carlos Mariátegui and the Rise of Modern Peru, 1890–1930* (Albuquerque: University of New Mexico Press, 1979); and in Spanish, Patricia Funes, *Salvar la nación: Intelectuales, cultura y política en los años veinte latinoamericanos* (Buenos Aires: Prometeo Libros Editorial, 2006); Alberto Flores Galindo, *La agonía de Mariátegui: La polémica con el Komintern* (Lima: DESCO, 1982); Estuardo Núñez, *La experiencia europea de Mariátegui* (Lima: Empresa Editora Amauta, 1978); and works by Robert París and José Aricó. Harry E. Vanden and Marc Becker, *José Carlos Mariátegui: an Anthology* (New York: Monthly Review Press, 2011) choose their selections well, despite occasionally problematic translations.

W. R. Grace or the Foundation Company does so with the satisfaction that she is elevating her social status.[50]

The second key distinction between Mariátegui and Haya de la Torre is that in adhering to the stageist paradigm that located Peru in a past of "Spanish feudalism," Haya viewed Peru's bourgeois failure as a departure from history's normal path, whereas Mariátegui saw Western bourgeois society as itself tired and decadent, ripe to be swept away by the winds of revolution. That revolution would presumably be socialist and in service to the masses, but it would also manifest the postwar spirit of regeneration, reflecting the anti-bourgeois sensibility of the European avant-garde.

To give a taste of Mariátegui's fascination with what he saw as a global moment of revolutionary possibility, his first published full book, *La escena contemporánea* (1925), discussed the ideas of Henri Barbusse, Oswald Spengler, Luigi Pirandello, Georges Sorel, Maxim Gorky, Italian futurism, Gandhi, Rabindranath Tagore, and Mustafa Kemal, among others.[51] One of the book's essays, "Orient and Occident," notes the passing of Western knowledge hegemony as the age of empire gave way to postwar crisis:

> In its vainglorious youth, Western civilization dealt disdainfully and arrogantly with the peoples of the East. The white man considered his dominion over the man of color necessary, natural, and legitimate. He used the words "oriental" and "barbarous" as if they were synonyms. He thought only Western things were civilized. . . . Today the West, relativist and skeptical, discovers its own decadence and foresees its coming twilight, and feels the need to explore and better understand the East. . . . Meanwhile the idea of democracy, grown old in Europe, sprouts in Asia and Africa. Imported by European capital, the doctrine of Marx penetrates. . . . Thus a vigorous will to independence appears in the East at the same time that in Europe the capacity to co-opt or suffocate that will is debilitated.[52]

50. José Carlos Mariátegui, *Ideología y política*, 16th ed. (Lima: Empresa Editora Amauta, 1986), 88–89. On the Peruvianism *huachafita*, which denotes a social climber of limited means and/or poor taste, see David S. Parker, "*Siúticos, Huachafos, Cursis, Arribistas* and *Gente de Medio Pelo*: Social Climbers and the Representation of Class in Chile and Peru, 1860–1930," in *The Making of the Middle Class: Toward a Transnational History*, ed. A. Ricardo López and Barbara Weinstein (Durham, NC: Duke University Press, 2012), 335–354.

51. José Carlos Mariátegui, *La escena contemporánea*, 14th ed. (Lima: Empresa Editora Amauta, 1987), 165.

52. Mariátegui, *Escena contemporánea*, 190–193.

Even if Mariátegui did not believe that Peru's middle class was sufficiently free from the thrall of the West to lead an anti-imperialist revolution, he did have faith in its working class and native majority and saw South American socialism as a genuine possibility given the crisis of Western capitalism. Again, in contrast to most of the writers considered in this chapter, Mariátegui did not portray the South American bourgeoisie as an inadequate version of its European counterpart, because for Mariátegui bourgeois failure was universal. Returning, though, to the qualities he identified in Peru's middle class—imitative cosmopolitanism and lack of national feeling—we see direct lines of descent from Rojas, Encina, and González Prada, and if we read between the lines, we still hear faint echoes of Bunge and perhaps even Alberdi. What had changed by the 1920s was not so much the critique of the middle class itself, but the way in which South Americans conceptualized their nations' bourgeoisies in relation to Europe—in evolving dialogue with the global ideological currents of their era.

Of course the ultimate irony is that the last half century of European historiography has called into question just about everything Latin Americans thought they knew about the European middle classes. Only a minority of historians today would validate Haya de la Torre's account of a *bourgeoisie conquérant* "who, having been strengthened as economic classes over a long period of growth, ultimately capture political power and more or less violently wrest it from the classes that represent feudalism."[53] Elements that South Americans took as signs of their divergence from the historical norm—their bourgeoisie's investment in "feudal" landed property, or their tendency to mimic "aristocratic" habits of consumption, or their attraction to the liberal professions and politics—turn out to be not so aberrational after all.[54] Sarah Maza may or may not have been right to speak of the French bourgeoisie as a *myth*, but at minimum there is some consensus that the bourgeois revolution paradigm oversimplifies far more nuanced histories.[55] In late nineteenth- and early twentieth-century South America, however, the conquering bourgeoisie paradigm

53. Haya de la Torre, *Anti-imperialismo y el APRA*, 114.

54. Hora, "Landowning Bourgeoisie," 594–598.

55. Sara C. Maza, *The Myth of the French Bourgeoisie: An Essay on the Social Imaginary, 1750–1850* (Cambridge, MA: Harvard University Press, 2003). Influential critiques of the bourgeois revolution paradigm include Dror Wahrman, *Imagining the Middle Class: The Political Representation of Class in Britain, c. 1780–1840* (Cambridge: Cambridge University Press, 1995); and William M. Reddy, *Money and Liberty in Modern Europe: A Critique of Historical Understanding* (Cambridge: Cambridge University Press, 1987), chapter 1. For thought-provoking alternative views, see Neil Davidson, *How Revolutionary Were the Bourgeois Revolutions?* (Chicago:

remained the unchallenged frame through which critical intellectuals perceived their own bourgeoisies as failures.

Conclusion

The same interconnectedness that put Argentine beef on British dinner tables and delivered Peruvian raw cotton to Manchester's power looms drew urban Latin Americans fully into the orbit of Europe's products, styles, manners, current events, letters, ideas, and people. Or to state the same point in a more specific way, the South American thinkers whose ideas have been profiled in this chapter were full-fledged members of the global bourgeoisie, as were their readers. Their education, networks, habits, material culture, diversions, values, aspirations, and fears were undoubtedly bourgeois if we adhere to this book's capacious definition. While patriotic lovers of country they were inescapably cosmopolitan, which should hardly surprise when we remember that South American raw materials and markets were essential parts of the machine that created the global bourgeoisie in the first place. But why, then, did these bourgeois South Americans so fervently believe that their nations were stuck in a pre-bourgeois age? A fatal paradox of globality was the way in which its asymmetries obliterated people's consciousness of the simultaneity they were in fact living and replaced it with an imaginary map of "advanced" and "backward" nations, hierarchically ordered and defined in part by race, each at its own stage of development, each living its particular moment in historical time. Those nations perceived as advanced got to define the normal march of history, and the rest had to contemplate their paths as retarded or deviant, a *Sonderweg*.[56]

Few peoples were more acutely aware of their *Sonderweg* than urban South Americans. Although they were no longer colonial subjects—any more than late-1800s US Americans were—they nevertheless experienced emotions not dissimilar to those that many colonized elites felt each time they returned home from overseas, each time they bought Paris couture or London flannels, each time they cited a French or Italian author to lend authority to their writings, each time they picked up a magazine filled with European news, each time they tried to imagine their countries' future. The "failed bourgeoisie" diagnosis was

---

Haymarket Books, 2012); and Vivek Chibber, *Postcolonial Theory and the Specter of Capital* (London: Verso, 2014).

56. David Blackbourn and Geoff Eley, *The Peculiarities of German History: Bourgeois Society and Politics in Nineteenth-Century Germany* (Oxford: Oxford University Press, 1984).

one facet of this larger metanarrative of deficiency. It reflected reality inasmuch as it was true—and unremarkable—that economies dominated by copper mines and sugar plantations and cattle ranches and import-export houses were different from those dominated by manufacturing. But the narrative was also built upon myths: the myth that industry was the only measure of modernity, the myth of Europeans' inherently superior business acumen, the myth of the conquering bourgeoisie overthrowing feudalism by force. To assess the significance of those myths, consider the following: How would it feel to spend one's life believing that one is "living in a previous century"? What kinds of economic choices and public policies arise from an all-consuming sense of being "behind" and needing to "catch up"? Questions such as these, still awaiting answers, are by no means trivial or purely academic. They lie at the heart of the global middle class condition.

14

The "Missing" or "Forgotten" Middle Class of Tsarist Russia

Alison K. Smith

THE LIFE STORY of Semën Prokofevich Vasilev exemplifies some of the challenges that face the historian trying to integrate Russia into a global history of the middle classes. Born in Moscow in 1709, Vasilev was placed in apprenticeship to a local merchant by his widowed mother. He prospered in trade, first opening a small textile shop and later expanding his operation to include foreign goods. This was not necessarily unusual—foreign goods came into the Russian Empire in ever greater quantities during the eighteenth century. Vasilev, however, was reportedly particularly successful, in part because of his God-fearing nature, and in part because he was actively engaged in expanding his trading circle, traveling abroad to find better-quality merchandise to import and to create and maintain personal ties with foreign producers. He was later credited with establishing direct commerce with England and thereby helping the Russian Empire establish itself firmly within the wider world of trade.

Vasilev's economic successes made him exactly the kind of productive bourgeois a growing state might want. His philanthropic acts also fit this vision: he donated monies to build a new bell tower at one monastery and gave other monies to a series of other church causes and buildings. For all this, though, his place within the global middle class was a bit less clear. On the one hand, he traveled abroad himself—he was as much a global citizen as one could be in the eighteenth century. But one anecdote included in the brief retelling of his life points to the problems with envisioning him in this way:

Once, two foreign merchants, who had sent Vasilev their wares many times [but] did not know him personally, came to Moscow in order to make the acquaintance of such a renowned and wealthy Moscow merchant and began to seek him out by his address.... It was morning. Semën Prokofevich at that time was busy sweeping the pavement near his house. The foreigners, not seeing anyone other than him on the street, called out to him and asked the location of the house of the merchant Vasilev, with whom they had mercantile connections and whom they had never seen. He indicated his house to them and came over from the other side to show them; he was dressed properly and, as was his habit, met them with courtesy. At this point they recognized him and, seeing his modest life, were amazed that he could manage such extensive trade. But, having conversed with him, they were convinced even more than before of his prudence, business sense, and integrity, and gained even more trust in him; because of this his trade grew even greater, and he in the course of his life amassed great wealth.[1]

Here, Vasilev is eventually recognized as wealthy and as an able businessman, a proper bourgeois, but only after he is first taken for a much simpler man. What marked him as such?

A large part of the difficulty in identifying Vasilev may have come simply from the fact that his visitors were foreigners (probably, based on other accounts of Vasilev's trade, Englishmen). Cases in which foreign visitors to Russia had trouble interpreting dress and behavior to identify an individual's social status abound.[2] It might, though, be a more general problem with identifying the Russian middle classes. Fairly consistently from that time on, Russians themselves were both interested in identifying their own middle class—or middle classes, or middle estates—and also uncertain as to what their middle classes actually were. Interest in the empire's "middlings" continued to develop through the revolutionary era at the beginning of the twentieth century, with Russia's middle class alternately found and dismissed, praised and lambasted, often in comparison with an idealized Western other. In a way, since at least the

1. Trifon Semenov Dobriakov, "O Moskovskom 1-i gil'dii kuptse Semene Prokof'eviche Vasil'eve" [On the Moscow first-guild merchant Semen Prokofevich Vasilev], *Dushepoleznye chtenie* 1, no. 8 (1860): 473–482, 478–479.

2. Alexander M. Martin, *Enlightened Metropolis: Constructing Imperial Moscow, 1762–1855* (Oxford: Oxford University Press, 2013), 4–5; on clothing, see Lina Bernstein, "Russian Eighteenth-Century Merchant Portraits in Words and in Oil," *Slavic and East European Journal* 49, no. 3 (2005): 407–429.

beginning of the nineteenth century, Russian contemporary commentators often engaged in a sort of self-othering, finding themselves to be exotic in comparison to a European normal.

Most often, Russia's middle classes have been envisioned as "missing," "insignificant," or "forgotten."[3] One reason is that they were masked on the one hand by masses of peasants and on the other by the powerful image of the Russian nobility. As of the 1897 first all-Russian census, 87 percent of the population lived in rural settings, and a full 75 percent of the population listed agriculture as its primary occupation. Only 4 percent of the population engaged in trade, and less than 1 percent in the professions.[4] This led to a situation in which, as one historian put it, "'was there a bourgeoisie?' is the question repeatedly posed by the Western layman, accustomed as he is to visualizing only wealthy, leisurely nobles and destitute, slaving peasants whenever prerevolutionary Russia is brought to his mind."[5] This vision of a "Western layman" speaks to the particular challenge of recognizing a middle in the context of a powerful alternative vision of Russian society divided into two groups of wealth and dearth, of the privileged and the unprivileged. A second reason for the invisibility or inscrutability of Russia's middle classes is the problem of economic development. As the story goes, until 1861 serfdom retarded the development of capitalism in Russia, thereby retarding the growth of a proper bourgeoisie. Even after that, industrialization progressed with unusual degrees of state intervention, again creating an economic background that made Russia distinctly different in comparison to an ideal Western other.[6] Moreover,

3. Richard Pipes, *Russia under the Old Regime*, 2nd ed. (London: Penguin, 1995), 191–220; Michael T. Florinsky, *Russia: A History and an Interpretation*, vol. 2 (New York: Macmillan, 1955), 720, 786; and Valentine T. Bill, *The Forgotten Class: The Russian Bourgeoisie from the Earliest Beginnings to 1900* (New York: Frederick A. Praeger, 1959). Elise Kimerling Wirtschafter comments on the problem of seeing the missing middle in *Social Identity in Imperial Russia* (DeKalb: Northern Illinois University Press, 1997), 72–73, 96–99. Other social histories that grapple with the question include Janet Hartley, *A Social History of the Russian Empire, 1650–1825* (London: Longman, 1998); and Boris Mironov, *A Social History of Imperial Russia, 1700–1917* (Boulder, CO: Westview, 2000).

4. *Pervaia vseobshchaia perepis'naseleniia Rossiiskoi imperii 1897 goda* [First general census of the population of the Russian Empire, 1897], vol. 8 (St. Petersburg: Tsent. Stat. komitetom M-va vn. del, 1905), 4–5.

5. Bill, *Forgotten Class*, viii.

6. Olga Crisp, *Studies in the Russian Economy before 1914* (London: Macmillan, 1976); Theodore H. von Laue, *Sergei Witte and the Industrialization of Russia* (New York: Columbia University Press, 1963).

historians who examine the social history of Russia's economic development tend to look at individual entrepreneurs, not at a wider entrepreneurial class.[7] Even here, the middle class disappears.

Thinking about the Russian middle requires addressing two problems. First, it requires grappling with language, particularly the complicated language of social estate (*soslovie*, pl. *sosloviia*). Defining the middle class has been and continues to be a challenge for historians everywhere; as Robert Darnton put it, even just a single word, "the tendentious term 'bourgeois' . . . is abusive, aggravating, inexact, and unavoidable. Historians have argued over it for generations, and are arguing still."[8] Comparisons between societies make the problem more acute: "middle class" is not quite the same as *bourgeoisie*, nor are either quite the same as *Bürgertum*.[9] In nineteenth-century Russia, this problem was all the more acute because as conceptions of class were emerging, they did so in the context of a society constructed out of legal social estates that continued to have real meaning. These associations and identities could imply middling status but at the same time obscure membership in a broader middle class, particularly when viewed in comparison with foreign conceptions of social structure.

Second, it requires thinking in terms not of numbers or of economic bases alone but also of a middle class conceived of as itself, as a social or cultural whole. As Louise McReynolds has put it, historians' focus on economic or political concepts of the middle class have largely doomed Russia's middle class to insignificance: "The paradigm historians constructed was skewed from the outset because it was based on a premise that accepted the western model as normative."[10] A shift to a focus on culture or self-identification helps to correct this; people believed themselves to be part of a middling status, or a middle class. However, placing that focus in a global context in some ways echoes the same

7. Henry Rosovsky, "The Serf Entrepreneur in Russia," *Explorations in Entrepreneurial History* 6, no. 4 (1954): 207–233; Alfred Rieber, *Merchants and Entrepreneurs in Imperial Russia* (Chapel Hill: University of North Caroline Press, 1982); and Galina Ulianova, *Female Entrepreneurs in Nineteenth-Century Russia* (London: Pickering and Chatto, 2009).

8. Robert Darnton, *The Great Cat Massacre and Other Episodes in French Cultural History* (New York: Vintage, 1984), 109.

9. Jürgen Kocka, "The Middle Classes in Europe," *Journal of Modern History* 67 (December 1995): 783–806, 783.

10. Louise McReynolds, *Russia at Play: Leisure Activities at the End of the Tsarist Era* (Ithaca, NY: Cornell University Press, 2003), 3.

problems of translation that plague discussions focused on social groups. Reading culture across borders could still obscure Russia's middle.

Social Estates and the Problem of Definitions

The search for Russia's middle classes begins first of all on a purely local level—and, indeed, even on a sub-local level based in social estate.[11] Many scholars have described tsarist Russia's social structure as one based on that used in the *Digest of the Laws*: a four-part division of the population into nobility, churchfolk, town inhabitants, and rural inhabitants. None of these categories, however, were as simple as this outline suggests; as Gregory Freeze put it, "the four-estate paradigm is manifestly deficient" because it implied consistency within each of the four estates.[12] In reality, each of the four estates was actually composed of an array of different statuses, and none of these categories were as consistently internally divided as the larger category of town inhabitants. Because of the system of legal estates, townspeople not only went by many names but also many of those who resided in towns regularly were not considered townspeople proper because they lacked official legal status. As a result, the potential middle class even in a single town was internally divided into separate groups, each with its own corporate body and, at least according to some, its own estate-based ethos.

The bulk of official town residents were the *meshchane* (sing. *meshchanin*; collective n. *meshchanstvo*), the lower-ranking townspeople or petty bourgeois. They were those whose fathers had been townspeople or those who had chosen the status if they were free to do so. They were subject to the same duties to the state as peasants and serfs: providing military recruits and paying the soul tax, the yearly tax paid by every male "soul." Both of these duties were assessed communally, making *meshchane* as bound to their towns as peasants were to the land or their lord—the ultimate mark of unprivilege in the empire. As a result, throughout the nineteenth century, the *meshchanstvo* came to be associated with among the most impoverished and most backward parts of urban (if not all of

11. Alison K. Smith, *For the Common Good and Their Own Well-Being: Social Estate in Imperial Russia* (New York: Oxford University Press, 2014); N. A. Ivanova and V. P. Zheltova, *Soslovnoe obshchestvo Rossiiskoi imperii* [The estate society of the Russian Empire] (Moscow: Novyi khronograf, 2010).

12. Gregory L. Freeze, "The Soslovie (Estate) Paradigm and Russian Social History," *American Historical Review* 91, no. 1 (1986): 11–36, 21.

Russian) society, rather than with the idea of towns as modern and modernizing places.

In principle, the word *meshchanstvo* could have served as a direct translation for "bourgeoisie" or "middle class," and at times it did just that. At the end of the eighteenth and beginning of the nineteenth centuries, *meshchanstvo* was not necessarily value-laden but instead was simply a word to indicate townspeople, and often townspeople as a whole, not as a specific category. When Catherine the Great (r. 1762–96) compiled her Charter to the Towns, the term *meshchane* most of all meant what a later commentator described as "all those who belonged to the *middle type of people*."[13] When the idea of *la cuisine bourgeoise* was translated into Russian, it came in as *meshchanskaia kukhnia*.[14] At this time, the word could be used at times as an unproblematic translation of a foreign concept of the middle class, or the third estate, or the bourgeoisie. By the middle of the nineteenth century, *meshchanstvo* was still used in this same general way but now with strongly negative undertones. In particular, it came under fire from the Russian intelligentsia. As Timo Vihavainen argues, Alexander Herzen focused the intelligentsia's critique on "the petty bourgeoisie and the petty bourgeois way of life (*meshchanstvo*)." In Herzen's vision of this problematic *meshchanstvo*—in this sense even translated as "philistinism" rather than as "bourgeois"—it "meant, of course, more a state of mind than a social category."[15] Although some criticized the *burzhuaziia* or a more general concept of *burzhuaznost′*, using a transliterated rather than translated word to express this negative sense of the bourgeoisie or bourgeois sensibility, the term *meshchanstvo* maintained its negative connotations through the tsarist era and on into the Soviet one.[16]

13. *Novoe obshchestvennoe ustroistvo S. Peterburga* [New social structure of St. Petersburg] (St. Petersburg: Ministerstvo vnutrennikh del, 1846), 4n.

14. Alison K. Smith, *Recipes for Russia: Food and Nationhood under the Tsars* (DeKalb: Northern Illinois University Press, 2008), 115–116.

15. Timo Vihavainen, *The Inner Adversary: The Struggle against Philistinism as the Moral Mission of the Russian Intelligentsia* (Washington, DC: New Academia, 2006), 31. The Russian version of Vihavainen's book translates "philistinism" back as *meshchanstvo*: Timo Vikhavainen, *Vnutrennii vrag: bor′ba s meshchanstvom kak moral′naia missiia russkoi intelligentsii* (St. Petersburg: Kolo, 2004). See also Catriona Kelly, *Refining Russia: Advice Literature, Polite Culture, and Gender from Catherine to Yeltsin* (Oxford: Oxford University Press, 2001), 108–109.

16. Jo Ann Ruckman, *The Moscow Business Elite: A Social and Cultural Portrait of Two Generations, 1840–1905* (DeKalb: Northern Illinois University Press, 1984), 39; Samuel D. Kassow, James L. West, and Edith W. Clowes, "Introduction," in *Between Tsar and People: Educated Society and the Quest for Public Identity in Late Imperial Russia*, ed. Edith W. Clowes, Samuel D.

Meshchane might have been the largest group of townspeople, but merchants (*kuptsy*) were the most prominent.[17] Catherine the Great distinguished merchants from *meshchane* by financial status, granting merchants their own societies and their own set of privileges, ranging from the significant (freedom from the soul tax and military service) to the cultural (the right to drive certain kinds of carriages). She also made them unique in the instability of their status, a fact that made it difficult for them to consolidate as a class. A business failure in a single year could force merchants back into the mass of *meshchane*—an act that was often temporary but that still meant that a person was suddenly no longer among the privileged of Russian society. Individual merchants could find themselves suddenly subject to the dreaded soul tax and military draft upon their business failure, and the names of those merchants who were demoted to a lower guild or the *meshchanstvo* were published in local papers, an act that both warned business associates and served as a kind of public shaming.[18]

There are other challenges to viewing Russia's merchants as a middle class. Some historians have sought to identify a real vibrancy in the world of Russia's merchants even in the seventeenth and eighteenth centuries.[19] Many, however, have seen them as overwhelmingly backward, entering some sort of comfortable bourgeois state only at the empire's very end. At times their words are explicitly orientalist in tone: "Bearded, patriarchal, semi-Asiatic in dress and manner, and fully versed in the arts of haggling and swindling, the Russian merchants in the early nineteenth century not only lacked the distinctive urban ethos of the West but also clung to their obscurantist cultural traditions."[20] This statement is barely different than the words of some nineteenth-century English travelers or even of nineteenth-century Russian authors themselves, whose

---

Kassow, and James L. West (Princeton, NJ: Princeton University Press, 1991), 3–14, 4–5; and Vera Dunham, *In Stalin's Time: Middleclass Values in Soviet Fiction*, enlarged and updated edition (Durham, NC: Duke University Press, 1990).

17. Many books examine merchants, but few focus on *meshchane* or other parts of town society. See Thomas C. Owen, *Capitalism and Politics in Russia: A Social History of the Moscow Merchants, 1855–1905* (Cambridge: Cambridge University Press, 1981); Rieber, *Merchants and Entrepreneurs*; and Ruckman, *Moscow Business Elite*; and a nearly uncountable number of books in Russian on merchants.

18. Smith, *For the Common Good*, 114.

19. Erika Monahan, *The Merchants of Siberia: Trade in Early Modern Eurasia* (Ithaca, NY: Cornell University Press, 2016); David L. Ransel, *A Russian Merchant's Tale: The Life and Adventures of Ivan Alekseevich Tolchenov, Based on His Diary* (Bloomington: Indiana University Press, 2009).

20. Owen, *Capitalism and Politics in Russia*, 1.

often negative images of merchants created, as Beth Holmgren calls it, "the problem of the merchant in Russian literature."[21] In this view, the merchants were old-fashioned, often Old Believers (followers of a version of Orthodoxy that had broken away from the official church in the seventeenth century in part because it rejected the church's modernizing reforms), and as a result simply not a proper middle class for the rapidly moving nineteenth century. Only at the end of the nineteenth century did they begin to seem like a proper business class, but even then, they were a particularly conservative one, tied to religion and of a certain Slavophile, anti-modern bent.

If it was difficult to conceptualize these statuses as a middle class within Russia, the problem was exacerbated by contact with the outside world. Indeed, there might never have been a question had there not been a comparison with an outside, idealized (though in retrospect largely imaginary) Western middle class. Many of the reforms that altered Russian social structures in the eighteenth century were influenced by practices in countries farther to Russia's west. Contemporary historians linked Catherine the Great's particular interest in developing an urban "middling sort" in explicitly national terms; one said that she aimed "to create in Russia a particular kind of middle condition, on the example of the middle estate of Western Europe, particularly of France."[22] Russia had long had merchants, even merchants engaged in global trade, and it had had artisans and nascent professionals. In this vision, however, they awaited transformation into a modern bourgeoisie. Catherine's reforms were intended to push forward that transformation.

Despite such efforts on the part of Russia's rulers, a certain mutual incomprehensibility of concepts of the middle class across international borders remained. In 1824, G. Le Cointe de Laveau, "secretary of the Imperial Moscow Society of Naturalists," published *Guide du voyageur à Moscou*, a simple guide for tourists. In it, Laveau gave a history of the city, described its physical plan, gave a few statistics about the place and its population, and pointed out "that which this capital offers that is curious and interesting, its most remarkable monuments" rather than providing a narrative traveler's account.[23] It was a

21. Beth Holmgren, *Rewriting Capitalism: Literature and the Market in Late Tsarist Russia and the Kingdom of Poland* (Pittsburgh: University of Pittsburgh Press, 1998), 17–53.

22. A. Gradovskii, *Nachala russkogo gosudarstvennogo prava* [The bases of Russian law], vol. 1: *O gosudarstvennom ustroistve* [On public order] (St. Petersburg: M. Stasiulevich, 1875), 295–296.

23. G. Le Cointe de Laveau, *Guide du voyageur à Moscou* (Moscow: De l'imprimerie d'Auguste Semen, 1824).

practical guide, not an ethnographic study, and yet it soon became the center of a cross-cultural dispute. The dispute began when the guide was reviewed in several French journals. One reviewer, M. Depping, found Laveau's portrayal of Moscow troubling because it failed to address what he saw as Russia's true despotic (and "oriental") nature. For him, Laveau's passing reference to the government of Moscow "buying" workers was taken as a sign "of the difference between the civilization of Russia and that of the rest of Europe." In Depping's interpretation, Russia might build monuments in the style of Greece and Rome, but in buying the workers to build those monuments, it seemed rather to be "of Bukhara," not properly European.

Depping also puzzled over something that Laveau included perhaps out of duty, not intending it to be the subject of such scrutiny: the city's population statistics. Depping exactly reported Laveau's listing of the population, including nobles, state servitors, churchfolk, merchants (*marchands*), foreigners, townspeople (*bourgeois*), and artisans, among others. Based on his own understanding of urban social structures, Depping claimed to think that there was something wrong with this listing: "This table was probably not drawn up in a very rigorous manner; how, for example, has a distinction been made between the *marchands* and the *bourgeois*?"[24] Depping apparently did not know that there was nothing wrong with the statistics; Laveau had simply translated the Russian estate terms—"merchant" as *marchand* and *meshchane* as *bourgeois*— as exactly as he could. But Depping's puzzlement over the distinction indicates both the difficulty in describing Russian social structures to a foreign audience and perhaps also an unwillingness to understand on the part of that foreign audience.

Nor was this the end of the confusion. Soon after Depping's review, another journal, the *Journal des voyages*, published an excerpt from Laveau's guide with a brief editor's introduction. Unlike Depping, who saw autocracy and arbitrariness, if not outright despotism, lurking in Laveau's descriptions, this editor found the book to be all it needed to be: a well-informed, well-written guide for the tourist, exactly as it promised. He also took it upon himself to answer one of Depping's criticisms of the text, and the criticism he decided to answer was Depping's question about population statistics. Depping had wondered, he noted, about the distinction between *marchands* and *bourgeois*. This author

---

24. M. Depping, review of *Guide du voyageur a Moscou* par G. Lecointe de Laveau, *Bulletin des sciences géographiques, etc., Economie publique, Voyages,* vol. 3 of 6th section of *Bulletin universel des sciences de l'industrie* (1825): 334–337, 334–335.

claimed that "it is easy to respond that if all the *marchands* are *bourgeois,* all the *bourgeois* are not *marchands,* and that one may make a class of those who are not."[25] The first part of this statement seems like the beginning of a logic puzzle: all merchants are townspeople, but not all townspeople are merchants. That was certainly true, probably held true in most European (and non-European) towns, and should probably have been understood by Depping, as well. The second part of his statement recognized that Russian law viewed townspeople as a separate legal social group within Russia's social structure of estates.

There followed yet another level of interrogation of this passage, for the *Bulletin universel* and the *Journal des voyages* had at least one Russian reader. Later that year, the Russian journal *Moskovskii telegraf* published an unsigned piece on "news of Russia and Russian literature in French journals." It discussed Laveau's book and the two reviews. It, too, focused on Depping's confusion over merchants and townspeople and on the second author's glib response.

> If these French statisticians had asked any sort of Russian, then he would have told them that here we call merchants those townspeople [*grazhdane,* also often translated as "citizen"] who pay taxes in their own way, not by the soul, but according to the capital amassed by the whole family; that these townspeople [*grazhdane*] are divided into three classes or guilds, depending on the amount they pay; and that merchants are given preference in trade and distinctions that common townspeople [*meshchane*] do not have, as they pay not according to their capital, but by the soul, and take part only in petty trade and crafts.[26]

For a Russian reader, this was again a completely logical, completely true description of the distinction between two social estates (and the three words denoting social status), but it seems unlikely that this particular description would actually have been much use for Depping, with its mention of guilds that were not craft guilds, but instead something to do with merchants, and its reference to paying "by the soul" in an age before Gogol had begun to write *Dead Souls,* let alone had the novel brought this peculiarity of Russian tax practices

25. M. de Laveau, "Topographie et statistique de Moscou," *Journal des voyages* 26, no. 79 (1825): 227–241, 228n.

26. "Izvestiia o Rossii i russkoi literature, pomeshchaemye vo frantsuzsk. zhurnalakh" [News of Russia and Russian literature published in French journals], *Moskovskii telegraf* 5, no. 17 (1825): 70–74, 73.

to a wider European audience. The language of Russian social estates proved difficult, if not impossible, to equate with the western middle class.

The Middle Class and the Imperial Town

This conversation emphasizes contradictions of language based in social estate on the one hand and a foreign (in this case, French) conception of the middle classes on the other. As such, it is embedded in an approach that focuses on a social understanding of the bourgeoisie: one in which the labels people carried—as merchants, as townspeople—had implication for their membership in a middle class. Sarah Maza has commented that the middle class is "the most obviously artificial among familiar social groupings" because it "exists by definition only in relation to other social groups."[27] In the Russian case, though, an understanding of the middle class (or classes) came to have at least one firm definition: it involved the empire's towns. In 1826, Petr Ivanov published a legal guide for "in general the whole middle estate."[28] What that meant in practice was a guide to laws about towns and about the various social estates associated with them. Likewise, a few decades later N. I. Sokolov equated "our middle estates" with "the so called *town societies*."[29]

This association came with yet more complications. For one, the people who actually lived in towns were much more socially diverse than official statistics and the existence of official town statuses might indicate. Town population statistics often included not only the formal town residents—the merchants and *meshchane*—but also the nobles, bureaucrats, soldiers, clergymen, and others who might find themselves living there. Elise Kimerling Wirtschafter has

27. Sarah Maza, "Luxury, Morality, and Social Change: Why There Was No Middle-Class Consciousness in Prerevolutionary France," *Journal of Modern History* 69, no. 2 (1997): 199–229, 201.

28. Petr Ivanov, *Obozrenie prav i obiazannostei Rossiiskogo kupechestva i voobshche vsego sred-nego sosloviia, s prisovokupleniem izlozheniia postanovlenii, otnosiashchikhsia kak do sudebnykh mest, uchrezhdennykh sosloviia sego, tak i lits izbiraemykh iz onogo k razlichnym dolzhnostiam* [Overview of the rights and duties of the Russian merchant estate and in general of the entire middle estate] (Moscow: P. Kuznetsov, 1826); see also L. O. Ploshinskii, *Gorodskoe ili srednee sostoianie russkogo naroda v ego istoricheskom razvitii ot nachala Rusi do noveishikh vremen* [Town or middle status of the Russian people in its historical development from the beginning of Rus' to the present day] (St. Petersburg: E. Veimar, 1852).

29. N. I. Sokolov, "O nashikh srednikh sosloviiakh" [On our middle estates], *Russkii vestnik* 24, no. 1 (1859): section "Sovremennaia letopis'," 21.

focused on a broader vision of these nonofficial residents based in the concept of the *raznochintsy,* or "people of various ranks." These were those who belonged to a "multiplicity of economic, service and protoprofessional subgroups" and who were initially largely of socially and economically marginal status.[30] Eventually, as more of society became ascribed to a social estate, and also as education gave rise to a new kind of outsider, the concept of the *raznochinets* took on a more abstract association. As Wirtschafter has put it, it entered "into the realm of social consciousness" and became identified with the Russian intelligentsia, explicitly not the middle class.[31]

Furthermore, over the course of the nineteenth century, differentiating the many separate legal estates of Russian towns became increasingly difficult. As many commentators at the time and many historians since have pointed out, "estate" simply failed to accurately describe the actual occupation of many individuals.[32] The problem was a fundamental one. In his 1832 statistical survey of Moscow, V. Androsov described one of the problems inherent in thinking of the city's population as one based in social estate because those divisions, stark as they might be on paper, were much more blurred in everyday life. One *meshchanin* might own property in the capital and live on its proceeds; another, however, might barely make a living. What meaning, then, did the word *meshchanin* have? Or, the growth of manufacturing within the city was creating another mixed-up world: manufacturers did not all come from "a particular social estate" but instead were a mixture of "merchants, *meshchane,* foreigners, artisans, peasants of all sorts, retired soldiers and even retired bureaucrats."[33]

30. Elise K. Wirtschafter, "The Groups Between: Raznochintsy, Intelligentsia, Professionals," in *The Cambridge History of Russia,* vol. 2: *Imperial Russia, 1689–1917,* ed. Dominic Lieven (Cambridge: Cambridge University Press, 2009), 245–263, 246; see also her *Structures of Society: Imperial Russia's "People of Various Ranks"* (DeKalb: Northern Illinois University Press, 1994).

31. Wirtschafter, "Groups Between," 249.

32. Historians include George E. Munro, *The Most Intentional City: St. Petersburg in the Reign of Catherine the Great* (Madison: University of Wisconsin Press, 2008), 57–59; and Catherine Evtuhov, *Portrait of a Russian Province: Economy, Society, and Civilization in Nineteenth-Century Nizhnii Novgorod* (Pittsburgh: University of Pittsburgh Press, 2011), 110–112. Other important contributions to the history of tsarist Russian urban society include J. Michael Hittle, *The Service City: State and Townsmen in Russia, 1600–1800* (Cambridge: Harvard University Press, 1979); and Manfred Hildermeier, *Bürgertum und Stadt in Russland, 1760–1870: Rechtliche Lage und soziale Struktur* (Köln: Böhlau, 1986).

33. V. P. Androsov, *Statisticheskaia zapiska o Moskve* [Statistical note of Moscow] (Moscow: S. Selivanovskii, 1832), 54, 59–60.

If this was the case in 1832, the problem was all the more acute by the end of the century as town populations swelled. Furthermore, in the latter parts of the nineteenth century, after a town reform in the 1870s altered the bases of town administration and self-government, the blurring of lines between separate town societies based in estate and a larger sense of a unified town society gained new relevance. An earlier reform of St. Petersburg had distinguished between town administrative bodies that were "general for all [town] society" and those that were "separate, by estate."[34] Now towns were supposed to be able to act more as single units, whatever their internal estate distinctions. Much of the town reform moved in this direction; it has been called one of the reforms that sought in principle to create not a non-estate but an all-estate consciousness in Russia.[35] However, this new all-town consciousness was in practice laid on top of the existing estate consciousness, creating an awkward mix.

On top of this was another complication: Russia was a multinational empire, and its towns and therefore its potential bourgeoisie reflected that fact. Much of the town population lived outside the boundaries of Russia proper. At the time of the 1897 census, St. Petersburg and Moscow were by far the two largest cities of the empire, with populations of over one million. Of the seventeen other cities with populations of more than one hundred thousand, only five were in what is now the modern Russian Federation. The remaining twelve were in the empire's periphery. They had large Russian populations, but many of the towns in Russia also had large non-Russian populations from around the empire—Jews, Germans, Armenians, Tatars. The laws regulating towns often ignored these differences in favor of recognizing distinctions of social status (in other words, being a German or a Tatar mattered less than being a merchant or a *meshchanin*), but not always (being a Jew always mattered). This had obvious implications for the ability of Russia's middling strata to cohere into a distinct middle class.

Perhaps as a result, by the beginning of the twentieth century, the definition of the middle classes or middle estates had shifted to something that implied association with towns but also focused more on other, more abstract qualities.

34. *Polnoe sobranie zakonov Rossiiskoi imperii* [Complete collection of the laws of the Russian Empire], 2nd collection (St. Petersburg: Tipografiia II Otdeleniia Sobstvennoi ego imperatorskogo velichestva kantseliarii, 1830–1885), vol. 21, no. 19721 (13 February 1846).

35. V. A. Nardova *Gorodskoe samoupravlenie v Rossii v 60-kh-nachale 90-kh godov XIX v* [Town self-government in Russia]. (Leningrad: Nauka, 1984), 49.

The author of a 1907 text on the "growth of the middle estate in Russia" actually defined what he meant by that phrase. For him, it was not simply synonymous with those who lived in towns but was something more: "the cultured, free, and learned stratum of the population."[36] Decades before, Sokolov had also moved in this direction. He commented that "under the name of town residents, or people of the middle sort, in particular are meant all those who, living in towns, occupy themselves with artisanal trades, trade, the arts and sciences."[37] This early twentieth-century definition took that association with learned (more or less) occupations to its natural end. Here, in a discussion of legal statuses, a vision of a middle class defined in part by a cultural unity begins to emerge.

Translating Culture

At some point during the nineteenth century, Russia had become home to people who behaved as if they were members of a proper (in the sense of echoing a model from western Europe) middle class. Alexander Martin dates it to "the middle third of the nineteenth century, when Russia was suddenly full of modern, middle-class Europeans: readers, shoppers, civic activists, urban *flâneurs*."[38] The stolid traditional culture of Russia's merchants that had obscured the eighteenth-century merchant Vasilev from his foreign visitors was falling away. As an English traveler put it in his 1861 account, "Twenty years ago the richest merchants in St. Petersburg wore beards, and caftans, and shoes made of bark. That is not the case now; and I myself dined in Moscow with a merchant of the first guild whose clothes might have been made by the best tailor in London or Paris; who had three or four kinds of French wine at table; whose daughters played airs from *Erani* and *Rigoletto*, and spoke French nearly as well as their French governess."[39] From this point through to the end of the tsarist regime, in periodicals, in middle-brow literature, in leisure activities, in advertisements, in charitable and philanthropic works, this middle-class cultural world became ever more firmly embedded in Russia's towns, bringing together

36. L. Sokal'skii, *Rost srednego sosloviia v Rossii kak sledstvie ostanovki v rost gosudarstvennoi territorii* [The growth of the middle estate in Russia as a consequence of the end of the growth of state territory] (Odessa: Slav, 1907), 6.

37. Sokolov, "O nashikh srednikh sosloviiakh," 23.

38. Alexander M. Martin, "History, Memory, and the Modernization of 19th-Century Urban Russia," *Kritika* 11, no. 4 (2010): 837–870, 838.

39. Henry Sutherland Edwards, *The Russians at Home* (London: Wm. H Allen, 1861), 160.

people of many different official statuses and at times also of many different nationalities and religions into a cultural whole.

This cultural middle, moreover, developed explicitly in conversation with ideas of the West; it is no coincidence that Martin refers to the appearance of "middle-class Europeans." As in many other non-Western nations in the age of empire, both culturally and intellectually, Russia's eighteenth and nineteenth centuries had one major source of confrontation: Russia versus the West. Initially, this distinction mapped onto social distinctions, as well, but in a way that seemed to leave out the middle—signified above all by the clothing (and facial-hair) reforms of Peter the Great. Western culture became elite culture, while Russian culture remained the culture of the masses. In the middle of the nineteenth century, Russian intellectuals split into Slavophile and Westernizer camps, each with implications for understanding both history and the current cultural climate. At the end of the century, spurred on by the nationalist Alexander III, this distinction became more complicated, as the elite embraced "Russian style," while popular culture took on a new interest in the modern.[40]

Weaving through this tension between Russian "tradition" and a modernity often viewed as Western, a cultural middle emerged over the course of the nineteenth century. In keeping with earlier discussions of the location of the middle classes, towns were the spaces in which this new culture, in part a consumer or a commercial culture, was learned and developed.[41] Clothing choices became markers of a separate middle path, perhaps particularly for women.[42] Women, in fact, become much more prominent in discussions of the Russian middle classes when the focus shifts to culture and the self. Women played particularly important roles in the creation of this hybrid middle culture—as both its producers and its consumers.[43] In the world of cookbooks, they became the guardians of a distinctly Russian middle status in the context

40. Richard Wortman, *Scenarios of Power: Myth and Ceremony in Russian Monarchy from Peter the Great to Nicholas II* (Princeton, NJ: Princeton University Press, 2006); Mark D. Steinberg, *Proletarian Imagination: Self, Modernity, and the Sacred in Russia, 1910–1925* (Ithaca, NY: Cornell University Press, 2002).

41. Sally West, *I Shop in Moscow: Advertising and the Creation of Consumer Culture in Late Tsarist Russia* (DeKalb: Northern Illinois University Press, 2011), 96.

42. Christine Ruane, "Caftan to Business Suit: The Semiotics of Russian Merchant Dress," in *Merchant Moscow: Images of Russia's Vanished Bourgeoisie*, ed. James L. West and Iurii A. Petrov (Princeton, NJ: Princeton University Press, 1998), 53–60.

43. Anna Fishzon, *Fandom, Authenticity, and Opera: Mad Acts and Letter Scenes in Fin-de-Siècle Russia* (Basingstoke: Palgrave Macmillan, 2013).

of growing luxury; in musical societies, they were among the most numerous students and performers.[44]

To foreign eyes, though, this cultural middle was still at least in part obscured. In the realm of cuisine, starting in the 1840s, a number of cookbook authors began to present Russian readers with a vision of proper middle-class cooking, a style that was above all a mix of the Russian and the Western. The prototypical meal might be cabbage soup and piroshki, followed by roast beef washed down with burgundy. To these authors, this was simply the way that Russian culture had developed, incorporating elements of the foreign and transforming them into something new. For foreign visitors to Russia, many of whom were themselves proper middle-class men and women, these distinctions were invisible. The foods they were presented with seemed at odds with, not a representation of, a recognizable middle class. The places in which they ate were similarly incomprehensible, the people around envisioned as either nobles or peasants based on the Westernness or Russianness of their dress, with no space for a prosperous middle.[45] The middle was invisible in the wider context of the Russian social and cultural world. As in the story of Vasilev and his foreign visitors and as in the exchange over definitions of merchants and *meshchane*, placing Russia's middle classes in a global context made them harder to interpret. It was in the context of a middle class defined according to a singular Western notion that Russia suffered from a "missing" one.

Conclusion

But of course, particularly by the end of the tsarist era, there were many individuals who were by almost any definition members of a middle class. They were employed in nonmanual labor and enjoyed a middle-class culture that looked out to the wider world. Somehow, though, they remained an afterthought. That might have been because they were demographically few, and so the still strong visions of an extreme distinction between wealth and poverty even within towns alone erased them.[46] Or it might have been because they remained individuals,

44. Lynn Sargeant, *Harmony and Discord: Music and the Transformation of Russian Cultural Life* (New York: Oxford University Press, 2011).

45. Alison K. Smith, "Eating Out in Imperial Russia: Class, Nationality, and Dining before the Great Reforms," *Slavic Review* 65, no. 4 (2006): 747–768.

46. Ilya Gerasimov, *Plebeian Modernity: Social Practices, Illegality, and the Urban Poor in Russia, 1906–1916* (Rochester, NY: University of Rochester Press, 2018).

not constituent members of a middle class—they were bourgeois, but not a bourgeoisie. The official structures of town society and administration before the reforms of the 1870s (and in many ways still after then) made uniting in a consistent and coherent middle class challenging if not impossible. In addition, the state's hostility to public associations and the absence of opportunities for political participation until the last decade of the empire made establishing a consistent political vision for the middle class nearly impossible. Although charitable and other associations, in particular, became spaces where some coherent identity could begin, they only went so far in the face of the larger structures of the tsarist administration and social constructs.[47]

In all of this Russia was, of course, not unique. The idea of the middle class, the bourgeoisie, may have been a construct, but it was a construct that has been a consistent source of comparison for societies around the world. The idea that a "missing" or mutant middle class has explanatory power for nineteenth-century (or for that matter, for twenty-first-century) political developments is likewise shared, at times even by those studying parts of the very "West" against which Russia compared itself.[48] This reification of an idealized Western other has been a persistent issue in Russian historiography more generally, one of many "explanations of non-European realities in terms of missing factors (missing in relationship to a mythical, stylized West)," as Alessandro Stanziani has put it.[49] But that is also too simple a way of thinking about the problem. In the Russian case, at least, the development of some sort of middle class modernity actively needed that idealized Western image—it gave shape to Russians' own vision of their middle. They, after all, published and corrected foreigners' accounts in their own journals; they conceived of their hybrid cuisine as a truly Russian and yet also truly middling one. At the same time, though, the association of the middle classes with the West also made it inimical for those Russians who, as Martin put it "embraced the preposterous notion that Western

47. Adele Lindenmeyr, *Poverty Is Not a Vice: Charity, Society, and the State in Imperial Russia* (Princeton, NJ: Princeton University Press, 1996); Joseph Bradley, *Voluntary Associations in Tsarist Russia: Science, Patriotism, and Civil Society* (Cambridge, MA: Harvard University Press, 2009).

48. Jonathan Sperber, "*Bürger, Bürgertum, Bürgerlichkeit, Bürgerliche Gesellschaft:* Studies of the German (Upper) Middle Class and Its Sociocultural World," *Journal of Modern History* 69, no. 2 (1997): 271–297, 273.

49. Alessandro Stanziani, *Bondage: Labor and Rights in Eurasia from the Sixteenth to the Early Twentieth Centuries* (New York: Berghahn, 2014), 140.

middle-class attitudes were somehow alien to their national character."[50] The association could be either generative or stifling to the conception of a middle class.

Perhaps this is why not only the Russian case, but also the many other alternative ways of conceptualizing the middle classes that do not quite fit the schema of the idealized Western image, are important. For one, they expand on the definition of the middle class, making of it a more vibrant and diverse set of people and practices. They also in a way reify elements of that dominant paradigm, as certain elements appear and reappear as they are transformed. And finally, and in a rather different way, they may actually suggest that the linkage of middle-class society with developed civil society and liberal government is the aberration, rather than the rule. In the Russian case, autocratic state policies based around social estate and urban administration at times hampered but also in some ways encouraged the development of a middle class—just not a political one.[51] Cases like the Russian one make it clear that economic, social, and cultural shifts associated with the rise of the middle class are simply not necessarily also associated with political change. They may, instead, be associated above all with a cycle of creating and recreating themselves, alternatively reaching out to wider middle-class cultures and concerns and looking within to their own histories and practices.

---

50. Martin, "History, Memory," 838.

51. Alison K. Smith, "Honored Citizens and the Creation of a Middle Class in Imperial Russia," *Slavic Review* 76, no. 2 (2017): 327–349.

15

Chinese Middle Classes between Empire and Revolution

Sabine Dabringhaus & Jürgen Osterhammel

FOR MANY CENTURIES China has been the most populous society in the world. To Western observers who brought back firsthand reports from about 1600 onward, Chinese society was marked by pervasive features that accounted for its amazing uniformity and set it apart from the fissiparous social landscape of early modern Europe: a social hierarchy with scholar-officials ("literati") at the top and humble merchants at the bottom,[1] a shared commitment to the inner-worldly ethics of Confucianism substituting for the belief in a transcendent god, and the popular practices of ancestor worship that kept families together and rooted people in their places of origin.[2] The divergence between China and the West seemed to increase even more during the nineteenth century. While western Europe developed a new kind of dynamic bourgeois society underpinned by industrialization and fueling imperial expansion, China seemed to remain static, unsusceptible to social change and institutional reform. The Taiping Revolution and other destructive uprisings of the middle decades of the nineteenth century threw the archaic nature of Chinese society into ever sharper relief.[3] Practices considered to be odious, such as infanticide and

---

1. In traditional visions of the social hierarchy, merchants (*shang*) were ranked below peasants (*nong*).

2. See Jürgen Osterhammel, *Unfabling the East: The Enlightenment's Encounter with Asia* (Princeton, NJ: Princeton University Press, 2018), chapter 11.

3. Qiao Zhiqiang, ed., *Zhongguo jindai shehui shi* [History of modern Chinese society] (Beijing: Renmin chubanshe, 1991), 43–45.

female foot-binding, underscored China's incomprehensible strangeness and provoked missionary efforts to civilize—as it was seen at the time—the depraved descendants of a once glorious civilization. Whereas Western models were emulated in Japan and an English-speaking urban class of businessmen and intellectuals emerged within a colonial context in Bengal, China in 1900, when spear-wielding Boxer insurgents clashed violently with the united imperial powers, seemed to represent a quintessentially non-bourgeois type of society. In a world of universal progress, China looked as if it were caught in a trap of backwardness. Quite a few Chinese observers shared this bleak diagnosis.

More than half a century later, around 1960, an entirely different image of Chinese strangeness gained ground not just in Europe but almost everywhere in the world. Mainland China was still, or rather again, an extremely non-bourgeois society, the polar opposite of the West. What was striking now was no longer the premodern, archaic character of Chinese society but its futuristic antagonism to any kind of liberal civility.[4] The radically collectivist communism that was propagated and partly practiced by the Chinese Communist Party (CCP) during the so-called Great Leap Forward (1958–61) surpassed even the most extreme excesses under Soviet Stalinism. China at that time turned against the Soviet leadership and accused it of succumbing to Western decadence and of taking the "capitalist road." Chinese society around 1960 was totalitarian, if ever that term made any sense. Private property was virtually nonexistent, a tightly controlled planned economy left no room for individual market activities, all everyday services were provided by agencies of the state or the party, and stirrings of cultural individualism and political dissidence were violently repressed or smothered under a torrent of relentless propaganda.

Campaigns against "feudal" and "bourgeois" thinking, invariably seen as being treasonably Western, were continued and even stepped up during the most excessive years (1966–69) of Mao Zedong's Great Proletarian Cultural Revolution. People with a "black"—rather than "red"—class background, which included any kind of non-proletarian family history and everyone whose lifestyle and outlook deviated even slightly from the egalitarian norms of Maoist orthodoxy were viciously persecuted. "Bourgeois humanitarianism," as exemplified in the music of Ludwig van Beethoven, of all things, came under vehement attack. As late as 1976, the year Mao died, there was no discernible middle class in China, and hardly anyone dared to predict that there would ever be one.

4. On the revolutionary changes in China, see the concise summary in Andrew G. Walder, *China under Mao: A Revolution Derailed* (Cambridge, MA: Harvard University Press, 2015).

This is the background to what the present chapter attempts to explain. China was first perceived as an exotic counterimage to modern bourgeois societies, from which it indeed differed enormously in structural terms. Then, after half a century of almost permanent social and political upheaval, it presented itself to the world as a socialist, and even communist, model system that had once and for all left behind the historical stage of capitalism and bourgeois hegemony. At the time of Mao's death, only two social classes were admitted to exist: workers and peasants, along with the two derivative categories of cadres and intellectuals, both drawn from the proletariat and the peasantry.[5] All other social elements had been eradicated through a protracted process of revolution that culminated in the deeply transformative social engineering implemented *after* the establishment of the CCP's dictatorship in 1949.

Post-Communist Middle Classes

Another forty years on, the overall situation has again changed dramatically. Where there had been no *visible* middle class—clandestine milieus and individual identification with the educational values of a delegitimized high culture certainly did exist—until the end of the Maoist era, China nowadays boasts the largest and most volatile middle class in the world—officially termed "China's new capitalist stratum" (*Zhongguo xin zhongchan jiecheng*).[6] This stratum did

5. On internal differentiation within these classes, see several chapters in James L. Watson, ed., *Class and Social Stratification in Post-Revolution China* (Cambridge: Cambridge University Press, 1984); on the special status of intellectuals, see Eddy U, "Reification of the Chinese Intellectual: On the Origins of the CCP Concept of *Zhizhifenzi*," *Modern China* 35 (2009): 604–631. For an independent Marxist view, see Alvin Y. So, "The Changing Pattern of Classes and Class Conflict in China," *Journal of Contemporary Asia* 33 (2003): 363–376.

6. On China's new middle class, see Jean-Louis Rocca, *The Making of the Chinese Middle Class: Small Comfort and Great Expectations* (Basingstoke: Palgrave Macmillan, 2017); Jean-Louis Rocca, *A Sociology of Modern China*, rev. ed. (London: Hurst, 2015); and a number of edited volumes: David S. G. Goodman, ed., *The New Rich in China: Future Rulers, Present Lives* (London: Routledge, 2008); Cheng Li, ed., *China's Emerging Middle Class: Beyond Economic Transformation* (Washington, DC: Brookings Institution Press, 2010); Chen Minglu and David S. G. Goodman, eds., *Middle Class China: Identity and Behaviour* (Cheltenham: Elgar, 2013); Hsin-Huang Michael Xiao, ed., *Chinese Middle Classes: Taiwan, Hong Kong, Macao and China* (London: Routledge, 2014). Systematic surveys of Chinese society since 1949 are Li Peilin, ed., *Chinese Society: Change and Transformation* (London: Routledge, 2012); and Guo Yingjie, ed., *Handbook on Class and Social Stratification in China* (Cheltenham: Elgar, 2016). A comparative perspective can be found in Christophe Jaffrelot and Peter van der Veer, eds.,

not burst onto the scene after the collapse of an explicitly anti-bourgeois regime—as in many countries within the former Soviet bloc. It owed its existence to a policy change at the top of a nominally socialist party-state that remained firmly in power. Of course, the Chinese state did not simply create a middle class out of nothing. By reintroducing personal property, encouraging an acquisitive mentality, opening up spaces for private enterprise, expanding the job market in urban white-collar employment, and reorganizing the educational system along strictly competitive and achievement-oriented lines, the CCP allowed latent processes of social differentiation to unfold with astonishing speed. Social engineering on the largest possible scale was not abandoned. It moved into a new stage.

In 1978, the CCP leadership under Deng Xiaoping decided to take first steps at liberalizing the economy. Later on, "capitalist" elements were cautiously introduced. Throughout the implementation of "reform," the party never abandoned the "commanding heights" of the economy and never stepped back from a tight control of the population. To mention just one example, a pervasive system of residency permits (*hukou*) continued to exist. Even today, residency status is used as an instrument to regulate the labor market, control entitlement to social services, and allot economic chances; it creates geographical identities (rural vs. urban) that are difficult to change. People without *hukou* or with a *hukou* inappropriate for the area where they live face considerable difficulties.[7] This is a strong factor in inhibiting autonomous class formation through activities in the market and also the reason why access to officials who are able to grant such favors as *hukou* remains essential. The right of abode, so important in the social development of the West, continues to be severely restricted.

Private business in the People's Republic of China (PRC) is still subordinated to overall state guidance. A great number of white-collar jobs requiring advanced skills have been created in the various state bureaucracies, in government-run companies, and in the exploding sector of secondary and university education. The state remains the most important employer of the middle classes. Hardly

Patterns of Middle Class Consumption in India and China (Los Angeles: Sage, 2008). There is also a more sensationalist type of literature, e.g., Helen H. Wang, *The Chinese Dream: The Rise of the World's Largest Middle Class and What It Means to You*, 2nd ed. (n.p.: Bestseller Press, 2012).

7. Eileen Yuk-Ha Tsang, *The New Middle Class in China: Consumption, Politics and the Market Economy* (Basingstoke: Palgrave Macmillan, 2014), 36–40, 179–80.

any other decision gave a greater boost to an individualistic middle-class mentality than the privatization of home ownership. It offered countless millions a stake in a system providing them with a chance to own property. At the same time it guaranteed the political stability always treasured by property owners; the reforming party proved its own indispensability. Under post-Mao reform, the population of China continued to be tied to the state through numerous bonds of dependence, though now as propertied managers of their own personal affairs rather than helpless objects of direct state alimentation. The new Chinese middle class is certainly "rising" in terms of quantity, and their impact on a voracious consumer culture provides vital demand for the national economy. It also increasingly defends its own interest within local contexts, showing cautious signs of civil society aspirations. However, the new middle class does not rise *against* the state but strictly within limits defined by the party that preserves its monopoly of power.

Who are the members of this brand-new Chinese middle class whose "cultured" lifestyle is today advertised in all kinds of media as the as the most conspicuous sign of the national upswing? Sociologists, among them quasi-official research teams of the Chinese Academy of Social Sciences that apply advanced methods of social surveying, disagree about the size and internal differentiation of this stratum and about the ways in which it can be demarcated from the subordinate classes of blue-collar workers, small farmers, and migrant workers on the one hand and—a much more difficult problem—from the dominant class and the very rich on the other.[8] Generally speaking, members of this social formation live in the rapidly expanding cities. They are employed in state administration, do office or technical work in private companies, or run their own small businesses, including professional services in areas formerly integrated into the state bureaucracy, such as medicine or law. They are consumption-oriented in a comprehensive way, tend to be proprietors of their own apartments or even houses, may possess their own car (or at least pin their hopes on acquiring one), and are keen on securing the best possible education for their children (an old priority of Chinese elites), preferably university training in North America, Europe, or Japan. They are modestly well-off without reveling in luxury and do not occupy positions of political or economic leadership or even power. Disregarding the more substantial entrepreneurs toward

8. An excellent discussion is David S. G. Goodman, *Class in Contemporary China* (Cambridge: Polity Press, 2014), 92–121.

the upper end of the social pyramid and menial office workers as well as the petty self-employed further down the scale of social stratification, the core of the middle classes—David Goodman calls them "the intermediate middle classes"—may comprise about 12 percent of the population of the PRC.[9] Interestingly, a much higher proportion of people surveyed—on the order of 60 percent or more—regularly identify themselves as "middle class."[10] The rise of the middle class hovers between fact and fantasy.

While the idea that any complex society is likely to show some kind of stratification was missing from an official discourse that warned against the dangers of bourgeois subversion, the Communist Party in 2002, in a remarkable volteface, proclaimed the expansion of the middle classes a key goal of national development.[11] It has since revised its aims upward several times with the goal of turning China into a middle-class society within a generation. Since Marxist, Leninist, and Maoist theory leaves little room for standard sociological criteria such as income, occupation, status, and lifestyle, the old politico-economic concept of class (*jieji*) had to be softened by admixtures of the non-Marxist notion of the social stratum (*jieceng*).[12] This terminological dilution has added to the empirical uncertainty as to who should count as middle class and who should not. The category remains at least as opaque and elusive for China as when it is applied to contemporary societies elsewhere, and the term "bourgeoisie" with its obnoxious political connotations is hardly ever related to the current situation and remains reserved for historical interpretations and Marxist theory. One might say that the new middle class in socialist China is a post-bourgeois social formation. It is also a huge segment of society "without a shared class identity."[13]

9. David S. G. Goodman, "Locating China's Middle Classes: Social Intermediaries and the Party State," *Journal of Contemporary China* 24 (2016): 1–13, 4.

10. Goodman, *Class in Contemporary China*, 4.

11. Goodman, *Class in Contemporary China*, 26.

12. On the implications of this terminological shift, see Ann Anagnost, "From 'Class' to 'Social Strata': Grasping the Social Totality in Reform-era China," *Third World Quarterly* 29 (2008): 497–519; on "class" in Maoist semantics, see Richard Curt Kraus, *Class Conflict in Chinese Socialism* (New York: Columbia University Press, 1981).

13. This is the conclusion of one of China's most prominent social scientists: Lu Chunlong, "China's Middle Class: Unified or Fragmented?" *Japanese Journal of Political Science* 14 (2013): 127–150, 127. One historian of Republican China links the modern development of the bourgeoisie to the rise of a working class: Shi Quansheng, "Guanyu Zhongguo zichan jieji de chansheng yu xingcheng" [On the Chinese bourgeoisie's origins and shape], *Anhui shixue* [Historical studies of Anhui] 2004.5: 44–49.

Where does all this leave the historian? In the Chinese case, focusing on the middle classes in the age of empire makes only limited sense if the broader and long-term picture is ignored. The current glorification of the Chinese middle class, both in discourse and reality, has to be the benchmark for historical interpretation. Without succumbing to teleological fallacies, one cannot avoid being overwhelmed by the fast-motion emergence of a huge middle class right before our eyes. At first sight, this amazing societal transformation looks like the culmination of a long process of sociogenesis, and it should not be too difficult to discover its origins and preparatory stages. Yet, in China there has never been a steady and continuous evolution of a stratified social system from "tradition" to "modernity."

This distinguishes China from western Europe and the post-aristocratic immigrant societies of North America and Australasia. In Japan, the Meiji regime conducted a moderate social revolution "from above" in removing vestiges of a feudal order; it never weakened the legal and economic basis of private property, and there was much more social continuity than in China at the level of individual families preserving high status and affluence. The degree of violent social rupture experienced in China between the 1940s and the 1970s finds parallels only in the Soviet Union and in those countries (Vietnam, North Korea, etc.) where the socially destructive effects of colonialism were exacerbated by a subsequent phase of anti-bourgeois socialist revolution. At the same time, the Soviet Union and its satellite states in Eastern Europe adopted European "high culture" under the class-neutral label of the "humanistic legacy." The educated middle class in the Eastern bloc watched ballet, listened to classical music in state-sponsored performances, and read the canonical novelists of the nineteenth century. Nothing remotely similar to the savage onslaught on everything traditional and foreign in Mao's Cultural Revolution happened during the entire Soviet period. Stalinist campaigns against aesthetic "formalism" were tame by comparison.

In contrast to China, Indian society experienced a rather smooth transition from Raj to republic; the present Indian middle class can retrace its origins to the colonial period in a way the Chinese middle class is unable to do. The demise of the Ottoman Empire—in many respects a historical twin of the Chinese Empire since the times of the Ming dynasty (1368–1644)—had grave effects on the non-Turkish minorities while the considerable change initiated "from above" during Kemal Atatürk's reforms of the 1920s did not amount to a wholesale destruction of an entire social order in the Anatolian core regions of the republic.

China, by contrast, experienced waves of intensified and irrevocable social dislocation:[14] in 1905 the abolition of state examinations and with them of the privileged mandarinate that had administered the empire during the past millennium; between 1946 and 1953 the extermination of the landlord class during the so-called land revolution that began in the CCP-controlled regions of North China prior to the nationwide assumption of state power; from 1949 to 1956 the socialization of private "capitalist" business in the cities;[15] from 1957 to 1983 in campaign after campaign that disciplined intellectuals, a group that was still very small in 1956 when the number of college graduates hardly exceeded a hundred thousand.[16]

Emerging after these waves of revolutions within the Revolution, the middle class that has taken shape in China since the 1990s is a post-revolutionary creation possessing only shallow roots in the past, a parvenu class with fragile cultural bearings. Family genealogies reaching back to earlier generations of businessmen, high-ranking officials in the pre-communist governments, and professors with contacts in the West remain scattered and particularistic and do not add up to a statistically significant bourgeois experience. As a rule, private fortunes could not be preserved and transmitted on the Chinese mainland after 1949, whereas other strategies of status maintenance might have yielded greater success; for instance, elite families ensuring during the crucial years around 1949 that their daughters married rustic CCP cadres. Where members of former "capitalist" families were again successful under the auspices of post-Mao reform, they owed this to connections with top party officials and to personal managerial skills that proved useful once the regime decided to value people for their ability rather than their class background. Whereas entrepreneurial dynasties rarely survived on the Chinese mainland, it was possible for

14. For a fruitful model of stages in modern Chinese history, see Wolfgang Franke, *A Century of Chinese Revolution 1851–1949* (Oxford: Blackwell, 1970).

15. Ceng Xin, "Luelun jianguo chuqi Zhongguo Gongchandang dui minzu zichan jieji zhengce bianhua de yuanyin" [Reasons for the change in the CCP's policy toward the bourgeoisie during the early period of the People's Republic], *Yan'an daxue xuebao* [Journal of Yan'an University] 31, no. 3 (2009): 34–38; Feng Xiaocai, "Rushing towards Socialism: The Transformation and Death of Private Business Enterprises in Shanghai, 1949–1956," in *The People's Republic of China at 60: An International Assessment*, ed. William C. Kirby (Cambridge, MA: Harvard University Asia Center, 2011), 240–258.

16. By 1982, it had risen to 4.5 million: Richard Curt Kraus, *Pianos and Politics in China: Middle-Class Ambitions and the Struggle over Western Music* (New York: Oxford University Press, 1989), 24.

some families to retain elite status by shifting their fields of activity. In a typical trajectory, a former capitalist might have professed his loyalty to the CCP in the relatively easygoing 1950s, thereafter somehow survived the Cultural Revolution, and under reform took up a new career in business.[17]

Yet, the top earners in the PRC rarely hail from entrepreneurial dynasties. They are in some ways comparable to the profiteers of the French Revolution and the Napoleonic years, nouveaux riches who benefit from a change of regime, in this case the transition from Maoism to managerial authoritarianism and "state neoliberalism"[18] under Deng Xiaoping and his successors. Given this general pattern of discontinuity, there is no consistent story to tell about piecemeal class formation in an undisturbed long run—the normal European and North American experience. The new Chinese middle class neither grew organically from stage to stage, nor did it, in line with orthodox Marxist expectations, triumph in the class struggle.

Business Elites in an Age of Empire

In search of equivalents on the Chinese mainland to a fully articulated bourgeoisie, one has to turn to the age of empire. The following sketch will leave aside the difficult question of middling ranks in Chinese society prior to sustained contact with the West. Of course, there were millions of people ranging in status and livelihood between the title-bearing and, as a rule, landowning elite and the poor and often-illiterate population at the bottom of society.[19] These respectable townspeople included merchants, artisans, priests, teachers, medical

17. A case study is Chen Minglu, "Being Elite, 1931–2011: Three Generations of Social Change," *Journal of Contemporary China* 21 (2012): 741–746; and a broader picture based on interviews is in David S. G. Goodman, "New Economic Elites: Family Histories and Social Change," in *State-Society Relations and Governance in China*, ed. Guo Sujian (Lanham, MD: Lexington Books, 2014), 15–38. Most valuable, though still rare, are multigenerational histories of individual families such as Joseph Esherick, *Ancestral Leaves: A Family Journey through Chinese History* (Berkeley: University of California Press, 2011); Sherman G. Cochran and Andrew Hsieh, *The Lius of Shanghai* (Cambridge, MA: Harvard University Press, 2013); and Brett Sheehan, *Industrial Eden: A Chinese Capitalist Vision* (Cambridge, MA: Harvard University Press, 2015).

18. Alvin Y. So and Chu Yin-wah, *The Global Rise of China* (Cambridge: Polity Press, 2016), 18–20, 56–85.

19. Li Mingwei, *Qingmo Minchu Zhongguo chengshi shehui jieceng yanjiu (1897–1927)* [Research on urban social classes from the Late Qing Period to the Early Republic] (Beijing: Shehui kexue wenxian chubanshe, 2005), 67–81.

practitioners, and so on.[20] They did not make the smooth transition to modernity that was analogous to the European standard trajectory "from burghers to bourgeoisie." It is almost impossible to reduce the enormous complexity of that shifting social world to a few abstract formulas. We shall focus on a tiny section among these intermediate social groups—the business elite—and ask the fairly precise question of how its development was affected by empire.

The age of empire is a difficult concept for China. Formally speaking, China's age as a *victim* of empire began with the Opium War of 1839–42. It ended with the expulsion of the last Western businessmen and missionaries from the Chinese mainland in the early 1950s. Alternatively, the abrogation of the remaining "unequal treaties" with the Western powers in 1943 or, more convincingly, the end of Japanese wartime occupation in September 1945 could serve as terminal dates; however, these dates do not immediately make sense in terms of social history.

The crucial question is how and with what intensity exogenous forces that became effective through the institutional framework of empire impacted Chinese society. Three preliminary points have to be made.

First, this impact was highly uneven in spatial terms. The sheer size of the country and the vast physical distance of many places in the interior from any borders and thus from sustained contact with the outside world have always militated against a powerful and pervasive transnational impact. Even if recent scholarship has revised the traditional image of a secluded and inward-looking Middle Kingdom,[21] the fact remains that only small sections of Chinese society

20. For summary descriptions of society under the Qing dynasty, see William T. Rowe, *China's Last Empire: The Great Qing* (Cambridge, MA: Belknap Press of Harvard University Press, 2009), 90–121; Richard J. Smith, *The Qing Dynasty and Traditional Chinese Culture* (Lanham, MD: Rowman and Littlefield, 2015), 124–68. There is little first-rate social history on the people below "middle" positions in prerevolutionary China, but see Janet Y. Chen, *Guilty of Indigence: The Urban Poor in China, 1900–1953* (Princeton, NJ: Princeton University Press, 2012). For the basic issues in Chinese social history, see an unsurpassed article from the 1980s: William T. Rowe, "Approaches to Modern Chinese Social History," in *Reliving the Past: The Worlds of Social History*, ed. Olivier Zunz (Chapel Hill: University of North Carolina Press, 1985), 236–296.

21. A remarkable and self-consciously "internalist" statement written without the foreknowledge of coming reform was Gilbert Rozman, ed, *The Modernization of China* (New York: Free Press, 1981). Early attempts to place China within a transnational or global context were Jürgen Osterhammel, *China und die Weltgesellschaft: Vom 18. Jahrhundert bis in unsere Zeit* (Munich: C. H. Beck, 1989); and Joanna Waley-Cohen, *The Sextants of Beijing: Global Currents in Chinese History* (New York: W. W. Norton, 1999).

developed a distinctly maritime and overseas-oriented identity. This changed slowly after the Opium War without ever leading to a social structure that, as a whole, was skewed toward distant markets and faraway target areas of emigration.[22] Speaking of Chinese society as such should always come with the qualification that several types of society coexisted within the borders of the empire or the nation-state, including frontier zones of mobile settlement and resource extraction.[23] The tension between maritime and continental remains important to this day.

Famously, the treaty ports were places where new social forces emerged earlier than elsewhere.[24] But of the fifty or so treaty ports that had been opened to foreign commerce by 1917, only a handful of major cities had become the sites of fully articulated Sino-Western hybrid societies of a quasi-colonial type: Shanghai, Guangzhou, Tianjin, Hankou (Wuhan), and Xiamen (Amoy). These cities contained foreign settlements under the autonomous administration of consuls or foreign-dominated municipal councils. Beijing was never a treaty port, and in many big cities of the interior, let alone isolated trading posts along the Chinese border, the direct presence of agents of Western empire, apart from missionaries, was minimal, even at the numerical peak of the Western presence around 1920.

Shanghai soon overshadowed all the other treaty ports.[25] It was unique in size and social dynamic and became by far the most important place for the

22. Though somewhat overstated, Murphey's anti-globalist case for Chinese self-centeredness should not be dismissed out of hand: Rhoads Murphey, *The Outsiders: The Western Experience in India and China* (Ann Arbor: University of Michigan Press, 1977).

23. Susan Naquin and Evelyn S. Rawski, *Chinese Society in the Eighteenth Century* (New Haven, CT: Yale University Press, 1987), 130–133; this book distinguishes between ten different "regional societies" within the empire. The best social history written today in China, too, has a regional focus. See Wang Xianming, "The Emergence of Modern Chinese Social History," in *Thirty Years of Chinese History Studies*, ed. Zhang Haipeng (Beijing: China Social Press, 2015), 413–440, especially 419–423; see also He Yimin, "Chinese Urban History Studies Face the Twenty-first Century," *Chinese Studies in History* 47 (2014): 73–99.

24. Zhang Kaiyuan, Ma Min, and Zhu Ying, eds., *Zhongguo jindai minzu zichan jieji yanjiu* [Research on the bourgeoisie in modern China] (Wuhan: Huazhong shifan daxue chubanshe, 2000), 84–92.

25. There is a huge literature on this, always containing bits and pieces on the bourgeoisie. See Marie-Claire Bergère, *Shanghai: China's Gateway to Modernity* (Stanford, CA: Stanford University Press, 2009); on the foreign presence, see Nicholas R. Clifford, *Spoilt Children of Empire: Westerners in Shanghai and the Chinese Revolution of the 1920s* (Hanover, NH: University Press of New England, 1991); Robert Bickers, *Britain in China: Community, Culture and*

entry of Western modernity into China, a matchless hub of shipping, trade, industry, and finance, globally connected to a much greater extent than any other Chinese city, with the exception of colonial Hong Kong. The disproportionate amount of first-rate research devoted to Shanghai tends to obscure the basic fact that Shanghai was not representative of the rest of the country, not even of the other major treaty ports.

Second, the temporality of empire in China is more uneven than in the case of the typical colonized country. Until the mid-1890s, the Western imperial presence was entirely urban. Thereafter, a few territorial colonies (some of them under the legal form of leased territories) were added to the picture, but they remained few, rather small (in China proper no entire province ever came under alien jurisdiction), and sparsely populated. Outside peripheral areas such as Manchuria and Taiwan, territorial colonialism was too marginal to leave a more than regional imprint on Chinese social history.

Thus, there was a life cycle of the treaty port "system" that lasted continuously from the 1860s, when the foreign concessions in Tianjin and Hankou were beginning to become important, to 1937–38, when the Japanese invasion brought a degree of violence to the cities of Eastern China and the middle Yangzi that had hitherto been unknown. Like everyone else, the middle classes had to cope somehow, but under emergency conditions that often continued into the subsequent periods of civil war and communist revolution.[26] While the Japanese had their stake in treaty port society since the 1890s, their own empire in China was of a different kind, and Japanese military occupation (in the Shanghai International Settlement and in Hong Kong beginning only in December 1941, after Pearl Harbor) was a much heavier burden on the Chinese civilian population than the rule of Western consuls and businessmen in the treaty ports had ever been. "Empire" in China meant quite different *types* of empire, partly coexisting, partly following one upon the other.

Third, the peculiarities of the pre-1937 business elite cannot be understood without reference to the unusual fluidity and malleability of social categories in late imperial China. The formal side of the system was the elite ranks obtained through competitive state examinations. The ranks were graded meticulously, as were the tiers within the bureaucracy. But that rationalist

Colonialism 1900–1949 (Manchester: Manchester University Press, 1999); Robert Bickers, *Out of China: How the Chinese Ended the Era of Western Domination* (London: Allen Lane, 2017).

26. Parks M. Coble, *Chinese Capitalists in Japan's New Order: The Occupied Lower Yangzi, 1937–1945* (Berkeley: University of California Press, 2003).

arrangement was undermined in the nineteenth century by the growing opportunity to purchase lower titles.[27] Thus, successful merchants gained access to a social elite that even traditionally had been permeable for upwardly mobile talent. Upper-class status had never been based on aristocratic bloodlines, and great wealth, though not translating automatically into elevated status, was no liability for social advancement. To a lesser extent even than in earlier centuries, there was no strictly defined upper class from which a middle class could distance itself through lifestyle, cultural choices, or political ambition.

Urban society before the onset of Western influence was not rigidly stratified in estates with graduated legal rights. While title bearers (the "gentry") enjoyed certain legal privileges—a strong reason for sparing no effort in the examinations or purchasing a title—the formal status of non-elite subjects was more or less the same. [28] Elite culture and popular culture overlapped and mixed in spaces such as the opera theater. Since Chinese cities enjoyed little corporate autonomy and had no Western-style governing councils, there were few elective offices that could constitute a patrician oligarchy. The city was ruled by magistrates appointed from above and was otherwise kept going by all sorts of informal networks. Self-regulating guilds (*gongsuo*) were important pillars of urban life.[29] So were the *huiguan*, native-place associations where residents originating from a particular province or city, and speaking a common dialect that might be incomprehensible to their neighbors, met to socialize and do business; running hostels was one their major tasks.[30] Often nationwide trades and branches of business were in the hands of people from one particular region. Thus bankers were frequently based in remote Shanxi province.[31] These translocal structures of solidarity enabled far-flung trading networks to operate throughout the empire and integrate its various regions. They also impeded European-style horizontal class formation since they introduced into urban

27. Zhang Kaiyuan, Ma Min, and Zhu Yin, eds., *Xinhai Geming qianhou de guan shen shang xue* [The education of officials, gentry and businessmen in the period of the Revolution of 1911] (Wuhan: Huazhong shifan daxue chubanshe, 2011), 171–190.

28. Rowe, *China's Last Empire*, 109–114.

29. Xu Dixin and Wu Chengming, eds., *Chinese Capitalism, 1522–1840* (Basingstoke: Macmillan, 2000), 181–183.

30. Bryna Goodman, *Native Place, City, and Nation: Regional Networks and Identities in Shanghai, 1853–1937* (Berkeley: University of California Press, 1995).

31. See Huang Jianhui, *Ming Qing Shanxi shangren yanjiu* [Studies on the Shanxi businessmen of the Ming-Qing period] (Taiyuan: Shanxi jingji chubanshe, 2002).

society an element of localism and a permanent distinction between natives and aliens. The eminent social historian William T. Rowe has argued that geographical distinctions were more important than class or status in late imperial society.[32]

The 1860s were a watershed decade for China. The destructive Taiping Revolution was defeated after taking a heavy toll of life, especially among the elite of the central and eastern provinces. The idea that moderate reforms were needed became thinkable for the first time. At the same time, foreign trade increased and commercial activities revived. Under these circumstances, title holders (many of them absentee landlords) and merchants drew ever closer and began to coalesce in what was already termed by contemporaries a *shen-shang*, or gentry-merchant class, though the degree of distance or fusion between the two elements is still disputed.[33] This composite class came together first in a common defense of local or provincial interests, and, second, in charity activities, social services, and other forms of civil engagement and Confucian community leadership.[34]

These people were notables with close links to officialdom. The characteristic blurring of social boundaries makes it difficult to describe them as a distinct class, let alone a rising bourgeoisie. Some represented the quintessential parasitic landlord of later communist propaganda. Others were business people with often mixed portfolios of investment and mercantile activities. Commercial opportunities increased during the last four decades of the nineteenth century with the expansion of foreign trade and the first attempts by central and provincial governments to raise capital for joint state-private projects of modernization in shipping, shipbuilding, mining, and railway building.

32. William T. Rowe, *Hankow: Commerce and Society in a Chinese City, 1796–1889* (Stanford, CA: Stanford University Press, 1984), 213.

33. Wang Xianming, "Zhongguo jindai shenshi jiecheng de shehui liudong" [The social mobility of the gentry stratum in modern China], *Lishi yanjiu* [Historical research] 1993.2: 80–95, 88; Ma Min, *Guan shang zhijian: shehui jubian zhong de jindai shenshang* [Between bureaucrats and merchants: The modern gentry-merchant class amid social change] (Wuhan: Huazhong shifan daxue chubanshe, 2003); Mary Backus Rankin, *Elite Activism and Political Transformation in China: Zhejiang Province, 1865–1911* (Stanford, CA: Stanford University Press, 1986).

34. Rowe, *Hankow*, 99–134; Kwan Man Bun, *The Salt Merchants of Tianjin: State Making and Civil Society in Late Imperial China* (Honolulu: University of Hawai'i Press, 2001), 89–103; Wang Jingyu, *Jindai Zhongguo ziben zhuyi de zongti kaocha he ge'an bianzhe* [Complete examination and discussion of capitalism in modern China] (Beijing: Zhongguo shehui kexue chubanshe, 2004), 225–249.

Some of these notables, especially in the big treaty ports, were compra-dors.[35] The comprador was a new type of Chinese merchant: a middleman at the interface of Western and Chinese business and in this sense a successor to the Hong merchants of pre–treaty-port days.[36] His task was to organize the commercial linkages between foreign export-import companies and the Chi-nese domestic market, to guarantee payments by Chinese partners, and to recruit and supervise the Chinese staff of Western firms. He had to be a busi-nessman of substantial standing and creditworthiness in his Chinese environ-ment. Being a comprador was in many cases combined with other mercantile roles or functions. Compradors sometimes amassed great fortunes and secretly provided loans or share capital to Western firms.[37]

For their daily business, compradors needed a good knowledge of English. This did not automatically turn them into agents of Westernization, although they were certainly more deeply involved with Western bourgeois culture than their counterparts, the expatriate businessmen who rarely left the treaty ports, were with their Chinese host culture. There was little in the way of cosmopoli-tan sociability in the treaty ports. The Western and Chinese worlds overlapped without ever merging into a third social space. It is difficult to see the compra-dors as the first generation of a Chinese entrepreneurial bourgeoisie. Chinese historians have argued that their historical significance lies in the fact that they broke with the traditional system of commercial guilds, thus opening up the countryside to the capitalist market system. Moreover, their influence on local officials paved the way to changes in social stratification at the village level.[38]

35. Hao Yen-p'ing, *The Comprador in Nineteenth-Century China: Bridge between East and West* (Cambridge, MA: Harvard University Press, 1970); Huang Yifeng et al., *Jiu Zhongguo de maiban jieji* [The comprador class in prerevolutionary China] (Shanghai: Shanghai renmin chubanshe, 1982).

36. On the far-flung international activities of these pre-1840 merchants, see John D. Wong, *Global Trade in the Nineteenth Century: The House of Houqua and the Canton System* (Cambridge: Cambridge University, 2016).

37. Hao Yen-p'ing, *The Commercial Revolution in Nineteenth-Century China: The Rise of Sino-Western Mercantile Capitalism* (Berkeley: University of California Press, 1986), 245–258; Xian Qiaoying, "Jianxi maiban yu Zhongguo zaoqi xiandaihua" [The compradors and the early mod-ernization of China], *Beijing lianhe daxue xuebao* [Journal of Beijing Union University] 2, no. 3 (2004): 31–37.

38. Jin Pusen and Yi Jichang, "Maiban yu Zhongguo jindai shehui jieceng de bianqian" [The compradors and the changes in Chinese social strata in modern times], *Zhejiang daxue xuebao* [Journal of Zhejiang University] 32, no. 3 (2002): 13–21.

Compradors belonged to a specific period in the contact between China and the West. Many Western businessmen regarded them as a necessary evil. Following the lead of Japanese trading houses, there was a general tendency in the early years of the twentieth century to replace the freewheeling comprador with young "Chinese managers" who were direct employees of the foreign firm and often received technical training on the job.[39] The compradors did not reinvent themselves as a new class of industrialists. Zhu Ying, one of the leading historians of Chinese capitalism, comes to the conclusion that the businessmen emerging in the early years of the twentieth century formed a new social group and did not evolve as direct successors to the compradors of treaty-port days.[40]

An Entrepreneurial Elite

When we marvel at the speed of social change in the PRC during the past thirty years and compare it to transformations in Europe that we believe to have taken much longer to unfold, a look back at China between, roughly, 1895 and 1930 reveals processes of hardly less stormy renewal.[41] At the time of the Boxer Rebellion, there was hardly any Chinese-run private enterprise on the China coast.[42] During the following decade, concurrently with the convulsive transition from empire to republic, several successful companies were established.[43] Within a very short time span, the first generation of Chinese industrialists

39. Andrew Smith, "The Winds of Change and the End of the Comprador System in the Hong Kong and Shanghai Banking Corporation," *Business History* 58 (2015): 179–206. A parallel development was the recruitment of young Chinese for the foreign-dominated Maritime Customs Service: Chang Chihyun, *Government, Imperialism and Nationalism in China: The Maritime Customs Service and Its Chinese Staff* (London: Routledge, 2013), 62–71.

40. Zhu Ying, "Jindai Zhongguo shangren yu shehui biange" [Businessmen in modern China and the transformation of society], *Tianjin shehui kexue* [Tianjin social sciences] 2001.5: 126–131.

41. For a brief survey of urban social change at China's fin de siècle, see Peter Zarrow, *China in War and Revolution, 1895–1949* (London: RoutledgeCurzon, 2005), 112–127; still valuable is Marianne Bastid, "Currents of Social Change," in *The Cambridge History of China*, vol. 11: *Late Ch'ing, 1800–1911*, pt. 2, ed. John King Fairbank and Liu Kwang-ching (Cambridge: Cambridge University Press, 1980), 536–602.

42. Li Mingwei, *Qingmo Minchu Zhongguo chengshi shehui jieceng yanjiu*, 30–40.

43. Wellington K. K. Chan, "The Organizational Structure of the Traditional Chinese Firm and Its Modern Reform," *Business History Review* 46 (1982): 218–235, especially 228–232. A classical case study is Sherman G. Cochran, *Big Business in China: Sino-Foreign Rivalry in the Cigarette Industry, 1890–1930* (Cambridge, MA: Harvard University Press, 1980).

appeared on the scene.[44] When the First World War broke out and Western firms retreated from Asian markets, Chinese manufacturers were well positioned to seize the opportunity and fill the void. The modern sector of the Chinese economy experienced a war boom. For the first time, Western dominance over the economy of the treaty ports was successfully challenged. Even though Japanese industrial capital rushed into China in the early twenties and major British firms held their own, many of the wartime gains could be preserved.[45]

For the second decade of the twentieth century it is possible to speak of the emergence of an entrepreneurial elite *after* the compradors and the modernizing bureaucrats of the Qing government. Its core element was a small stratum of entrepreneurs who were most successful in five sectors: shipping, banking, light industry (cotton, cement, flower mills, tobacco, etc.), department stores, and publishing.[46] The rise of Chinese-owned enterprises that often successfully competed with Japanese and Western firms was accompanied by the emergence of related economic functions and social roles: the manager, the banker, the stockbroker (the Shanghai Stock Exchange first appeared under that name in 1905, although a Chinese-controlled exchange was established only in 1920), and the lawyer who specialized in commercial law and was a cultural broker in his own right, mastering Western as well as Chinese law.[47]

44. Wang Jingyu, *Jindai Zhongguo ziben zhuyi de zongti kaocha*, 3–14; Xu Dixin and Wu Chengming, eds., *Zhongguo ziben zhuyi fazhan shi* [History of capitalist development in China], vol. 2: *Jiu minzhu zhuyi geming shiqi de Zhongguo ziben zhuyi* [Capitalism in the period of China's Old Democracy Revolution] (Beijing: Shehui kexue wenxian chubanshe, 2007), 485–525. For an abridged translation of this work see n. 29 above.

45. Du Xuncheng, *Minzu ziben zhuyi yu jiu Zhongguo zhengfu (1840–1937)* [Chinese capitalism and the old Chinese government] (Shanghai: Shanghai shehui kexueyuan chubanshe, 1991), 104–159.

46. Chao Kang, *The Development of Cotton Textile Production in China* (Cambridge, MA: Harvard University Press, 1977); Elisabeth Köll, *From Cotton Mill to Business Empire: The Emergence of Regional Enterprises in Modern China* (Cambridge, MA: Harvard University Press, 2003); Cheng Linsun, *Banking in Modern China: Entrepreneurs, Professional Managers and the Development of Chinese Banks, 1897–1937* (Cambridge: Cambridge University Press, 2002); Ji Zhaojin, *A History of Modern Shanghai Banking: The Rise and Decline of China`s Finance Capitalism* (Armonk, NY: Sharpe, 2003); Brett Sheehan, "Urban Identity and Urban Networks in Cosmopolitan Cities: Banks and Bankers in Tianjin, 1900–1937," in *Remaking the Chinese City: Modernity and National Identity, 1900–1950*, ed. Joseph W. Esherick (Honolulu: University of Hawai'i Press, 1999), 47–64; Christopher A. Reed, *Gutenberg in Shanghai: Chinese Print Capitalism, 1876–1937* (Honolulu: University of Hawai'i Press, 2004).

47. Bryna Goodman, "'The Crime of Economics': Suicide and the Early Shanghai Stock Market," in *Citadins et citoyens dans la Chine du XXe siècle: Essais d'histoire sociale*, ed. Yves

The war boom does not explain everything. These new urban milieus sprang up under a few more facilitating conditions. Three of them were particularly important. First, based on a new discourse about the legitimacy of self-interest, modern economic thinking gained ground in China.[48] Second, after the disaster of the Boxer Rebellion of 1900–1901, the Qing state turned to an ambitious policy of modernization known as the New Policies.[49] Essential for forging the new social character of the "businessman" were two innovations of the year 1904: the court's approval of the establishment of chambers of commerce throughout the empire, and the first company law (*gongsi fa*).[50] It created a legal basis for stock corporations, thus opening up the possibility of attracting capital from anonymous strangers and weakening the traditional dependence on family networks and investments by people from one's own province of origin.[51]

The third factor was education. There had been an older tradition of missionary education in quite worldly subjects and even of sending young

Chevrier, Alain Roux, and Xiaohong Xiao-Planes (Paris: Éditions de la Maison des sciences de l'homme, 2010), 183–205; Xu Xiaoqun, *Chinese Professionals and the Republican State: The Rise of Professional Associations in Shanghai, 1912–1937* (Cambridge: Cambridge University Press, 2001), 50–77, 215–228.

48. Chi Kong Lai, "Merchant Discourse on Self-interest in Modern China," in *Creating Chinese Modernity: Knowledge and Everyday Life, 1900–1940*, ed. Peter Zarrow (New York: Peter Lang, 2006), 99–115, 107–113; on a leading protagonist of this reorientation, see Wu Guo, *Zheng Guanying: Merchant Reformer of Late Qing China and His Influence on Economics, Politics, and Society* (Amherst, NY: Cambria Press, 2010).

49. The consequences for the business community of this policy are discussed in: Zhang Kaiyuan, Ma Min, and Zhu Ying, *Zhongguo jindai minzu zichan jieji yanjiu*, 658–662.

50. Zhu Ying, *Xinhai Geming shiqi xinshi shangren shetuan yanjiu* [Research on the new form of business groups during the Revolution of 1911] (Wuhan: Huazhong shifan daxue chubanshe, 2011), 46–97; a good case study is Zhang Fanglin, *Shichang huanjing yu zhidu bianqian: Yi Qingmo zhi Minguo Nanchang shangren yu shanghui zuzhi wei shijiao* [The environment of the market and changes in the system: From the perspective of businessmen and chambers of commerce in Nanchang during the Late Qing and Republican Periods] (Beijing: Renmin chubanshe, 2013); see also Yu Heping, "Shanghui yu Zhongguo zichan jieji de 'ziwei' hua wenti" [Chambers of commerce and the question of autonomization of the Chinese bourgeoisie], *Jindaishi yanjiu* [Modern history studies] 31 (1991): 25–41. A case study for Tianjin is Hu Guangming, "Lun zaoqi Tianjin shanghui de xingzhi yu zuoyong" [The character and effect of the early chamber of commerce of Tianjin], *Jindaishi yanjiu* 26 (1986): 182–223.

51. David Faure, *China and Capitalism: A History of Business Enterprise in Modern China* (Hong Kong: Hong Kong University Press, 2006), 43, 46.

students abroad, especially to the United States and Japan. But only around the turn of the century did the impression gain general acceptance that China should engage with the knowledge of the modern world. The Qing state as well as provincial governments sent students abroad for civil and military trading in large numbers. Families invested, as they do again today, in overseas educations for their sons and sometimes even daughters. Soon a new generation of returned students with degrees from foreign universities and fluent in English or Japanese were available on the job market or entered directly into their families' businesses.[52] Those who did not join the private economic sector found employment as teachers in the rapidly expanding schools and universities (not just in the treaty ports); others tried to make a living as freelance intellectuals.[53]

The historiography of the Chinese revolution that began in the 1920s has drawn attention to the sharp political disagreements which by 1927 had turned into the initial stage of a civil war.[54] Marxist historians have conventionally separated the social spectrum behind ideology and political action into divisions ranging from the *Lumpenproletariat* to big landlords and wealthy capitalists, with a "national bourgeoisie" being the favorite of orthodox commentators. This should not obscure certain commonalities in the urban society of 1920s Shanghai, and to a lesser extent of other big cities.[55]

First, this modern urban elite—from the shipping magnate to the radical journalist—shared a background in the upper-class world of the late empire. Even the protagonists of early socialism, anarchism, and communism rarely originated from the low peasantry or the industrial proletariat. Second, whatever their diverging views on the desirable political order, they were united in

52. Huang Xiaojian, *Guiguo huaqiao de lishi yu xianguang* [The returned overseas Chinese: Past and present] (Hong Kong: Xianggang shehui kexue chuban she, 2005), 34–40; Zhang Fuji, *Jindai Zhongguo shehui yanhua yu geming* [Change and revolution in modern Chinese society] (Beijing: Renmin chubanshe, 2002), 167–186.

53. Zhang Kaiyuan, Ma Min, and Zhu Ying, *Xinhai Geming qianhou de guan shen shang xue*, 515–541.

54. That this was not a binary juxtaposition of the Communists and their enemies is shown by Edmund S. K. Fung, *The Intellectual Foundations of Chinese Modernity: Cultural and Political Thought in the Republican Era* (Cambridge: Cambridge University, 2010); see also Timothy Cheek, *The Intellectual in Modern Chinese History* (Cambridge: Cambridge University Press, 2015).

55. On different proximities between bourgeoisie and intellectuals, see Xu Jilin, "The Urban 'Cultural Nexus of Power': Intellectual Elites in Shanghai and Beijing, 1900–1937," *Frontiers of History in China* 9 (2014): 32–55.

their nationalism and their resistance to Western and Japanese imperialism.[56] Third, this opposition did not prevent them from being heavily influenced by Western culture and ideas. They typically—and this is true for no previous generation—received a dual education in the Chinese tradition as well as in foreign knowledge. The young industrialist with a US degree in textile technology or business administration, the Japanese-trained military officer, or the student reader of Karl Marx—they all lived in a composite mental world. Fourth, nobody doubted that China should enter industrial modernity as forcefully as possible. There was little room in these years for rural nostalgia or fanciful communist utopianism. Sun Yat-sen's book *The International Development of China*, published in English in 1922, captured the mood of the time with its grand schemes for industrial and infrastructural modernization.[57] Fifth, all these people were immersed in the rapidly emerging consumer culture, especially in Shanghai. These were the golden years of the new department stores, of advertising, of fashion, of new role models for women, of the acquisition of prestigious gadgets from abroad.[58] At the same time,

56. Feng Xiaocai, *Zai shang yan shang: Zhengzhi bianju zhong de Zhejiang shangren* [At business talking business: Zhejiang businessmen during political change] (Shanghai: Shanghai shehui kexueyuan chubanshe, 2004), 190–193. The contradictory psychology of these people is discussed in Qiao Zhiqiang and Zhao Xiaohua, "Qingmo Minchu minzu zichan jieji xintai chutan" [A tentative analysis of the mentality of the national bourgeoisie of the Late Qing and early Republican Periods], *Shanxi daxue xuebao* [Journal of Shanxi University] 1995.4: 7–13.

57. Sun Yat-sen, *The International Development of China* (New York: Putnam, 1922). On the hopes pinned on the benefits of industry, see Sheehan, *Industrial Eden*, 2 and passim.

58. Frederic Wakeman and Yeh Wen-hsin, eds., *Shanghai Sojourners* (Berkeley, CA: Institute of East Asian Studies, 1992); Yeh Wen-hsin, "Shanghai Modernity: Commerce and Culture in a Republican City," *China Quarterly* 150 (1997): 375–394; Yeh Wen-hsin, *Shanghai Splendor: Economic Sentiments and the Making of Modern China, 1843–1949* (Berkeley: University of California Press, 2007); Sherman G. Cochran, ed., *Inventing Nanjing Road: Commercial Culture in Shanghai, 1900–1945* (Ithaca, NY: Cornell University Press, 1999); Karl Gerth, *China Made: Consumer Culture and the Creation of the Nation* (Cambridge, MA: Harvard University Press, 2003); Frank Dikötter, *Exotic Commodities: Modern Objects and Everyday Life in China* (London: Hurst, 2006); Antonia Finnane, *Changing Clothes in China: Fashion, History, Nation* (New York: Columbia University Press, 2008), 101–175; Andreas Steen, *Zwischen Unterhaltung und Revolution: Grammophone, Schallplatten und die Anfänge der Musikindustrie in Shanghai, 1878–1937* (Wiesbaden: Harrassowitz, 2006); Xu Tao, *Zixingche yu jindai Zhongguo* [The bicycle and modern China] (Shanghai: Shanghai renmin chubanshe, 2015); Qiao Yigang and Liu Kun, "The Emerging of 'Female Citizen': The Subject Identity of Modern Chinese Women through Literary Practices," *Frontiers of History in China* 4 (2009): 107–123.

untrammeled hedonism was challenged by the ideals of frugality and admonitions to buy Chinese-made goods.[59]

Business, too, had to be conducted in a modern way. The only chance to compete with formidable foreign rivals (who were likely to have their own factories in the treaty ports) was to join them, often from a position of weakness, in the game of capitalist enterprise. However, the Chinese entrepreneurs did not simply adopt Western methods of running a company. They combined some of these methods—such as a formalized in-house hierarchy and a clearly defined division of responsibilities—with Chinese networking experience and a personal capitalism based on family solidarity and lineage ties.[60]

The business elite of the 1900s to 1940s—whose "golden age," as Marie-Claire Bergère, the outstanding expert on the Chinese bourgeoisie, has established in her authoritative works, was limited to the quarter century from 1912 to 1937 (more narrowly defined, from 1912 to 1927)—was the closest mainland China came to developing a modern bourgeoisie.[61] It was weakened during the war of 1937/41 to 1945 and the subsequent civil war when rampant inflation took its additional toll. It was eventually destroyed by the communist regime between 1952 and 1956.[62] Whether the anti-communist Guomindang regime of the early and mid-thirties with its notoriously greedy "four big families" already put debilitating pressure on the private capitalists remains a moot point.[63] Be that as it may, the Chinese bourgeoisie rose and fell within one

59. Margherita Zanasi, "Frugal Modernity: Livelihood and Consumption in Republican China," *Journal of Asian Studies* 74 (2015): 391–409.

60. Sherman G. Cochran, *Encountering Chinese Networks: Western, Japanese, and Chinese Corporations in China, 1880–1937* (Berkeley: University of California Press, 2000); Gary G. Hamilton, *Commerce and Capitalism in Chinese Societies* (London: Routledge, 2006), 220–236; Marie-Claire Bergère, *The Golden Age of the Chinese Bourgeoisie, 1911–1937* (Cambridge: Cambridge University Press, 1990), 152–164.

61. Bergère, *Golden Age*; Bergère, *Shanghai*, 147–176; Bergère, *Capitalisme et capitalistes en Chine: XIXe–XXIe siècle* (Paris: Perrin, 2007). See also Tang Lixing, *Shangren yu Zhongguo jinshi shehui* [Businessmen and modern Chinese society] (Hangzhou: Zhejiang renmin chubanshe, 1993), 292–293.

62. Bergère, *Capitalisme et capitalistes*, 203–213; Yang Kuisong, "The Evolution of the Chinese Communist Party's Policy on the Bourgeoisie (1949–1952)," *Journal of Modern Chinese History* 1 (2007): 13–30.

63. Parks M. Coble, *The Shanghai Capitalists and the Nationalist Government, 1927–1937* (Cambridge, MA: Harvard University Press, 1980); more nuanced is Bergère, *Capitalisme et capitalistes*, 145–167.

generation.[64] Its political imprint remained limited to the extent that members of the business elite supported ideas of participatory and rights-based citizenship that were put forward by intellectuals.[65] These ideas failed to be implemented on the Chinese mainland. The history of the Chinese bourgeoisie confirms a general observation: the rise and flourishing of bourgeois milieus with their characteristic values and lifestyle cannot be separated from the issue of power. It requires at least a minimum of protection on the part of the state.[66]

Epilogue: Business Elites in the Diaspora

There is a different story to tell: Chinese capitalism was rescued by colonialism. It rose and flourished in British Hong Kong and Singapore, hardly hampered by a laissez-faire colonial regime. Chinese business, too, had benefited from the legal protection of property and the authoritarian control of the work force available in the Shanghai International Settlement. The same protection and support under British law was offered from 1842 to 1997 in the crown colony. Without revolutionary interruption, a Chinese upper class of merchant-notables in the globally connected port city had time to evolve into a modern entrepreneurial elite.[67] After the Japanese invasion of the Chinese mainland in the summer of 1937, and again ten years later, when a Communist victory in the civil war came to look ever more likely, wealthy Chinese, many active entrepreneurs among them, fled to Hong Kong, taking with them substantial amounts of financial capital in addition to the cultural capital of their experience and skills.[68]

64. This contradicts the view of Chinese historians that the development of a bourgeoisie began with the opening of the first Treaty Ports. e.g., Chen Xulu, *Metabolism of Modern Chinese Society*, vol. 1 (Singapore: Silkroad Press, 2013), 130.

65. Merle Goldman and Elizabeth J. Perry, eds., *Changing Meanings of Citizenship in Modern China* (Cambridge, MA: Harvard University Press, 2002).

66. Zhang Kaiyuan, Ma Min, and Zhu Ying, *Zhongguo jindai minzu zichan jieji yanjiu*, 666–670.

67. On this elite in the nineteenth century, see John M. Carroll, *Edge of Empires: Chinese Elites and British Colonials in Hong Kong* (Cambridge, MA: Harvard University Press, 2005); Elizabeth Sinn, *Power and Charity: A Chinese Merchant Elite in Colonial Hong Kong*, 2nd ed. (Hong Kong: Hong Kong University Press, 2003).

68. Gary G. Hamilton, *Cosmopolitan Capitalists: Hong Kong and the Chinese Diaspora at the End of the Twentieth Century* (Seattle: University of Washington Press, 1999).

As part of a general process of Chinese emigration that already began during the Ming dynasty, Chinese settlements and communities developed in many parts of Southeast Asia, later also in the United States and several countries of Latin America and the Caribbean. Capitalist businessmen—export merchants, shipowners, mining entrepreneurs, bankers, planters—always formed a minority within these ethnic minorities.[69] Much of their business was conducted with the mainland and among the Chinese diaspora.[70] The assets accumulated by the successful among them were often reinvested on the Chinese mainland. This happened already in the late Qing period, when patriotic overseas Chinese made substantial contributions to the modernization of the mother country.[71] Remittances from Chinese living abroad have made a vital contribution to many family budgets and regional economies ever since the late nineteenth century.

In our time, the stories merge. The Chinese state and its officials, private entrepreneurs in the PRC, and expatriate Chinese business people, not to mention the capitalists on Taiwan, form a complex web of modern economic actors who operate freely within the world of an integrated Greater China—and beyond. The members of this archipelago of managerial and mercantile elites share a basic attitudinal and behavioral disposition that can vaguely be termed "Confucian" and is also, in modified shapes, to be found in Japan,

69. Philip A. Kuhn, *Chinese among Others: Emigration in Modern Times* (Lanham, MD: Rowman and Littlefield, 2008); Wang Gungwu, *The Chinese Overseas: From Earthbound China to the Quest for Autonomy* (Cambridge, MA: Harvard University Press, 2000); Yen Ching-hwang, *The Ethnic Chinese in South and Southeast Asia: Business, Culture and Politics* (Singapore: Times Academic Press, 2002); Yen Ching-hwang, *Ethnic Chinese Business in Asia: History, Culture and Politics* (Singapore: World Scientific, 2014); Rajeswary Ampalavanar Brown, ed., *Chinese Business Enterprise in Asia* (London: Routledge, 1995); Rajeswary Ampalavanar Brown, *Chinese Big Business and the Wealth of Asian Nations* (Basingstoke: Palgrave Macmillan, 2000); Carl A. Trocki, "Boundaries and Transgressions: Chinese Enterprise in 18th- and 19th-century Southeast Asia," in *Ungrounded Empires: The Cultural Politics of Modern Chinese Transnationalism*, ed. Aihwa Ong and Donald Nonini (New York: Routledge, 1997), 61–85; Shinya Sugiyama and Linda Grove, eds., *Commercial Networks in Modern Asia* (Richmond: Curzon Press, 2001).

70. On this intra-diaspora trade, see Jason Lim, *Linking an Asian Transregional Commerce in Tea: Overseas Chinese Merchants in the Fujian-Singapore Trade, 1920–1960* (Leiden: Brill, 2010), 30–32.

71. Michael R. Godley, *The Mandarin-Capitalists from Nanyang: Overseas Chinese Enterprise in the Modernization of China, 1893–1911* (Cambridge: Cambridge University Press, 1981); Yen Ching-hwang, "The Overseas Chinese in Late Ch'ing Economic Modernization," *Modern Asian Studies* 16 (1982): 217–232.

Korea, and other parts of the Sinic sphere.[72] This extended commonality cannot disguise a crucial difference between those who have been exposed to Western ways of life since colonial times and the citizens of the PRC who began to catch up with Western consumer society and its values only in the 1990s. The parvenu excesses of the wealthy in mainland China, starkly contrasting with both Confucian and Maoists ideals of frugality, can partly be explained by a pent-up desire to draw level with a still-distant West. Elites in the Pacific Rim diaspora, by contrast, are able to afford a more relaxed attitude. In many respects, they arrived in the West long ago. This is not least reflected in politics. For all their patriotism and willingness to explore economic opportunities on the mainland, the overseas Chinese business elite is careful to maintain and defend its freedom of action beyond the grip of the Chinese Communist Party.

72. Gilbert Rozman, ed., *The East Asian Region: Confucian Heritage and Its Modern Adaptation* (Princeton, NJ: Princeton University Press, 1991); Daniel A. Bell, *China's New Confucianism: Politics and Everyday Life in a Changing Society* (Princeton, NJ: Princeton University Press, 2008); Sabine Dabringhaus, *Geschichte Chinas im 20. Jahrhundert* (Munich: C. H. Beck, 2009), 226–228.

PART VI

Global Social History

16

Race, Culture, and Class

EUROPEAN HEGEMONY AND GLOBAL CLASS
FORMATION, CIRCA 1800–1950

Richard Drayton

IN 1837, three years into the period of "apprenticeship" that followed the Emancipation Act coming into force, two American abolitionists visited Barbados. They sought out the small community of wealthy free colored businessman who clustered in the capital city Bridgetown. They visited the home of Joseph Thorne, who had been a slave until the age of twenty:

> On one side was a large library of religious, historical, and literary works, the selection of which displayed no small taste and judgment. On the opposite side of the room was a fine cabinet of minerals and shells. In one corner stood a number of curious relics of the aboriginal Caribs, such as bows and arrows, etc., together with interesting fossil remains. On the tops of the books-cases and mineral stand, were birds of rare species, procured from the South American Continent.[1]

Thorne's respectability was buttressed by his decision to adhere to the Anglican Church, of which he was a lay catechist, rather than, as most people of color had, to seek the more welcoming congregations of the "low church" Methodists, Baptists, and Moravians. But his political activity still put him into

---

1. James A. Thorne and J. Horace Kimball, *Emancipation in the West Indies: A Six Months' Tour in Antigua, Barbadoes, and Jamaica in the Year 1837* (New York: American Anti-Slavery Society, 1838), 73.

confrontation with the white planters and merchants with whom he shared the pew.

With other members of that small urban prosperous group of "colored" brokers and middlemen, Thorne was one of the sponsors of the newspapers *New Times* and the *Liberal*, published by the free colored journalist Samuel Jackman Prescod from 1836 and 1837.[2] These pressed for the removal of disabilities suffered by people of color, for the end of apprenticeship, and for radical parliamentary reform that would allow educated propertied men, whatever their skin shade, to vote for and sit in the House of Assembly. In 1839, an anonymous column in the *Liberal*, probably by Prescod, proposed that in the future the "middle orders," rather than the "excessively rich," should govern society. Versus the guzzling corruption of the rich, which was characterized by "habits of gratification, of adulation, producing mental incapacity, and moral deadness," it offered a government of a frugal, educated, industrious "middle class."[3] It was a political claim that had sponsors in any European city circa 1840, except that in the context of Barbados or Jamaica or Trinidad, those "middle orders" were middle in more senses than property. The color of their skins lay usually between the "black" of the slave and the "white" of the master class. At the same time they were key brokers in the social life of the city, while taking on special responsibilities of leadership, protection, and patronage toward that majority of unlettered manual workers that in 1838 emerged from slavery. They sought to propagate both religion and new respectable modes of marriage and family life in the same way that, as Prashant Kidambi has argued, the emerging middle class of nineteenth-century India sought to encourage "purity," "thrift," and "public decency" among the vulgar masses of Bombay.[4]

2. On the Free Coloured of Barbados, and in particular the place of Joseph Thorne, see Jerome S. Handler, *The Unappropriated People: Freedmen in the Slave Society of Barbados* (Baltimore: Johns Hopkins University Press 1974); and Melanie Newton, *The Children of Africa in the Colonies: Free People of Colour in Barbados in the Age of Emancipation* (Baton Rouge: Louisiana State University Press, 2008).

3. *Liberal*, 8 May 1839, quoted in Newton, *Children of Africa in the Colonies*, 180.

4. Prashant Kidambi, *The Making of an Indian Metropolis: Colonial Governance and Public Culture in Bombay, 1890–1920* (Aldershot: Ashgate, 2007), 211–212. See also Tanika Sarkar, *Hindu Wife Hindu Nation: Community, Religion, and Cultural Nationalism* (Bloomington: Indiana University Press, 2001); Margrit Pernau, *Ashraf into Middle Class: Muslims in Nineteenth-Century Delhi* (New York: Oxford University Press, 2013).

Global Historical Sociology and the Problem
of Its Weights and Measures

How do we make sense of this social formation in early nineteenth-century Barbados, which had its equivalents in every society across the Americas and in cities like Cape Town and Freetown in Africa?[5] It is unclear sometimes whether class and class formation are even recognized as global phenomena: it is striking, for example, that Julian Go and George Lawson in their 2017 manifesto work *Global Historical Sociology* do not even address class as a key analytic and problem.[6] Where there is a mature literature on a global middle class, it concerns twentieth- and twenty-first-century social formations, in particular those of the postcolonial and neoliberal moments.[7] For the nineteenth century, it is largely true that the kinds of middle class that emerged outside Europe are largely invisible to a variety of historical and social scientific literatures that make an assumption, usually tacit, that the bourgeoisie, if it was not in fact "a myth," had its locus classicus in nineteenth-century Europe.[8] It was Europe, indeed in its North-West capitalist climax, that we

5. Rex Nettleford, "Freedom of Thought and Expression: Nineteenth-Century West Indian Creole Experience," *Caribbean Quarterly* 36 (1990): 13–45; Matthias Röhrig Assunção and Michael Zeuske, "'Race', Ethnicity and Social Structure in 19th Century Brazil and Cuba," *Ibero-amerikanisches Archiv, Neue Folge* 24, no. 3/4 (1998): 375–443, 397–398; Robert Ross, *Status and Respectability in the Cape Colony* (Cambridge: Cambridge University Press, 1999); Saul Dubow, *A Commonwealth of Knowledge: Science, Sensibility and White South Africa 1820–2000* (Oxford: Oxford University Press, 2006); T. C. McCaskie, "Cultural Encounters: Britain and Africa in the Nineteenth Century," in *The Oxford History of the British Empire*, vol. 3: *The Nineteenth Century*, ed. Andrew Porter (Oxford: Oxford University Press, 1999), 665–690.

6. Julian Go and George Lawson, eds., *Global Historical Sociology* (Cambridge: Cambridge University Press, 2017).

7. Leo Kuper, *An African Bourgeoisie: Race, Class and Politics in South Africa* (New Haven, CT: Yale University Press, 1965); Brian P. Owensby, *Intimate Ironies: Modernity and the Making of Middle Class Lives in Brazil* (Stanford, CA: Stanford University Press, 1999); A. Richard López and Barbara Weinstein, eds., *The Making of the Middle Class: Towards a Transnational History* (Durham, NC: Duke University Press, 2012); Hagen Koo, "The Global Middle Class: How Is It Made, What Does It Represent?," *Globalizations* 13, no. 4 (2016): 440–453; Henrike Donner, *Domestic Goddesses: Maternity, Globalization and Middle-Class Identity in Contemporary India* (London: Routledge, 2016).

8. See the subtle survey of the literature in the crucial chapter 15 of Jürgen Osterhammel, *The Transformation of the Modern World: A Global History of the Nineteenth Century* (Princeton, NJ: Princeton University Press, 2014), 761–778; and Sarah Maza, *The Myth of the French Bourgeoisie: An Essay on the Social Imaginary, 1750–1850* (Cambridge, MA: Harvard University Press, 2003).

assume that the ideal type of a social class attached to an idea of *Bildung* and with a particular political self-consciousness emerged. It is assumed that non-Western colonial bourgeoisies are simply derivative of metropolitan forms, the products of acculturation, in particular in the late twentieth century, rather than being their historical partners. We confront here two pervasive problems of the postcolonial social sciences. First, we see the persistence of diffusionism, particularly where the problem of the modern is assayed. Second, there is the more profound issue that for comparative sociology, as for history, even when we essay at non-Eurocentrism, our norms and references, all the weights and measures of the social sciences, are taken from European experience.[9] The corollary of this is that we are often less sensitive to European phenomena as the products, rather than drivers, of transnational processes.

Jürgen Osterhammel in his masterwork on the nineteenth century urges us to examine how "the greater social differentiation fueled by population growth and with the general expansion of regional and supraregional trade and business activity" led to the growth in the weight of middle ranks in societies around the world.[10] His question is comparative, extending that distinguished tradition of the pursuit of *Universalgeschichte* via mapping parallels for which Max Weber remains the doyen. The comparative approach can lead to powerful interpretative insight. The brilliance of Weber's essay "Class, Status, Party" is to propose three axes for social analysis—group formation around the division of labor and property, group formation around honor, and group formation around identity as collective agency and cultural property—that come very close to transcending their modern European anchorage.[11] But their provenance drags on them still. They reproduce the anthropological imagination of liberal Europe circa 1900, presuming the existence of discrete disconnected distinctive national and regional experiences. They do not guide us to the alternative possibility of presuming interaction and connections and overlap and what, to coin a word, we might call "multiethnogenesis," that is to say, the simultaneous generation of many ethnicities in one system of

9. For a discussion of this theme, see, for example, Richard Drayton and David Motadel, "The Futures of Global History," *Journal of Global History* 13, no. 1 (2018): 1–21.

10. Osterhammel, *Transformation of the Modern World*, 766.

11. Max Weber, "The Distribution of Power within the Political Community: Class, Status, Party," in *Economy and Society: An Outline of Interpretive Sociology*, by Max Weber, ed. Guenther Roth and Claus Wittich (Berkeley: University of California Press, 1968), 926–939.

related status identities. As such they are tools for the analysis of distinct societies rather than a theory of social convergence. From this vantage point we might then ask how "middle" elements were coproduced in different places, and how we might identify forms of convergence between varieties of "middling" elements in international society over nineteenth- and twentieth-century history.

What Weber achieves in *Economy and Society*, however, is to clarify the work that "class" and other instruments of status distinction are doing in social life. On the one hand, they organize forms of monopolization, in which groups command privileged positions relative to material or ideal resources or social roles, from which they exclude other groups present in the society. Charles Tilly, in a 2001 intervention, extends the Weberian approach in arguing that the inequality is organized and propagated across time and space through the "inequality-generating mechanisms" or exploitation, when one group involves others in the production of value that they do not share, and "opportunity hoarding," in which a value-producing resource is kept to members of an in-group.[12] On the other hand, the flip side of this proposition is that status distinctions organize spaces of encounter among those who share a rank, they create the terrain for commensality and nuptuality, for negotiation and alliance, opening up the possibility of those who are not kin entering into networks of collective action, support and sympathy, and trust. The middle class in every society is both "middle" in terms of status and "middle" in terms of its capacity for engagement with social groups above or below, its capacity, in a word, for mediation. It is to this global history of mediation that we should turn to identify the ground for a global bourgeoisie.

Toward a Connective History of the Global Middle Class

If we seek to explore the question of the global middle class via connective rather than comparative history, we need to ask how the registers of social differentiation were transformed on a global scale, with European class, status, and party identities as much as product of this transnational turn as those in Latin America or Asia. It is my hypothesis that the global history that surrounded the construction of the early modern European imperial globalization, and which reached maturity in the early nineteenth century, the

12. Charles Tilly, "Relational Origins of Inequality," *Anthropological Theory* 1, no. 3 (2001): 355–372.

culmination of the first *Sattelzeit*, had three key effects. First, the moment of European hegemony from about 1750 to 1950 was correlated with the internal integration of Western Christendom of which ideas of civilization and whiteness, indeed of Europe as a discrete continent, were consequences, and with an ever-expanding external regime of linkages between Western European and non-European social formations. Second, connected to these linked processes of integration (often in the midst of competitive warfare) and external linkage (again often associated with violence and constrained consent) was the production of, and ascent in importance of mediating groups—negotiators, brokers, merchants, translators, middlemen, subaltern fixers (in the original meaning of the word "subaltern"), overseers, work captains, gang masters, accountants, managers, skilled artisans, pilots—in every part of the world, for which European *Bürgertum*, the bourgeois, the middle class were local and privileged expressions. Third, linked to that violent integration of international society, and the associated premium on mediation and mediators, was a process of standardization of social imaginaries, manners, customs, a pressure driving toward the reduction of specific complexity into general categories, toward uniformity. That convergence of manners across the court milieu of postmedieval Europe which Norbert Elias explored in *The Civilizing Process*, had perhaps a later global equivalent in the constitution of a transnational *Ständegeist* or esprit de corps among those who mediated the making of the modern world.[13] An integrated world could only be made sense of, indeed could only be massified, through forms of simplification, of the ignoring of complexity, or the performance of simplicity. The key question then becomes, how were regimes of status standardized around the world, mass produced, mass marketed, and made exchangeable?

Several of the contributions to this volume focus attention explicitly on how the material history of mediation as a dimension of modern global history threw up middle classes. Sabine Dabringhaus's and Jürgen Osterhammel's compradors, Kris Manjapra's "service professionals," Adam Mestyan's *efendi*, David Parker's luxury-consuming *porteños*, and Houchang Chehabi's constitutional revolutionaries emerged in the zones of linkage, where the local and global were coupled. This is a refreshing advance on the somewhat idealist

---

13. See Norbert Elias, *The Civilizing Process*, vol. 1: *The History of Manners* (Oxford: Blackwell, 1969). My argument here was stimulated by Peter Burke's provocative essay "The Language of Orders in Early Modern Europe," in *Social Orders and Social Classes in Europe since 1500*, ed. M. L. Bush (London: Longman, 1992), 1–12.

approach of Dror Wahrman, later globalized by David Cannadine, which seeks class in forms of social imagination.[14] Social ideas clearly mattered, but their purchase on the world depended on the work they do and did, on their value as lenses to particular interests and for forms of collective action. The rise of a global bourgeoisie certainly depended on particular psychocultural formations, but it was equally the expression of ever-denser and more dynamic forms of economic and political local and global activity and integration; its members were the men (and women) in the middle of an ever-expanding set of connections.

We should begin to think about the making of global social history as not just associated with but formally similar to the processes that produced regional and international market economies. In thinking about economies of status, we have the encouragement of Weber himself, who compared racial exclusion with the cartel behavior of economic actors.[15] Cartel behavior is of course a posture relative to a market. The key to the market is the principle of fungibility: that everything can or should be violently simplified to an exchange value that allows it to enter into conversation with any other thing through some currency—silver, Spanish piastres, gold, pounds sterling, or dollars—that operates as a material lingua franca. Global history from about 1500 to 1800 produced an analogous international bourse of honor, an analogous set of currencies of status through which both European integration and global social linkages could take place, premised on violent simplifications. It is in this process of integration, standardization, and simplification that race, class, and culture become, I am arguing, the critical axes of status identity and group dynamics in international society.[16] To the extent that we can talk

14. Dror Wahrman, *Imagining the Middle Class: The Political Representation of Class in Britain, c. 1780–1840* (Cambridge: Cambridge University Press, 1995); and David Cannadine, *Class in Britain* (London: Penguin, 2000); and David Cannadine, *Ornamentalism: How the British Saw Their Empire* (London: Penguin, 2002).

15. Weber, *Economy and Society*, 385–393, applies to his analysis of the uses of race and ethnicity that language of "monopolization" which he had first explored in discussing the sociology of economic behavior (344–348). See also Ernst Moritz Manasse, "Max Weber on Race," *Social Research* 14, no. 2 (1947): 191–221; and Andrew Zimmerman, "German Sociology and Empire: From Internal Colonization to Overseas Colonization and Back Again," in *Sociology and Empire: Colonial Studies and the Imperial Entanglements of a Discipline*, ed. George Steinmetz (Durham, NC: Duke University Press, 2013), 166–187.

16. I am in conversation here with Catherine Hall, *White, Male and Middle Class: Explorations in Feminism and History* (London: Routledge, 1992).

about a global history of the bourgeoisie, its members recognized themselves both locally and in international society through its locations within, and membership of, particular simplified modern meanings of ethnic, rank, and ideological and aesthetic community.

By race, class, and culture I mean concretely ideas of whiteness versus others understood as on a spectrum or as an amalgamated nonwhiteness; of bi- and tri-class social cleavage around the division of labor, property, and social prerogative; of civilization for which Christianity, education, aesthetic taste and manners, forms of collective voluntary action, and charity, were, in varying ways, signifiers. Those who wished to participate in a world dominated by Europe had to negotiate their place relative to these ways of seeing, institutions, and practices; they had to submit to the weights and measures of the global status market, or they had to reach within and form alternative registers of honor, status, and collective identity that might formally be compared to, and traded with, Western norms. Joseph Thorne and his circle in early nineteenth-century Barbados were only one example of a global phenomenon.

Christopher Bayly at the opening of *The Birth of the Modern World* argued how by the era of the First World War, a certain uniformity of dress and deportment was visible at the meeting places of international society.[17] This was not simply for him an emblem of Von Laue's "world revolution of westernization."[18] He recognized how the Maori chiefs who by 1900 wore frock coats and bow ties also sported ritual tattoos, and that kinds of formal uniformity and convergence were combined with extravert expressions of difference, such as the fez. We might push his argument harder to examine how the contemporary regime of power was shaping social identities and ideas of honor, as much as common modes of dress. In particular I am suggesting that rather than a simple conversion of manners, we are seeing a tactical and constrained participation of non-Western actors in the norms of dominant contemporary actors. Bayly, one notes, does not examine why people wore suits, or indeed, to take his later work in *Recovering Liberties*, why non-European groups invested in the political language of Liberalism, contenting himself

17. C. A. Bayly, *The Birth of the Modern World, 1780–1914: Global Connections and Comparisons* (Oxford: Blackwell, 2004), 13.

18. Theodore H. von Laue, *The World Revolution of Westernization* (New York: Oxford University Press, 1987).

with asking how.[19] But the decision to wear a suit, or to write of India or Brazil in terms of Comte or Spencer or Mill, was a response to a particular location of power and status in the contemporary world, a world in which white, propertied, Christian, suit-wearing men set the terms of encounter of international society.

The consolidation of European hegemony across the long nineteenth century, associated in particular I argue with postindustrial means of production, communication, and warfare, created a cultural space in which, to borrow the language of the Martinique poet and philosopher Edouard Glissant, a kind of "forced poetics" operated, in which to enjoy political, economic, even psychological personhood demanded that one performed membership in the community of the dominant group.[20] The mediating groups of international society, generated by the material history of early and late modern globalizations, were compelled to negotiate their status in a field of power relations for which race, class, and culture, understood in particular nineteenth-century ways, were significant dimensions. The taking of "middle-class" identities and manners by people in the spaces subject to European domination was in part constrained consent, in part resistance to, their predicament. Mimesis of social class behavior, in which aspiring colonial bourgeoisies rehearsed elements of the European bourgeois cultural habitus, is certainly, in some ways, simple West to non-West transfer and diffusion.[21] But mimicry of status norms can often be a form of self-defense, in which dissent is coded in the agency of the performer, a claiming of membership in the "modern."[22] We may see this complex of mimesis and subversive mimicry, for example, in Marcus Garvey's decision to bestow the titles of "Duke of the Nile" and "Baron of the Zambezi" on his Pan-African allies.

I might brutally summarize my argument into two key claims. First, that globalization—understood as an articulation of capitalism and governmentality—required mediators of all kinds and created the global

---

19. C. A. Bayly, *Recovering Liberties: Indian Thought in the Age of Liberalism and Empire* (Cambridge: Cambridge University Press, 2011).

20. Edouard Glissant, "Free and Forced Poetics," in *Ethnopoetics: A First International Symposium*, ed. Michel Benamou and Jerome Rothenberg (Boston: Boston University, 1976), 95–101.

21. For a discussion of the role of mimesis in generating social class identities, see Sharon Zukin, "Mimesis in the Origins of Bourgeois Culture," *Theory and Society* 4, no. 3 (1977): 333–358.

22. Michael Taussig, *Mimesis and Alterity: A Particular History of the Senses* (London: Routledge, 1993).

middle classes *an sich*, creating a space of social predicament and opportunity simultaneously across a number of societies. But second, that European hegemony compelled these people in the middle to negotiate their value in the international bourse of honor, creating the global middle classes *für sich*. The partner of the European integration of the world, which had on its inner substance the creation of modern class identities and relationships within Europe, was a transnational process of social-class identity formation in the periphery. Middle classes, each specific to their local context but in each also in mimetic conversation with social formations elsewhere, emerged across the world. For these global bourgeoisies, ideas of race, social rank, and culture and civilization became entangled in claims to status that themselves were mediators of claims to rights.

Ethnic Difference as Marker of Origin versus Ethnic Difference as a Marker of Status

We are scarcely at the beginning of understanding the complex entangled global histories of status and class formation. This is, first, because race and ethnic difference, while the central metal in all the transnational alloys of status across the modern era, is a neglected term of social scientific analysis.[23] But second, and more fundamentally, we have not usually thought about how different kinds of domination, subordination, and inequality can be connected in economies of status. Some productive beginnings in this direction have come in the new literatures on "intersectionality" and "kyriarchy," which have emerged out of critical race and gender studies.[24] These have suggested that class and status group formation has for millennia been quietly entangled with ideas of gender and ethnicity.

---

23. See Mills's discussion of the suppression of both race and the history of racism in the Western political tradition in Charles W. Mills, "Racial Liberalism," *Proceedings of the Modern Language Association* 123 (2008): 1380–1397.

24. See inter alia Kimberlé Crenshaw, "Demarginalizing the Intersection of Race and Sex," *University of Chicago Legal Forum*, no. 1 (1989): 139–167; and Kimberlé Crenshaw, "Mapping the Margins: Intersectionality, Identity Politics and Violence against Women of Colour," *Stanford Law Review* 43, no. 6 (1991): 1241–1299; Patricia Collins, *Black Feminist Thought: Knowledge, Consciousness and the Politics of Empowerment* (London: Routledge, 2000); and Elisabeth Schüssler Fiorenza and Laura Nasrallah, eds., *Prejudice and Christian Beginnings: Investigating Race, Gender, and Ethnicity in Early Christian Studies* (Minneapolis, MN: Fortress Press, 2009).

The modern global history of the bourgeoisie appealed to a far older infrastructure of stereotyped and simplified orders of identity and status. The ideological management of status and inequality in relationship to cultural identity
and difference took characteristic forms in every society but, with the rise of
ancient imperial systems, came into exchange and convergence. For Western
registers of status difference, the clear point of origin lies in the legacies of
Roman imperial assumptions. The Barberini polyptych, a carved ivory leaf in
the Louvre Museum from the early sixth-century Byzantine Empire, which
depicts probably, the Emperor Justinian, provides us with a luminous window
onto the overlapping of registers of distinction that organized antique society
and that shaped modern European ideas of status (Fig. 16.1). It correlates imperial power with a variety of other kinds of dominance. Divine power anoints
the emperor from above, while his mastery of a well-broken elegant horse
dominates the work, complemented by the submission of Tellus, the female
earth goddess who touches his foot while vainly seeking his approving gaze,
while in the register below ethnically different peoples—bearded men from
the West and Indians from the East, with lions and elephants among them,
supplicate themselves and bring tribute.[25] Imperial power long before Byzan-
tium, and into our own time, has always been correlated with particular con-
stellations of human-animal, gender, ethnic, and class dominance and
subordination.

When Western Eurasians sailed outward to Africa and the Americas circa
1500, they carried with them this complicated economy of macro and micro
scales of domination and status difference. They found terms of exchange with
the status regimes they encountered, and a vast, scarcely mapped hybrid history of social imaginaries of human-animal, gender, ethnic, and status group
identities opened up.[26] The central category within this emerged as race at the

25. For a general discussion of Byzantine imperial iconography, see Alicia Walker, *The Emperor and the World: Exotic Elements and the Imaging of Middle Byzantine Imperial Power, Ninth
to Thirteenth Centuries C. E.* (Cambridge: Cambridge University Press, 2012).

26. For the early colonial Spanish imperial spaces, see Marcy Norton, "The Chicken and the
Iegue: Human-Animal Relations and the Columbian Exchange," *American Historical Review* 120,
no. 1 (2015): 28–60; Irene Silverblatt, *Moon, Sun, and Witches: Gender Ideologies and Class in Inca
and Colonial Peru* (Princeton, NJ: Princeton University Press, 1987); Ramón Gutiérrez, *When
Jesus Came, the Corn Mothers Went Away: Marriage, Sexuality and Power in New Mexico, 1500–
1846* (Stanford, CA: Stanford University Press, 1991); Verena Stolcke, "Invaded Women: Sex,
Race and Class in the Formation of Colonial Society," *European Journal of Development Research*

FIGURE 16.1. Barberini diptych. Constantinople, late Roman Theodosian style, early sixth century. Musée du Louvre. Peiresc Collection; Barberini Collection; purchase, 1899.

core of new kinds of ethnic and status identities across a world of European trading and colonial enclaves.[27] The intrusion of plantation and mining economies had profound consequences on modern status identities, in particular because indigenous and chattel slavery were their recurrent partner. It is important to insist that plantation society was not a social form located only in Brazil, the Caribbean, and the American South. The entire West was a plantation society, shaped by the commodities and identities being generated in the tropical hotspots of early modern globalization. It is a convenient myth that there were parts of Europe, say London or Amsterdam, involved in overseas trade, while other places, far from the ocean, continued with their innocent inner-European life. From the opening of Habsburg power in the sixteenth century, it was the capacity of maritime powers to mobilize the entire continent, selling sugar in Geneva and coffee in Dresden, that made these empires possible, and thus every educated European, even deep in the hinterlands of the continent, participated in European imperial globalization and consumed and retailed, along with coffee and sugar, the idea of whiteness and of the difference of Europeans from Africans and Asians.

We might be so bold as to argue that the modern racialized identity of Europeans relative to others was generated overseas as part of the regime of multiethnogenesis that accompanied slavery and colonialism. It is in Brazil in the 1640s, that a scientific observer noted with surprise that the Portuguese, Dutch, German, French, and English were collectively referred to, in their difference from Africans and indigenous, as "Europeans": "In genere autem vocant omnes Europaeos."[28] The parallel of this was the construction of an idea of Africans not as merely sharing a continental provenance but also a persistent set of civilizational characteristics. The "science" of race was not first made in the books of philosophers nor, pace Winthrop Jordan, in primordial

---

6, no. 2 (1994): 7–21; Matthew Restall, *The Maya World: Yucatec Culture, 1550–1850* (Stanford, CA: Stanford University Press, 1997); and Stephanie Mawson, "Philippine Indios in the Service of Empire: Indigenous Soldiers and Contingent Loyalty," *Ethnohistory* 63, no. 2 (2016): 381–413.

27. James Sidbury and Jorge Cañizares-Esguerra, "Mapping Ethnogenesis in the Early Modern Atlantic," *William and Mary Quarterly* 68, no. 2 (2011): 181–208.

28. Willem Piso and Georg Marcgrave, *Historia Natvralis Brasiliae* (Amsterdam: Apud Franciscum Hackim Apud Lud. Elzevirium, 1648), 268, quoted in Staffan Müller-Wille, "Linnaeus and the Four Corners of the World," in *The Cultural Politics of Blood, 1500–1900*, ed. Kimberly Anne Coles, Ralph Bauer, Zita Nunes, and Carla L. Peterson (Basingstoke: Palgrave Macmillan, 2015), 191–209.

attitudes. It acquired its meaning in the structures of social practices. Plantation slavery indelibly marked those with by dark skins for servitude.[29] The
transfer of the fact of servitude into an idea of natural subordinacy, and of
difference into inferiority, happened easily and influenced religious and scientific ideas about human diversity and its meaning. As we pay attention to how
racialization in the early modern world was interlocked with the simultaneous
construction of internal colonial and global divisions of labor, forms of political domination via the state form, and the imagination of cultural hierarchy
through religion and science, it becomes increasingly difficult to use "class"
without examining the ways it was lived and seen as "race" and "culture" (or
"civilization").

These material life of early modern globalization shaped ways of seeing that
found their expression in the work of Buffon, Linnaeus, and Blumenbach and
in the science of race in eighteenth-century Europe.[30] The idea of "race" began
as a claim of what was shared by the people who lived in one place and their
kin, a kind of local or regional identity, as in the European nations that met in
Marcgrave's Brazil. But by the climax of the European seaborne empires, "race"
become portable—descriptive of kinds of people rather than of the inhabitants of a locale—and became a currency of status. In Buffon's appendix to the
Histoire Naturelle, for example, we find the critical shift from older ideas of race
as geographically defined, he writes for example of "la race espagnole," to a
modern idea; a "real race" he writes "can propagate itself, multiply itself, and
conserve in perpetuity through generation all the characteristics that may distinguish it from other races." This proposition that people were marked with
heritable characteristics, rather than the mark of descent from a community
fixed in one locale, was shaped by that human experience of mass uprooting
and relocation that European imperialism imposed on Europe and Africa and
Amerindia after 1500, and itself then became an instrument for further

29. For the classic statement of this view, see Eric Williams, *Capitalism and Slavery* (Chapel
Hill: The University of North Carolina Press, 1944).

30. Stephen Jay Gould, *The Mismeasure of Man*, rev. ed. (New York: W. W. Norton, 1996);
Sara Eigen and Mark Larrimore, eds., *The German Invention of Race* (Albany: State University
of New York Press, 2006); Bruce Baum, *The Rise and Fall of the Caucasian Race: A Political His-
tory of Racial Identity* (New York: New York University Press, 2006); Andrew S. Curran, *The
Anatomy of Blackness: Science and Slavery in an Age of Enlightenment* (Baltimore: Johns Hopkins
University Press, 2011); Anne Lafont, "How Skin Color Became a Racial Marker: Art Historical
Perspectives on Race," *Eighteenth-Century Studies* 51, no. 1 (2017): 89–113.

advances of trade, war, and government. Its impact would be seen into the nineteenth century, and far beyond the Atlantic context.

The New World idea of race as heritable natural difference that marked whiteness and its others signs of civilizational capacity came to shape how Europeans met people in Asia and the Pacific. The Japanese and Chinese, for example, were discovered to be "yellow," while the Papuans were described as "oceanic negroes."[31] George Everest, of the eponymous mountain, writing to the president of the Royal Society in 1839, offered a fascinating document of the migration of New World racism to the old: "when an Englishman arrives in India, and finds himself accosted by groups of people he looks on as Niggers and Infidels."[32] A Google Books Ngram Viewer search for the appearance of the word "nigger" in English-language books identifies its climax only from the 1830s onward, paradoxically, but not, as we shall see so surprisingly, correlated with the ends of formal slavery. Pace Peter Mandler, by the 1830s, ideas of race which we would recognize were certainly in circulation in the international system.[33] This idea of the "Nigger," brought in the baggage of the nineteenth-century Englishman to India, Egypt, Malaya, and even China, is one of the clearest examples of that simplified way of imagining social identity which became globalized in the nineteenth-century. Its impact can be seen in how non-Western mediating social groups and elites had to construct strategies of status making through property, manners, culture, and civility.

It might be said that the strategies of status making applied by non-European middle classes were merely based on the importing of European bourgeois norms, whether high collars or piano lessons. But they were influenced also by another legacy of early modern globalization: side-by-side ideas

31. Chris Ballard, "'Oceanic Negroes': British Anthropology of Papuans, 1820–1869," in *Foreign Bodies: Oceania and the Science of Race 1750–1940*, ed. Chris Ballard and Bronwen Douglas (Canberra: Australian National University Press, 2008), 157–202; Michael Keevak, *Becoming Yellow: A Short History of Racial Thinking* (Princeton, NJ: Princeton University Press, 2011); Rotem Kowner, *From White to Yellow: The Japanese in European Racial Thought, 1300–1735* (Montreal: McGill-Queen's University Press, 2014).

32. George Everest, *A Series of Letters Addressed to the Duke of Sussex* (London: W. Pickering, 1839), 93.

33. For a dogged refusal to admit race as a key category of British thought, see Peter Mandler, "Race and Nation in Mid-Victorian Thought," in *History, Religion, and Culture: British Intellectual History 1750–1950*, ed. Stefan Collini, Richard Whatmore, and Brian Young (Cambridge: Cambridge University Press, 2000), 224–244.

of radical racial difference had emerged the possibility of a religious, cultural, or civilizational *embranquecimento*, to take the Brazilian term, through mixture and through the transformation of the non-whites through Christian conversion and Western education. Within the locus classicus of plantation society, middling groups defined by mixed racial ancestry, by property, and by conversion to Christianity—the kinds of people who staffed the "*pardo* militias" of Spanish America—were the necessary basis of white and colonial domination and privilege. On the other side of the world, in Asia, the possibility of inducting non-Europeans into the manners and civilization of the West, if not to Christianity, was an equivalent project. In the East, from the Ottoman Empire to Persia, to India and China, Europeans negotiated with local systems of rank and status, approximating those at their higher echelons to themselves. From those confronting European xenologies, forms of mimicry and adaption could provide spaces of negotiation. Thus ideas of ethnicity, civilization and civilizational potential, and social rank were entangling in complex ways, "racing" class into subtle hybrid hierarchical regimes of status. This was certainly the case in the core regimes of the plantation system, but one might argue that it was also informing social relations in other parts of the world.

European Hegemony and the Nineteenth-Century Global Bourse of Honor

Where nonwhites, whether in Europe, Asia, the Near East, or Africa, met Europeans on terms of relative equality, race and nation were less important in the economies of status than social rank and religion.[34] At the climax of European power in the nineteenth century, however, new industrial means of transport, communications, and waging war opened up a power gap between the West and the non-Rest, which had multiple consequences. Europeans were now able to penetrate the interior of continents and to wrest concessions from polities that previously had been able to keep them at arms length. This

34. Christian Windler, *La diplomatie comme expérience de l'autre: Consuls français au Maghreb 1700–1840* (Geneva: Librairie Droz, 2002); Tseng-Tsai Wang, "The Audience Question: Foreign Representatives and the Emperor of China, 1858–1873," *Historical Journal* 14, no. 3 (1971): 617–626; Antony Best, "The Role of Diplomatic Practice and Court Protocol in Anglo-Japanese Relations, 1867–1900," in *The Diplomats' World: The Cultural History of Diplomacy, 1815–1914*, ed. Markus Mösslang and Torsten Riotte (Oxford: Oxford University Press, 2008), 231–253; David Motadel, "Qajar Shahs in Imperial Germany," *Past and Present* 213 (2011): 191–235.

generated new kinds of both economic ambition, to include territory and people into the circuit of capital, and political ambition, in which colonial states claimed a developmental power and prerogative. A new arrogance of the European powers was hardened by the ways in which the repeating rifle and machine gun allowed Europeans to do violence to others that could not be returned. In this context, the dynamic identified by Tacitus in *The Agricola*— "Proprium humani ingenii est odisse quem laeseris" (It is in the nature of men to hate those whom we hurt)—revealed itself in the nineteenth-century world in which an ascendant European looked down on those who appeared to be lagging behind in civilizational terms. It is in this context that Osterhammel correctly identifies a "dominant racism."[35]

Indeed from circa 1850 we see the consolidation of an idea of a white international, for which the idea of "civilization" (understood as Christian and Western) was a key signifier, which would have a powerful influence on international society, even through the twentieth century, in and after the Cold War, into our own time.[36] In that period, we might argue, race was "classed," and ethnic difference as written on the body acquired powerful weight as a primary indicator of status and group identity. Race penetrated all other indices of status. Whiteness mattered more, rather than less, paradoxically, with the crisis of plantation slavery and its ultimate end. Instead of the clear and rigid orders of status, inclusion, and exclusion, new orders of race and class organized an economy of personhood. Weber's examination of race and ethnicity is, in part, sensitive to this. He discusses, for example, the problem of the "poor whites" in the United States, in which a form of honor compensated for another kind of status inferiority: "The social honour of the 'poor whites' was dependent on the social *déclassement* of the Negroes."[37] Eugene Genovese in *The World the Slaveholders Made* notes how in the United States, democratic politics and the end of slavery was associated with a more virulent racism, the violent manufacture of status difference aimed at a new democratic form of

35. Osterhammel, *Transformation of the World*, 891. I am, however, less persuaded than he is that the countercurrent we find in the kind of opposition that Mill gave to Carlyle's form of racism, Antenor Firmin's riposte to Gobineau, and the anti-racist social theory of Weber, Du Bois, or Boas represented more than marginal phenomena at the high-water mark of European imperial power.

36. David Todd, "Transnational Projects of Empire in France, c. 1815–1870," *Modern Intellectual History* 12, no. 2 (2015): 265–293.

37. Weber, *Economy and Society*, 391. See also Lawrence A. Scaff, *Max Weber in America* (Princeton, NJ: Princeton University Press, 2011).

"monopolization" and "opportunity hoarding."[38] It seems clear too that within Europe in Weber's own time, in a similar way, class inequality was being made more stable by the idea that there was a world of racial and colonial subordinates. In Britain, the partner of the expansion of the franchise was the promotion by the Conservative Party of a popular pro-imperial and militarist sentiment tied to a clear implicit white supremacist program of solidarity across economic classes.[39] There are some students of Weber who argue that he came actively to envision how, similarly, Germany's participation in imperialism (and the overseas projection of power) might solve class antagonism and weaken the appeal of the politics of socialism.[40] What seems certain is that Edmund Morgan's and Genovese's models of how racism worked in a conservative *Sammlungspolitik* in the United States might more generally be applied to understanding the politics of imperialism across Europe and, perhaps, the more somber passages of European history between 1933 and 1945.

While we think of the period from 1850 to 1945 as one of violent competition between the European powers, reaching a catastrophic climax in 1914–45, the other dimension of this period was an unprecedented degree of collaboration and integration of the empires into an imagined "international system" for which Europe was arbiter.[41] In the age of steam, "imperium" and "dominium" entered a fundamentally new relationship. The rule of European imperial powers over colonists overseas had from the outset been understood as that of a superintending "imperium," the supremacy of the center, versus a "dominium" constituted on the ground through settlement, property rights, and administration. But although from about 1650 to 1800, "imperium" was understood in nation state terms as revolving around the power of the British or French crowns, post 1800—the age of Napoleonic emancipatory conquest,

38. Eugene Genovese, *The World the Slaveholders Made* (New York: Pantheon Books, 1969); and Edmund Morgan, *American Slavery, American Freedom* (New York: W. W. Norton, 1975).

39. Bernard Semmel, *Imperialism and Social Reform: English Social-Imperial Thought* (London: George Allen and Unwin, 1960); Martin Pugh, *The Tories and the People* (Oxford: Basil Blackwell, 1985).

40. Wulf D. Hund, "Racism in White Sociology: From Adam Smith to Max Weber," in *Racism and Sociology*, ed. Wulf D. Hund and Alana Lentin (Vienna: Lit, 2014), 23–68; Kieran Allen, *Max Weber: A Critical Introduction* (London: Pluto Press, 2004), 28.

41. For an argument about the role of collaboration among the European powers since 1500, as a counterpoint to the more usual historical theme of imperial competition, see Richard Drayton, *Masks of Empire: The World History underneath Modern Empires and Nations, c. 1550 to the Present* (London: Palgrave Pivot, 2019).

systems of unequal treaties, and the principle of "extra-territoriality," of free trade and cosmopolitan utopias—the idea of "imperium" now began to appeal ultimately to the rights, interests, and prerogatives of mankind and nature as a whole. Before one conquered in the name of the Crown, with the male sword-bearer as the consecrated local expression of sovereignty, now European powers took territory in the interest of all of humanity, including the conquered themselves.

The climax of European hegemony in the international system we might see as a moment of "multiethnogenesis," in the sense that it generated, side by side, and entangled together, a set of new racial identities. The corollary of the consolidation of a tighter idea of Europe's difference from the rest of the world was an amalgamation of others into either an earlier or lower state of cultural and social evolution. The invention of a "white" race, with its own internal hierarchies, was levered not just on the African body but in a system of imagined others—the Chinese (now degenerate rather than enlightened), the Indian (thuggish and vile rather than noble)—with other races, Amerindian and aborigine, imagined as fit for extinction. This was only a later moment in a process that had begun with eighteenth-century anthropology and race theory. But now difference was radically entwined with status and historical destiny.

Modern personhood, to put it another way, constructed side-by-side European domination, was initially highly raced, with Europe as the civilizational equivalent to the Caucasian in Blumenbach's race theory, closest to the divine or natural point of origin, relative to which other ethnic groups were at varying degrees of degeneration. Some like the Japanese or Iranians, perhaps more competent to become "modern" than others like those of African descent, all had to fight to prove their capacity for full membership in the modern world. If one looks at J. James Thomas's response to Froude's racist dismissal of the post-emancipation Caribbean in the 1860s or the fin de siècle Asian intellectuals discussed by Charles Kurzman or Pankaj Mishra, we can see a familiar defensive claim on a kind of modern personhood.[42] Securing such membership of the "modern" was the principle goal of the global middle classes.

---

42. On J. J. Thomas and his milieu, see Faith Smith, *Creole Recitation: John Jacob Thomas and Colonial Formation in the Late Nineteenth-Century Caribbean* (Charlottesville: University of Virginia Press, 2002); Charles Kurzman, *Democracy Denied, 1905–1915: Intellectuals and the Fate of Democracy* (Cambridge, MA: Harvard University Press, 2008); and Pankaj Mishra, *From the Ruins of Empire: The Intellectuals Who Remade Asia* (London: Farrar, Straus and Giroux, 2012).

Education, political nationalism, literature, theater, music, and projects of reform and state making—these were the battlefields on which the Third Estate in Europe had sought to make itself central to public life. For the mediating groups of the non-European world, elite and middling, similar campaigns would have to be fought in order to negotiate the status of simply being fully human in the early twentieth-century world.

Conclusion

The bourgeoisie, in and out of Europe, emerged in the interstices of relations of domination. It was a social class that mediated economic life and came to seek political inclusion and, afterward, a kind of hegemony. In crises spread across the long nineteenth and twentieth centuries, members of the European and colonial *tiers état* laid claim to a special historic role. Their demand was premised on ideas of their central role in collective life and of how their manners and habitus gave them special capacities to lead toward the imagined futures of liberalism, nationalism, and the paternalist varieties of socialism. The modern history of the world was marked by this class's conflicts and alliances with various agents of the Old Regime, and its struggles with and against old and new subaltern classes.

It has been this essay's burden to argue that their local histories of class formation, each peculiar to its own society and clumped into particular regional patterns, were, all the same, global convergent. There is, *en bref*, a common global history of the bourgeoisie. This convergence began in global economic connections. Violence, linked to forms of co-option, patronage, cooperation, transfer, and mimicry, organized an international division of labor and regime of production and exchange. With this came new simplified global currencies of status and honor, transacted through the connected logics of race, class status, and civilization. Each global bourgeoisie might have emerged in its peculiar space, but each came to understand itself as related, via these currencies, to others elsewhere in the world, in particular via explicit or implicit racial imaginaries. A historical sociology that seeks to do justice to global history must take seriously this problem of how race ordered class, at a variety of scales of collective life, periphery shaping center and vice versa, with enduring effects.

INDEX

Persons

Places

Subjects

A NOTE ON THE TYPE

This book has been composed in Arno, an Old-style serif typeface in the classic Venetian tradition, designed by Robert Slimbach at Adobe.